Learning Web Design

SECOND EDITION

Learning Web Design

A Beginner's Guide to HTML, Graphics, and Beyond

Jennifer Niederst

O'REILLY®

Beijing • Cambridge • Farnham • Köln • Paris • Sebastopol • Taipei • Tokyo

Learning Web Design, Second Edition
A Beginner's Guide To HTML, Graphics, and Beyond

by Jennifer Niederst

Published by O'Reilly & Associates, Inc., 1005 Gravenstein Highway North, Sebastopol, CA 95472.

O'Reilly & Associates books may be purchased for educational, business, or sales promotional use. Online editions are also available for most titles (*safari.oreilly.com*). For more information, contact our corporate/institutional sales department: 800-998-9938 or *corporate@oreilly.com*.

Print History:

March 2001: First edition.

June 2003: Second edition.

Editor: Paula Ferguson

Production Editor: Matt Hutchinson

Cover Designer: Edie Freedman

Interior Designer: David Futato

0-596-00484-2
[C]

Contents

Part II. Learning HTML

Preface

I've had the opportunity to teach web design to hundreds of absolute beginners. My classes and workshops have been filled to capacity with seasoned graphic designers, office assistants, recent college graduates, programmers looking for a more creative outlet, work-at-home moms, and anyone else looking to get a start in web design. Despite the variety of backgrounds, I find that I hear the same questions and concerns over and over. Similarly, I've noticed that there are certain concepts that regularly trip up my students and other topics that they master with ease.

Through a certain amount of trial and error, I've developed a successful method for teaching beginning web design, and that method forms the structure of this book. Reading this book is a lot like sitting in my classroom.

I wrote my last book, *Web Design in a Nutshell, Second Edition* (O'Reilly 2001), because it was the book I needed to do my job as a web designer. I wrote this book because it is the book I wish I had been able to give my students. While *Web Design in a Nutshell* is comprehensive and contains detailed explanations, it is most appropriate for intermediate-level and professional web designers. *Learning Web Design* addresses the specific needs and concerns of beginners. I like to think of it as the "prequel" to the Nutshell book.

Although this book is for newcomers, I haven't "dumbed down" or glossed over anything. I dig deep into HTML coding and web graphics production. This edition also introduces style sheets and is mindful of current web standards, so you'll learn the right way of doing things. You will certainly find plenty of technical information, as you'd expect from an O'Reilly book.

This new edition features hands-on exercises throughout the book that allow you to try out new techniques along the way. All of the materials you need for the exercises, as well as trial versions of popular web development software, are provided on the accompanying CD. I've included short quizzes at the end of each chapter to make sure you're up to speed with key concepts.

On the Companion CD

The CD included with this book contains:

- Materials for all the exercises
- Trial versions of Macromedia® Fireworks® MX and Macromedia® HomeSite® v5
- Time-limited tryout versions of Adobe® Photoshop® 7 and Adobe® ImageReady® 7
- BareBones' BBEdit 7.0 demo

I do assume you have a certain level of knowledge. Obviously, you need to know your way around a computer and have a basic familiarity with the Web, even if you've just surfed a little. Also, this book doesn't teach basic principles of graphic design such as color theory, type design, or balance and proportion. However, I do provide some design tips in Chapter 21. Finally, I assume that you know how to use an image-editing software package to create graphics; I'll teach you how to make graphics appropriate for the Web.

Whenever possible, I provide pointers on how current web design tools, both for authoring web pages and creating web graphics, can help you create web sites more quickly and easily. Unfortunately, I can't include every available web-related product in this book, so I've stuck with the most popular tools: Macromedia Dreamweaver, Adobe GoLive, and Microsoft FrontPage for web authoring, and Adobe Photoshop, Macromedia Fireworks, and JASC Paint Shop Pro for creating web graphics. In most cases, the general principles apply to whichever tool you prefer, so don't be dismayed if your favorite tool isn't featured here. If it works for you, that's all that matters.

Whether you are reading this book on your own or using it as a companion to a web design course, I hope it gives you a good head start toward becoming a web designer. And more importantly, I hope you have fun.

Contents

The book is divided into four parts, each covering a general subject area.

Part I: Getting Started

Part I provides answers to the common questions people have when getting started in web design. It lays a foundation for understanding the medium, before jumping into the nitty-gritty of tags and file formats.

Chapter 1, Where Do I Start?, answers the big questions: where to start, what you need to learn, what you need to buy, and so on.

Chapter 2, How the Web Works, introduces the Web, URLs, servers, browsers, and the anatomy of basic web pages.

Chapter 3, Getting Your Pages on the Web, provides a step-by-step demonstration of how to upload a web page. This chapter also addresses finding a hosting service and registering domain names.

Chapter 4, Why Web Design Isn't Like Print Design, is a summary of the unknown factors that affect the web design process, as well as tips for coping with them.

Chapter 5, The Web Design Process, takes you through the steps of creating a web site, from conceptualization through final testing.

The Companion Web Site

Be sure to visit the companion web site for this book at *www.learningwebdesign.com*. It features color charts, lists of links from the book, updates, and other good stuff.

Part II: Learning HTML

Part II focuses on HTML tags and their uses. I provide complete instructions for tagging by hand and offer tips on using popular web-authoring tools that can do the job for you.

Chapter 6, Creating a Simple Page, shows how to create a basic web page, and includes explanations of how HTML works and the tags necessary to structure a document.

Chapter 7, Formatting Text with HTML, explains all the tags and attributes used to control the display of text in web pages.

Chapter 8, Formatting Text with Style Sheets, provides an introduction to Cascading Style Sheets for controlling text display.

Chapter 9, Adding Graphic Elements, explores the HTML tags related to adding graphics and horizontal rules to the page.

Chapter 10, Adding Links, focuses on the tags used for adding hypertext links to a page.

Chapter 11, Tables, provides a thorough introduction to tables: how they're used, how they're tagged, and how they can go wrong.

Chapter 12, Frames, covers the structure and creation of framed documents, including explanations of frame-related HTML tags as well as tips and tricks for using frames effectively.

Chapter 13, Color on the Web, explains the options for specifying colors for HTML elements.

Part III: Creating Web Graphics

Part III covers what you need to know about creating graphics for the Web. I provide background information on web graphics file formats, overviews of available tools, and practical tips for graphics production and optimization.

Chapter 14, All About Web Graphics, introduces important concepts that apply to all web graphics: appropriate file formats, image resolutions, production tips, and more.

Chapter 15, Creating GIFs, discusses all aspects of creating graphics in the GIF format, including transparency, optimization tips, and the web palette.

Chapter 16, Creating JPEGs, describes the process of creating and optimizing JPEGs.

Chapter 17, Animated GIFs, looks at the creation and optimization of animated GIFs.

Chapter 18, Slicing and Rollovers, provides step-by-step instructions for creating sliced images and rollover buttons.

Part IV: Form and Function

Part IV returns to the big-picture issues of what makes a web site work well and look professional.

Chapter 19, Web Design Techniques, uses a combination of the skills established in Parts II and III to create a number of common web design elements.

Chapter 20, Building Usable Web Sites, introduces the basic principles of information design, interface design, and navigation.

Chapter 21, Web Design Dos and Don'ts, provides a rapid-fire list of tips for what to do and what *not* to do in web design.

Chapter 22, How'd They Do That: An Introduction to Advanced Techniques, introduces advanced techniques and technologies, so you can recognize them when you see them.

Conventions Used in This Book

The following typographic conventions are used in this book:

Italic
> Used to indicate URLs, email addresses, filenames, and directory names, as well as for emphasis.

Colored roman text
> Used for special terms that are being defined and for cross-references.

`Constant width`
> Used to indicate code examples and keyboard commands.

`Colored constant width`
> Used to indicate HTML tags and attributes, and used for emphasis in code examples.

`Constant width italic`
> Used to indicate placeholders for values in HTML attributes.

G   Used to indicate a figure that appears in full color in the gallery insert.

Acknowledgments

I want to thank my editor, Paula Ferguson, for her valuable input to this new edition. Thanks also to the others who have contributed hands-on time to the project: Edie Freedman for the series cover design, David Futato for the series interior design, Chris Reilley for his top-notch figures and information design, Matt Hutchinson for copyediting the manuscript, Tom Dinse for writing the index, and everyone else who contributed to the construction of this book.

O'Reilly Would Like to Hear from You

Please address comments and questions concerning this book to the publisher:

O'Reilly & Associates, Inc.
1005 Gravenstein Highway North
Sebastopol, CA 95472
(800) 998-9938 (in the United States or Canada)
(707) 829-0515 (international or local)
(707) 829-0104 (fax)

We have a web page for this book, where we list errata, examples, or any additional information. You can access this page at:

http://www.oreilly.com/catalog/learnweb2

To comment or ask technical questions about this book, send email to:

bookquestions@oreilly.com

For more information about our books, conferences, Resource Centers, and the O'Reilly Network, see our web site at:

http://www.oreilly.com

I also want to thank my ace technical reviewers, Linda Bean Pardee, Joe Sharrino, and Josh Wood, whose comments truly made this a better book. Warm thanks also go to Jason Carlin (my Windows and indie-rock consultant), Ellie Lee for cheerleading and for her homemade dim sum that got me through the home stretch, and Starbucks in Wayland Square for the gallons of iced chai that fueled the writing of the majority of this edition.

As always, I want to thank my Mom and Dad for their unending encouragement, optimism, and humor. Warm thanks go to my brother, Liam, for being an inspiration and for generously contributing images for several figures in this book. Thanks also go to the whole Robbins family for their enthusiastic support of my writing endeavors, with a special tip of the hat to Neil for his time and PC and to Laura for contributing content for figures.

And last, but certainly not least, my love and appreciation go to my husband, Jeff, for providing valuable tidbits of web wisdom, general technical assistance, and a good life overall.

Getting Started

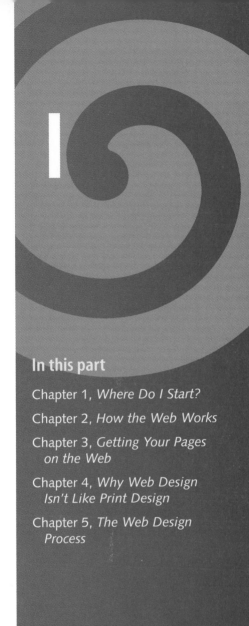

There's a lot more to the art of web design than HTML and GIF files. If you're just getting started, chances are you have some big questions. Where do I start? How does it all work? How do I get my stuff on the Web? How is web design different from print design?

Part I answers all of these questions and more. Before we get into the nitty-gritty of tags and file formats, it is important that you have a good feel for the web design environment. Once you understand the medium and its quirks, you'll have a good head start toward using your tools and making design decisions. All the rest will fall into place.

Where Do I Start?

The buzz about the Web has been so loud it is impossible to ignore. For many people, it's a call to action—a new career opportunity, an incentive to keep up with competitors, or just a chance to get stuff out there for the world to see. But the Web can also seem overwhelming.

Through my experience teaching web design courses and workshops, I've had the opportunity to meet people of all backgrounds who are interested in learning how to build web pages. Allow me to introduce you to just a few:

> "I've been a print designer for 17 years, and now all my clients want web sites."

> "I work as a secretary in a small office. My boss has asked me to put together a small internal web site to share company information among employees."

> "I've been a programmer for years, but I want to try my hand at more visual design. I feel like the Web is a good opportunity to explore new skills."

> "I am an artist and I want to know how to get samples of my paintings and sculpture online."

> "I'm a designer who has watched all my colleagues switch to web design in the last few years. I'm curious about it, but I feel like I'm too late."

Whatever the motivation, the first question is always the same: "Where do I start?" With something as seemingly vast and fast-moving as the Web, it's not easy to know where to jump in. But you have to start somewhere.

In this chapter, I will answer the most frequently asked questions from people who are ready to make the leap into web design.

Am I Too Late?

That's an easy one—absolutely not! Although it may seem that everyone in the whole world has a personal web page, or that your colleagues are all light-years ahead of you in web experience, I can assure you that you're not too late. Keep in mind that this medium and industry are still relatively new. You're still in time to be a pioneer.

Now that the dust has settled after the dot-com rise and its spectacular crash, the Web has become an essential part of standard business practice. We're at the point where we just assume that a business, regardless of its size, will have a useful web site. So, web design—and a steady need for web designers and developers—is here to stay.

Where Do I Start?

The first step is understanding the fundamentals of how the Web works, including a working knowledge of HTML, the role of the server, and the importance of the browser. This book has been written specifically to address these topics, so you are certainly on the right track. Once you learn the fundamentals, there are plenty of resources on the Web and in bookstores for you to further your learning in specific areas.

The first step is understanding the fundamentals of how the Web works.

One way to get up to speed quickly is to take an introductory web design class. If you don't have the luxury of a full-semester course, even a weekend or one-day seminar can be extremely useful in getting over that first hump.

If your involvement in web design is purely at the hobbyist level, or if you have just one or two web projects you'd like to publish, you may find that a combination of personal research (like reading this book) and solid web design tools (such as Macromedia Dreamweaver) may be all you need to accomplish the task at hand.

If you are interested in pursuing web design as a career, I recommend building some sample web sites to show to potential employers. These sites can be the result of class assignments, personal web sites, or a sample site for a small business. What's important is that they look professional and have clean, working HTML behind the scenes. Getting an entry-level job and working as part of a team is a great way to learn how larger sites are constructed and can help you decide which specific area of web design you would like to pursue.

What Do I Need to Learn?

This one's a big question. The answer depends on where you are starting and what you want to do. I know, that answer sounds like a cop-out, but it's true, given the wide variety of tasks involved in web design.

The term "web design" has become a catch-all for a process that actually encompasses a number of different disciplines, from graphic design to programming. We'll take a look at each of them.

If you are designing a small web site on your own, you will need to wear many hats. The good news is that you probably won't notice. Consider that the day-to-day upkeep of your household requires you to be part-time chef, housecleaner, accountant, diplomat, gardener, and construction worker—

but to you it's just the stuff you do around the house. In the same way, as a solo web designer, you'll be part-time graphic designer, writer, producer, and information architect, but to you, it'll just feel like "making web pages." Nothing to worry about.

Large-scale web sites are almost always created by a team of people, numbering from a handful to hundreds. In this scenario, each member of the team focuses on just one facet of the design process. If you are not interested in becoming a jack-of-all-trades solo web designer, you may choose to specialize and work as part of a team. If that is the case, you may be able to simply adapt your current set of skills and interests to the new medium.

The following are some of the core disciplines involved in the web design process, along with brief descriptions of the skills required in each area.

Graphic design

Because the Web is a visual medium, web pages require attention to presentation and design. The graphic designer makes decisions regarding everything you see on a web page: graphics, type, colors, layout, etc. As in the print world, graphic designers play an important role in the success of the final product. If you work as a graphic designer in the web design process, you may never need to learn any backend programming languages. (I didn't.)

If you are interested in designing commercial sites professionally, I strongly recommend formal graphic design training as well as a strong proficiency in Adobe Photoshop (the industry standard). If you are already a graphic designer, you will be able to adapt your skills to the Web easily. Because graphics are a big part of web design, even hobbyist web designers will need to know how to use some image-editing software, at minimum.

In addition, you may also want to do some personal research on the fundamentals of good design. I recommend *The Non-Designer's Web Book*, Second Edition by Robin Williams and John Tollett (Peachpit Press, 2000) and *Robin Williams Web Design Workshop* by Williams, Tollett, and Rohr (Peachpit Press, 2001). Both provide sound graphic design advice, specifically applied to the web medium. For more general instruction on design principles, check out *Design Basics*, Fifth Edition by David Lauer and Stephen Pentak (Harcourt College Publishers, 2000).

Information design

One easily overlooked aspect of web design is information design: the organization of content and how you get to it. Information designers (also called "information architects") deal with flow charts and diagrams and may never touch a graphic or text file; however, they are a crucial part of the creation of the site.

AT A GLANCE

"Web design" actually combines a number of disciplines, including:

- Graphic design
- Information design
- Interface design
- HTML production
- Programming and scripting
- Multimedia

Frontend Versus Backend

You'll often hear web designers and developers say that they specialize in either the frontend or backend of web site creation.

Frontend design

"Frontend" refers to any aspect of the design process that appears in or relates directly to the browser. This book focuses primarily on frontend web design.

The following tasks are commonly considered to be frontend disciplines:

- Graphic design
- Interface design
- Some aspects of information design (when it pertains to the user's experience of the site)
- HTML production, including style sheets, JavaScript, XHTML, and usually DHTML

Backend development

"Backend" refers to the programs and scripts that work behind the scenes to make web pages dynamic and interactive. In general, backend web development falls in the hands of experienced programmers, but it is good for all web designers to be familiar with backend functionality.

The following disciplines are considered to be backend:

- Some aspects of information design (when it pertains to how the information is organized on the server)
- CGI programming
- Database programming
- Dynamically generated pages
- XML implementation
- Java programming

See the sidebar Servers and Clients in Chapter 2, for more background on the distinction.

If you think you may be interested in this aspect of web development, read *Information Architecture for the World Wide Web*, Second Edition by Lou Rosenfeld and Peter Morville (O'Reilly, 2002) for a good overview.

It is possible to find courses specifically about information design, although they are likely to be at the graduate level. Again, some personal research and experience working on a team will go a long way toward rounding out this skill. We will look at some basic principles of information design in Chapter 20.

Interface design

If graphic design is concerned with how the page looks, interface design focuses on how the page works. The interface of a web site includes the methods for doing things on a site: buttons, links, navigation devices, etc., as well as the functional organization of the page. In most cases, the interface, information archictecture, and graphic design of a site are tightly entwined. I discuss interface design further in Chapter 20.

Often, the interface design falls into the hands of a graphic designer by default; in other cases, it is handled by an interface design specialist or the information designer. Some interface designers have backgrounds in software design. It is possible to find courses on interface design; however, this is an area that you can build expertise in by a combination of personal research, experience in the field, and common sense.

HTML and graphics production

A fair amount of the web design process involves the creation and troubleshooting of the HTML documents that make up a site. Production people need to have an intricate knowledge of HTML (the tagging language used to make web documents), and usually some additional scripting or programming skills. At large web design firms, the team that handles HTML and coding may be called the "development" or "production" department.

Fortunately, basic HTML is easy to learn on your own, and there are new and powerful tools (such as Macromedia Dreamweaver, Adobe GoLive, and Microsoft FrontPage) that can reduce errors and speed up the production process.

In addition to the HTML document, each of the graphics that appear on the page need to be produced in a way that is appropriate and optimized for web delivery. Graphics production techniques are covered in Part III.

Programming and scripting

Advanced web functionality (such as forms and interactivity) requires traditional programming skills for writing scripts, programs, and applications, and for working with databases, servers, and so on. The stuff behind the scenes makes web pages work their real magic, and there is a always a demand for such programmers. Professional programmers may never touch a graphic file or have input on how the pages look. If you want to become a programmer, definitely pursue a degree in Computer Science. Although some programmers are self-taught, formal training is beneficial.

It is possible to turn out competent, content-rich, well-designed sites without the need for programming, so hobbyist web designers should not be discouraged. However, once you get into collecting complex information via forms, or serving information on demand, it is necessary to have a programmer on the team.

Multimedia

One of the cool things about the Web is that you can add multimedia elements to a site, including sound, video, animation, and interactivity. If you are interested in specializing in multimedia for the Web, I recommend becoming a power-user of multimedia tools such as Macromedia Flash and/or Director. A background in sound and video production may also be beneficial. Web development companies usually look for people who have mastered the standard multimedia tools, and have a good visual sensibility and an instinct for intuitive and creative multimedia design. Audio, video, and Flash are discussed further in Chapter 22.

Do I Need to Learn Java?

You'd be surprised at the number of times I've heard the following: "I want to get into web design so I went out and bought a book on Java." I usually respond, "Well, go return it!" Before you spend money on a big Java book, I'm here to tell you that you don't need to know Java programming to be a web designer.

The following is a list of "languages" associated with the creation of web sites. They are listed in general order of complexity and in the order that you might want to learn them. Bear in mind, the only *requirements* are HTML and style sheets. Where you draw the line after that is up to you.

HTML (HyperText Markup Language)

This is the language used to write web page documents (we'll discuss it further in Part II and throughout this book). Writing HTML is not programming, it's more like word processing in longhand.

Everyone involved with the Web needs a basic understanding of how HTML works. Its limitations and quirks define what can be done on web pages. If

---

AT A GLANCE

Web-related programming "languages" in order of increasing complexity:

- HTML
- Style sheets
- JavaScript
- DHTML
- CGI and web scripting
- XML
- Java

---

you're in web production, you'll live it and breathe it. The good news is that it's simple to learn the basics. Plus, there are HTML-editing tools that will make the work even easier for you.

Style sheets

Once you've mastered HTML for structuring your web documents, you'll want to take on Cascading Style Sheets (CSS) to control the way they look. Style sheets are now the official and standard mechanism for text and page formatting. They are also a great tool for automating production, because you can make a change to a single style sheet document and have it affect all the documents in your site. Style sheets are now supported by the overwhelming majority of browsers in current use.

Style sheets are discussed further in Chapter 8.

JavaScript

Despite its name, JavaScript is not at all related to Java. JavaScript is a web-specific scripting language that makes browsers do tricks. Special instructions can be inserted in web pages to add functionality, such as popping up new windows or making something change when the pointer is passed over it (known as a "rollover").

Learning to write JavaScript from scratch means learning a programming language, so the learning curve is steep. The good news is that most web-authoring tools come with standard scripts that you can just drop into place. Depending on your role in the web design process, the tools you use, and the people you hire or work with, you may never need to learn to write JavaScript yourself. JavaScript is discussed a little more in Chapter 22.

DHTML (Dynamic HTML)

DHTML is not a separate programming language; it refers to the use of a combination of HTML, JavaScript, and style sheets in a way that makes page elements move or change (thus the term "dynamic"). Because browsers have different ways of handling DHTML content, making DHTML work correctly is tricky. Writing DHTML code is an advanced web production skill—useful to learn if you want to specialize in web production and programming, but not essential for everyone. Fortunately, tools such as Macromedia Dreamweaver provide an easy interface for adding basic DHTML tricks such as animation to your pages. For a more detailed introduction, see Chapter 22.

The World Wide Web Consortium

The World Wide Web Consortium (called the W3C for short) is the organization that oversees the developement of web technologies. The group was founded in 1994 by Tim Berners-Lee, the inventor of the Web, at the Massachusetts Institute of Technology (MIT).

In the beginning, the W3C concerned itself mainly with the HTTP protocol and the development of the HTML. Now, the W3C is laying a foundation for the future of the Web by developing dozens of technologies and protocols that must work together in a solid infrastructure.

For the definitive answer on any web technology question, the W3C site is the place to go:

www.w3.org

For more information on the W3C and what they do, see this useful page:

www.w3.org/Consortium/

Server-side programming and scripting

Some web pages, including those that use forms and databases, rely on special programs on the server to send information to and from the user. These programs are sometimes called CGI (Common Gateway Interface) scripts, and can be written in a number of programming languages, such as Perl, Python, or C. PHP, ASP, and JSP are other tools that can be used to create complex web applications that interact with databases on the server.

Server functionality is typically programmer territory and is not expected of all web designers. Your hosting service may provide a few "canned" CGI scripts for common functions such as an email form or guest book along with instructions for adapting them to your own needs.

XML

If you hang around the web design world at all, you are sure to hear the acronym XML (which stands for eXtensible Markup Language). XML is not a specific language in itself, but rather a robust set of rules for creating other markup languages. Where HTML is useful in defining the elements of a page (headings, paragraphs, etc.), other XML languages that are customized to specific types of information can be created.

To use a classic example, if you were publishing recipes, you might create a set of XML tags that included <ingredient>, <instructions>, and <servings>. A bank might use a set of XML tags to identify the <account>, <balance>, <date>, etc. Special style sheets tell the browser how to display the XML content. This makes XML a powerful tool for transferring data between applications and handling the data in complex databases, as well as displaying it on a web page. Since most of this happens on the backend (see the sidebar Frontend Versus Backend), the responsibility for XML development usually falls in the hands of programmers.

XHTML

One of the first things the developers of the Web did when they had the rules of XML in place was to apply XML to the previously hacked-together HTML language. The result was XHTML. For now, you can just think of XHTML as a really strict version of HTML in which you can't have a single character out of place. One day, all browsers will expect pages to be in XHTML format. For now, they are rather forgiving of regular HTML.

This book teaches you how to write HTML the "right" way, but does not go as far as presenting all XHTML-compliant code examples. The XML-based rules that make XHTML different from HTML are outlined in Chapter 22. They are worth learning and putting into practice if you plan on becoming a professional web developer.

Java

Although Java can be used for creating small applications for the Web (known as "applets"), it is a complete and complex programming language that is typically used for developing large, enterprise-scale applications. Learn Java only if you want to become a Java programmer. You can live your life as a web designer without knowing a stitch of Java (as I do).

What Do I Need to Buy?

It should come as no surprise that professional web designers require a fair amount of gear, both hardware and software. One of the most common questions I'm asked by my students is, "What should I get?" I can't tell you specifically what to buy, but I will provide an overview of the typical tools of the trade.

Bear in mind that while I've listed the most popular commercial software tools available, many of them have freeware or shareware equivalents which you can download if you're on a budget (try CNET's Download.com). With a little extra effort, you can get a full web site up and running without big cash.

Equipment

For a comfortable web site–creation environment, I recommend the following equipment:

A solid, up-to-date computer. Either a PC running Windows or a Mac is fine, but most creative departments in professional web development companies tend to be Mac-based. Although it is nice to have a super-fast machine, the files that make up web pages are very small and tend not to be too taxing on computers. Unless you're getting into sound and video editing, don't worry if your current setup is not the latest and greatest.

Extra memory. Because you'll tend to bounce between a number of software programs, it's a good idea to have enough RAM installed on your computer to be able to leave those programs running at the same time. It depends on the programs you're running, but as a ballpark figure, 64 MB is an absolute minimum, and 128 MB and up is preferable.

A large monitor. While not a requirement, a large or high-resolution monitor (1024 × 768 pixels and up) makes life easier. The more monitor real estate you have, the more windows and control panels you can have open at the same time. You can also see more of your page to make design decisions.

While not a requirement, a large monitor makes life easier.

A second computer. Many web designers find it useful to have test computers that use different platforms than their primary computers (i.e., if you design on a Mac, test on a PC). Because browsers work differently on Macs than on Windows machines, it's critical to test your pages in as many environments as possible. If you are a hobbyist web designer working at home, check your pages on a friend's machine.

A scanner and/or digital camera. If you anticipate making your own graphics, you'll need some tools for creating images or textures. I know a designer who has two scanners: one is the "good" scanner, and the other he uses to scan things like dead fish and rusty pans. Because web graphics are low resolution, you don't need a state-of-the-art, mega-pixel digital camera to get decent results.

Software

There's no shortage of software available for creating web pages. In the early days, we just made do with tools originally designed for print. Today, there are wonderful tools designed with web design specifically in mind that make the web design process more efficient. Although I can't list every available software release (you can find other offerings as well as the current version numbers of the following programs in software catalogs), I'd like to introduce you to the most common and proven tools for web design. Note that you can download trial versions of many of these programs from the company web sites, as listed in the At a Glance: Popular Web Design Software sidebar later in this chapter.

Web page authoring

Web-authoring tools are similar to desktop publishing tools, but the end product is a web page document (an HTML file). These tools provide a visual "WYSIWYG" (What You See Is What You Get; pronounced "whizzy-wig") interface and shortcuts that save you from typing repetitive HTML code. Some of the more powerful packages also generate JavaScript and DHTML. The following are some popular web-authoring programs:

Macromedia Dreamweaver. This is the industry standard due to its clean code and advanced features.

Adobe GoLive. GoLive is another top-of-the-line tool with advanced features.

Microsoft FrontPage. This program is quite popular in the business world, but notorious for adding extra proprietary code to its files, so it tends to be shunned by professional web designers. Another drawback is that some functions require special Microsoft software on the server, so check with your server administrator if you plan to use FrontPage.

HTML editors

HTML editors (as opposed to authoring tools) are designed to speed up the process of writing HTML by hand. They do not allow you edit the page visually like WYSIWYG authoring tools (listed previously) do. Many professional web designers actually prefer to create HTML documents by hand, and they overwhelmingly recommend the following two tools:

Macromedia HomeSite (Windows only). This tool includes shortcuts, templates, and even wizards for more complex elements.

BBEdit by Bare Bones Software (Macintosh only). Lots of great features make this the editor of choice for Mac-based web developers.

Graphics software

You'll probably want to add pictures to your pages, so you will need an image-editing program. We'll look at some of the more popular programs in greater detail in Part III. In the meantime, you may want to look into the following popular web graphics–creation tools:

Adobe Photoshop. Photoshop is undeniably the industry standard for graphics creation in both the print and web worlds. If you want to be a professional designer, you'll need to know Photoshop thoroughly.

Adobe ImageReady. Bundled with Adobe Photoshop, this program helps make smaller, better web graphics and provides special functions such as animation and "rollover" effects.

Macromedia Fireworks. This web graphics–creation program combines a drawing program with an image editor. Its real power lies in its web-specific functions for creating optimized graphics, animated graphics, and interactive buttons. It is well-integrated with Dreamweaver.

Adobe Illustrator. This drawing program is often used to create graphics, which are then brought into Photoshop for fine-tuning.

JASC Paint Shop Pro (Windows only). This full-featured image editor is very popular with the Windows crowd, primarily due to its low price (only $99 at the time of this printing).

Multimedia tools

Because this is a book for beginners, I won't focus on advanced multimedia elements; however, it is still useful to be aware of the software that is available to you should you choose to follow that specialty:

Macromedia Flash. This is the hands-down favorite for adding animation, sound, and interactive effects to web pages due to the small file size of Flash movies.

On the Companion CD

The CD included with this book contains some software to help you get started:

- Trial versions of Macromedia Fireworks MX and Macromedia HomeSite v5
- Time-limited tryout versions of Adobe Photoshop 7 and Adobe ImageReady 7
- BareBones' BBEdit 7.0 demo

Adobe LiveMotion. Adobe's multimedia package for creating interactive Flash content. It is well-integrated with other Adobe products.

Apple Quicktime. You can use the QuickTime Player and QuickTime Player Pro do to basic audio and video editiong and exports.

Apple Final Cut Pro. For more advanced video editing, Final Cut Pro is an industry favorite.

Macromedia Director. Director can also be used to generate movies and interactive elements (called "Shockwave" files) for web delivery; however, it grows less popular for the Web as the scripting capabilities of Flash improve.

Internet tools

Because you will be dealing with the Internet, you need to have some tools specifically for viewing and moving files over the network:

A variety of browsers. Because browsers render pages differently, you'll want to test your pages on as many browsers as possible (Netscape Navigator and Microsoft Internet Explorer, at minimum), as well as a text-only browser such as Lynx.

A file-transfer program (FTP). This enables you to transfer (upload) your files to the computer that will serve your pages to the Web. There are many utilities that do file transfer exclusively, including Fetch (for the Mac) and WS_FTP (Windows). File-transfer functions are built into some web page–authoring tools such as Macromedia Dreamweaver and Adobe GoLive. See Chapter 3 for more information on file uploading.

Telnet. If you are advanced and know your way around the Unix operating system, you may find a telnet program helpful for manipulating files on the server. If not, you can probably get along without one.

AT A GLANCE

Popular Web Design Software

Web Page Authoring

Macromedia Dreamweaver
  www.macromedia.com

Adobe GoLive
  www.adobe.com

Microsoft FrontPage
  www.microsoft.com/catalog/

HTML Editing

Macromedia HomeSite
  www.macromedia.com

BBEdit by Bare Bones Software
  www.barebones.com

Graphics

Adobe Photoshop

Adobe ImageReady

Macromedia Fireworks

JASC Paint Shop Pro
  www.jasc.com

Adobe Illustrator

Macromedia Freehand

Multimedia

Macromedia Flash

Macromedia Director

Apple Final Cut Pro, Final Cut Express, and iMovie

Adobe Premier

Adobe After Effects

Macromedia SoundEdit

Internet Tools

Netscape Navigator (browser)
  home.netscape.com/browsers/

Microsoft Internet Explorer (browser)
  www.microsoft.com/windows/ie/
  www.microsoft.com/mac/ie/

Lynx (text-only browser)
  lynx.browser.org

File transfer programs (FTPs)

Telnet

The Moral of the Story

Well, it's not really a moral, but the lesson of this chapter should be "you don't have to learn everything." And even if you want to learn everything eventually, you don't need to learn it all at once. So relax, don't worry...

As you'll soon see, it's easy to get started designing web pages—you will be able to create simple pages by the time you're done reading this book. From there, you can continue adding to your bag of tricks and find your special niche in web design.

Test Yourself

Each chapter in this book ends with a few questions that you can answer to see if you picked up the important bits of information. Answers appear in the Appendix.

1. What is the difference between frontend and backend web development?

2. There are roles and responsibilities within web design. Who does not need to learn any HTML?

3. What is the difference between a web-authoring program and an HTML-editing tool?

4. What is the best way to change the font and color of text on a web page?

5. What web language is used to pop up a new browser window?

TRY IT

Exercise 1-1: Taking Stock

Now that you're taking that first step in learning web design, it might be a good time to take stock of your assets and goals. Using the lists in this chapter as a general guide, try jotting down answers to the following questions:

- What are your web design goals? To become a professional web designer? To make personal web sites only?
- Which aspects of web design interest you the most?
- What current skills do you have that will be useful in creating web pages?
- What skills will you need to brush up on?
- What hardware and software tools do you already have for web design?
- What tools do you need to buy? What tools would you like to buy eventually?

How the Web Works   2

I got started in web design in early 1993—pretty close to the start of the Web itself. In web time, that makes me an old-timer, but it's not so long ago that I can't remember the first day I looked at a web page. Frankly, I was a bit confused. It was difficult to tell where the information was coming from and how it all worked.

This chapter sorts out the pieces and introduces some basic terminology you'll encounter. If you've already spent time perusing the Web, some of this information will be a review. If you're starting from scratch, it is important to have all the parts in perspective. We'll start with the big picture and work down to specifics.

The Internet Versus the Web

No, it's not a battle to the death, just an opportunity to point out the distinction between these two words that are increasingly being used interchangeably.

The Internet is a network of connected computers. No company owns the Internet (i.e., it is not equivalent to America Online); it is a cooperative effort governed by a system of standards and rules. The point of connecting these computers together, of course, is to share information. There are many ways information can be passed between computers, including email and file transfer (FTP), as well as outdated modes such as WAIS and gopher. A mode of communication is known as a protocol, and it requires special programs that know how to handle that flavor of information.

The World Wide Web (known affectionately as "the Web") is just one of the ways information can be shared; it is a subset of the information on the Internet, and it has its own protocol.

There are several aspects that make the Web unique among other protocols. First, and probably most significantly, you can easily link one document to another—the documents and their links form a huge "web" of connected information.

In this chapter

An explanation of the Web, as it relates to the Internet

The role of the server

Introduction to URLs and their components

The anatomy of a web page

The function of a browser

The formal name for linked text is hypertext and the technical term for the way the Web transfers information is the Hypertext Transfer Protocol, or HTTP for short. If you've spent any time using the Web, that acronym should look familiar since it is the first four letters of nearly all web site addresses. We'll look more closely at web addresses later in this chapter.

Serving Up Your Information

Let's talk more about the computers that make up the Internet. Because they "serve up" documents upon request, these computers are known as servers. More accurately, the server is the software (not the computer itself) that allows the computer to communicate with other computers; however, it is common to use the word "server" to refer to the computer, as well. The role of server software is to wait for a request for information, then retrieve and send that information back as soon as possible.

There's nothing special about the computers themselves...picture anything from a high-powered Unix machine to a humble personal computer. It's the server software that makes it all happen. In order for a computer to be part of the Web, it must be running special web server software that allows it to "speak" the Hypertext Transfer Protocol. Web servers are also called "HTTP servers." Apache is a popular web server. It is available for free for Unix-based computers, including Macs running Mac OS 10.2; there is also a Windows version. Microsoft also offers a family of web servers for Windows-based computers.

Each server is assigned a unique number (its IP address) and a corresponding name (its domain or hostname), such as *oreilly.com*. The number and name are used to identify that particular server on the Internet, so you can connect to the right information. On the Web, there is a convention that machines running web servers have a name starting with "www" (such as *www.oreilly.com*), but this is by no means a hard and fast rule.

Web Page Addresses (URLs)

With all those web pages on all those servers, how would you ever find the one you're looking for? Fortunately, each document has its own special address called a URL (Uniform Resource Locator). The Web is so popular now, it's nearly impossible to get through a day without seeing a URL (pronounced "U-R-L," not "erl") plastered on the side of a bus, printed on a business card, or broadcast on a television commercial.

URLs may look like crazy strings of characters separated by dots (periods) and slashes, but each part has a specific purpose.

A Brief History of the Web

The Web was born in a particle physics laboratory (CERN) in Geneva, Switzerland in 1989. There, a computer specialist named Tim Berners-Lee first proposed a system of information management that used a "hypertext" process to link related documents over a network. He and his partner, Robert Cailliau, created a prototype and released it for review. For the first several years, web pages were text-only. It's difficult to believe that in 1992 (not long ago), the world had only 50 web servers, total!

The real boost to the Web's popularity came in 1992 when the first graphical browser (NCSA Mosaic) was introduced. This allowed the Web to break out of the realm of scientific research into mass media. The ongoing development of the Web is overseen by the World Wide Web Consortium (W3C).

If you want to dig deeper into the Web's history, check out these sites:

Web Developers' Virtual Library

   WDVL.com/Internet/History

W3C's History Archives

   www.w3.org/History.html

The parts of a URL

A complete URL is generally made up of four components, as shown in Figure 2-1. Let's examine each one.

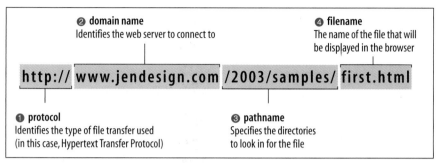

Figure 2-1. The parts of a URL.

❶ `http://`

The first thing the URL does is define the protocol that will be used for that particular transaction. As we discussed earlier, the letters HTTP let the server know to use Hypertext Transfer Protocol, or get into "web-mode."

> **NOTE**
>
> *Sometimes you'll see a URL that begins with https://. This is an indication that it is a secure server transaction. Secure servers have special encryption devices that hide delicate content, such as credit card numbers, while they are transferred to and from the browser.*

❷ `www.jendesign.com`

The next portion of the URL indicates the server to connect to. In most cases, the URL identifies a server by its domain name, but it could also call the server by its number (it's just easier for humans to ask for it by name). In this URL, I am asking to see a file on the "jendesign" server. The "www" is just a convention for indicating that this is a web server.

❸ `/2003/samples/`

If you see a series of words separated by slashes, that indicates a path through directory levels to a specific file. Because the Internet was originally comprised of computers running the Unix operating system, our current way of doing things still follows many Unix rules and conventions.

❹ `first.html`

The last part of the URL is the name of the file itself. It must end in *.htm* or *.html* in order to be recognized as an HTML document.

Intranets and Extranets

When you think of a web site, you generally assume that it is accessible to anyone surfing the Web. However, many companies take advantage of the awesome information-sharing and gathering power of web sites to exchange information just within their own business. These special web-based networks are called intranets. They are created and function like ordinary web sites, only they are on computers with special security devices (called firewalls) that prevent the outside world from seeing them. Intranets have lots of uses, such as sharing human resource information or providing access to inventory databases.

An extranet is like an intranet, only it allows access to selected users outside of the company. For instance, a manufacturing company may provide its customers with passwords that allow them to check the status of their orders in the company's orders database. Of course, the passwords determine which slice of the company's information that user is allowed to see. Sharing information over a network is changing the way many companies do business.

Our example URL is saying it would like to use the HTTP protocol to connect to a web server on the Internet called *jendesign.com* and request the document *first.html* (located in the *samples* directory, which is in the *2003* directory).

URL shortcuts

Obviously, not every URL you see is so convoluted. Often, you see URLs that are short and sweet, like *www.oreilly.com*. Here's how that works.

http://

Since all web pages use the Hypertext Transfer Protocol, "http://" is usually just omitted because it is implied. In addition, browsers are programmed to add that part automatically if it is not typed in explicitly. It's always in there, you just don't always need to deal with it.

Index files

Another implied part of a URL is any reference to a document called *index.html*. Most servers have a built-in default that causes them to search for a file called *index.html* if no filename is specified in the URL.* So, if I type in *www.oreilly.com*, the browser will try to retrieve the document *http://www.oreilly.com/index.html*. By naming the top-level document in your directory *index.html*, you can keep your URL simple (Figure 2-2).

Figure 2-2.   Short and sweet URLs have implied components that you don't need to type in.

The index file is also useful for security. If a directory doesn't contain a file called *index.html*, and the server is set up to look for one, when someone types in a URL without a specific filename, the browser will display a list of all the files in that directory. One way to prevent people snooping around your files is to be sure there is an index file in every directory (Figure 2-3). Your system administrator may also add other protections to prevent your directories from displaying in the browser.

---

* The default file might have a different name, such as *default.html*. It depends on how the server software is configured, so be sure to ask your server administrator for the proper default filename.

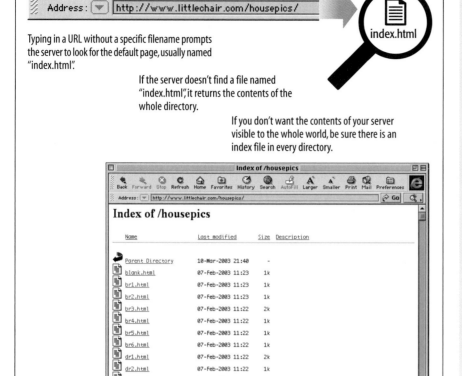

Typing in a URL without a specific filename prompts the server to look for the default page, usually named "index.html".

If the server doesn't find a file named "index.html", it returns the contents of the whole directory.

If you don't want the contents of your server visible to the whole world, be sure there is an index file in every directory.

Figure 2-3. Index files protect your directories from snoopers.

One way to prevent people from snooping around your files is to be sure there is an index file in every directory.

TERMINOLOGY

Servers and Clients

As we discuss in this chapter, server software sends information upon request. Sometimes the word "server" is used to refer to the computer running that software.

The other half of this equation is the software that makes the request. This software is called a "client."

On the Web, the browser is the client software that makes requests for documents. The web server returns the documents for the browser to display.

Often in web design, you'll hear reference to "client-side" or "server-side" applications. These terms are used to indicate which machine is doing the processing. Client-side applications run on the user's machine, while server-side applications and functions use the processing power of the server computer.

The Anatomy of a Web Page

Finally, we get to the real meat of the Web—web page documents. You know what they look like when you view them on your computer, but what's happening "under the hood?" Let's take a quick look at the stuff web pages are made of.

In Figure 2-4, you see a basic web page as it appears in a browser. Although you can view it as one coherent page, it is actually made up of three separate files: an HTML document (*simple.html*) and two graphics (*flower.gif* and *simpleheader.gif*). The HTML document is running the show.

```
<html>
<head>
<title>A Story</title>
</head>

<body>
<p><img src="flower.gif"><img src="simpleheader.gif"> <img src="flower.gif">
<h1>A Story</h1>
<p>Once there was a <em>very</em> simple web page. This page looked at
all the really cool web pages and felt a little inferior. But then the
little web page remembered, "HEY! I'm a web page all the same, and isn't
that cool enough?"</p>
<hr>
<p><b>The End</b>
</body>

</html>
```

simple.html

The simple web page displayed in this example is made up of three separate files: an HTML text document and two graphics.

flower.gif

simpleheader.gif

The browser brings these separate elements together in the window. Tags in the HTML file give the browser instructions for how the page is to be displayed.

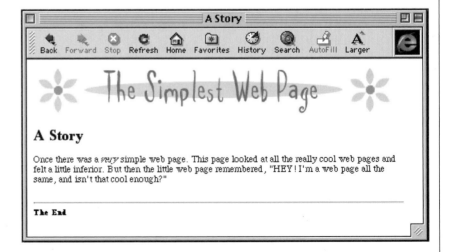

Figure 2-4. The source file and images of a simple web page, and how that page appears in a browser.

HTML documents

You may be as surprised as I was to learn that the graphically rich and interactive pages we see on the Web are generated by simple, text-only documents.
That's right: plain old ASCII text (meaning it has just letters, numbers, and
a few symbol characters).

Take a look at *simple.html*, the text document that makes up our sample web
page. You can see it contains the text content of the page; the "magic" lies in
the special tags (indicated with angle brackets, < and >). They explain how the
text is to be displayed, where the graphics should go, and where links occur.
This system of tagging is called the HyperText Markup Language, or HTML
for short, and the tags are commonly known as HTML tags.

But where are the pictures?

Obviously, there are no pictures in the HTML file itself, so how do they get
there when you view the final page?

You can see in Figure 2-4 that each image is a separate graphic file. The
graphics are placed in the flow of the text with an image placement tag
(<img>) that tells the browser where to find the graphic (its URL). When the
browser sees the <img> tag, it goes out and gets the graphic from the server
and displays it seamlessly on the web page. It's the browser that brings all the
separate pieces together.

More about tags

You'll be learning about HTML in detail in Part II, so I don't want to bog you
down with too much detail right now, but there are a few things I'd like to
point out. Read through the HTML document and compare it to the browser results in Figure 2-4. It's easy to see how the page elements and tags relate.

First, you'll notice that anything within brackets does not display in the final
page. Tags simply provide the browser with instructions for how the text or
element is to be rendered on the page. Usually, the tag uses an abbreviation
of the instruction, such as "h1" for "heading level 1," or "em" for "emphasized
text."

Second, you'll see that most HTML tags appear in pairs (sometimes called
containers), the first one turning that instruction "on" and the second one
(containing a slash) turning it "off." In our HTML document, <h1> indicates
that the following text should be a heading level 1; </h1> ends the heading
and switches back to normal text.

There are some tags that don't use a closing tag. These are usually called
"standalone" tags, and they are used for placing an element or instruction on
a page. In our sample, the <hr> means "draw a horizontal rule (line) here."

TIP

View Source

You can see the HTML file for
any web page by choosing
View → Source or View →
Page Source in your browser's
menu. It is a good way to
peek at the tagging that is
responsible for an effect you
like. Your browser will open
the source document in a
separate window.

Keep in mind that while
learning from others' work is
fine, the all-out stealing of
other people's code is poor
form (or even illegal). If you
want to use code as you see
it, ask for permission and
always give credit to those
who did the work.

The HTML Concept

It's significant to note that in "pure" HTML, tags merely specify the type of information that follows, not instructions for how the information should look. It's just like the style categories you might create in a word-processing program or desktop-publishing application.

So, when tagging a document properly, you indicate that a particular headline is a heading level 1 (<h1>), but it's the browser (controlled by the end user) that determines what an h1 looks like. Most browsers render first-level headings in the largest bold font available.

During the early years of the Web, some tags for controlling the appearance of text got slipped into the HTML standard, but the original intent of HTML was to keep style information separate from the content and structure of the document.

Fortunately, style sheets have come along to handle the formatting of text and basic page elements, so HTML is again free to simply structure documents as it was designed to do.

NOTE

Because the browser is fundamental to how web pages appear to the end user, designers need to be especially aware of some of the complex issues surrounding browser software. We'll talk about some of those in Chapter 4.

Browsers

As you probably know, a browser is a piece of software that displays web pages. It is the tool you use to view the Web, a little like a television set is used to view television programs. More technically, it is the "client" software that requests documents from the server.

The browser reads through the HTML file and renders the text and tags as it encounters them. When I first began writing HTML, it helped me to think of the tags and text as "beads on a string" that the browser deals with one by one, in sequence. Understanding the browser's method can be helpful when troubleshooting a misbehaving HTML document.

A browser is really a one-trick pony: it requests web pages and displays their contents. You can't use the browser to edit the web file (you have to open the original file in an editor to do that)—you can only view it. Some "browsers" are bundles of programs that include a browser, email functionality, file transfer capabilities, even an HTML editor. Their capabilities are enhanced by the use of helper applications and plug-ins that help the browser present media other than HTML documents, including audio, video, and interactive presentations.

The most popular browsers are Microsoft Internet Explorer and Netscape, but there are hundreds of smaller, lesser-known browsers out there.

One browser in particular you should know about is Lynx, a browser that displays only text and no graphics (Figure 2-5). Because it works on simple terminals, it is often used in academic and scientific networks. Sight-impaired users may have web pages spoken to them by a device that reads from a text-only browser. Web designers often use Lynx to test their pages for functionality under the most rudimentary viewing conditions.

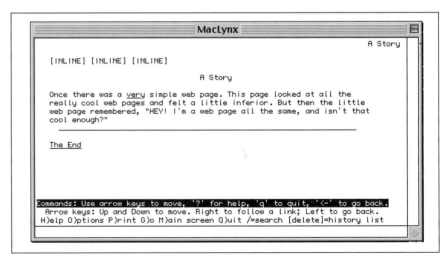

Figure 2-5. The way our simple web page looks in Lynx, a text-only browser.

Putting It All Together

To wrap up our introduction to how the Web works, let's trace the stream of events that occur with every web page that appears on your screen (Figure 2-6).

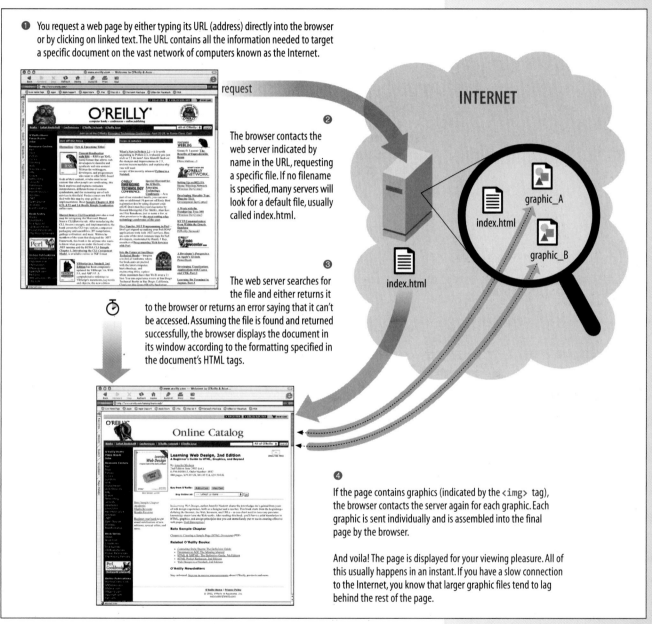

1 You request a web page by either typing its URL (address) directly into the browser or by clicking on linked text. The URL contains all the information needed to target a specific document on the vast network of computers known as the Internet.

request

INTERNET

2 The browser contacts the web server indicated by name in the URL, requesting a specific file. If no filename is specified, many servers will look for a default file, usually called index.html.

graphic_A

index.html

graphic_B

index.html

3 The web server searches for the file and either returns it to the browser or returns an error saying that it can't be accessed. Assuming the file is found and returned successfully, the browser displays the document in its window according to the formatting specified in the document's HTML tags.

4 If the page contains graphics (indicated by the `<img>` tag), the browser contacts the server again for each graphic. Each graphic is sent individually and is assembled into the final page by the browser.

And voila! The page is displayed for your viewing pleasure. All of this usually happens in an instant. If you have a slow connection to the Internet, you know that larger graphic files tend to lag behind the rest of the page.

Figure 2-6. How browsers display web pages.

Test Yourself

Let's play a round of "Identify that Acronym!" The following are a few basic web terms you should be able to define. Answers are in the Appendix.

1. HTML   a) Home of Mosaic, the first graphical browser

2. W3C   b) The location of a web document or site

3. CERN   c) The tagging language used for all web documents

4. HTTP   d) The organization that monitors web technologies

5. URL   e) Particle physics lab where the Web was born

6. NCSA   f) Protocol for transferring web documents on the Internet

Answers: _____

TRY IT

Exercise 2-1: Getting to Know Your Browser

We've talked about the components of a web page and the basic functions of the browser, but there's nothing like experiencing it first-hand. You'll need a web browser and web access to work along.

ACTIVITY I

Launch your browser and enter this URL (either type into the location field, or select File → Open Location from the application menu):

> *www.learningwebdesign.com/materials/chap02/ contents/*

Instead of a web page, you should see all the files that are stored in that directory. That's because there is no default *index.html* file. Fortunately, that directory is full of dummy documents, but you can see how exposed your files are if you neglect to name the top document in each directory *index.html*.

ACTIVITY 2

1. Let's take a look under the hood of a web page. Enter this URL into your browser:

   > *www.learningwebdesign.com/materials/chap02/ simple.html*

   You should see the web page from Figure 2-4.

2. To look at the HTML source for that page (or any web page you're viewing), select View → Source (or View → Page Source on Netscape) from the application menu. A window will open containing the raw HTML that makes up the page.

   For a more complicated example, open the following URL and view the source:

   > *www.learningwebdesign.com*

   You're looking at the source for the file *index.html*. The HTML source can get long and complicated even for a fairly straightforward page like this. Don't worry if you don't understand what's going on in the code; much more of it will look familiar by the time you're done with Part II of this book.

Getting Your Pages on the Web

3

Because your browser can display documents right from your hard drive (i.e., "locally"), you do not need an Internet connection to create web pages. However, eventually, you'll want to get them out there for the world to see. That is the point, right?

Putting a page on the Web is easy… just transfer your files to your web server and *ta da*—you're on the Web! But what if you don't have a web server? This chapter will tell you where to look for one (you might even have server space and not know it).

But first, I want to show you how easy it is to put a page online. If you're one of those instant-gratification types (and have access to a web server), you can follow along and publish your first web page before the next chapter.

Putting Files Online (FTP)

Publishing on the Web requires that you transfer your web documents from your desktop computer to your web server computer. If you are in an office or at a school that has a web server as part of its network, you may be able to move the files directly over the network, as you would with any other file transfer.

More likely, your server will be in a remote location, accessible via the Internet. Files are transferred between computers on the Internet via a protocol called FTP (File Transfer Protocol). Because FTP is a special Internet protocol, you need to use software made for the job.

In addition, you need to know these four things to FTP files:

The name of your web server (host). For example, *www.jenware.com*.

Your login name or user ID. You'll get a login name from the server administrator when you set up your server account (or if you're a freelancer, you'll need access to your client's login).

In this chapter

A step-by-step demonstration of how to upload a web page

Finding a server to host your web site

Registering your own domain name

Your password. This will also be provided by the server administrator or client.

The directory where your web pages reside. Your server administrator should also tell you which directory to use for your web pages (usually, it's *www* or *html*). Your server might be set up to send you to the correct directory when you log in, in which case, if you leave the directory blank, you will automatically be forwarded to the proper directory. Again, get directions from the administrator.

FTP software

FTP functionality is now built into the better WYSIWYG web-authoring tools, such as Macromedia Dreamweaver, Adobe GoLive, and Microsoft FrontPage (just to name a few). This is a great feature, because you can build your pages and upload them all in one program. See the Tool Tip:Uploading Files Via FTP later in this chapter.

If you haven't yet invested in one of these tools, there are a number of dedicated FTP programs with simple interfaces that make file transfer as easy as moving files around on your own computer. For the Mac, both Fetch and Interarchie allow "drag and drop" transfers. On the PC, WS_FTP and AceFTP are quite popular. You can download these programs at CNET's *www.download.com*.

A real, "live" web page: Step-by-step

Finally. Let's go through the process of putting a page on the Web. In this scenario, I had an idea for a cooking resources web site, so I registered my own domain name, *jenskitchen.com** (we'll discuss registering domain names later in this chapter). Now I want to put a page online to let folks know when the site will launch and the content will be available.

Don't worry if you don't understand the contents of the HTML file. We'll get to that soon. For now, I just want you to be familiar with the contents of the file we're uploading.

Before you can upload your files, you need to have FTP (file transfer) software and certain information about your web server.

---

* This is a fictitious domain used for demonstration purposes only. It bears no relation to any site that may appear one day at that location.

Step 1: Start with a web page

I used an HTML editor to type out a simple HTML document, and saved it with the name *index.html* in a directory on my desktop called *mysite* (Figure 3-1). Before I put it on the server where everyone can see it, I check the page in a browser by opening the file that I just saved on my hard drive. This is called viewing the file "locally"—on your own machine. Since it looks fine, I'm ready to upload.

Viewing a file "locally" means viewing a file that is stored on your own computer.

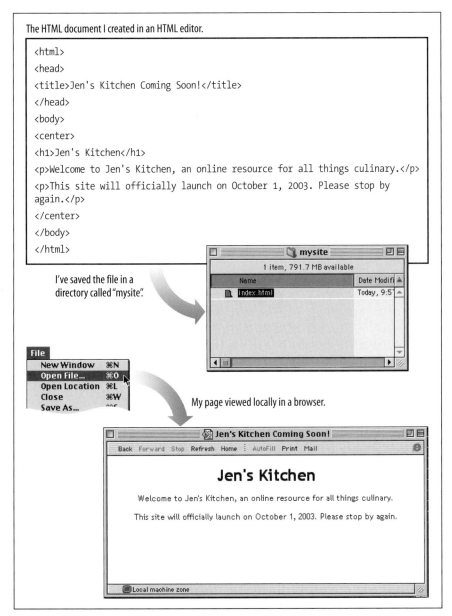

The HTML document I created in an HTML editor.

```
<html>
<head>
<title>Jen's Kitchen Coming Soon!</title>
</head>
<body>
<center>
<h1>Jen's Kitchen</h1>
<p>Welcome to Jen's Kitchen, an online resource for all things culinary.</p>
<p>This site will officially launch on October 1, 2003. Please stop by again.</p>
</center>
</body>
</html>
```

I've saved the file in a directory called "mysite".

mysite
1 item, 791.7 MB available

Name	Date Modifi
index.html	Today, 9:5

File
New Window	⌘N
Open File...	⌘O
Open Location	⌘L
Close	⌘W
Save As...	⌘S

My page viewed locally in a browser.

Jen's Kitchen Coming Soon!

Back Forward Stop Refresh Home AutoFill Print Mail

Jen's Kitchen

Welcome to Jen's Kitchen, an online resource for all things culinary.

This site will officially launch on October 1, 2003. Please stop by again.

Local machine zone

Figure 3-1. Creating and viewing a web page before uploading it.

Step 2: Connect to the server with an FTP program

Since I work on a Mac I often use Fetch for transferring files, but the steps and options are essentially the same on all other FTP programs, so this demo is useful for everyone.

The first thing I do, of course, is make sure that I'm connected to the Internet. I like my cable modem because it is always on, but you may need to dial in over a modem. Once I'm online, I can launch Fetch and connect to the server.

When I select New Connection (Figure 3-2), Fetch pops up a window that asks me the name of the server I want to connect to (in my case, it's *jenskitchen.com*) ❶. For security reasons, it asks for my username and password (I got these when I set up the server account) ❷. The last thing it asks for is the directory ❸. My server administrator told me to use *www*.

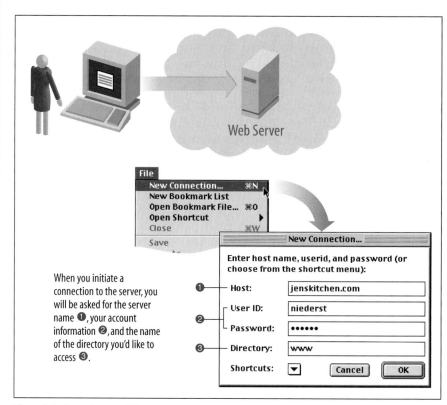

Figure 3-2. Connecting to an FTP server.

Step 3: Upload the file

Once I'm connected, Fetch gives me a window that shows the directory structure on the server (Figure 3-3). Since I want to "put" a file onto the server, I click the Put File button (other FTP programs may call this function "send" or "upload") ❶.

Clicking the Put File button gives me a window where I can browse through the directories on my desktop. I just select my *index.html* file and click Open to continue ❷.

The final bit of information I need to provide is the format of the file I am uploading ❸. For HTML documents like this one, select Text from the Format menu (other FTP programs call text ASCII). For images or other media, select Raw Data or Binary, depending on the FTP program you're using.

Once I select Text and hit OK, my file starts whizzing over the lines and onto the server. It'll take a moment to upload, but soon, you'll see the file pop up in the server directory in the main Fetch window ❹.

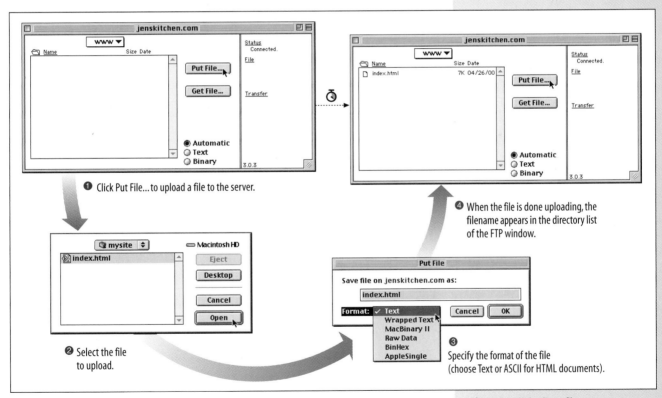

Figure 3-3. Uploading a file.

Organizing and Uploading a Whole Site

We uploaded only one document in this example, but chances are your site will consist of more than one page. If your site contains more than a dozen or so documents and graphics files, you should organize your files into directories and subdirectories. This requires some work and careful planning, but it makes site management much easier in the long run.

One common convention is to keep all of the graphics in a directory called *graphics* or *images*. In most cases, the overall directory structure is based on the structure of the site itself (for instance, if you have a "News" category on your site, there would be a corresponding *news* directory for those files). Site structure is discussed in more detail in Chapter 20.

The good news is that you can upload an entire site in one go. When you select a directory to be FTPed (whether in an authoring tool or with an FTP program), it will upload *everything* within that directory—leaving the subdirectory structure intact. Follow the instructions shown here, but select the directory name instead of a single filename for upload.

The FTP program will check the format of each file and select "text" or "raw data" as appropriate during the upload.

It is a good idea to set up your site directory structure as you want it on your local hard drive first, then upload everything to the final server once it is ready.

Step 4: Check the page in a browser

Now my page is officially on the Web. Just to be sure, I can check it with a browser (Figure 3-4). I open my favorite browser and enter the URL *www.jenskitchen.com/index.html*, and there it is.

Figure 3-4. Verifying the results of an FTP transfer.

Uploading Files Via FTP

Here's how you upload files in three of the more popular authoring programs. See the documentation that comes with your software for more detailed instructions.

Dreamweaver MX

❶

Before you can upload documents, you must set up a new "site" (Dreamweaver's word for a project).

Enter the standard FTP information in the Remote Info category of the Define Sites... dialog box.

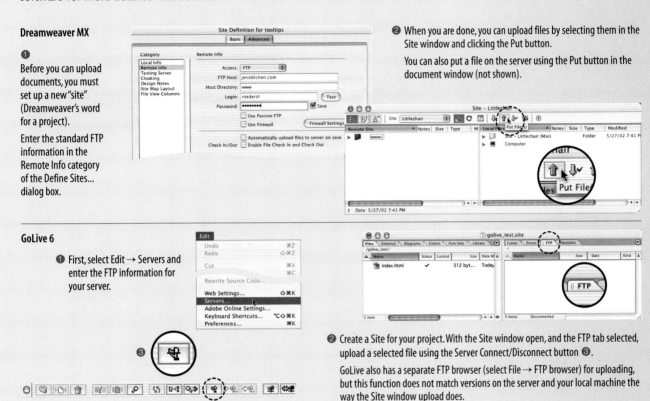

❷ When you are done, you can upload files by selecting them in the Site window and clicking the Put button.

You can also put a file on the server using the Put button in the document window (not shown).

GoLive 6

❶ First, select Edit → Servers and enter the FTP information for your server.

❸

❷ Create a Site for your project. With the Site window open, and the FTP tab selected, upload a selected file using the Server Connect/Disconnect button ❸.

GoLive also has a separate FTP browser (select File → FTP browser) for uploading, but this function does not match versions on the server and your local machine the way the Site window upload does.

FrontPage 2002

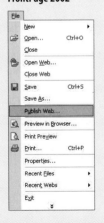

❷

NOTE: To FTP your files, be sure to type "ftp://" at the beginning of the domain name. The dialog box prompts you with an "http://" example, but HTTP transfer works only if the server has the FrontPage 2002 Extensions installed.

❶ Select File → Publish Web to select files to upload. The first time you do this, you will be prompted to enter the remote site info. There is a separate window for entering your username and password.

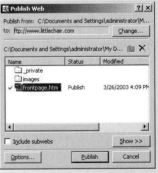

❸ Once you've entered the information, select the file or folder you want to upload in the Publish Web dialog box.

Finding Server Space

By now you know that in order for your pages to be on the Web, they must reside on a web server. Chances are, the desktop machine you are working on is not set up with HTTP server software, so you'll need to get access to a computer that is equipped for the job. Looking for space on a web server is also called finding a host for your site.

Fortunately, there are many hosting options, ranging in price from free to many thousands of dollars a year. The one you choose should match your publishing goals. Will your site be business or personal? Will it get a few hits a month or thousands? How much can you (or your client) afford to pay for hosting services?

In this section, I'll introduce you to some of the options available for getting your web pages online. This should give you a general idea of what type of service you need. However, you should still count on doing a fair amount of research to find the one that's right for you.

One of the first tasks in launching a new web site is finding a host (server space) for your files.

Inherit a server

If you are working as a web designer in an office, especially at a web design company, it is likely that there will be a server connected to your company's network. If this is the case, you can just copy your files to the specified server machine.

If you are a student, you may be given some space to publish personal pages as part of your school account. Ask the department that gives you your email account how to take advantage of web space.

If you are working as a freelancer, your clients will probably assume the responsibility of setting up server space for their sites. But smaller clients may ask for your assistance in finding space, in which case the rest of this chapter is for you.

Online publishing communities

If you just want to publish a personal site and don't want to sink any money into it, you might try picking up some free web space from an online publishing community such as Yahoo! GeoCities (*geocities.yahoo.com*) or Tripod (*www.tripod.lycos.com*). These services (and others like them) provide of free server space in exchange for the opportunity to place *their* advertising on *your* content. The ads are annoying (especially if you go for the pop-up window option), but it might be an acceptable sacrifice if you're on a budget.

Advantages:	Disadvantages:
It's free!	You're stuck with annoying ad banners or pop-up windows.
Good for personal and hobbyist web pages. Also a good option for teens with limited budgets.	Not appropriate for business sites.
	Usually lacks advanced options such as script support.

Online services and ISPs

If you have an account with an online service such as America Online (*www.aol.com*) or CompuServe (*www.compuserve.com*), you probably already have some web server space just waiting to be filled. The online services usually provide tools and assist with making web pages and getting them online. (Of course, after reading this book, you won't need 'em, right?!)

Likewise, ISPs (Internet Service Providers) such as Earthlink provide as much as 10 MB of web server space for their members.

Advantages:	Disadvantages:
A low-cost alternative if you already have the service, or if you are shopping for both a hosting service and Internet access—in the range of $15–40 per month.	Not desirable for business sites because of the limited space and the ISP-based domain name in the URL (for example, *www.earthlink.com/members/~niederst*).
Good for small sites, such as personal and hobbyist web pages.	Service may be slow because you are sharing servers with hoards of other members.
	They may not offer functionality (CGI scripts) necessary for business transactions.

Professional hosting services

If you are working on a serious business site, or if you are just serious about your personal web presence, you will probably want to rent server space from a professional hosting service. Hosting services focus their energies and resources on providing server space, dependable connections to those servers, and related services. Unlike ISPs, they do not offer Internet access.

Hosting companies usually offer a range of server packages, from just a few megabytes (MB) of space and one email address to full-powered e-commerce

ISPs vs. Hosting Services

There are two types of Internet services, and they are easily confused.

An ISP (Internet Service Provider) is the company you go to if you want access to the Internet from your home or office. You can think of an ISP as a provider of a pipeline from your computer to the worldwide network of the Internet via dial-up, DSL, cable modem, or ISDN connections. AOL, CompuServe, and Earthlink are examples of nationwide ISPs, but there are also smaller, local ISPs in nearly every urban area.

In this chapter, we're talking about hosting services. Their business is based on renting out space on their computers. They take care of the server software, keeping the lines working, and so on. They also provide email accounts and may also include special features such free mailing lists or guestbooks for your site. There are thousands of hosting services out there.

The slightly confusing part is that many ISPs also give you some space on a server to host your personal pages. If you put your pages here, you will be stuck with the ISP name in your URL (in other words, they generally don't host other domain names; you need a hosting service for that).

Professional hosting services, however, do not tend to offer Internet access. They expect you to take care of that yourself. In most cases, you'll need both an ISP and a hosting company.

solutions with lots of bells and whistles. Of course, the more server space and more features, the higher your monthly bill will be, so shop wisely.

Advantages:

Scalable packages offer solutions for every size of web site. With some research, you can find a host that matches your requirements and budget.

You get your own domain name (for example, *www.littlechair.com*). We'll talk about domain names shortly.

Disadvantages:

Finding the right one requires research (see the Shopping for Hosting Services sidebar).

Robust server solutions can get expensive, and you need to watch for hidden charges.

TIP

Shopping for Hosting Services

When you set out to find a host for your web site, you should begin by assessing your needs. The following are some of the first questions you should ask yourself or your client:

Is it a business or personal site? Some hosting services provide space for personal sites only; others charge higher rates for business sites than for personal sites. Make sure you are signing up for the appropriate hosting package for your site, and don't try to sneak a commercial site onto a personal account.

How much space do you need? Most small sites will be fine with 10 MB or 15 MB of server space. You may want to invest in more if your site has hundreds of pages, a large number of graphics, or a significant number of audio and video files (which take up more space).

How much traffic will you get? Be sure to pay attention to the amount of data transfer you're allowed per month. This is a function of the size of your files and the amount of traffic you'll get (i.e., the number of downloads to browsers). Most hosting services offer 5–10 gigabytes (GB) of throughput a month (which is perfectly fine for low- or moderate-traffic sites), but after that, they start charging a few cents a megabyte. If you are serving media files such as audio or video, this can really add up. I once ran a popular site with a number of movies that turned out to have over 30 GB of data transferred a month. Fortunately, I had a service with unlimited data transfer (there are some out there), but with another hosting company I could have racked up an extra $300 per month in fees.

How many email accounts do you need? Consider how many people will want email at that domain when you're shopping for the right server package. If you need many email accounts, you may need to go with a more robust and higher-priced package.

Do you need extra functionality? Many hosting services offer special web site features—some come as part of their standard service and others cost extra money. They range from libraries of spiffy scripts (for email forms or guestbooks) all the way up to complete, secure e-commerce solutions. When shopping for space, consider whether you need extra features, such as shopping carts, secure servers (for credit card transactions), a RealMedia server (for streaming audio and video), mailing lists, and so on.

Once you've identified your needs, it's time to do some hunting. First, ask your friends and colleagues if they have hosting services that they can recommend. There's nothing like firsthand experience from someone you trust. After that, the Web is the best place to do research. The following sites provide reviews and comparisons of various hosting services; they can be good starting points for your server shopping spree:

HostSearch
www.hostsearch.com

CNET Web Services
webhostlist.internetlist.com

HostIndex
www.hostindex.com

TopHosts.com
www.tophosts.com

www."YOU".com!

Your home page address is your identity on the Web. If you are posting a just-for-fun page and want to save money, an ISP URL (such as *www.earthlink.com/members/~niederst*) might be fine. More likely, you'll want your own domain name that better represents your business or content. For a small yearly fee, anyone can register a domain name.

What's in a name?

A domain name is a human-readable name associated with a numeric IP address (the "IP" stands for Internet Protocol) on the Internet. While computers know that my site is on a server space numbered 206.151.75.9, you and I can just call it "littlechair.com." The IP address is important, though, because you'll need one (well, two, actually) to register your domain name.

Registering a domain

Registering a domain name can be a fairly painless, one-stop transaction. Most hosting companies will register a domain for you as part of the process of setting up a server account. But be sure to ask specifically—some still require you to register your domain on your own.

If you do need to register a domain on your own, you can go to a company that specializes in domain name registration. While there used to be just one source for domains, there are now hundreds of domain sellers, and they are highly competitive. On the up side, this has resulted in lower prices, but on the down side, it's hard to know who to trust.

Two of the most popular companies in the domain-selling arena are Network Solutions (*www.networksolutions.com*) and Register.com (*www.register.com*). A list of others can be found at *yahoo.com* under Internet and World Wide Web → Domain Name Registration. All companies can register domain names ending in *.com*, *.net*, or *.org*, while some offer newer and international extensions (see the sidebar, Dot What?).

A domain registration company will ask you for the following:

- An administrative contact for the account (name and address)

- A billing contact for the account (name and address)

- A technical contact for the account (generally the name and address of your hosting service)

- Two IP addresses for the server on which the domain will be hosted

The standard price for registering a domain is $35 per year; however, it is fairly easy to find lower prices if you shop around.

Dot What?

The vast majority of web sites that you hear about end with *.com*, but there are other suffixes available for different purposes. These suffixes, used for indicating the type of site, are called top-level domains. The following are the most common top-level domains (also called TLDs) in the United States and their uses:

.com	commercial/business
.org	nonprofit organization
.edu	educational institutions
.net	network organizations
.mil	military
.gov	government agencies

In late 2000, the governing body for top-level domains announced a list of additional suffixes. Now you can register *.us*, *.tv*, *.biz*, *.info*, *.ws*, *.cc*, as well as a variety of international domain extensions.

If you don't have IP addresses, most domain registry services will offer to "park" the site for you for an additional fee. Parking a site means that you have reserved the domain name, but you can't actually *do* anything with it until you get a real hosting package. Basically, you're paying for the privilege of borrowing some IP addresses. There are a few scams out there, so shop wisely. In addition to the $35 per year registration fee, do not spend more than $35 to $50 per year to park a site. Some domain registration companies also offer basic hosting services.

Is it available?

You might have already heard that the simple domain names in the coveted *.com* top-level domain are heavily picked over. Before you get too attached to a specific name, you'd better do a search to see if it is still available. All of the domain name registration sites feature a domain name search right on the front page. This is the first step for setting up a new domain. Some people will even base the name of their company on what domain names are still available.

If "your-domain-name" at ".com" is not available, try one of the other top level domain suffixes, such as *.org*, *.info*, or *.us*. You may also try variations on the name itself. For example, if I found that *jenniederst.com* wasn't available, I might be willing to settle for *jen-niederst.com* or *jenniferniederst.com*.

Test Yourself

Before we move on, let's see if the important parts of this chapter have been uploaded to your brain. Answers appear in the Appendix.

1. What does FTP stand for?

2. Once you have a server, what bits of information do you need to FTP?

3. What format should you select to upload a graphic file? an audio file? an HTML file?

4. In an FTP program, what does the "Get File" function do?

5. How do you upload a whole directory of files at once?

6. What is an IP address? How does it relate to the domain name?

Why Web Design Isn't Like Print Design

4

Like many people, I designed for print for years before I started designing for the Web. My transition was full of interesting twists and turns, and a few brick walls. The Web is a unique medium, and in my opinion...a little strange. By its nature, it forces designers to give up control over the very things they are traditionally responsible for controlling. Many elements, such as colors, fonts, and page layout, are determined by the user or that user's browser software.

There is no guarantee that people will see your pages the same way you design them on your screen. The experience can be a shock until you get used to it. Then it can be downright frustrating.

Designing for the Unknown

Much of web design is, as I call it, "designing for the unknown": unknown users, unknown browsers, unknown platforms, unknown monitor sizes, and so on. In this chapter, I'll discuss how these unknowns impact your role as designer.

Becoming a good web designer requires a solid understanding of the web environment in order to anticipate and plan for these shifting variables. Eventually, you'll develop a feel for it.

Unknown browsers

You may be familiar with the two biggies in the browser arena, Netscape and Microsoft Internet Explorer, but did you know that there are actually hundreds of browsers in use today? In fact, there are dozens of versions of Internet Explorer alone, once you count all the past releases, partial releases, and the various platform versions of each.

In this chapter

The unknown factors that affect the web design process

Tips on surviving the frustration of "designing for the unknown"

The importance of knowing your audience

Becoming a good web designer requires a solid understanding of the web environment.

What you'll quickly learn is that these browsers may display the same page differently (see Figure 4-1). This is due in part to built-in defaults for rendering fonts and form elements. Some browsers, such as Lynx, do not display graphics at all. Each browser has its own slight variation on how to interpret standard HTML tags in terms of fonts and sizes. And to make matters worse there are sets of tags that work *only* in Netscape or *only* in Internet Explorer (they were created by each company to give their browser a competetive edge). If you use these tags, users with the competing browser won't see your content the way you intended.

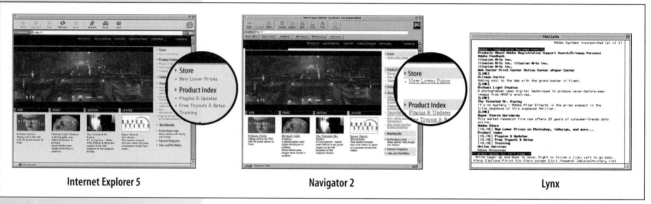

| Internet Explorer 5 | Navigator 2 | Lynx |

Figure 4-1. The same web page may look different on different browsers. Dealing with browser variations is the trickiest part of web design.

The area where browser difference has the most impact is in the support of newer web development technologies such as Cascading Style Sheets (a method for advanced control of text and page formatting) and DHTML (a method for adding interactivity and motion to web pages). While they tend not to be an issue in the latest browser versions, there are enough out of-date browsers still in use that your special effects may be missed by a significant percentage of your audience.

Pressure from web developers finally forced the major browser companies to get on the same page and support one set of web standards (see the Working Toward a Standard sidebar), so the situation has improved over the last four years. However, the fact that your pages will be at the mercy of a myriad of browser interpretations is unlikely to change anytime soon.

Another twist is that users can choose to turn off certain browser functions, such as JavaScript or Java support. The site in Figure 4-2 (the name has been blurred to protect the innocent) uses a Java applet for its navigation bar at left. The applet makes the buttons appear to press down and makes a little "click-click" sound as you pass the mouse over them. But look what happens when users don't have Java activated on their browsers—no navigation at all! This is the danger of relying on a technology trick for crucial page elements.

AT A GLANCE

When you design web pages, there are many unknown factors that affect how your page will look and function, including:

- Browser usage
- Platform
- User preference
- Window size/monitor resolution
- Connection speed
- Color support
- Font support

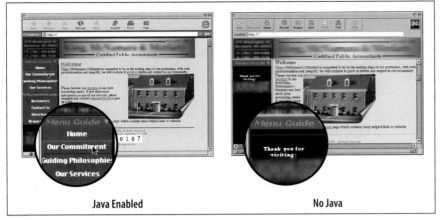

Java Enabled   No Java

Figure 4-2. This web site uses a Java applet for its basic navigation. The applet changes the appearance of the buttons and adds a little clickety sound when the pointer passes over the button graphics. Unfortunately, for users with browsers that aren't Java-enabled, the applet doesn't appear at all, and the page is a dead end.

Similarly, it is impossible to know whether your users will have the browser plug-ins necessary to play multimedia files such as Flash, Windows Media, or QuickTime movies. When you require a plug-in, make sure that you make it easy for users to download a copy.

Unknown platforms

Another variable that affects how users see your pages is the platform, or operating system, of their computers. Although most web users have personal computers running some version of the Windows operating system, a significant portion view the Web from Macintosh computers and Unix/Linux systems. Each operating system has its own characteristics and quirks that affect how your page will look and perform.

For instance, Windows machines and Macs have different ways of displaying type, leading to the same size type appearing much larger on Windows than on Mac. If you set the type on your web page to be small on your Windows machine, it may be completely illegible for Mac users.

Form elements such as scrolling lists and pull-down menus take on the general appearance of the operating system, and therefore appear quite differently (and as different sizes), depending on the machine you view them from.

The viewers' platforms also have an effect on the way they see colors. See the section Unknown colors later in this chapter.

In addition, there is usually a slight discrepancy between the functionality of browsers across different platforms. In general, browser and plug-in releases for the Macintosh lag behind the Windows versions. And although Unix was the platform upon which the Web was built, it is often ignored by software developers eager to hit the dominant Windows market.

Working Toward a Standard

Since the beginning, the World Wide Web Consortium (W3C), the organization that monitors and guides the development of the Web, has set the standards for how the Web should work. This includes minutely detailed specifications for HTML and how browsers should interpret them.

Not surprisingly, since the beginning the browser companies have been trying to stay one step ahead by introducing their own "improvements" to the standards. The result has been browser incompatibility, especially in emerging technologies such as style sheets and DHTML. Trying to get web features to work for all browsers is the single biggest frustration for web developers.

Fortunately, the web development community has made enough noise that the browser companies seem be listening. Both Netscape and Microsoft have vowed to be standards-compliant (as demonstrated by the efforts they put into Netscape 6 and Internet Explorer 5 and higher), which will result in more predictability for web page look and performance. Of course, Version 4 and earlier browsers haven't disappeared from the earth entirely—but hopefully, it won't be long now.

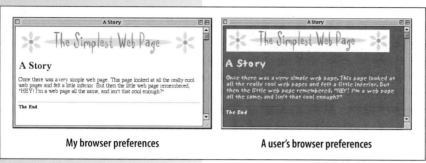

| My browser preferences | A user's browser preferences |

Figure 4-3. A document viewed on the same browser version can look very different as a result of the user's browser settings.

| Graphics On | Graphics Off |

Figure 4-4. This web site looks great with all the graphics on, as the designers intended it to be seen. But if someone decides to turn off graphics (because of a slow modem connection) or views it on a text-only browser, none of the links are labeled, and the page is a dead end.

This could have been avoided if the designer had used alternative text labels in the image tags. This is discussed in Chapter 9.

TRY IT

Exercise 4-1: Playing with Preferences

See how bad you can get your favorite web pages to look. Keep in mind that some users may be doing this to you!

- Launch your browser. Select Edit → Preferences from the menu.
- Select Appearance (Netscape) or Web Content and Language/Fonts (Internet Explorer).
- Go crazy setting new text and background colors. Change the size and fonts of the text. Be sure to check or uncheck boxes so that your preferences will override the document's settings. Try turning off image display.

Now have a look at some web pages. How do you like their makeover?

Unknown user preferences

At the heart of the original web concept lies the belief that the end user should have ultimate control over the presentation of information. For that reason, browsers are built with features that enable users to set the default appearance of the pages they view. The users' settings will override yours, and there's not much you can do about it. Figure 4-3 shows how the same page might look for different users.

Now that web page design has become more exciting, I think users are less likely to alter the color settings in their browsers than they were when most web pages were comprised of black text on gray backgrounds. However, they can still tinker with the default font settings. I've seen CAD designers with super-high monitor resolution set their default type at 24 points to make it easily readable from a comfortable distance. I've looked over the shoulder of a kid who set his browser to render all text in a graffiti font, just because he could. You simply don't know how your page will look on the other end.

Users might also opt to turn off the graphics completely. You'd be surprised at the percentage of people who do this to alleviate the wait for bandwidth-hogging graphics over slow modem connections. Make sure your pages are at least functional with the graphics turned off. The web page in Figure 4-4 becomes unusable with the graphics turned off because the navigation elements lose their labels.

Unknown window size and monitor resolution

When you design a printed piece, you know that your page is a certain size, so you design elements to fit that space. Another tricky thing about the Web is that you really have no idea how big your "page" will be. The available space is determined by the size of the browser window when the page is opened.

Web pages are also more fluid than print; they reflow to fill the available space. Although you may prefer the way your page looks when the window is just larger than the headline graphic, the fact is users can set the window as wide or narrow as they please. This is one of the most vexing aspects of web design. Figure 4-5 shows how the elements on the page rewrap to fill the available space when a browser window is resized. Notice how the text fills the width of the large window. Notice also how the flower graphic gets pushed to the next line when the window is really small.

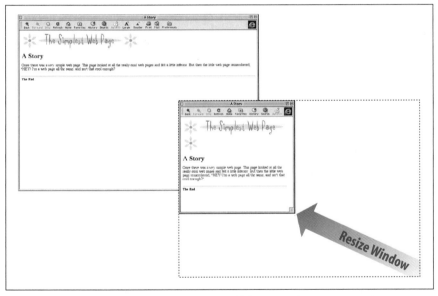

Figure 4-5. Web page elements shift around to fill the available browser window space.

Because browser windows can only be opened as large as the monitors displaying them, standard monitor resolution (the total number of pixels available on the screen) is useful in anticipating the likely dimensions of your page. This is particularly true on Windows machines, since the browser window is typically optimized to fill the monitor.

For instance, one of the lowest standard monitor resolutions still in use today is 640 × 480 pixels. After you allow for the space that the browser and all its rows of buttons and scrollbars take up, that leaves a space as small as 623 × 278 pixels for your page. That's not very much space, but if you are designing a site for students or people who are likely to be using slightly older machines, you should keep this dimension in mind.

> *The tricky thing about the Web is that you really have no idea how big your "page" will be.*

TRY IT

Exercise 4-2:
Resize Your Window

If you have a browser and access to the Web, take some time to get a feel for how web pages respond when the browser window is resized. Make sure your browser window is not optimized to fill the screen.

Activity I

Enter the following URL into your browser:

www.w3.org/MarkUp/

Make the browser as wide as your monitor will allow. Now make it extremely narrow. How many lines of text are at the top? What happens to the headline? What happens to the pink box?

Activity II

Now look at:

www.oreilly.com/

Play around with the width of the browser. Do you notice how the text and page elements always fill the width of the screen? What happens when the page gets very narrow? Can you see the information in the right column?

Other common pixel dimensions are 800 × 600, 1024 × 768, and 1280 × 1024 (although they do go even higher). At the highest resolutions, it's difficult to predict the browser window size because users are likely to resize the window smaller, or open several pages at once. Most commercial web sites today are designed to fit in an 800 × 600 monitor.

How do you cope with the unknown-window-size dilemma? One approach is to use a table to fix the dimensions of your content to a specific pixel width. That way, when the window is resized smaller, the elements do not shift, and users have a better chance of viewing the page as you intended.

Sounds great, right? Unfortunately, this solution has its drawbacks. When the window is resized smaller than the contents of the page, the content outside the browser window is simply no longer visible without horizontal scrolling. Users with smaller monitors may not even know it's there.

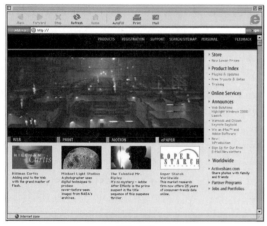

800 x 600

640 x 480

Figure 4-6. This page uses a table to fix the width of the page to 800 pixels wide. Notice how the navigation system falls out of view on the smaller monitor size. This is the risk of designing rigid page layouts. (In Adobe's case, a larger page size makes sense for their audience.)

Figure 4-6 shows a web site that has been designed to fit an 800 × 600 pixel browser window. Notice, however, that when the page is viewed on a smaller monitor (640 × 480), there's no way of knowing that there is a whole navigation system off the screen unless you happen to scroll to the right. This is one of the problems of fixing web pages to a particular width, especially if the width is larger than the lowest common denominator.

If you know that your audience is likely to have an up-to-date monitor, you can comfortably make the decision to design for a larger screen size. For instance, it's safe to assume that graphic designers are not working on a 640 × 480 screen, so a web page layout that fills 800 × 600 pixels is appropriate for a site of design resources.

You might choose to tell your users how you'd like them to size their screens. Every now and then (although not as often as in the early days of web design), you'll run into a friendly note at the top of a web page that says, "For optimal viewing of this site, please size your browser this wide," followed by a graphical bar of a certain width. The best you can do is hope that users will play along.

Another way to deal with unknown window size is to just accept it as the nature of the medium. It is possible to design for flexibility—good web pages are functional and not seriously compromised by a certain amount of shape-shifting. Learning to let go of some control is part of becoming a seasoned web designer.

DESIGN TIP

Designing "Above the Fold"

Newspaper editors know the importance of putting the most important information "above the fold," that is, visible when the paper is folded and on the rack. This principle applies to web design as well.

Web designers have adopted the term "above the fold" to refer to the first screenful of a web page. It's what users will see without scrolling, and it bears the burden of holding their attention and enticing them to click in further. Some elements you should consider placing above the fold include:

- The name of the site and your logo (if you have one)
- Your primary message
- Some indication of what your site is about (e.g., shopping, directory, magazine, etc.)
- Navigation to key parts of the site
- Crucial calls to action, such as "Register Now"

- Any other important information, such as a toll-free number
- An advertising banner (your advertisers may require it)

But how much is a "screenful"? Unfortunately, this varies by browser window size. Your available space could be as small as 623 × 278 pixels in a browser on a 640 × 480 monitor.

In general, the level of confidence in what will be seen on the first "page" is highest in the top-left corner of the browser window and then diminishes as the pages moves down and to the right. When the browser window is made very small, the bottom and the right edge are the most likely to be cut off. One strategy for page layout is to put your most important elements and messages in that top-left corner and work out from there through hierarchies of importance.

Unknown connection speed

Remember that a web page is published over a network, and it will need to go zipping through the lines as little bundles of data before it reaches the end user. In most cases, the speed of that connection is a mystery. On the high end, folks with T1 connections, cable modems, ISDN, and other high-speed Internet access may be viewing your pages at a rate of up to 500 KB per second. On the other end of the scale are people dialing in with modems whose speed can range from 56 Kbps to as slow as 14.4 Kbps. For these users, data transfer rates of 1 KB per second are common.

There are many factors that affect download times, including the speed of the server, the amount of traffic it is receiving when the web page is requested, and the general congestion of the lines.

It should be fairly intuitive that larger amounts of data will require more time to arrive. When you are counting on maintaining the interest of your readers, every millisecond counts. For this reason, it is wise to follow the golden rule of web design: *keep your files as small as possible!*

One of the worst culprits for hogging bandwidth is graphics files, so it is especially important that you spend time optimizing them for the Web. (I discuss some strategies for doing this in Chapters 15 and 16.) HTML files, although generally just a few kilobytes (KB) in size, can be optimized as well by removing redundant tags and extra spaces. Audio, video, and multimedia content also consume lots of bandwidth.

Keep your files as small as possible!

Unless you are designing specifically for high-bandwidth applications, assume the worst when it comes to connection speeds. Since you know a web page is designed to travel, do your best to see that it travels light.

Unknown colors

I'll never forget my first lesson in web color. I had designed a headline graphic that used a rich forest green as a background. I proudly put the page up on the server, and when I went into my boss's office to show him my work, the graphic came up on his screen with a background of *pitch black*. It was then that I learned that not everyone (including my boss) was seeing my colors the way I intended them.

When you are publishing materials that will be viewed on computer monitors, you need to deal with the varying ways computers handle color. The differences fall under two main categories: the number of colors and the brightness of colors.

Number of colors

Monitors differ in the number of colors they are able to display. They typically display 24-bit (approximately 17 million colors), 16-bit (approximately 65,000 colors), or 8-bit color (256 colors).

A full-color photograph may contain many thousands of shades of blended colors to produce a smooth image—not a problem for 24- or 16-bit monitors. But what happens to all those colors on an 8-bit monitor with only 256 available colors?

On 8-bit monitors, the image will be approximated out of the set of colors (called a palette) that the browser has on hand. Some colors from that full-color photo will shift to the nearest palette color. Others will be approximated by dithering (using a speckled pattern of two palette colors to create a color not in the palette, as in Figure 4-7 Ⓖ). Be aware that colors may behave differently depending on the monitor used to view them.

Brightness

That rich forest green I described in my example above was a victim of varying gamma settings. Gamma refers to the overall brightness of a computer monitor's display, and its default setting varies from platform to platform. Images created on a Macintosh will generally look much darker when viewed on a Windows machine or Unix system (which is what happened to me). Images created under Windows will look washed out on a Mac. Figure 4-8 Ⓖ shows the same page viewed at different gamma settings.

The image below shows a graphic as it might appear on a monitor that displays millions or thousands of colors (24-bit or 16-bit monitors). These monitors can smoothly display an enormous range of colors.

8-bit monitors, on the other hand, can display only 256 colors at a time. Within the browser, there are only 216 available colors to choose from.

The image above shows what happens to the same graphic when viewed on an 8-bit monitor. The close-up shows how the real color is approximated by mixing colors from the available palette of colors. This effect is called dithering.

Figure 4-7. Browsers with a limited color palette will approximate unavailable colors by dithering. Ⓖ

Since the majority of the web audience today uses Windows machines, this shift is especially significant for designers using Macs. Try setting the gamma of your monitor darker to approximate the Windows viewing conditions (Adobe Photoshop comes with a Gamma utility for the Mac), and, as always, be sure to test your pages to make sure your color details aren't fading to black. There are also new web graphics tools that will give gamma previews and make brightness adjustments automatically.

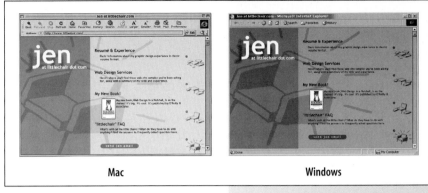

Mac Windows

Figure 4-8. Gamma refers to the overall brightness of monitors. Windows machines tend to be darker (the result of higher gamma settings) than Macs. G

Unknown fonts

Another aspect of web design that you may find shocking is that you have virtually no control over the fonts used to display your content. The way text appears is a result of browser settings, platform, and user preferences.

Even though there are methods for specifying a font face (style sheets and the HTML <font> tag), the font will display only if it is already installed on the end user's machine. It's more like "suggesting" a font than controlling it. There's no guarantee your chosen font will be available. If it is not found on the user's computer, a default font will be used instead.

About the only thing you can be sure of is that you have two fonts to work with: a proportional font (such as Times or Helvetica) that is used for the majority of body copy and headlines on a page, and a monospaced font (such as Courier) that is used for code or text tagged with the "preformatted" tag <pre>.

There are technologies for embedding fonts into a file, but they are not supported by most browsers. This lack of control over fonts is something you have to get used to. The only way to absolutely control type is to put it in a graphic, but that has its drawbacks and is obviously not appropriate for the main body text on a site. Make your font suggestions, and let it go.

Many traditional graphic designers are also frustrated by the lack of control over other typographical features such as leading and letterspacing. While HTML alone does not offer a solution, fortunately, these aspects may be controlled to some degree using style sheets (see Chapter 8).

You may find it shocking that you have virtually no control over the fonts used to display your content.

Surviving the Unknown

I can still remember my reaction to learning about this "unknown" stuff—it was somewhere between confusion and despair. If I couldn't control the size of the page, or the colors, or the type, what were they asking me to "design". Why did they need a designer at all? The answer is that the Web is a visual medium, and designers are needed for all the same reasons they've been needed in the past, including:

- Organizing information for the most effective communication

- Guiding readers' eyes through the page

- Creating an exciting visual experience that is in keeping with the company's brand message

My number-one bit of advice for conquering the medium is to let go.

As a word of consolation, I can tell you that you will develop a feel for designing around the unknowns on the Web. If you've worked as a print designer, you know that you develop a feel for how an ink color will work on a particular paper. It takes practice. But after you've done a certain amount of testing, you'll know the things that are likely to go wrong, and you can avoid them. It just takes time to develop those chops.

My number-one bit of advice for conquering the medium is to *let go*. Elements are going to shift, and pages will look different to different people. Accept it as part of the medium and move on. You'll go crazy trying to control every little thing. Sometimes, you just have to go with the flow.

Keep the Lowest Common Denominator in Mind

When you design for the Web, bear in mind that not everyone is equipped with the latest browser on a souped-up computer system with a lightning-fast connection. Although it's good to take advantage of the latest features in web publishing, you also have to design with the lowest common denominator in mind. In the web biz, this is also referred to as designing web pages that "degrade gracefully."

For instance, some of your users will not see your graphics because they have chosen to turn them off, or because they are using a text-only browser such as Lynx. Furthermore, some sight-impaired users will have your web pages read to them by a speech device attached to a text-only browser. For this reason, you should design so that your pages are at least *functional* (although not beautiful) with the graphics turned off. Avoid putting important text, such as headlines and contact information, in graphics. When you do use a graphic, be sure to provide alternative text for the image (alternative text is discussed in Chapter 9).

You should also avoid relying on effects that use special technologies for your main message. For example, if the whole point of your web site is to distribute an "800" number, do not put that number in a Java applet that makes it scroll across the screen. A significant percentage of users do not have Java activated on their browsers and will miss it altogether. The safest way to present your most important information is in plain old HTML text; that way, everyone is sure to see it. It's okay to play with more adventurous web techniques, but use them as "icing."

I'll repeat this because it is the most important guideline for web design: keep your files as small as possible. Assume the worst when it comes to connection speed, and everyone will benefit.

Take time to test your designs under less-than-optimum conditions before you put them online. Is it just a little less attractive (disappointing, but not critical) or is it totally unusable (back to the drawing board, as they say)?

Know Your Audience

We've established that there are a lot of unknown factors to consider when designing a web page. But there is something that you hopefully do know when you begin the design process: your target audience. In professional web development companies, researching the characteristics and needs of the target audience is one of the most important parts of the design process.

Having a good understanding of your audience can help you make better design decisions.

A good understanding of your audience can help you make better design decisions. Let's take a look at a few examples:

Scenario 1: A site that sells educational toys. If your site is aimed at a consumer audience, you should assume that a significant portion of your audience will be using your site from home computers. They may not keep up with the very latest browser versions, or they may be using an AOL browser or even surfing the Web with their TV, so don't rely too heavily on cutting-edge web technologies. They may also be connecting to the Internet through modem connections, so keep your files extra small to prevent long download times. When your bread and butter depends on sales from ordinary consumers, it's best to play it safe with your page design. You can't afford to alienate anyone.

Scenario 2: A site with resources for professional graphic designers. Because graphic designers tend to have larger computer monitors, this is a case for which you might safely design for an 800 × 600 pixel screen size or even larger. In addition, if they are accessing your pages from work, they are likely to have a connection to the Internet that is faster than the standard modem connection, so you can be a little more lax with the number of graphics you put on the screen (plus, a good-looking site will be part of the draw for your audience).

Scenario 3: A site used to share company information for in-house use only (also known as an intranet). This is the ideal situation for a web designer because many of the "unknowns" become easily known. Often, a company's system administrator will install the same browser on all machines and keep them up-to-date. Or you might know that everyone will be working on Windows machines with standard 800 × 600 monitors. Bandwidth becomes less of an issue when documents are served internally, as well. You should be able to take advantage of some features that would be risky in the standard web environment.

Test Yourself

This chapter covers a number of the quirks of the Web that every new web designer will need to become accustomed to. Describe how each of these factors affect your role as a web designer. Be specific. Answers appear in the Appendix.

1. The variety of browsers in use

2. Macs, PCs, and Unix/Linux systems

3. Each user's browser preferences

4. Resizable browser windows

5. The fonts installed on a user's computer

The Web Design Process

Web sites come in all shapes and sizes—from a single page about a favorite furry friend, to mega-sites conducting business for worldwide corporations such as American Express or FedEx. Regardless of the scale, the process for developing a site involves the same basic steps:

1. Conceptualize and research.

2. Create and organize content.

3. Develop the "look and feel."

4. Produce graphics and HTML documents.

5. Create a working prototype.

6. Test, test, test!

7. Upload and test again.

8. Maintain.

Of course, depending on the nature and scale of the site, these steps will vary in proportion, sequence, and number of people required, but in essence, they are a necessary journey for the creation of a site. This chapter examines each step of the web design process.

1. Conceptualize and Research

Every web site begins with an idea. It's the result of some*one* wanting to get some*thing* online, be it for personal or commercial ends. This early phase is exciting. You start with the core idea ("photo album for my family," "shopping site for skateboarding gear," "online banking," etc.) then brainstorm on how it's going to manifest itself as a web page. This is a time for lists and sketches, whiteboards and notebooks. What's going to make it exciting? What's going to be on the first page?

RESEARCH TIP

Some Questions Before You Begin

The following are just a few of the questions you should ask your clients during the research phase of design.

Strategy

- Why are you creating this web site? What do you expect to accomplish?
- What are you offering your audience?
- What do you want users to do on your web site? After they've left?

General Site Description

- What kind of site is it? (Purely promotional? Info-gathering? A publication? A point of sale?)
- What features will it have?
- What are your most important messages?
- Who are your competitors? What are they doing right? What could be improved upon?

Target Audience

- Who is your primary audience?
- How Internet-savvy are they? How technically savvy?
- Can you make assumptions about an average user's connection speed? Platform? Monitor size? Browser use?
- How often do you expect them to visit your site? How long will they stay during an average visit?

Content

- Who is responsible for generating original content?
- How will content be submitted (process and format)?
- How often will the information be updated (daily, weekly, monthly)?

Resources

- What resources have you dedicated to the site (budget, staff, time)?
- Will updates require completely new page designs with graphics?
- Can maintenance be handled by your staff?
- Do you have a server for your site?
- Have you registered a domain name for your site?

Graphic Look and Feel

- Are you envisioning a certain look and feel for the site?
- Do you have existing standards, such as logos and colors, that must be incorporated?
- Is the site part of a larger site or group of sites with design standards that need to be matched?
- What are some other web sites you like? What do you like about them?

Many web development and design firms spend more time on researching and identifying clients' needs than on any other stage of production.

Don't bother launching an HTML editor until you have your ideas and strategy together. This involves asking your client (or yourself) a number of questions regarding resources, goals, and, most importantly, audience. The Some Questions Before You Begin sidebar provides just a sampling of the sorts of questions you might ask before you start a project.

Many large web development and design firms spend more time on researching and identifying clients' needs than on any other stage of production. For large sites, this step may include case studies, interviews, and extensive market research. There are even firms dedicated to developing web strategies for emerging and established companies.

You may not need to put that sort of effort (or money) into a web site's preparation, but it is still wise to be clear about your expectations and resources early on in the process, particularly when attempting to work within a budget.

2. Create and Organize Content

The most important part of a web site is its content. Despite the buzz about technologies and tools, content is still king on the Internet. There's got to be something of value, whether it's something to read or something to do, to draw visitors and keep them coming back. Even if you are working as a freelance designer putting your client's ideas online, it is wise to be sensitive to the need for good content.

Content creation

When designing for a client, you need to establish immediately who will be responsible for generating the content that goes on the site. Some clients arrive full of ideas but empty-handed, assuming that you will create the site, including all of the content in it. Ideally, the client will be responsible for generating its own content and will allocate the appropriate resources to do so. Solid copy writing is an important, yet often overlooked component of a successful site.

Information design

Once you've got content—or at least a very clear idea of what content you will have—the next step is to organize the content so it will be easily and intuitively accessible to your audience. For large sites, the information design may be handled by a specialist in information architecture. It might also be decided by a team made up of designers and the client. Even personal sites require attention to the division and organization of information.

Again, this is a time for lists and sketchbooks. Get everything that you want in the site out there on the table. Organize it by importance, timeliness, category, and so on. Decide what goes on the home page and what gets divided into sections.

The result of the information design phase is usually a diagram (often called a site map) that reveals the overall "shape" of the site. Pages in diagrams are usually represented by rectangles; arrows indicate links between pages or sections of the site. The site map gives designers a sense of the scale of the site and how sections are related, and aids in the navigation design.

The most important part of a web site is its content.

DESIGN TIP

Viva la Pen and Paper!

There's still no beating pen and paper when it comes to firing up and documenting the creative process. Before you delve into the HTML and GIFs, there's no better way to hash out your ideas than in your handy notepad, on a napkin or whiteboard, or whatever surface is available. It's about creativity!

Make lists. Draw diagrams. Figure out that home page. Do it fast and loose, or include every minute detail and copy it faithfully online. It all comes down to your personal style.

Figure 5-1 shows the site diagram for my simple *www.littlechair.com* site. It is quite small compared to the diagrams for big e-commerce sites. I once saw a site diagram for a high-profile commercial site that, despite using postage stamp–sized boxes to represent pages, filled the length and height of the hallway.

The effectiveness of a site's organization can make or break it. Don't underestimate the importance of this step. For a more thorough introduction to information and interface design, see Chapter 20.

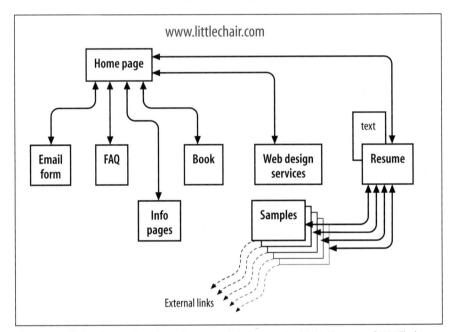

Figure 5-1. This is a diagram of my simple site, www.littlechair.com, as it existed in the spring of 2000. The boxes indicate pages and the arrows indicate links. The site diagrams for commercial web sites are usually much more complicated, and even at this scale the printouts can be large enough to fill a wall.

3. Develop the "Look and Feel"

The "look and feel" of a site refers to its graphic design and overall visual appearance, including its color scheme, typography, and image style (for example, photographic versus illustrative). As in the print world, this phase of design is often referred to as "art direction."

Sketch it

This is another chance to get out pads of paper and markers. Or perhaps you prefer to work out ideas right in Photoshop. Either way, it's your chance to be creative and try things. The result is one or more sketches (sometimes called a "look and feel study") that show off your proposed visual style for the site.

A sketch is usually just a flat graphic file in the approximate dimensions of the browser window (usually 800 × 500 pixels). When it is necessary to show interactivity (such as a "rollover" button effect), some designers use a layer in Photoshop that can be switched on and off to simulate the effect.

In some cases, it may be necessary to create a prototype home page in HTML to show off interactive and animated features, particularly if you have a client with no imagination (but a big budget to cover development costs). Keep in mind that the art direction phase is for exploring how the site will look, so flat graphic sketches are usually adequate.

The art direction process

In most professional web development jobs, the client receives two or three sketches showing its home page in various visual styles. In some cases, a second- or third-level design might be included if it is important to show how the design plays out through several levels. Figure 5-2 shows a set of look-and-feel studies I created for a women's site several years ago.

The designer is usually provided with a basic list of elements and a manuscript for what should be included in the sketches, but don't be too surprised if you are asked to make stuff up on occasion.

Ideally, the client will choose one sketch, but with a list of changes, requiring another round of design until the final design is agreed upon. In my experience, clients usually see elements they like in each style and ask for some sort of hybrid. In this respect, web designers face the same frustrations as traditional graphic designers.

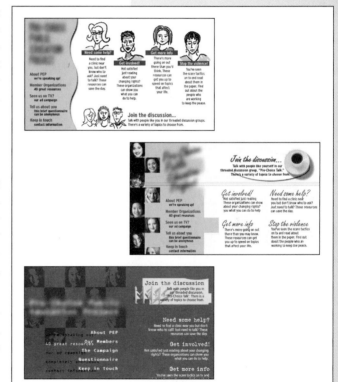

Figure 5-2. As part of the art direction phase, I created three sketches for this women's site, demonstrating how the same material might look in three different visual styles.

4. Produce Graphics and HTML Documents

Once the design is approved and the content is ready to go, the site enters the production phase. For small sites, the production may be done by one person. It is more common in commercial web design to have a team of people working on specialized tasks.

The art department uses its graphics tools to create all the graphics needed for the site. The content will be formatted into HTML documents by HTML whizzes who may write the code by hand or use a full-featured WYSIWYG program (such as Dreamweaver). There may also be multimedia elements produced and scripts and programs written. In short, all the elements of the site must be created.

5. Create a Working Prototype

At some point, all the pieces are brought together into a working site. This is not necessarily a distinct step; it is more likely to be an ongoing process as the HTML files and graphics are being produced (particularly if they are produced by the same person). E-commerce sites typically require a fair amount of programming on the backend to make them functional. This programming is part of the production and prototype building phases as well.

Once the pages are viewed in a browser, it is necessary to tweak the HTML documents, graphics, and scripting until everything fits smoothly in place and works as intended. As a solo web designer, I make a lot of rounds between my graphics program, HTML editor, and browser.

As in software design, the first prototype is often called the "alpha" release. It might be made available only to people within the web team for review and revisions before it is released to the client. The second release is called the "beta" and is generally the version that is sent to the client for approval. At this point, there is still plenty to do before the site is ready to go live on the Web.

6. Test, Test, Test!

Just because a page is working well on your machine doesn't mean it will look that way to everyone. As we discussed in Chapter 4, your page will be viewed through seemingly infinite combinations of browsers, platforms, window sizes, and user settings.

For this reason, I strongly recommend (and many clients require) that you test your pages under as many conditions as possible. Professional web design firms build time and resources into the production schedule for rigorous testing. This phase is often called QA (short for "quality assurance"). They check that the site is in working order, that all the links work, and that the site performs appropriately on a wide variety of browsers and platforms. These firms have banks of various computer configurations, running numerous browser versions on various monitor setups.

Even if you're working on your own and can't afford to turn a room of your house into a testing lab, try viewing your web pages in a number of the following situations:

- On another browser. If you developed your pages using Microsoft Internet Explorer, open them in Netscape. Hang onto old versions of browsers so you can open the pages in a less technically advanced browser as well.

- On a different kind of computer than the one on which you developed the pages. You may need to visit a friend and use her computer. If you worked on a Windows machine, you may be surprised to see how your pages look on a Mac, and vice versa.

- With the graphics turned off, and with a text-only browser, such as Lynx. Is your page still functional?

- With the browser window set to different widths and lengths (be sure to check the extremes). Try changing the resolution of your monitor to a lower setting.

- With your monitor set to 8-bit color. Are your graphics still clear?

- Over a slow modem connection, particularly if you have fast Internet access where you are working.

You may need to make some adjustments to make the page (at the very least) acceptable even in the worst of conditions.

Another type of testing that is important to perform is user testing. This process involves sitting ordinary people down with your site and seeing how easily they can find information and complete tasks. User testing is generally conducted as early in the production process as possible so changes can be made to the final site.

7. Upload and Test Again

Once you have all the kinks worked out of the site, it's time to upload it to the final server and make it available to the world. It's a good idea to do one final round of testing to make sure everything was transferred successfully and the pages function properly under the configuration of the final server. Check that the graphics still appear and the links are still working (link management is a big part of quality assurance).

This may seem like extra work, but if the reputation of your business (or your client's business) is riding on the success of the web site, attention to detail is essential.

I strongly recommend (and many clients require) that you test your pages under as many conditions as possible.

8. Maintain

Another aspect of web site production to be considered is how it's going to be maintained. A web site is never truly "done"; in fact, the ability to make updates and keep content current is one of the advantages of the web medium.

Although maintenance is an ongoing process that happens after the site is initially created, decisions regarding maintenance should be made early in the process. For instance, you should be clear up front about who will be responsible for site upkeep. If you are a freelancer, this should be included in the contract you sign when you begin the job. You should also decide what parts of the site will be updated, and how frequently. The refresh rate will likely impact the way you organize information and design the site.

You should also consider the lifespan of the site. If it is a site promoting a specific event, what happens to the site when the event is over? Even sites that are designed to be around a while will usually require a redesign after a few years to keep up with current technologies and changes in content requirements.

Test Yourself

How familiar are you with these basic terms in the web design process? Answers can be found in the Appendix.

1. What is a site diagram for? At what point in the process would you make one?

2. What is a "look and feel" study?

3. What pieces go into a working prototype?

4. Name at least three ways to test your web pages.

Learning HTML

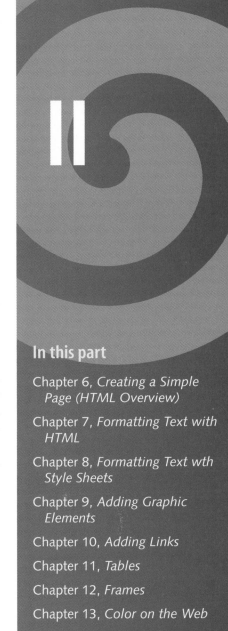

II

As we've already discussed, HTML is the stuff web pages are made of. In this section of the book, we finally dig into the details. I believe that it is useful to learn HTML the old-fashioned way—writing it by hand (I explain why in Chapter 6). Don't worry, it's easy to get started.

However, I recognize that you most likely will use a web-authoring tool to create your pages (I do). For that reason, I have included "Tool Tips" in each chapter that show how to access the tags we discuss in three popular authoring programs: Macromedia Dreamweaver MX, Adobe GoLive 6, and Microsoft FrontPage 2002. There are plenty of other web tools out there, so if you've found one that works for you, feel free to stick with it. Understanding the tags and how HTML works will make using your tools even easier.

The chapters in Part II cover the major HTML topics in detail.

Creating a Simple Page (HTML Overview)

6

Part I provided a general overview of the web design environment. Now that we've covered the big concepts, it's time to roll up our sleeves and start creating a real web page. It will be a simple page, but even the most complicated pages are based on the principles described in the following example.

In this chapter, we'll create a simple web page step by step so you can get a feel for what it's like to mark up a document with HTML tags. The "Try It" exercises allow you to work along. The files required for the exercises are provided on the CD (in the *chap06* directory), or online at the book's web site (*www.learningwebdesign.com/materials/chap06*).

The important lessons here are:

- How HTML tagging works

- How browsers display tagged documents

- How an HTML document is structured

Don't worry about learning specific text-formatting tags at this point. All the tags will be discussed in detail in the following chapters. For now, just pay attention to the process and the overall structure of the document. Once you understand the basics, adding tags to your bag of tricks is simple.

HTML the Hard Way

With all the wonderful web-authoring tools out there today, chances are you will be using one to create your pages. In fact, I recommend it; the time and sanity savings are too good to pass up.

You may be asking, "If the tools are so great, do I need to learn HTML at all?" The answer is yes, you do. You may not need to have every tag memorized, but some familiarity is crucial for everyone who wants to make web pages. If you apply for a job as a "web designer," employers will expect that you know your way around an HTML document.

I stand by my method of teaching HTML the old-fashioned way—*by hand*. There's no way to truly understand how HTML works other than typing it out, one tag at a time, then opening your page in a browser. It doesn't take long to develop a feel for tagging documents properly.

Understanding HTML will make using your authoring tools easier and more efficient. In addition, you will be glad that you can look at an HTML source file and understand what you're seeing. Say you see a really cool web page trick. You can always view the source to see how it's done, but if the source looks like gibberish to you, it won't do much good. Understanding HTML is also crucial for troubleshooting broken pages or fine-tuning the default formatting that web tools produce.

Once you know the basics, you can continue your learning by reading *Web Design in a Nutshell*, Second Edition (O'Reilly, 2001) or *HTML & XHTML: The Definitive Guide*, Fifth Edition by Chuck Musciano and Bill Kennedy (O'Reilly, 2002).

Introducing...the HTML Tag

By now, you know that web pages are formatted using HTML tags. The characters within the tag are usually an abbreviation of a formatting instruction or page element.

Most HTML tags are container tags (Figure 6-1, top). They consist of two tags (a beginning and an end tag) that are wrapped around a range of text. The tag instruction applies to all the content contained within the tags. Think of them as an "on" switch and "off" switch. The end tag looks the same as the start tag, only it begins with a slash (/). Be careful not to use the similar backslash character (see the tip Slash vs. Backslash on the following page).

A few tags are standalone tags: you just drop them into place where you want an element to appear (Figure 6-1, bottom). Standalone elements do not get a closing tag.

We'll be using both types of tags when we create our simple page.

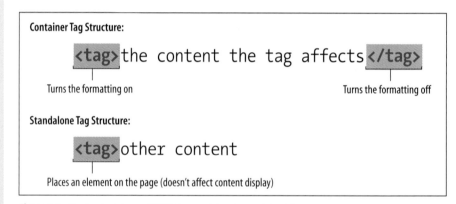

Figure 6-1. The two basic types of HTML tags: container tags and standalone tags.

Assembling a Web Page

We are ready to make a web page. This demonstration has four steps that will give you a feel for HTML mark-up:

Step 1: Setting up the HTML document. You'll learn about the tags used to give an HTML document structure.

Step 2: Formatting text. We'll use container tags to format the text.

Step 3: Adding graphical elements. We'll use standalone tags to add lines and pictures to the page. We'll also look at how tag attributes work.

Step 4: Adding a hypertext link. Since the Web is about linking, a web page demo would be incomplete without a brief introduction to linking.

The examples in this chapter show the HTML being typed by hand using Notepad on a PC. You could also use Macromedia HomeSite or, if you're on a Mac, BareBones BBEdit—but don't use the shortcut features just yet. (See the sidebar, Free Software Samples, for information on where to get these programs). Word-processing or page layout programs are not appropriate because they add hidden information to the code, and what we're after is pure text characters (ASCII).

We'll be checking our work in a browser frequently throughout this demonstration—probably more than you would in real life—but since this is an introduction to HTML, it is helpful to see the cause and effect of each small change to the source file.

The end result will be a simple home page for a site called "Jen's Kitchen" (Figure 6-2) that links to a number of my favorite recipes.

TIP

Slash vs. Backslash

HTML tags and URLs use the slash character (/). The slash character is found under the question mark (?) on the standard QUERTY keyboard.

It is easy to confuse the slash with the backslash character (\), which is found under the bar character (|). The backslash key will not work in tags or URLs, so be careful not to use it.

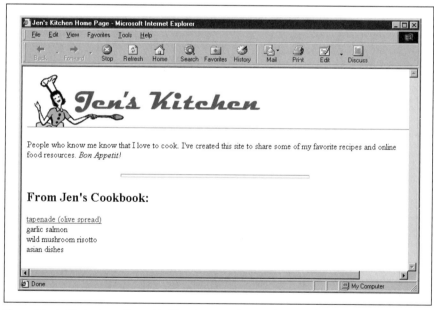

Figure 6-2. In this chapter, we'll assemble this web page step by step. It's not very fancy, but we have to start somewhere.

Free Software Samples

The two most popular HTML editors are Macromedia HomeSite (once Allaire HomeSite) for the PC and BBEdit for the Mac. Trial versions of each of these packages are provided on the CD that came with this book. You can also download trial versions online.

For BBEdit, go to the BareBones Software site and download a free demo:

www.barebones.com/products/ bblite/index.shtml

You can download a trial version of Macromedia HomeSite 5 at:

www.macromedia.com/ software/homesite/trial/

Step 1: Setting up the HTML document

There are two things that make an ordinary text file a browser-readable web document. The document must have a name that ends in *.htm* or *.html* in order to be recognized by the browser as a hypertext document, and it must contain the basic HTML tags that define the structure of the web document.

Giving the document basic structure

All web pages require a set of structural tags that help the browser sort out the parts of the document. These tags do *not* affect how the content looks in the browser window. We'll get to those tags later.

HTML documents have two parts: a head (also called the header) and a body. The head contains descriptive information about the document (its title, for example); the body contains the actual content that displays in the browser window. These parts are identified using the <head> and <body> container tags.

In addition to labeling these two parts, you must identify the document as being written in HTML by enclosing everything within <html> container tags. This tells the browser to interpret and render the tags in the file according to the rules of HTML.

The basic structure of an HTML document is shown in Figure 6-3.

In the exercise that follows, we'll open a text document and give it a basic HTML skeleton.

<aside>
To Capitalize or Not to Capitalize

Throughout this book, I have written my tags in all lowercase letters, but they could also be uppercase. In other words, tags are not "case-sensitive" in HTML. The choice is yours, but here are some things you should consider:

- On the one hand, using all capital letters makes the tags stand out against a sea of code. This is helpful when you are writing your HTML code from scratch.

- On the other hand, as HTML evolves, related tagging systems (such as XML and XHTML) require lowercase tags only. If you are learning HTML for the first time and you anticipate becoming a web professional, you should get in the habit of writing all lowercase tags from the start. Web authoring tools such as Dreamweaver and GoLive write tags in all lowercase by default. It is quickly becoming the proper way to write HTML, which is why I've stuck to all lowercase.
</aside>

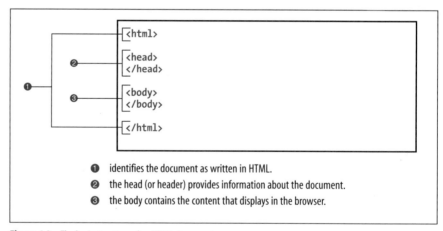

```
<html>

<head>
</head>

<body>
</body>

</html>
```

❶ identifies the document as written in HTML.
❷ the head (or header) provides information about the document.
❸ the body contains the content that displays in the browser.

Figure 6-3. The basic structure of an HTML document.

⟨4⟩

...w me know that I love to cook. I've
...ite to share some of my favorite
...line food resources. Bon Appetit!

From Jen's Cookbook:

```
Jen's Kitchen

People who know me know that I love to cook. I've
created this site to share some of my favorite
recipes and online food resources. Bon Appetit!

From Jen's Cookbook:

tapenade (olive spread)
garlic salmon
wild mushroom risotto
asian dishes
```

3. First, tell the browser that the text is in HTML format by
   labeling the entire document as "HTML." Place the
   "start HTML" tag (`<html>`) at the very beginning of the
   text and the "end HTML" tag (`</html>`) at the end.
   Next, identify the head and the body of the document.
   We want all of the text to show up in the browser
   window, so put a `<body>` tag at the beginning and a
   `</body>` tag at the end of the text.

```
tapenade (olive spread)
garlic salmon
wild mushroom risotto
asian dishes
</body>
</html>
```

4. The head, or header, of the document contains
   information about the document itself. We'll add some
   header content later, but for now, we'll leave it empty.
   Add `<head>` and `</head>` tags just before the body:

```
<html>
<head>
</head>
<body>
Jen's Kitchen...
```

5. Great...now the document has its basic structure. Set the
   file aside for now and read on; we'll get back to it in a
   moment.

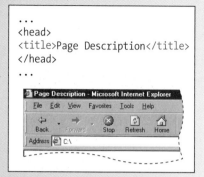

```
...
<head>
<title>Page Description</title>
</head>
...
```

Figure 6-4. The title is placed within the header of the document. The browser displays the title in the title bar.

> Make sure your document title is descriptive and useful.

<meta> Information

Another element that typically goes in the <head> of the document is the <meta> tag. The <meta> element is used to provide additional information about the document, such as search keywords, the author of the document, or a description of the type of content it contains. Web-authoring tools often use a <meta> tag to show what tool was used to create the document. <meta> tag functionality is beyond the scope of a beginner book, but it is useful to at least be able to recognize it.

Giving the page a title

Another essential part of a document is its title. The title is the name you give to the page; it shows up in the title bar at the top of the browser window. If you don't give the document a title, the filename is used instead. The title, indicated by the <title> container tag, goes within the head of the document (Figure 6-4).

Don't underestimate the importance of the title. It is one of the most important pieces of information you provide about your web page. In addition to appearing in the title bar of the browser, it is listed in the Favorites (or Bookmarks) menu when someone bookmarks your page. The title is also the first thing search engines look at when indexing pages. Make sure it is descriptive and useful. Include the name of the site and a description of the page, if possible. A generic title like "Welcome" or "My Home Page" will not help users identify your page later.

Now let's add a title to our document already in progress.

TRY IT

Exercise 6-1 *(continued)*

① Give It Structure ② Format Text ③ Add Graphics ④ Add a Link

6. Make sure the *kitchen.txt* document is open.

7. Give the document a title. You can use the one shown here or make up your own. The title element must be placed within the header of the document (that is, between the <head> tags). Use the <title> container tags to identify the title. The result should look like this:

```
<html>
<head>
<title>Jen's Kitchen Home Page</title>
</head>
<body>
Jen's Kitchen

People who know me know that I love to cook. I've created this
site to share some of my favorite recipes and online food resources.
Bon Appetit!

From Jen's Cookbook:

tapenade (olive spread)
garlic salmon
wild mushroom risotto
asian dishes
</body>
</html>
```

Saving and viewing the page

We have a document with the proper HTML structure and some content, but in order to view it in the browser, we need to save the file and give it a name. The filename needs to end in *.htm* or *.html* in order to be recognized by the browser as a web document. See the sidebar Naming C........ f

Naming Conventions

It is important that you follow th

8. Save the document and name it *kitchen.html*. The suffix *.html* tells the browser to open it as a web page. Be sure to save the file in the *chap06* directory on your hard drive.

9. Launch a browser, such as Internet Explorer, and choose Open Page or Open Local from the File menu. Locate your file using the dialog box that appears. Your web page should look something like this:

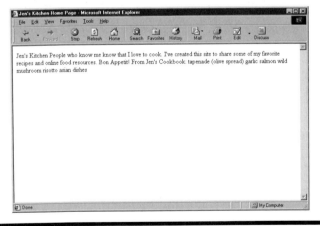

#, /, :, ;, •, etc. Limit filenames to letters, numbers, underscores, hyphens, and periods.

Filenames are case-sensitive in HTML. Consistently using all lowercase letters in filenames, while not necessary, makes your filenames easier to manage.

Keep filenames short. If you really must give the file a long, multi-word name, you can separate words with capital letters, such as *ALongDocumentTitle.htm*, or with underscores, such as *a_long_document_title.htm*, to improve readability.

Self-imposed conventions. It is helpful to develop a consistent naming scheme for huge sites. For instance, always using lowercase with underscores between words. This takes some of the guesswork out of remembering what you named a file when you go to link to it later.

Whoa! The text is all run together—that's not how it looks in the original text document. The page title is in the title bar of the browser, so that's a start. But let's look at what else happened. Notice how the browser ignored all of the line breaks. It also ignored the extra character spaces I added to indent the recipe names.

The lesson here is this: a browser will make a new paragraph or add a space *only* if it sees a tag in the file that specifically tells it to do so. Otherwise, it just ignores returns, tabs, and consecutive spaces in the source file.

Browsers ignore returns, tabs, and consecutive spaces.

This feature comes in handy, in a way, since you can enter as many returns and indents in your HTML document as you like. This makes it easier to read while it's in the editor and won't affect your final product. The sidebar What Browsers Ignore provides some useful insights on how browsers interpret HTML code.

TIP

What Browsers Ignore

Some information in an HTML document will be ignored when it is viewed in a browser, including:

Line breaks (carriage returns). Line breaks are ignored. Text and elements will wrap continuously until a paragraph (`<p>`) or line break (`<br>`) tag is encountered in the flow of the document text.

Tabs and multiple spaces. When a browser encounters a tab or more than one consecutive blank character space, it displays a single space. So if the document contains:

long,   long   ago

the browser displays:

long, long ago

Extra spaces can be added by using the "nonbreaking space" character string (` `) for each desired character space. (See the section Some Special Characters at the end of Chapter 7.)

Unrecognized tags. A browser simply ignores any tag it doesn't understand or that was incorrectly specified. Depending on the tag and the browser, this can have varied results. Either the browser displays nothing at all, or it may display the contents of the tag as though it were normal text.

Text in comments. Browsers will not display text between the special `<!--` and `-->` elements used to denote a comment. Here is a sample comment:

```
<!-- This is a comment -->
<!-- This is a
multiple-line comment
that ends here. -->
```

There must be a space after the initial `<!--` and preceding the final `-->`, but you can otherwise put nearly anything inside the comment.

Multiple `<p>` tags. When a browser sees a `<p>` (paragraph) tag, it adds a line space; however, a series of `<p>` tags (or empty paragraph containers, `<p></p>`) with no intervening text is interpreted as redundant and displays as though it were only a single `<p>` tag. Most browsers will display multiple `<br>` tags as multiple line breaks.

Document Structure

When you create a new file in a web-authoring tool such as Macromedia Dreamweaver or Adobe GoLive, the structural tags are added automatically. The tools usually add some extra document information to the header as well (such as

`<meta>` tags that say what software [participated...] file). The figures below sh[ow...] document in th[e...]

Dreamweaver MX

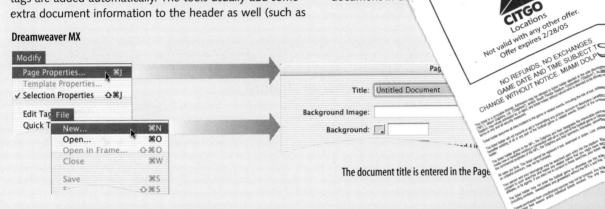

The document title is entered in the Page[...]

GoLive 6

Enter the document title in the Page Inspector palette. To open the palette, click on the page icon in the header section at the top of the document window. You can also just type in the title next to the icon.

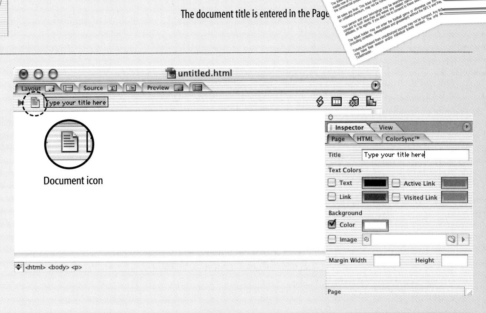

Document icon

FrontPage 2002

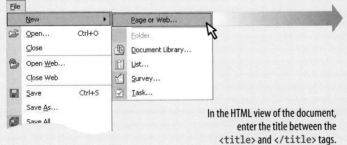

In the HTML view of the document, enter the title between the `<title>` and `</title>` tags.

Step 2: Formatting text

We're done setting up the document structure. Now let's quickly put some text formatting tags in there to whip our text into shape. At this point, don't worry too much about the specific tags—I just want you to get acquainted with the tagging process. (We'll discuss text-formatting tags in detail in Chapter 7.) In the following exercise, we break our document into paragraphs and headings.

TRY IT

Exercise 6-2: Formatting Text

1—Give It Structure 2—Format Text 3—Add Graphics 4—Add a Link

1. Open your new document, *kitchen.html*, in the HTML editing program if it isn't open already.

2. Make the first text line, "Jen's Kitchen," into a first-level heading by putting a "start Heading Level 1" tag (`<h1>`) at the beginning and an "end Heading Level 1" tag (`</h1>`) at the end, as shown. The browser will display text between `<h1>` tags in the largest, boldest text available.

   ```
   <h1>Jen's Kitchen</h1>
   ```

3. Turn the line "From Jen's Cookbook" into a second-level heading using the `<h2>` container tag in the same manner. Second-level headings display a bit smaller than first-level.

4. Turn the remaining blocks of text into paragraphs using the `<p>` container tag. Remember to put a `</p>` tag at the end of each paragraph. Check your progress against the finished code sample:

   ```
   <h1>Jen's Kitchen</h1>
   <p>People who know me know that I love to cook.
   I've created this site to share some of my
   favorite recipes and online food resources. Bon
   Appetit!</p>
   <h2>From Jen's Cookbook</h2>
   <p>
   tapenade
   garlic salmon
   wild mushroom risotto
   asian dishes
   </p>
   ```

   Let's stop and see how the page looks so far in a browser. You must save the document before your changes will be visible in the browser window. Just save

it with the same name, *kitchen.html*, and in the same directory so it overwrites the previous version. If you already have the document open in the browser window, you can just hit the Reload or Refresh button. Otherwise, just open the file locally, as before.

Your page should look like the screenshot below. Notice that the `<h1>`, `<h2>`, and `<p>` tags caused lines to break. They also added extra space above and below each text element.

5. This page is looking better, but we need to get the recipe names on separate lines. This time, I don't want any extra space between them. To cause a line to break without extra space, use break tags (`<br>`) where you want line breaks to occur (such as a carriage return). Add `<br>`s after each recipe name:

   ```
   <p>
   tapenade<br>
   garlic salmon<br>
   wild mushroom risotto<br>
   asian dishes
   </p>
   ```

Exercise 6-2 *(continued)*

6. Let's add a bit more text formatting. For emphasis, make the words "Bon Appetit!" italic, using the `<i>` (for italic) tag, as follows:

```
<i>Bon Appetit!</i>
```

This tag will not add line breaks or extra space; it only changes the style of the enclosed text.

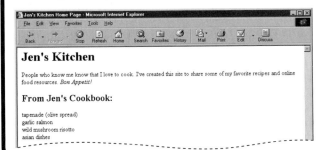

That's all the text formatting we will going to do for now, but it should give you a good taste of what it's like to format text with HTML tags. Once again, save the file and open it in the browser window. If it's already open, you can just hit the Refresh button.

Having trouble?

If you don't see any changes, you probably didn't save your file before you hit the Refresh button, or perhaps you saved the file with a new name or in a new directory and the browser is still pointing to the old version of the file.

A Brief History of HTML

Before HTML there was SGML (Standard Generalized Markup Language), which established the system of describing documents in terms of their *structure*, independent of appearance. SGML tags work the same way as the HTML tags we've seen, but there can be far more of them, enabling a more sophisticated description of document elements.

Publishers began storing SGML versions of their documents so that they could be translated into a variety of end uses. For example, text that is tagged as a heading may be formatted one way if the end product is a printed book, but another way for a CD-ROM. The advantage is that a single source file can be used to create a variety of end products. The way it is interpreted and displayed (i.e., the way it *looks*) depends on the end use.

Because HTML is one application of an SGML-based tagging system, this principle of keeping style information (instructions for how elements look) separate from the structure of the document remains inherent to the HTML purpose. In the early days of the Web, this ideal got muddied by the creation of HTML tags that contained explicit style instructions. The most glaring example is the `<font>` tag, which controls font, size, and color.

The solution is to use Cascading Style Sheets instead of HTML to format text. Style sheets keep style information out of the content by storing all style instructions in a separate document (or separate section of the source document).

Let's consider an example to see how style sheets work. Within the document, a heading is labeled with a standard `<h1>` to indicate the type of information (that it is a first-level heading). Elsewhere, in the style sheet, the designer specifies, "I'd like H1s to be 36 point, blue Helvetica type centered on the page." This pleases both the designers and the HTML purists.

Style sheets are covered in Chapter 8.

About Attributes

Here are some important things to know about attributes:

- Attributes go only in the opening container tag. The closing tag includes just the tag name, even if the opening tag is loaded with attributes.
- Most (but not all) attributes take values, which follow an equals sign (=) after the attribute's name. The value might be a number, a word, a string of text, a URL, or a measurement.
- The attribute value should always appear within quotation marks. In the next generation of HTML (called XHTML), quotation marks are a strict requirement.
- You can add several attributes within a single tag.
- Some attributes are required; for example, the src attribute within the <img> tag.

Step 3: Adding graphical elements

By now, I'm sure you're getting the hang of container tags. Let's drop in some graphical elements to make the page more interesting. Again, don't worry too much about the specific tags at this point; they'll be covered in Chapter 9.

In the next exercise, we'll add a simple graphic and a horizontal rule (a fancy term for a divider line) to break up the page. These elements will give us a good opportunity to look at how standalone tags and attributes work.

Introducing attributes

The real power and flexibility of HTML lies in the attributes—instructions added within a tag to modify its behavior or appearance. The formula (or syntax) for using attributes in a standalone tag is as follows:

```
<tag attribute="value">
```

For container tags, the attributes go in the opening tag only:

```
<tag attribute="value">affected text</tag>
```

Figure 6-5 looks at each of the components of attributes added to an <hr> (horizontal rule) tag. Take a moment to read the sidebar About Attributes for more useful attribute rules.

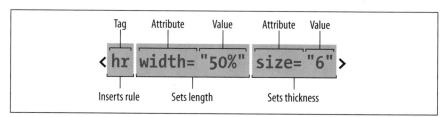

Figure 6-5. HTML attributes.

Exercise 6-3: Adding Graphical Elements

Give It Structure   Format Text   Add Graphics   Add a Link

1. In the *kitchen.html* file, delete the Jen's Kitchen headline (and the `<h1>`s) because we are now going to replace it with a spiffier graphic heading.

2. Place a graphic on the page by insterting an `<img>` tag where you want the graphic to appear. The `<img>` tag is a good example of a standalone tag—there's no closing or end tag; you just plop it into place. In place of the deleted headline, add the following HTML code:

   ```
   <img src="kitchen.gif">
   ```

   The `src=` part of the `<img>` tag is an attribute that tells the browser the source of the image (its URL). This is an example of a required attribute—without it, the browser wouldn't know which graphic to grab.

3. Now add a horizontal rule (line) above the second-level heading using the `<hr>` standalone tag. Inside the tag, we'll use attributes to change the length (`width=`) and thickness (`size=`) of the rule:

   ```
   <hr width="50%" size="6">
   ```

   The attributes in the `<hr>` tag are optional. Without the attributes, the default horizontal rule would be one pixel thick and the width of the browser window.

We're almost done. Check your progress against the code below. Then, save the page and view it again in the browser.

```
<html>
<head>
<title>Jen's Kitchen Home Page</title>
</head>
<body>
<img src="kitchen.gif">
<p>People who know me know that I love to cook.
I've created this site to share some of my
```

```
favorite recipes and online food resources. Bon
Appetit!</p>
<hr width="50%" size="6">
<h2>from Jen's Cookbook</h2>
<p>tapenade<br>
garlic salmon<br>
wild mushroom risotto<br>
asian dishes</p>
</body>
</html>
```

Having trouble?

If the graphic is not showing up, the graphic file is probably not in the proper location. The graphic file, *kitchen.gif*, which was provided on the CD, needs to be in the same directory as your *kitchen.html* file. Make sure they are both in the same directory on your hard drive, then try opening the document in the browser again.

Step 4: Adding a hypertext link

A web page isn't very useful without links, so let's add one. Don't worry about learning everything about linking from this example. Linking is an important part of web design, and I've dedicated a whole chapter to it (Chapter 10). For now, I just want to give you a taste of how it's done.

In the end, I'd like each of my recipe names to link to their respective recipe pages, so we'll start with the first one in this exercise.

Links are added with a container tag called an anchor (<a>...</a>). Like other container tags, anchor tags are placed around the text that you want to serve as a link (like "on" and "off" switches).

You also have to specify which page you want to link to; this is where the href= attribute comes in. It is a required attribute that gives the browser the URL of the target page. In my example, I've used a relative URL (a URL that points to a document on the same server, in the same directory) to create a link to the tapenade recipe page (*tapenade.html*).

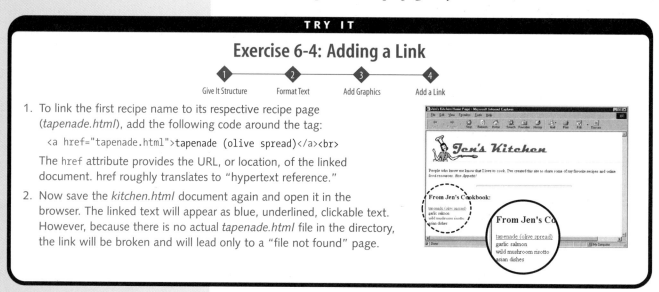

TRY IT

Exercise 6-4: Adding a Link

① Give It Structure ② Format Text ③ Add Graphics ④ Add a Link

1. To link the first recipe name to its respective recipe page (*tapenade.html*), add the following code around the tag:

   ```
   <a href="tapenade.html">tapenade (olive spread)</a><br>
   ```

   The href attribute provides the URL, or location, of the linked document. href roughly translates to "hypertext reference."

2. Now save the *kitchen.html* document again and open it in the browser. The linked text will appear as blue, underlined, clickable text. However, because there is no actual *tapenade.html* file in the directory, the link will be broken and will lead only to a "file not found" page.

Our simple web page is done. At this point, we could upload it to a server if we had one. See Chapter 3 for step-by-step instructions on uploading.

I know what you're thinking, "That page is really boring." That's okay, I'm thinking the same thing. But it is a real web page nonetheless, and we picked up some key concepts on the way. In future chapters, we'll add to your bag of tricks so you can make pages that are more sophisticated.

When Good Pages Go Bad

The previous demonstration went very smoothly, but it's easy for small things to go wrong when typing out HTML code. Unfortunately, one missed character can break a whole page. I'm going to break my page on purpose so we can see what happens.

What if I had forgotten to type the slash (/) in the closing header tag (</h1>)? With just one character out of place (Figure 6-6), the entire document displays in big, bold heading text. That's because without that slash, there's nothing telling the browser to turn "off" the heading formatting, so it just keeps going.

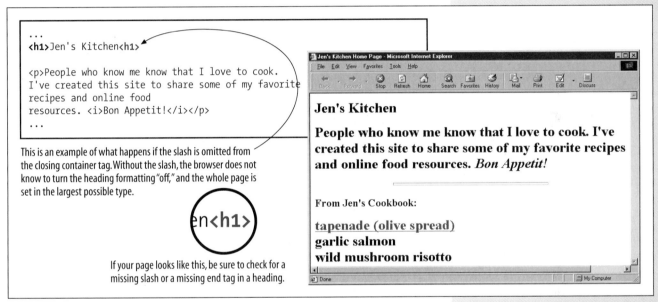

```
...
<h1>Jen's Kitchen<h1>

<p>People who know me know that I love to cook.
I've created this site to share some of my favorite
recipes and online food
resources. <i>Bon Appetit!</i></p>
...
```

This is an example of what happens if the slash is omitted from the closing container tag. Without the slash, the browser does not know to turn the heading formatting "off," and the whole page is set in the largest possible type.

en<h1>

If your page looks like this, be sure to check for a missing slash or a missing end tag in a heading.

Figure 6-6. The effects of a missing end slash.

I've fixed the slash, but this time, let's see what would have happened if I had accidentally omitted a bracket from the end of the first <h2> tag (Figure 6-7, following page).

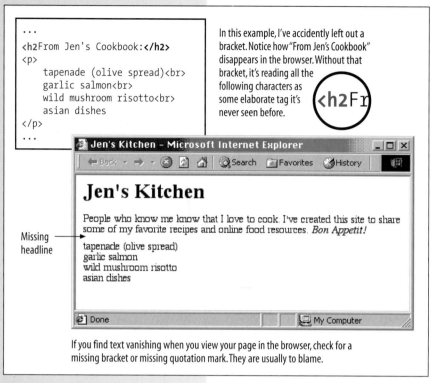

```
...
<h2From Jen's Cookbook:</h2>
<p>
    tapenade (olive spread)<br>
    garlic salmon<br>
    wild mushroom risotto<br>
    asian dishes
</p>
...
```

In this example, I've accidently left out a bracket. Notice how "From Jen's Cookbook" disappears in the browser. Without that bracket, it's reading all the following characters as some elaborate tag it's never seen before.

‹h2Fr

If you find text vanishing when you view your page in the browser, check for a missing bracket or missing quotation mark. They are usually to blame.

Figure 6-7. Missing brackets can cause text to vanish.

See how a whole chunk of text is missing? That's because without the closing tag bracket, the browser assumes that all the following text—all the way up to the next closing bracket (>) it finds—is part of that <h2> tag. Browsers don't display any text within a tag, so my heading disappeared. The browser just ignored the foreign-looking tag and moved on to the next element.

Making mistakes in your first HTML pages and fixing them is a great way to learn. If you write your first pages perfectly, I'd recommend fiddling with the code as I have here to see how the browser reacts to various changes. This can be extremely useful in troubleshooting pages later. I've listed some common problems in the sidebar, Having Problems? Note that these problems are not specific to beginners. Little stuff like this goes wrong all the time, even for the pros.

TROUBLESHOOTING

Having Problems

The following are some typical problems that crop up when creating web pages and viewing them in a browser:

I've changed my document, but when I reload the page in my browser, it looks exactly the same.

It could be you didn't save your HTML document before reloading or you saved it in a different directory.

All the text on my page is HUGE!

Did you start a heading tag and forget to close it? Make sure each tag you've used has its end tag. Also, make sure that each end tag has a slash (/).

Half my page disappeared!

This could happen if you are missing a closing bracket (>) or a quotation mark within a tag. This is a common error when writing HTML code by hand.

I put in a graphic using the <img> tag, but all that shows up is a broken-graphic icon.

The broken graphic could mean a couple of things. First, it might mean that the browser is not finding the graphic. Make sure that the URL to the graphic is correct. (We'll discuss URLs further in Chapter 10.) Make sure that the graphic is actually in the directory you've specified. If the graphic is there, make sure it is in one of the formats that web browsers can display (GIF, JPEG, or PNG) and that it is named with the proper suffix (*.gif*, *.jpeg* or *.jpg*, or *.png* respectively).

Test Yourself

Now is a good time to make sure you're understanding the basics of HTML tagging. Use what you've learned in this chapter to answer the following questions. Answers are in the Appendix.

1. What makes a container tag different from a standalone tag?

2. Write out the code for the basic skeleton of a web document.

3. Mark whether each of these filenames is an acceptable name for a web page by circling "Yes" or "No". If it is not acceptable, provide the reason why.

   a. *Sunflower.html*   Yes   No _____

   b. *index.doc*   Yes   No _____

   c. *cooking home page.html*   Yes   No _____

   d. *Song_Lyrics.html*   Yes   No _____

   e. *games/rubix.html*   Yes   No _____

   f. *%whatever.html*   Yes   No _____

4. All of the following tags are incorrect. Describe what is wrong with each one, then write them correctly.

   a. `<img "birthday.jpg">`

   b. `<i>Congratulations!<i>`

   c. `<a href="file.html">linked text</a href="file.html">`

   d. `<p>This is a new paragraph<\p>`

TRY IT

Exercise 6-5: Break Your HTML

Try breaking the HTML file you just created on purpose to learn more about how browsers interpret code. Make a copy of the *kitchen.html* file and make the changes listed below. Remember to save your document each time before you refresh it in the browser window. Also, remember to fix it before trying the next one.

- Delete the quotation mark after `kitchen.gif` (e.g., `<img src="kitchen.gif >`)

- Change the slash to a backslash in the closing `</a>` tag.

- Delete the close bracket (`>`) after the first `<p>` tag (`<p `).

- Try breaking other things and viewing the results in the browser. You'll find that some changes have big impacts; others don't.

HTML Review: Structural Tags

In this chapter, we covered the tags that establish the structure of the document. The remaining tags introduced in the Try It exercises will be treated in more depth in the following chapters.

Tag	Function
`<!-- -->`	Denotes a comment that will not display in the browser
`<html>`	Identifies the whole document as HTML
`<head>`	Identifies the head of the document
`<body>`	Identifies the body of the document
`<meta>`	Contains information about the document
`<title>`	Gives the page a title

Formatting Text with HTML

By this point, you should have an understanding of how HTML markup works. Now we'll take an intensive look at formatting text, one tag at a time. This chapter covers the HTML tags that are used to give structure to content and add simple styles. The following chapter introduces style sheets for more sophisticated text formatting.

But, before we begin, I want to reiterate a point we touched on in Chapter 4.

"Typesetting" on the Web

Marking up text for the Web is not the same as specifying type for print. For one thing, there is no way of knowing exactly how your text is going to look. Scary, but true.

Take a look at your browser's preferences and you will find that you (and every other surfer out there) are able to specify the fonts and sizes that you prefer for online viewing. To access the font controls in Internet Explorer, choose Edit → Preferences, then select Language/Fonts under the Web Browser category. In Netscape, choose Edit → Preferences and select Fonts from the Appearance category. This is where users can choose any font for the browser default. Most browsers also have a text zoom feature that allows users to change the font size on the fly.

Although there are ways to specify a font in an HTML document or style sheet, the text won't show up in that font unless it is already installed on the user's machine.

Another tricky thing is that you don't know how wide the window will be, so there is no guarantee that the lines will break the way they do on your machine. In addition, HTML alone does not provide a way to control indentation or spacing between lines and paragraphs (that's what style sheets are for). With HTML, you are stuck with the browser's default interpretation of each tag. There is much that is out of your control.

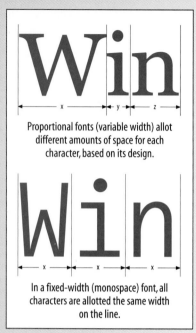

Proportional fonts (variable width) allot different amounts of space for each character, based on its design.

In a fixed-width (monospace) font, all characters are allotted the same width on the line.

Figure 7-1. Proportional and constant-width font examples.

Two fonts

What you can be certain of is that there are two fonts that will make up your page: a proportional font and a constant-width font (Figure 7-1).

The majority of your page—body text, headings, lists, blockquotes, etc.—will appear in the proportional font. A proportional font (called "Variable Width Font" in Netscape) is one that allots different amounts of space to each character; for example, a capital "W" takes up more space on the line than a lowercase "i". The default proportional font for the majority of web browsers is Times or Helvetica; as a very general guideline, you can assume body text will display in one of these two fonts at 10 or 12 points.[*]

The other available font is a constant-width font, which is used for special types of information. A fixed-width font (also known as a "fixed-width" or "monospace" font) allots the same amount of horizontal space to all the characters; the capital "W" takes up no more space than the lowercase "i". Browsers use the fixed-width font for a few specific tags, usually related to the display of code, such as `<pre>` or `<tt>` (we'll discuss these later in this chapter). You can usually assume these elements will display in some variation of Courier.

If you look in your browser's font preferences, you can see what fonts are set up for your default proportional and constant-width fonts. You even set them to any font you prefer. Unfortunately, however, you cannot change these settings for the users who visit your site.

Serif and Sans-Serif

Another way to characterize a font design is whether it is serif or sans-serif.

Serif typefaces have small slabs at the ends of letter strokes. Times and Courier are both serif fonts. In general, serif fonts are a more classic type design and can make large amounts of text easier to read.

serif

Sans-serif fonts do not have serif slabs; their strokes are square on the end. Helvetica and Arial are popular examples of sans-serif fonts. In general, sans-serif fonts appear sleeker and more modern.

sans-serif

Text in graphics

The only way to have absolute control over the display of type is to make it part of a graphic. It is common to see headlines, subheads, callouts, even whole web pages, put into big graphics rather than HTML text.

While the temptation of total control may be strong, there are some very compelling reasons why you should resist sinking text into GIF files. First, graphics take much longer to download than text, and on the Web, download speed is everything. Second, any information in a graphic cannot be indexed or searched; in essence, it is removed from your document. And last, this content will be lost on nongraphical browsers or to users with graphics turned off. While using "alternative" text in the graphic tag may help, it is limited and not always reliable.

That said, let's look at some tags for formatting text.

---

[*] Internet Explorer 5.5 and Netscape 6.0 started defining type sizes in pixels since point sizes are interpreted differently on Windows systems and Macs. The default size is 16 pixels, which will probably feel quite large to Mac users accustomed to smaller type.

Building Blocks

Many HTML tags are used to describe content—for instance, to identify a paragraph or a headline. The distinct parts that make up a document are known as block elements, and they are defined by block element tags.

When a browser sees a block element tag, it automatically inserts a line break and adds a little space above and below the element. This is the characteristic that all block elements have in common. You cannot start paragraph text on the same line as a heading; it will always start as a new "block" of text.

This section covers the basic block elements one tag at at time: paragraphs, headings, quotations, and preformatted text. The next section covers lists. Tables, rules, and divisions are also block elements, but they will be covered in later chapters.

Browsers automatically add space above and below block elements.

Paragraphs

`<p>...</p>`

Body text paragraph

One of the simplest things you can do to text is break it into paragraphs. Paragraphs display in the browser's default proportional font with extra space above and below (Figure 7-2).

Although most browsers will also recognize a single `<p>` placed between blocks of text as a paragraph break, many technologies, such as Java-Script and style sheets, require both opening and closing tags. If you are learning HTML for the first time, you should start making paragraphs the proper way with container tags.

Browsers will not recognize a string of `<p></p>` tags, so you can't use empty paragraphs to add extra space between elements, the way you can in a word-processing program (Figure 7-3).

```
<p>Rinse fillets & pat dry. Add to marinade for 20 minutes. Drain and
discard ginger.</p>
<p>Heat oil in wok. Add seasonings & stir fry for 10 seconds. Add Fish
Sauce; heat 2 minutes, stirring constantly. Pour over fillets in baking
dish.</p>
```

Rinse fillets & pat dry. Add to marinade for 20 minutes. Drain and discard ginger.

Heat oil in wok. Add seasonings & stir fry for 10 seconds. Add Fish Sauce; heat 2 minutes, stirring constantly. Pour over fillets in baking dish.

Figure 7-2. Paragraphs display in the default font with space above and below.

```
<p>Rinse fillets & pat dry. Add to marinade for 20 minutes. Drain and
discard ginger.</p>
<p></p>
<p></p>
<p></p>
<p></p>
<p>Heat oil in wok. Add seasonings & stir fry for 10 seconds. Add Fish
Sauce; heat 2 minutes, stirring constantly. Pour over fillets in baking
dish.</p>
```

Rinse fillets & pat dry. Add to marinade for 20 minutes. Drain and discard ginger.

Heat oil in wok. Add seasonings & stir fry for 10 seconds. Add Fish Sauce; heat 2 minutes, stirring constantly. Pour over fillets in baking dish.

Figure 7-3. Multiple empty paragraphs are ignored by the browser.

```
2 slices ginger<br>
1 T. rice wine or sake<br>
1 t. salt<br>
2 T. peanut oil
```

2 slices ginger
1 T. rice wine or sake
1 t. salt
2 T. peanut oil

Figure 7-4. Line breaks: the `<br>` tag starts a new line in a block element, but it doesn't add any extra space.

First Level Heading
Second Level Heading
Third Level Heading
Fourth Level Heading
Fifth Level Heading
Sixth Level Heading

Here's a little default body text for comparison.

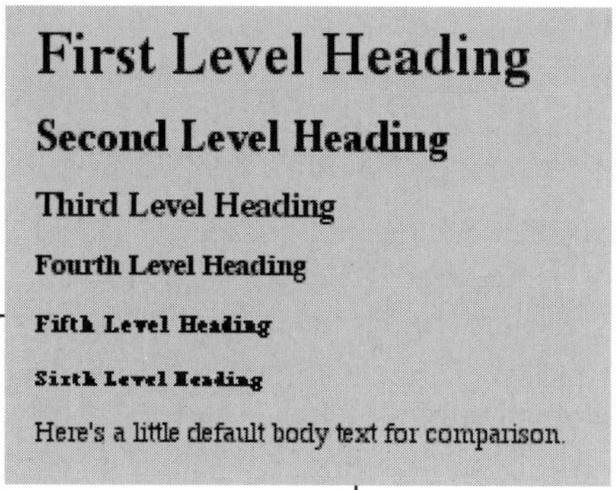

```
<h1>First Level Heading</h1>
<h2>Second Level Heading</h2>
<h3>Third Level Heading</h3>
<h4>Fourth Level Heading</h4>
<h5>Fifth Level Heading</h5>
<h6>Sixth Level Heading</h6>
<p>Here's a little default body text for comparison.</p>
```

Figure 7-5. Headings: there are six HTML heading levels. `<h1>` is the largest and each consecutive level gets smaller.

TRY IT

Exercise 7-1: Compare the Code with the Results

While you're still getting used to HTML tagging, I encourage you to read through the code in the figures in this chapter and compare it to the accompanying screen shots of the results. See if you can follow the logic of how the browser interprets the tags. It will be good practice for when you begin to scan your own HTML files.

`<br>`
Line break

While not a block element, I find it useful to introduce the break tag in relation to paragraphs. If you want to break a line of text, but *not* add extra space around it, you can insert a `<br>` tag within a paragraph or other block element (Figure 7-4). The `<br>` tag works like a simple carriage return. Multiple `<br>` tags are displayed as a stack of blank lines by most browsers.

Headings

`<h#>...</h#>`
Heading level-#
(where "#" can equal 1–6)

In the last chapter, we used the `<h1>` and `<h2>` tags to indicate headings for our page. There are actually six levels of headings, `<h1>` through `<h6>` (Figure 7-5).

Headings are displayed in bold text. The first-level heading (`<h1>`) is displayed at the largest heading size, and the consecutive levels get smaller and smaller. In fact, fifth- and sixth-level headings tend to be even smaller than regular text, and may be difficult to read. As a general rule, `<h3>` is as low as you'd want to go.

Since headings are used to provide logical structure to a document, it is proper to start with the `<h1>` heading and work down in numerical order. If you don't like how big and clunky a first- or second-level heading looks, use a style sheet to change its appearance. This is preferable to using a third-level heading out of order just because you want it to be smaller.

Long quotations

`<blockquote>...</blockquote>`
Blockquote

The `<blockquote>` tag is used for long quotations. Blockquotes are generally displayed with indented left and right margins, with a little extra space added above and below (Figure 7-6). For this reason, blockquotes were often used as a fudge to create narrow text columns, but now, style sheets offer better indent control, making that technique obsolete.

Preformatted text

`<pre>...</pre>`
Preformatted text

Preformatted text is a unique animal in the HTML world. It is displayed in the browser's constant-width font (usually Courier) with extra space added above and below. What makes it special is that text between `<pre>` tags is displayed exactly as it is typed—including all carriage returns and multiple character spaces (Figure 7-7). As we saw in Chapter 6, browsers normally ignore returns and spaces in the HTML source code.

Preformatted text was originally created for the display of code, where spacing, indents, and alignment are important, but you can use it to control spacing and alignment of any content (as long as you don't mind everything set in Courier).

```
<p>The true test that meat is fully cooked is its
internal temperature. Cooks Illustrated Magazine had
this to say about safe internal temperatures
for poultry:</p>

<blockquote>The final word on poultry safety is this:
As long as the temperature on an accurate instant-
read thermometer reaches 160 degrees when inserted
in several places, all unstuffed meat (including
turkey) should be bacteria free. Dark meat is
undercooked at this stage and tastes better at 170
or 175 degrees.</blockquote>
```

The true test that meat is fully cooked is its internal temperature. Cooks Illustrated Magazine had this to say about safe internal temperatures for poultry:

> The final word on poultry safety is this: As long as the temperature on an accurate instant-read thermometer reaches 160 degrees when inserted in several places, all unstuffed meat (including turkey) should be bacteria free. Dark meat is undercooked at this stage and tastes better at 170 or 175 degrees.

Figure 7-6. **Blockquotes** are indented on the left and right margins.

```
<pre>
1/4 c. chicken stock

        1 T. soy sauce

1 T. rice wine or sake

        1/2 t. sugar
</pre>
```

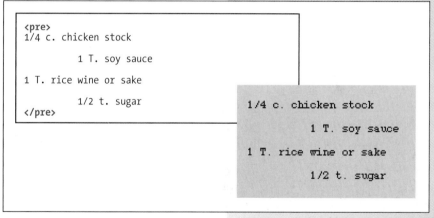

Figure 7-7. **Preformatted text** is unique in that the browser displays the text as it is typed, including carriage returns and extra spaces.

Exercise 7-2: Match the Sample—Block Elements

Use the block element tags you've learned so far to construct the sample HTML page shown below. There will be some variation due to browser preference differences. To save typing time, I've provided the raw text on the CD that accompanies this book (as well as online at *www.learningwebdesign.com/materials/chap07*). The resulting code for this exercise is provided in the Appendix.

HINT: Don't forget to add the structural tags to the document (including a title) and save it with the suffix *.html* (or *.htm*), as we learned in Chapter 6.

1. Copy the directory *chap_07* from the CD to your hard drive. Open the document *tapenade.txt*.

2. Add the necessary block element tags to make your document match this example. Note that the background, font, font size, and line length will probably look different because your browser settings are different than mine. Pay attention to the structure of the document and how text is broken up.

   Save and view the document as many times as you need along the way. Chances are you'll need to tweak and redo tags until you get it just right.

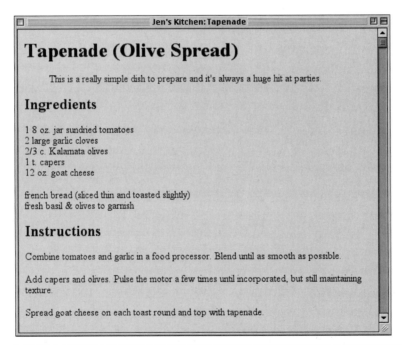

Jen's Kitchen: Tapenade

Tapenade (Olive Spread)

This is a really simple dish to prepare and it's always a huge hit at parties.

Ingredients

1 8 oz. jar sundried tomatoes
2 large garlic cloves
2/3 c. Kalamata olives
1 t. capers
12 oz. goat cheese

french bread (sliced thin and toasted slightly)
fresh basil & olives to garnish

Instructions

Combine tomatoes and garlic in a food processor. Blend until as smooth as possible.

Add capers and olives. Pulse the motor a few times until incorporated, but still maintaining texture.

Spread goat cheese on each toast round and top with tapenade.

Paragraph Styles

Here's how you access paragraph controls in three of the more popular authoring programs.

Dreamweaver MX

❶ With your text element highlighted, choose a paragraph style from the Format pull-down menu on the Properties palette.

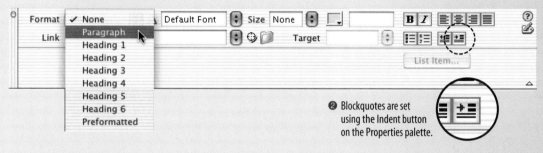

❷ Blockquotes are set using the Indent button on the Properties palette.

GoLive 6

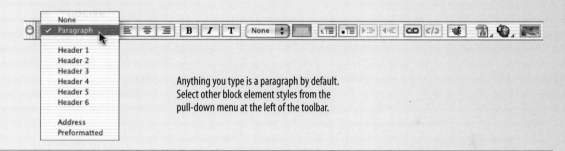

Anything you type is a paragraph by default. Select other block element styles from the pull-down menu at the left of the toolbar.

FrontPage 2002

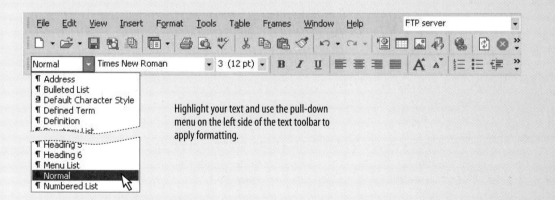

Highlight your text and use the pull-down menu on the left side of the text toolbar to apply formatting.

Lists

Sometimes it is necessary to itemize information instead of presenting it in paragraphs. For instance, you might need a list of items with bullets or detailed instructions that must appear in numerical order. Lists are block elements, which means that the browser will add space above and below the whole list.

There are three kinds of lists you can define with HTML: ordered lists (numbered lists), unordered lists (bulleted lists), and definition lists (for terms and their definitions). Each list type has its own tag that indicates the beginning and end of the whole list. You must also identify each item within the list.

Let's look at how to create formatted lists in HTML. Again, we'll look at each list tag one at a time, and you will have the opportunity to try them for yourself at the end of the section. There is also a Tool Tip that shows how to format lists using a web-authoring program.

```
<p><b>Instructions:</b></p>
<ol>
<li>Rinse fillets & pat dry. Add to marinade for 20 minutes. Drain and
discard ginger.</li>
<li>Heat oil in wok. Add seasonings & stir fry for 10 seconds. Add Fish
Sauce; heat 2 minutes, stirring constantly. Pour over fillets in baking
dish.</li>
<li>Fill wok with water to bottom of steamer tray. Heat til boiling. Steam
fish for 10 minutes, covered, high heat until flakey.</li>
</ol>
```

Instructions:

1. Rinse fillets & pat dry. Add to marinade for 20 minutes. Drain and discard ginger.
2. Heat oil in wok. Add seasonings & stir fry for 10 seconds. Add Fish Sauce; heat 2 minutes, stirring constantly. Pour over fillets in baking dish.
3. Fill wok with water to bottom of steamer tray. Heat til boiling. Steam fish for 10 minutes, covered, high heat until flakey.

Figure 7-8. Ordered (numbered) lists are indicated by the `<ol>` tag. Each item in the list is preceded by a list item tag `<li>`. The numbers are added automatically by the browser.

Ordered lists

`<ol>...</ol>`
Ordered list

`<li>`
List item

An ordered (numbered) list is used when the sequence of items is important. Browsers automatically insert a number before each list item, so you do not need to type the number in yourself (if you type in a number, you'll get two numbers when the document displays). The advantage of using a numbered list is that the list will be renumbered automatically if you insert or delete an item (plus, you get a nicely indented left edge).

The `<ol>` container tag identifies the entire list as "ordered." Each item within the list is then indicated with an `<li>` (list item) tag (Figure 7-8). Although the closing list item tag (`</li>`) is optional, it is good practice to include it, particularly if you are working with style sheets or JavaScript.

You can get fancy with ordered lists and change the style of numbering with the type attribute. There are five possible values: 1 (numbers), A (uppercase letters), a (lowercase letters), I (uppercase roman numerals), and i (lowercase roman numerals). Regular numbers are the default. The other variations are shown in Figure 7-9. Remember that attributes go in the opening tag only (e.g., <ol type="a">...</ol>).

When you use an ordered list, the browser adds the numbers automatically, so you don't need to type them yourself.

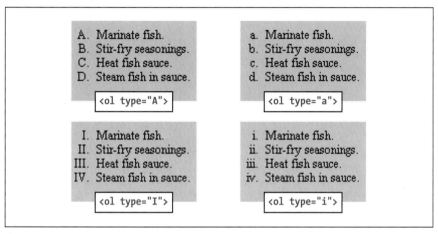

Figure 7-9. You can change the numbering style with the type attribute and the values shown above.

You can also start the list with a number (or letter value) other than "1" by using the start attribute as shown in Figure 7-10.

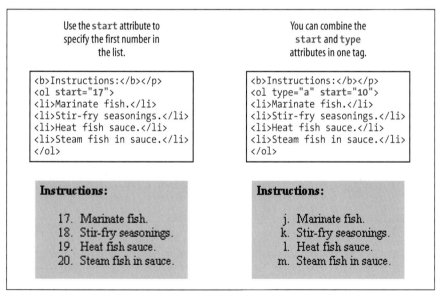

Figure 7-10. The start attribute sets the first number in the ordered list.

Unordered lists

`<ul>...</ul>`
Unordered list

`<li>`
List item

The bullets in an unordered list are added automatically by the browser.

Use the unordered list (`<ul>`) tag to make a bulleted list. The browser adds bullets automatically and sets the items on an indent. The `<ul>...</ul>` tags indicate the beginning and end of the bulleted list. Like ordered lists, each item within the list must be marked with `<li>` (list item) tags (Figure 7-11).

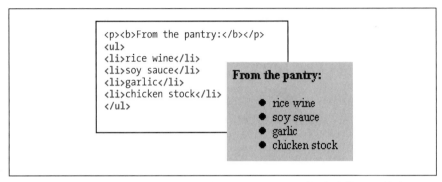

```
<p><b>From the pantry:</b></p>
<ul>
<li>rice wine</li>
<li>soy sauce</li>
<li>garlic</li>
<li>chicken stock</li>
</ul>
```

Figure 7-11. Unordered (bulleted) lists are indicated by the `<ul>` tag. Notice that the bullets are added automatically for each list item (`<li>`).

If you aren't excited about black dot bullets, you can use circles or squares. The `type` attribute in the `<ul>` tag gives you minimal control over the appearance of bullets. The values may be `disc` (the black dot default), `circle`, or `square` (Figure 7-12). If you want to use one of your own graphics as bullets, you'll need to use one of the tricks demonstrated in Chapter 19.

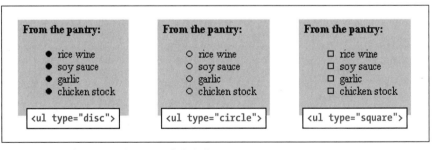

Figure 7-12. Use the `type` attribute to specify the bullet type.

TIP

By default, the browser does not put any extra space between list items. If you'd like extra space, add a `<br>` after each item or use a style sheet to add a specific amount of space above the `<li>` element.

Part II: Learning HTML

Definition lists

`<dl>...</dl>`
Definition (or dictionary) list

`<dt>`
Dictionary term

`<dd>`
Dictionary definition

Definition (or dictionary) lists are used for displaying lists of words with blocks of descriptive text. They are a bit different from the other two HTML lists in format. The `<dl>...</dl>` tags are used to mark the beginning and end of the entire list. Within the list, each word (term) is marked with the `<dt>` tag, and its definition is marked with a `<dd>`. The `</dt>` and `</dd>` tags may be omitted, but it is better to include them, particularly if you are working with style sheets or JavaScript.

Terms are displayed against the left margin with no extra space above or below. The definition is displayed on an indent (Figure 7-13).

Nesting lists

Any list can be nested within another list (Figure 7-14). For instance, you could add a bulleted list item under an item within a numbered list, or add a numbered list within a definition list, and so on. Lists can be nested several layers deep; however, since the left indent is cumulative, it doesn't take long for the text to end up pressed against the right margin.

```
<dl>
<dt>rice vinegar</dt>
<dd>Rice vinegar is made from fermented rice and has a
light, clean flavor that goes well with ginger.</dd>
<dt>soy sauce</dt>
<dd>This sauce based on fermented soy beans is probably
the best-known Asian seasoning.</dd>
<dt>fermented black beans</dt>
<dd>A staple of Chinese cuisine, these beans are preserved
in salt. The salt must be rinsed off before the beans
are used.</dd>
</dl>
```

rice vinegar
> Rice vinegar is made from fermented rice and has a light, clean flavor that goes well with ginger.

soy sauce
> This sauce based on fermented soy beans is probably the best-known Asian seasoning.

fermented black beans
> A staple of Chinese cuisine, these beans are preserved in salt. The salt must be rinsed off before the beans are used.

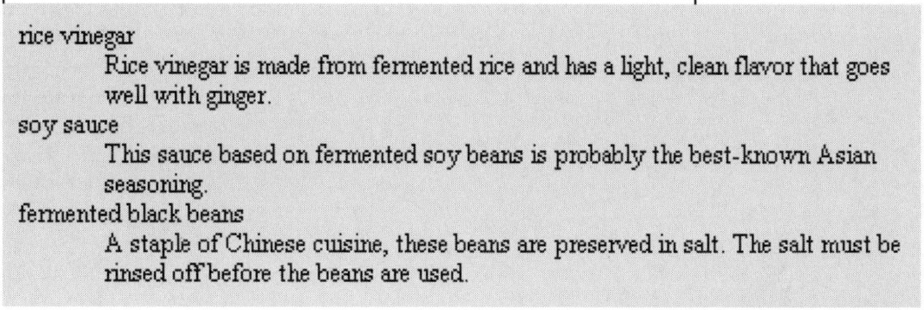

Figure 7-13. Definition lists are marked with `<dl>` tags. Terms are indicated by `<dt>` tags; definitions use `<dd>`.

```
<ol>
<li>Mix Marinade</li>
        <ul>
        <li>2 slices ginger <em>(smashed, then pinched
in marinade)</em></li>
        <li>1 T. rice wine or sake</li>
        <li>1 t. salt</li>
        <li>2 T. peanut oil</li>
        </ul>
<li>Stir-fry seasonings</li>
<li>Add fish sauce</li>
</ol>
```

This example nests an unordered list within an ordered (numbered) list.

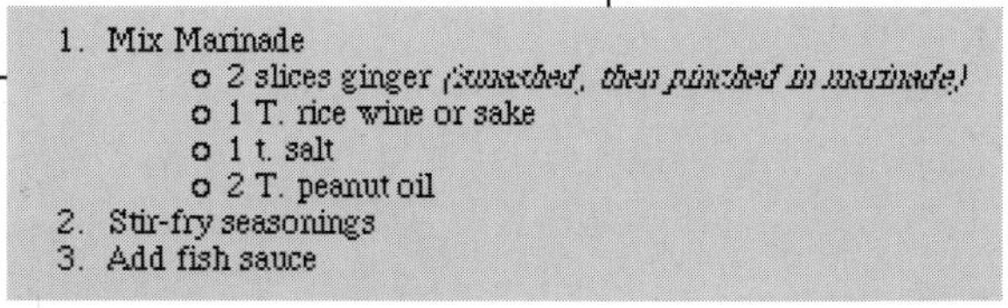

1. Mix Marinade
   - 2 slices ginger *(smashed, then pinched in marinade)*
   - 1 T. rice wine or sake
   - 1 t. salt
   - 2 T. peanut oil
2. Stir-fry seasonings
3. Add fish sauce

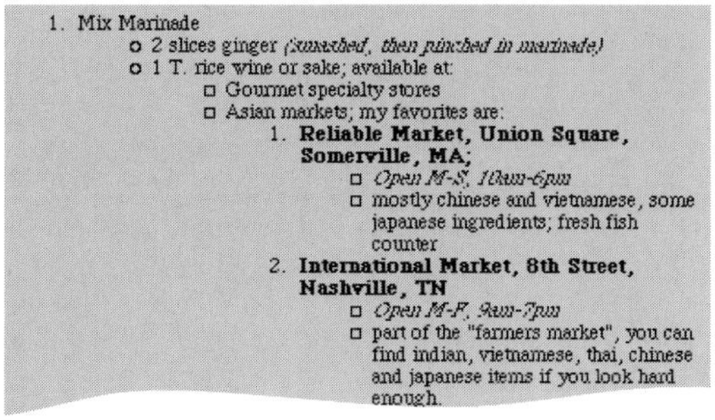

If you use too many nested lists, your content will end up shoved against the right margin.

Figure 7-14. Nesting lists.

Exercise 7-3: Match the Sample—Lists

Use the list tags we've just discussed to construct the sample page shown to the right.

Open the document *lists.html* from the *chap07* directory. The structure of the document is set up in HTML, but you'll need to format the three lists to match the samples shown here. The resulting code is provided in the Appendix.

List Practice

List A

A. Spread the pesto on the pizza crust as thick or thin as you like.
B. Cover the top evenly with tomato slices.
C. Spread the red onion (to taste) over the top and sprinkle with pine nuts.
D. Add globs and crumbles of goat cheese randomly. (Kalamata olives are a nice topping as well.)
E. Bake in a 400 degree oven for 10 to 15 minutes until sizzling and fragrant.

List B

5 Simple Pleasures

- Lemonade from scratch
- Warm bread
- Tomato soup with pepper
- A ripe plum
- Saltines

List C

Shrimp & Celery Bisque
This recipe makes enough for 2 or 3 meals or 4 opener soup courses. It's one of my favorite meals in cold weather.
Wild Mushroom Bowtie Pasta
I use this wild mushroom "ragout" as the base of a number of recipes: wild mushroom risotto, wild mushroom & brie phyllo packets, etc. I use the following mushrooms:
- chanterelle
- cremini
- morel
- shiitake
Chocolate-Kahlua Trifle
This is the easiest possible dessert recipe, and it's so yummy. It's also very portable if you put it together in a tall storage canister, so it's a good dish to bring to a party. People love dessert in a bucket!

Formatting Lists

Here's how you access list controls in three of the more popular authoring programs.

Dreamweaver MX

❶

With the entire list selected, choose the appropriate list style from the Text → List menu.

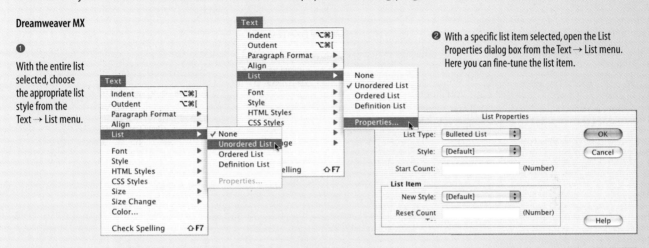

❷ With a specific list item selected, open the List Properties dialog box from the Text → List menu. Here you can fine-tune the list item.

GoLive 6

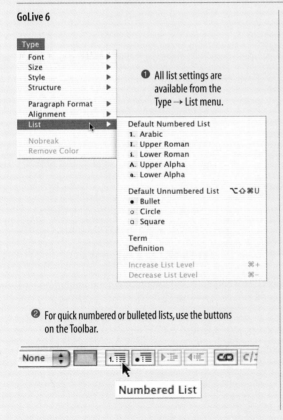

❶ All list settings are available from the Type → List menu.

❷ For quick numbered or bulleted lists, use the buttons on the Toolbar.

Numbered List

FrontPage 2002

❶ Insert the cursor where you'd like to start a numbered list. Then select Format → Bullets and Numbering. Click the Numbers tab and select the style.

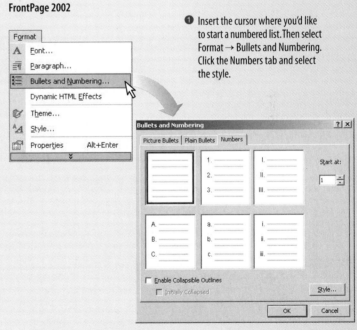

❷ A quick method is to type the list items and select them. Then click the Numbering icon on the toolbar. The items will automatically format to the default number list.

Inline Styles

So far, we've looked at block element tags for setting up content structure. The other type of tags is inline style tags, which affect the appearance of text right in the text flow. Inline tags don't introduce line breaks or extra spaces. The following are the most commonly used inline styles.

```
<p>2 slices ginger <i>(smashed, then pinched in marinade)</i></p>

<p>2 slices ginger <em>(smashed, then pinched in marinade)</em></p>
```

> 2 slices ginger *(smashed, then pinched in marinade)*
>
> 2 slices ginger *(smashed, then pinched in marinade)*

Figure 7-15. Italics: both `<i>` and `<em>` (for emphasized) tags make text italic.

```
<p>2 slices ginger <b>(smashed, then pinched in marinade)</b></p>

<p>2 slices ginger <strong>(smashed, then pinched in marinade)</strong></p>
```

> 2 slices ginger **(smashed, then pinched in marinade)**
>
> 2 slices ginger **(smashed, then pinched in marinade)**

Figure 7-16. Bold: both `<b>` and `<strong>` tags make text bold.

`<i>...</i>`
Italic text

This style tag makes the enclosed text italic (Figure 7-15). Use italic text sparingly, as browsers just slant the regular text font to achieve an "italic." The result is often unreadable, especially for large quantities of text.

`<em>...</em>`
Emphasized text

Another way to make text italic is the emphasized text tag. `<em>` is the "logical" style equivalent (see the Logical vs. Physical sidebar) to the `<i>` tag, since most browsers display emphasized text in italics (Figure 7-15).

> **TIP**
>
> *Avoid using italics for more than just a few words of text; the result is often unreadable.*

`<b>...</b>`
Bold text

The `<b>` tag specifies that the text be rendered in bold type (Figure 7-16).

`<strong>...</strong>`
Strong text

This is the "logical" style equivalent to `<b>`, as most browsers render strong text in bold type (Figure 7-16).

TERMINOLOGY

Logical vs. Physical

The whole point of HTML is to define the logical structure of a document, not its appearance (see the sidebar A Brief History of HTML in Chapter 6). With this in mind, there are a few "logical" style tags built into the HTML specification. Logical styles describe the enclosed text's meaning or context. By contrast, "physical" style tags give the browser specific display instructions. To achieve a style effect such as italics, you have your choice of either a logical tag (e.g., `<em>`, for emphasized text) or a physical tag (e.g., `<i>`, for italic). While logical tags are preferred conceptually, physical tags are by far more popular in practical use. However, logical tags really shine when used in conjunction with a style sheet that can make your emphasized text appear in whatever style and color you like, not just italic text.

`<tt>`...`</tt>`
Teletype (or typewriter text)

Text between `<tt>` tags displays in the browser's constant-width font (usually Courier) (Figure 7-17). Unlike preformatted text (`<pre>`), teletype text can be used inline, and extra character spaces or returns will be ignored by the browser (compare to Figure 7-7).

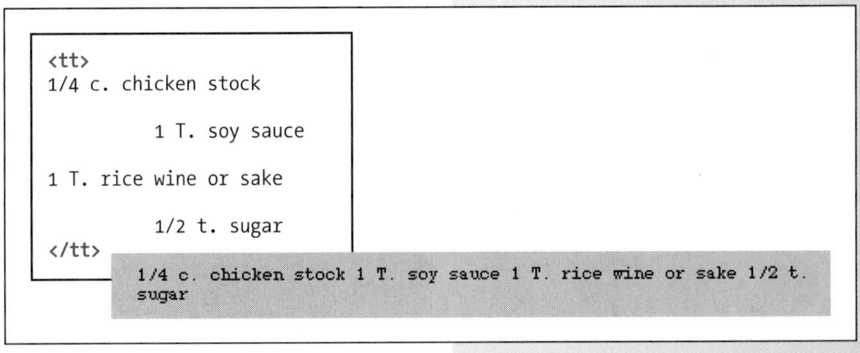

`<u>`...`</u>`
Underlined text

The `<u>` style tag causes the enclosed to be underlined. Be careful using this tag—underlined text may be confused with a link (Figure 7-18).

`<strike>`...`</strike>`
`<s>`...`</s>`
Strikethrough text

You can use either of these tags to make text appear with a line through it to suggest edited or deleted text (Figure 7-18).

`<sub>`...`</sub>`
Subscript

`<sup>`...`</sup>`
Superscript

These tags format enclosed text as subscript (smaller and slightly below the baseline) and superscript (smaller and slightly above the baseline), respectively (Figure 7-18).

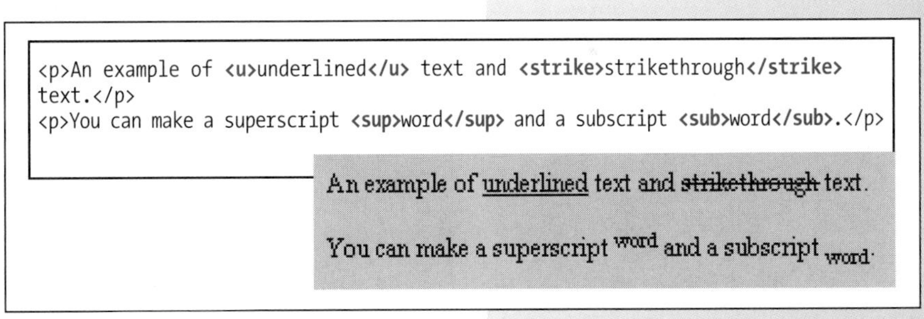

```
<tt>
1/4 c. chicken stock

        1 T. soy sauce

1 T. rice wine or sake

        1/2 t. sugar

</tt>
```
```
1/4 c. chicken stock 1 T. soy sauce 1 T. rice wine or sake 1/2 t.
sugar
```

Figure 7-17. Teletype: `<tt>` displays text in a constant-width font, but ignores line breaks and extra spaces, unlike `<pre>`.

```
<p>An example of <u>underlined</u> text and <strike>strikethrough</strike>
text.</p>
<p>You can make a superscript <sup>word</sup> and a subscript <sub>word</sub>.</p>
```
An example of underlined text and strikethrough text.

You can make a superscript word and a subscript word.

Figure 7-18. Examples of **underlined, strikethrough, superscript,** and **subscript** text

Combining styles

In HTML, you can apply several styles to the same piece of text by wrapping one set of style tags around another. This is known as nesting styles. It is similar to nesting block elements, such as lists.

The only rule is that one set of inline tags must be completely enclosed within the other—no overlapping. In the following example, the word "Caution!" is formatted in bold and italic text:

```
<i><b>Caution!</b></i>
```

Notice how the `<b>` container tags are completely within the `<i>` container tags? That's important. Let's compare that to an incorrect example:

```
<b><i>Caution!</b></i>
```

This may not display properly in a browser (although some browsers are more forgiving than others), and you'll certainly run into trouble with style sheets if your tags are not properly nested.

TRY IT

Exercise 7-4: Match the Sample—Inline Styles

See if you can get your recipe document to match this sample page.

Start with the final *tapenade.html* file you formatted in Try It: Exercise 7-2 with block element tags. Change the instructions to an ordered list, then use the various inline style tags we've learned to make the spans of text match the sample. The resulting code is in the Appendix.

Tapenade (Olive Spread)

This is a really simple dish to prepare and it's always a huge hit at parties.

Ingredients

```
1 8 oz. jar sundried tomatoes
2 large garlic cloves
2/3 c. Kalamata olives
1 t. capers
12 oz. goat cheese
```

french bread *(sliced thin and toasted slightly)*
fresh basil & olives to garnish

Instructions

1. **Combine tomatoes and garlic in a food processor.** Blend until as smooth as possible.
2. <u>Add capers and olives.</u> Pulse the motor a few times until incorporated, ~~but still maintaining texture~~.
3. Spread goat cheese on each toast round and top with tapenade.

Text Styles

Here's how you access style controls in three of the more popular authoring programs.

Dreamweaver MX

❶ The most common text style adjustments are available right on the Properties palette when text is highlighted.

❷ Additional styles are available under the Text → Style menu.

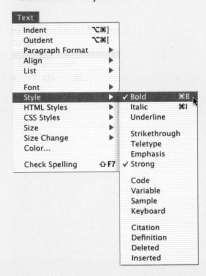

GoLive 6

❶ Basic style settings are available on the toolbar.

❷ Physical styles are available under the Type → Style menu.

❸ Logical styles are available under the Type → Structure menu.

FrontPage 2002

❶ Basic style settings are available on the toolbar.

❷ Additional style settings can be found under Format → Font.

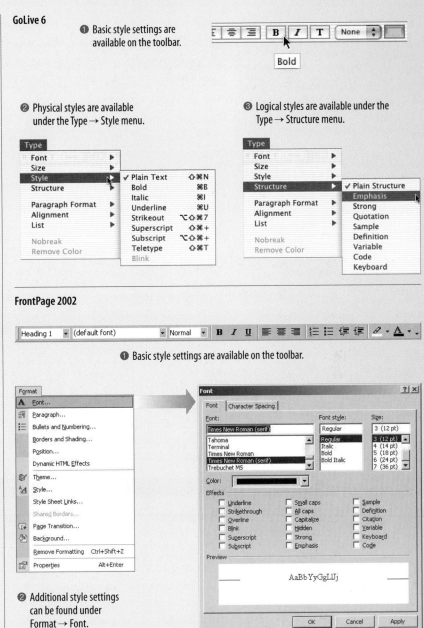

The Problem with <font>

While the <font> tag offers a way to make text look more interesting, it does have some downsides. First, it is not "good" HTML practice, in that it does nothing to structure the document logically and instead inserts display information right into the document (see the sidebar A Brief History of HTML in Chapter 6 for why this is undesirable). Furthermore, in practical terms, it is more cumbersome to make changes to the styles, because every <font> tag needs to be changed individually.

The <font> tag is finally being kicked to the curb by the web development community in favor of style sheets. In fact, the W3C has officially declared the <font> tag to be "deprecated" in the latest HTML specification. This means that browsers will support it, but its use is discouraged.

Style sheets are an easy and attractive alternative. They allow for more sophisticated formatting and store the formatting information in a separate document. You can make one change in the style sheet and apply it to a whole document... even a whole site. That saves having to pick through hundreds of <font> tags to change colors or sizes. Style sheets are introduced in Chapter 8.

The <font> tag still works, and web-authoring tools still make generous use of it. If you are working on a professional site, explore using style sheets for efficiency and use the <font> tag sparingly.

The <font> Tag

As we've seen so far, the formatting you can do with the basic set of HTML text tags is fairly limited. Before style sheets came along, designers were starving for ways to control the look of text; browser developers responded with the <font> tag.

The <font> tag is an inline style tag that uses attributes to control the typeface, size, and color of text. It made a big impact on the appearance of web pages; however, it was not without its drawbacks. Now that style sheets are widely supported, the <font> tag looks downright clunky, inefficient, and in poor form. See The Problem with <font> sidebar for more detailed information.

In this section, we'll see how to specify the size, typeface, and color of text using the <font> tag. All of these adjustments are made with tag attributes. If you need a refresher in how attributes work, see Chapter 6.

Controlling font size

`<font size="number">...</font>`
Font size

The size attribute within the <font> tag controls the size of the enclosed text. Unfortunately, the <font> tag does not allow you to specify type by point or pixel size. In HTML, you can only specify the size of the text relative to the default font size.

Frankly speaking, the system HTML uses for sizing type is strange. First, you need to know that the browser's default font size is given the value of "3." Some users set their default font size small; others set it large enough to view from a distance. Whatever the size the user has set it, the browser's default text has the value of 3.

With that established, the size attribute specifies larger and smaller type relative to the default value of 3. The value of the size attribute can be either absolute or relative.

Absolute values

Absolute values are the numerals 1 through 7, with each size increment about 20% larger than the size before. Therefore, type set to size="4" is approximately 20% larger than type set to size="3" (the default text size, whatever that might be). Similarly, type that is set to size="2" is approximately 20% smaller than the surrounding default text. The largest size the browser will display using the <font> tag is 7; if you try to specify a higher value, it will just display at the same size as text set to 7.

In Figure 7-19, I've adjusted the size of various spans of text using absolute values for the size attribute. Compare the code to the resulting text as displayed in the browser.

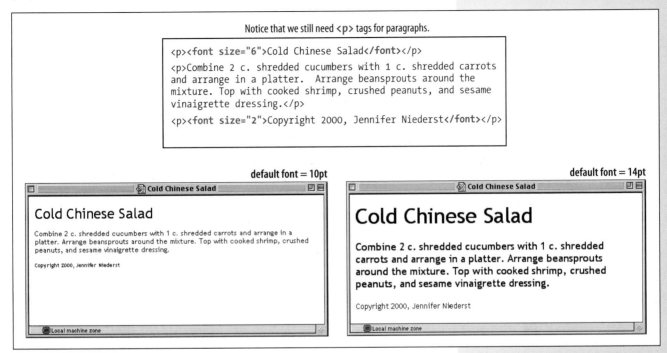

Figure 7-19. The resulting text size depends on the default browser font setting. See how text set to size="6" is much larger when the default font is set larger.

Relative values

The other way to specify font size is to use a relative value. The size is still specified on a scale of 1 through 7. However, instead of providing the actual number, relative values use a plus or minus sign to say how many increments larger or smaller than the default size the text should be.

Sounds confusing, but it's actually simple. If I want a span of text to appear one increment smaller than the default text, I specify size="-1". The result is exactly the same as specifying size="2" (because 3–1=2). Likewise, size="+2" displays exactly the same as size="5" (because 3+2=5). Because the browser won't display text with a size value higher than 7, the highest relative value that will work is +4 (3+4=7).

In Figure 7-20, I've used the <font> tag with relative values to specify text that is larger and smaller than the default text. Notice how the result is the same as when I used absolute values. Whether you use absolute or relative values is largely a matter of preference. Figure 7-21 shows the relationship between possible size values and the resulting text size.

In HTML, you can only specify the size of the text relative to the default font size.

```
<p><font size="+3">Cold Chinese Salad</font></p>

<p>Combine 2 c. shredded cucumbers with 1 c. shredded carrots
and arrange in a platter.  Arrange beansprouts around the
mixture. Top with cooked shrimp, crushed peanuts, and sesame
vinaigrette dressing.</p>

<p><font size="-1">Copyright 2000, Jennifer Niederst</font></p>
```

default font = 10pt

default font = 14pt

Figure 7-20. The relative size values in this figure are numerically equivalent to the absolute values in Figure 7-19. The browser displays the text exactly the same for both approaches.

		default					
Absolute Values	1	2	3	4	5	6	7
Relative Values	−2	−1	—	+1	+2	+3	+4
On a browser with its default font set to 10 points, these values might translate to approximately	6pt	8pt	10pt	12pt	14pt	18pt	27pt

Figure 7-21. The relationship between absolute and relative font sizes.

DESIGN TIP

Avoid Big Changes

As a rule of thumb, you should avoid changing the size of large blocks of text more than +1 or −1. Because type displays differently across platforms and for each user, you risk making your text too large and clunky or too small to be legible.

Changing the default text size

```
<basefont size="number">
```
Sets the base (default) size

You're not stuck with the default font set at 3. You can use the \<basefont> tag to set the default size of the text. When you use \<basefont>, any relative size specifications you make (with a plus or minus sign) in the document will be applied to the new base font size.

When placed in the \<head> of the document, the \<basefont> tag affects all the text in the document. So if you wanted the text in the whole document to be slightly larger than standard, set \<basefont size="4"> in the header, like this:

```
<html>
<head>
<title>Sample Document</title>
<basefont size="4">
</head>
<body>...
```

If you want to change the default text for a portion of the document, you can place the \<basefont> tag in the flow of text. All the text following the tag will

---

D E S I G N   T I P

Changing \<basefont>

Although you can change the default font size for a page, that doesn't mean you should. Keep in mind that users are likely to be viewing the text on their browsers at a size that is comfortable for them. You're not necessarily doing them a favor by changing it.

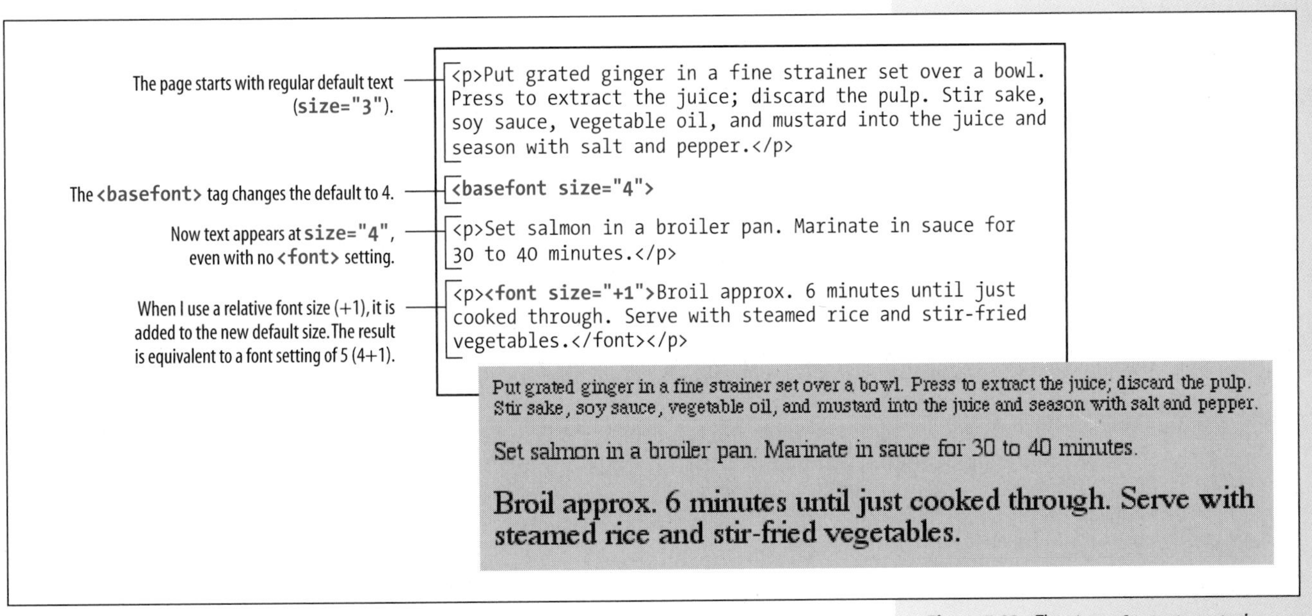

The page starts with regular default text (**size="3"**). →

```
<p>Put grated ginger in a fine strainer set over a bowl.
Press to extract the juice; discard the pulp. Stir sake,
soy sauce, vegetable oil, and mustard into the juice and
season with salt and pepper.</p>
```

The \<basefont> tag changes the default to 4. →

```
<basefont size="4">
```

Now text appears at **size="4"**, even with no \<font> setting. →

```
<p>Set salmon in a broiler pan. Marinate in sauce for
30 to 40 minutes.</p>
```

When I use a relative font size (+1), it is added to the new default size. The result is equivalent to a font setting of 5 (4+1). →

```
<p><font size="+1">Broil approx. 6 minutes until just
cooked through. Serve with steamed rice and stir-fried
vegetables.</font></p>
```

Put grated ginger in a fine strainer set over a bowl. Press to extract the juice; discard the pulp. Stir sake, soy sauce, vegetable oil, and mustard into the juice and season with salt and pepper.

Set salmon in a broiler pan. Marinate in sauce for 30 to 40 minutes.

Broil approx. 6 minutes until just cooked through. Serve with steamed rice and stir-fried vegetables.

be the new base font size. And of course, any relative font size settings will be relative to that size (Figure 7-22).

Figure 7-22. The \<basefont> tag sets size globally, so further relative changes will be based on the new \<basefont> setting.

Common Web Fonts

A specified font will only be used if it is already available on the user's machine, so there's no way to guarantee that your chosen typeface will be seen. Therefore, it is best to stick with the few fonts that are available on the majority of machines. The following fonts are the most commonly used on commercial web sites.

Serif fonts:

Times

Available for PC, Mac, and Unix, this is the most common default browser serif font.

Georgia

Georgia is was designed specifically for legibility at low resolutions, such as computer monitors. It is distributed for free by Microsoft.

Sans-serif fonts:

Helvetica

This is the most common sans-serif default browser font.

Arial

This is a standard system font on Macs and Windows systems. Many feel it is more attractive than the more common Helvetica. It is one of the most safe fonts to specify for a web page.

Verdana

This font was designed to be clear at screen resolutions, making it a highly legible font for web pages. It comes with Internet Explorer.

Trebuchet MS

Trebuchet was also designed for good legibility at screen resolutions. It comes with Internet Explorer.

Specifying a Typeface

`<font face="`*fontname*`">...</font>`
Specifies typeface

To suggest a typeface for a span of text, use the `face` attribute within the `<font>` tag. You can provide just one font name, or a list names separated by comments and spaces (Figure 7-23).

Remember that the specified typeface will be used only if it is found on the user's machine. If the browser looks for the font and doesn't find it, the default proportional font will be used instead. For this reason, it is common to provide a list of fonts for the `face` attribute, from specific to more generic, as shown here:

`<font face="Verdana, Helvetica, sans-serif">...</font>`

If the browser can't find Verdana, it will use the more widely available Helvetica; and if it can't find Helvetica, it will use some other sans-serif font. The generic font families are serif, sans-serif, monospace, cursive, or fantasy. They should be used as the last choice in your list, so if your specific font can't be found, at least the general style will be matched.

Unfortunately, there aren't many fonts that are commonly found on all computers. See the sidebar Common Web Fonts for recommendations.

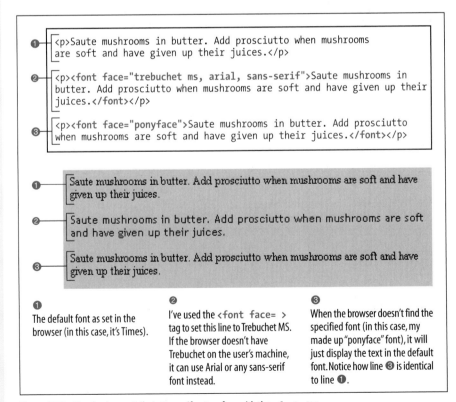

❶ The default font as set in the browser (in this case, it's Times).

❷ I've used the `<font face= >` tag to set this line to Trebuchet MS. If the browser doesn't have Trebuchet on the user's machine, it can use Arial or any sans-serif font instead.

❸ When the browser doesn't find the specified font (in this case, my made up "ponyface" font), it will just display the text in the default font. Notice how line ❸ is identical to line ❶.

Figure 7-23. Use the `face` attribute to specify a typeface with the `<font>` tag.

Specifying type color

`<font color="color">...</font>`
Specifies font color

You can change the color of type by using the color attribute within the `<font>` tag. The value of this attribute can be one of 140 standard color names, or it can be a numeric value that describes any color you choose. The sample in Figure 7-24 shows two methods for making the text color gray. The systems for specifying colors on the Web are explained in Chapter 13.

```
<p><font color="gray">Fish in Black Bean Sauce</font></p>
<p><font color="#808080">Fish in Black Bean Sauce</font></p>
```

Fish in Black Bean Sauce

Fish in Black Bean Sauce

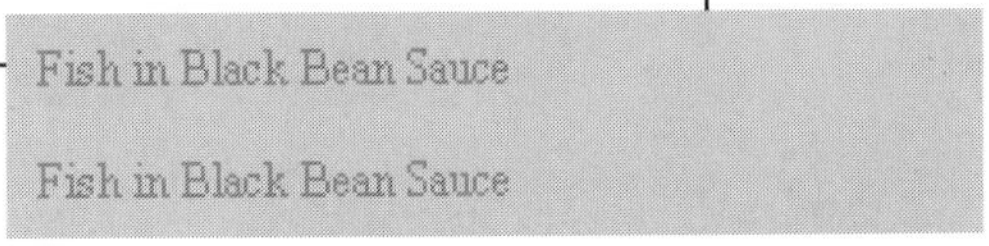

Figure 7-24. The color attribute is used to specify text color. Colors can be specified by name or numeric value.

Combining styles

We've just seen the separate attributes of the `<font>` tag that control size, typeface, and color. But what if you want to make a headline large, Helvetica, and blue? Do you have to use the `<font>` tag three times?

Not at all. You can put many attributes within a single opener tag. The order doesn't matter. So you can control the size, font, and color of your text in one fell swoop, as shown here:

```
<font size="+2" face="Helvetica" color="teal">...</font>
```

The `<font>` tag can also be nested with other inline style tags. What do you think the following HTML code will look like when viewed in a browser?

```
<b><i><font color="red"
size="6">CAUTION!!</font></i></b>
```

First of all, we can see it displays the word "CAUTION!!". The `<font>` tag around that word makes it large and red. But we also have an italic tag (`<i>`) and a bold tag (`<b>`) wrapped around everything. I bet you've guessed by now that the word will display in large, red text that is also italic and bold. (Or you could just look at Figure 7-25.)

When nesting style tags, be sure that one set is completely enclosed within the other and the tags are not overlapping.

```
<b><i><font color="red" size="6">CAUTION!!</font></i></b> Melted sugar
is very hot!
```

CAUTION!! Melted sugar is very hot!

Figure 7-25. Applying multiple font attributes and styles to text.

Exercise 7-5: Playing with the <font> Tag

It's time to get a little hands-on experience with the <font> tag.

1. Start by opening the file *trifle.html* from the *chap07* directory. It has been formatted with block element tags and looks something like this:

Chocolate-Kahlua Trifle

This is the easiest possible dessert recipe, and it's so yummy. It's also very portable if you put it together in a tall storage canister, so it's a good dish to bring to a party. People love dessert in a bucket!

1 devils food cake mix
1 3.9 oz. package chocolate (or devils food) instant pudding mix
1 tub of Cool Whip
4 toffee bars (such as Skor or Heath)
1/2 cup Kahlua (if you're tempted to use more, don't. This works well.)

2. First, let's change the font of all of the text to Verdana (and if that isn't available, we'll use Arial or a sans-serif font). Wrap all the text in <font> tags with the face attribute, as shown here:

```
<body>
<font face="Verdana, Arial, Helvetica, sans-serif">
<p><b>Chocolate-Kahlua Trifle</b></p>
<p>This is the easiest possible dessert recipe, and
  it's so yummy. It's also very portable if you
  put it together in a tall storage canister, so
  it's a good dish to bring to a party. People
  love dessert in a bucket!</p>
<p>1 devils food cake mix<br>
  1 3.9 oz. package chocolate (or devils food)
    instant pudding mix<br>
  1 tub of Cool Whip<br>
  4 toffee bars (such as Skor or Heath)<br>
  1/2 cup Kahlua (if you're tempted to use more,
    don't. This works well.) </p>
</font>
</body>
```

3. Next, make the headline green and two sizes larger than the default text. The bold tags can go inside or outside the <font> tag, but make sure that they are properly nested:

```
<p><font color="green" size="5"><b>Chocolate-Kahlua
    Trifle</b></font></p>
```

4. Finally, make the intro paragraph purple and slightly smaller than the default text:

```
<p><font color="purple" size="-1">This is the
    easiest possible dessert recipe ...in a
    bucket!</font></p>
```

The resulting page should look something like this sample. Feel free to continue playing around with the <font> tag until you feel comfortable with it.

Chocolate-Kahlua Trifle

This is the easiest possible dessert recipe, and it's so yummy. It's also very portable if you put it together in a tall storage canister, so it's a good dish to bring to a party. People love dessert in a bucket!

1 devils food cake mix
1 3.9 oz. package chocolate (or devils food) instant pudding mix
1 tub of Cool Whip
4 toffee bars (such as Skor or Heath)
1/2 cup Kahlua (if you're tempted to use more, don't. This works well.)

Font Size, Face, and Color Settings

Here's how you access `<font>` tag controls in three of the more popular authoring programs.

Dreamweaver MX

Font size, face, and color settings are available on the Properties palette.

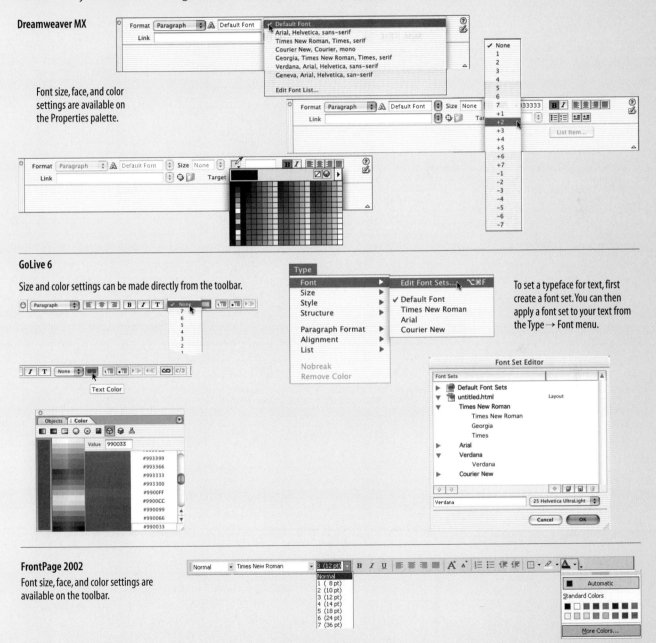

GoLive 6

Size and color settings can be made directly from the toolbar.

To set a typeface for text, first create a font set. You can then apply a font set to your text from the Type → Font menu.

FrontPage 2002

Font size, face, and color settings are available on the toolbar.

HTML alone provides few tools for adjusting text alignment.

Aligning Text

HTML alone gives designers precious little control over text alignment. As you might have guessed, style sheets offer more sophisticated control over alignment, margins, line spacing, indents, and so on. These techniques are covered in Chapter 8.

However, HTML can handle simple margin alignment. Paragraphs and headlines can be aligned on the left margin (left-justified), aligned on the right margin (right-justified), or centered using the `align` attribute in the <p> or <h#> tag. If you want to realign multiple elements on the page with the `align` attribute, you need to put it in every tag. Let's look at a few examples.

Left and right alignment

<p align="left">

Left alignment

This is the default value for the `align` attribute. So if you want text aligned on the left margin, you don't have to do anything; it will be displayed that way automatically.

<p align="right">

Right alignment

When you set the `align` value to `right`, the text will align on the right margin (Figure 7-26). Notice that it works in both paragraphs and headings.

```
<h2 align="right">Fish in Black Bean Sauce</h2>
<p align="right">The Chinese fermented black beans in this recipe give
the dish an unusual earthy aroma.</p>
<p align="right">It is a richly flavored dish that is also low in fat.</p>
```

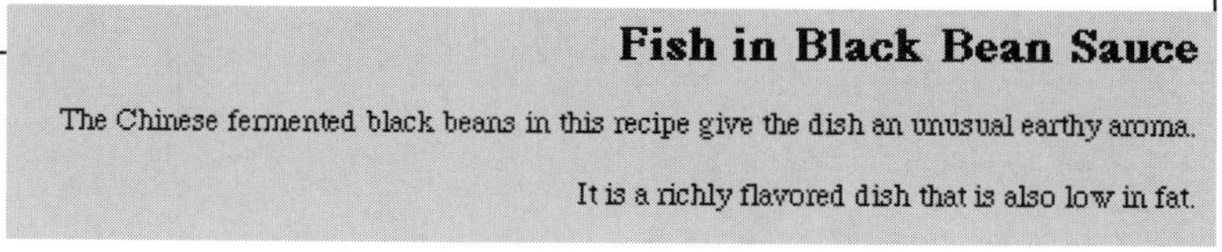

Figure 7-26. To align text flush-right, use the `align="right"` attribute.

> **NOTE**
>
> *The `align` attribute has been "deprecated" in the latest HTML specification in favor of style sheet alignment control. This means that it is still supported by browsers, but it will be omitted from future versions of HTML.*

Centering text

There are a couple of ways to center text using HTML.

<p align="center">
Center alignment

Set the value of the `align` attribute to `center` to center the paragraph or heading on a page. Remember, to center the whole page with this method, every element needs to have the `align="center"` attribute in its opening tag (Figure 7-27).

```
<h2 align="center">Fish in Black Bean Sauce</h2>
<p align="center">The Chinese fermented black beans in this recipe give
the dish an unusual earthy aroma.</p>
<p align="center">It is a richly flavored dish that is also low in fat.</p>
```

Fish in Black Bean Sauce

The Chinese fermented black beans in this recipe give the dish an unusual earthy aroma.

It is a richly flavored dish that is also low in fat.

Figure 7-27. These headings and paragraphs are centered using the `align="center"` attribute in each tag.

<center>
Center alignment

Another way to center text is to use the `<center>` container tag (Figure 7-28). This tag centers all of the text within it—you could center your whole page this way, if you like. Because it is so straightforward to use, the `<center>` tag is a popular way to center; however, it is not part of the official HTML specification. The proper way to center the whole page with HTML is to use a `<div>` (division) tag (see The `<div>` Tag sidebar).

```
<center>
<h2>Fish in Black Bean Sauce</h2>
<p>The Chinese fermented black beans in this recipe give the
dish an unusual earthy aroma.</p>
<p>It is a richly flavored dish that is also low in fat.</p>
</center>
```

Fish in Black Bean Sauce

The Chinese fermented black beans in this recipe give the dish an unusual earthy aroma.

It is a richly flavored dish that is also low in fat.

Figure 7-28. You can center many elements at once (or a whole page) using the `<center>` tag.

The <div> Tag

The `<div>` (division) tag is used to identify a generic block element. A division can contain multiple text elements such as headlines or paragraphs.

Once you put the `<div>` container tags around a part of a page, any style attributes (such as alignment) you apply to the division will apply to all the elements it contains.

The generic `<div>` tag is especially useful when used in conjunction with style sheets. (It's covered in better detail in Chapter 8.) I mention it here because it can be used with the `align` attribute to apply left, right, or center alignment to multiple headings and paragraphs at once. This saves having to put `align` attributes in every tag on the page.

In the example below, the `<div>` tag is used to center a whole page (similar to the `<center>` tag shown in Figure 7-28):

```
<div align="center">
<h1>Headline</h1>
<p>Paragraph content...</p>
<p>Another paragraph...</p>
<p>Yet another paragraph...</p>
</div>
```

Even blockquotes and lists, which can't use the `align` tag themselves, can be realigned when placed within a `<div>`.

You'll find that web-authoring programs such as Macromedia Dreamweaver use the `<div>` tag liberally to format pages. It's a good tag to be familiar with, even if you're a beginner.

Indents

It's generally not a good idea to write illegal HTML to achieve a visual effect. It can come back to bite you later.

Unfortunately, there is no "indent" function in standard HTML, so in the past, designers resorted to the creative misuse of existing tags to get text to indent. Once again, style sheets are the way to go for indenting text. But because web-authoring tools still use the old-school hacks, it doesn't hurt to be able to recognize them.

A few popular HTML cheats include (Figure 7-29):

- Using the `<blockquote>` tag to produce an indent on both the left and right margins

- Using an unordered list (`<ul>`...`</ul>`) with no list items (`<li>`) to display text as indented

- Using a dictionary list (`<dl>`...`</dl>`) with only definitions (`<dd>`) and no terms to display text as indented

```
<blockquote>Heat oil in wok. Add seasonings & stir fry for 10
seconds. Add Fish Sauce; heat 2 minutes, stirring constantly.
Pour over fillets in baking dish.</blockquote>

<ul>Heat oil in wok. Add seasonings & stir fry for 10 seconds.
Add Fish Sauce; heat 2 minutes, stirring constantly. Pour over
fillets in baking dish.</ul>

<dl>
<dd>Heat oil in wok. Add seasonings & stir fry for 10 seconds.
Add Fish Sauce; heat 2 minutes, stirring constantly. Pour over
fillets in baking dish.</dd>
</dl>
```

> Heat oil in wok. Add seasonings & stir fry for 10 seconds. Add Fish Sauce; heat 2 minutes, stirring constantly. Pour over fillets in baking dish.
>
> Heat oil in wok. Add seasonings & stir fry for 10 seconds. Add Fish Sauce; heat 2 minutes, stirring constantly. Pour over fillets in baking dish.
>
> Heat oil in wok. Add seasonings & stir fry for 10 seconds. Add Fish Sauce; heat 2 minutes, stirring constantly. Pour over fillets in baking dish.

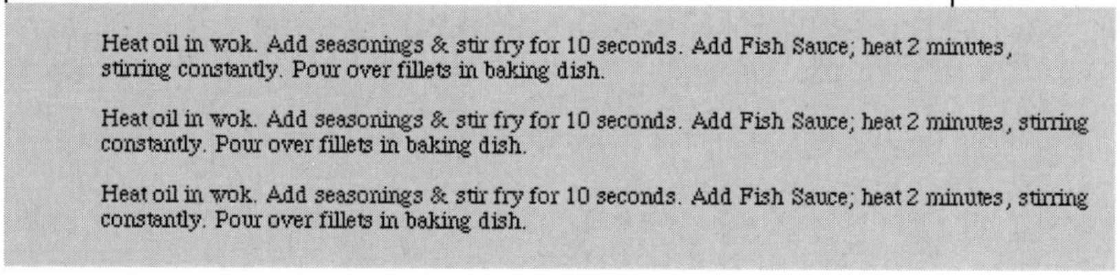

Figure 7-29. Three "cheats" for indenting HTML text.

Even with these workarounds, you only get an automatic indent of about a half-inch on the left or both margins. You can't indent just the first line or specify the amount of indentation as you can with style sheets.

Another popular technique for aligning large amounts of contents is to use a table. Using tables for alignment is discussed in Chapter 11. Some designers use 1-pixel transparent graphics, which they size to push text out of the way. This technique is discussed in Chapter 19.

Preventing line breaks

Say you want to keep a line of text all on one line, even if the window is resized. There's a tag for that. It's the "no break" tag (<nobr>). Text and graphics that appear within this tag will not be broken by the automatic wrapping function of the browser (Figure 7-30). If the string of elements is very long, it will continue off the browser page, and users will have to scroll to the right to see it. This tag may be useful for holding a row of individual graphics (such as a navigational toolbar) together, even when the window is resized very small; however, a table is a better solution.

Text or images between "no break" tags will stay on one line, regardless of the width of the browser window.

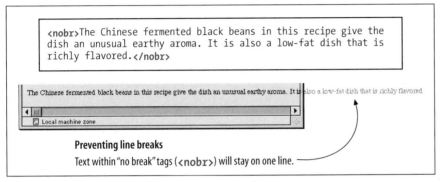

Figure 7-30. Preventing line breaks.

Preformatted text

As we saw earlier in this chapter, the preformatted text tag (<pre>) gives you character-by-character control over text alignment. Of course, you have to live with your text displayed in Courier. Since <pre> text honors blank character spaces, it's possible to use this tag to align other elements precisely on the page (although you'd probably be better off using tables). Figure 7-31 shows preformatted text used for precise alignment.

Preformatted text is unique in that it displays extra characters and carriage returns just as they are typed.

```
<pre>
                     calories        carb (g)       fat (g)
French Fries            285             38             14
Fried Onion Rings       550             26             47
Fried Chicken           402             17             24
</pre>
```

	calories	carb (g)	fat (g)
French Fries	285	38	14
Fried Onion Rings	550	26	47
Fried Chicken	402	17	24

Figure 7-31. An example of precise text alignment using preformatted text (<pre>).

Some Special Characters

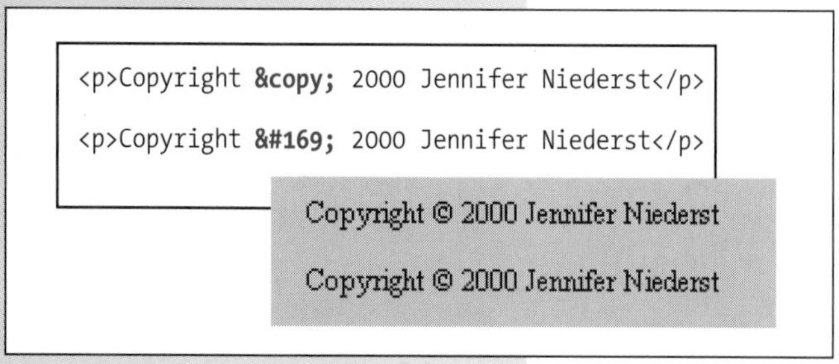

There's just one last text-related topic before we move on.

Some common characters, such as ©, are not part of the standard set of ASCII characters, which contains only letters, numbers, and a few basic symbols. To get these characters on a web page, you have to call them by their character entity names in the HTML document. A character entity is a string of text that identifies a specific character. Characters can be defined by name or by their numeric values.

An example will make this clear. I'd like to add a copyright symbol to my page. The typical Mac keyboard command, *Option-g*, which works in my word processing program, won't work in HTML. Instead, I must use the character entity name © (or its numerical value ©) where I want the symbol to appear (Figure 7-32).

Remember how extra character spaces in an HTML document are ignored by browsers? If you need to add a hard character space (or a string of them) to a page, you can insert them using the character entity for a "nonbreaking space,"   (Figure 7-33).

Table 7-1 lists some commonly used character entities. Of course, there are many more than are listed here. For a complete list, check out Webmonkey's useful Special Characters Quick Reference at *hotwired.lycos.com/ webmonkey/reference/special_characters/*.

Figure 7-32. Most special characters can be called by name or by number. The browser displays the special character in place of the character entity string.

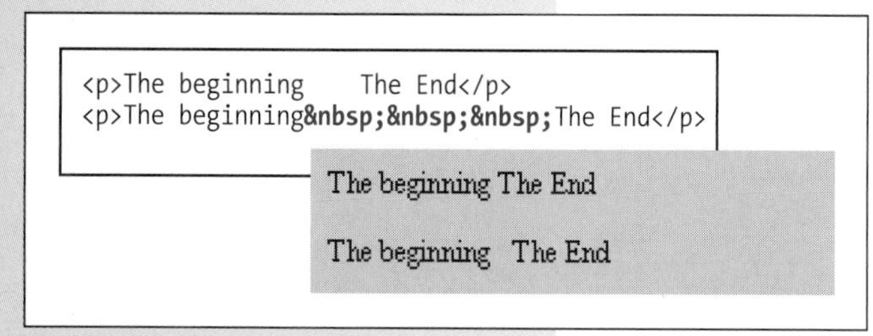

Figure 7-33. Browsers ignore multiple character spaces in an HTML file, but you can add hard spaces using the "nonbreaking space" character entity.

Table 7-1. Common special characters and their character entities

Character	Description	Name	Number
	Character space (nonbreaking space)		
©	Copyright	&copy;	&#169;
®	Registered trademark	&reg;	&#174;
™	Trademark	&trade;	&#153;
£	Pound	&pound;	&#163;
¥	Yen	&yen;	&#165;
"	Left curly quotes	none	&#147;
"	Right curly quotes	none	&#148;
<	Greater-than symbol; left bracket (useful for displaying tags on a web page)	none	&#155;
>	Less-than symbol; right bracket (useful for displaying tags on a web page)	none	&#139;

Character Entities

Here's how you add character entities in three of the more popular authoring programs.

Dreamweaver MX

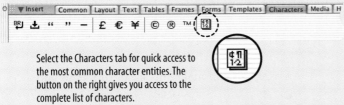

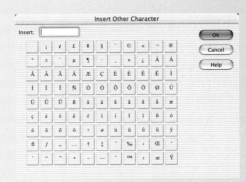

Select the Characters tab for quick access to the most common character entities. The button on the right gives you access to the complete list of characters.

GoLive 6

Open the Web Settings window from the Edit menu.

In the Inspector panel, select the character from the indicated text box. Copy the character and paste it into your web page.

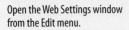

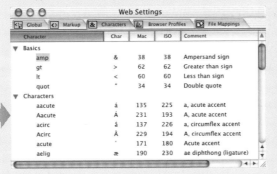

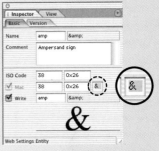

When you select a character from the Web Settings list, information about it appears in the character Inspector panel.

FrontPage 2002

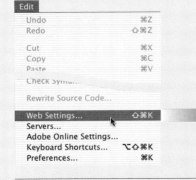

Place the insertion point where you want to insert a character. Go to Insert → Symbol. Select the character you want to insert, and click Insert.

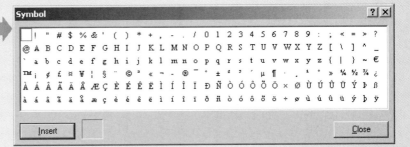

Exercise 7-6: Format Your Résumé

Now is your chance to put together all the tags we've learned so far. This time, I'm kicking you out of the nest and you'll be creating your own page from scratch. There are no answers in the back of the book for this one, since every person's document will be different.

1. In the text or HTML editor of your choice, write your résumé as though you were really putting it online and inviting prospective employers to see it. I recommend just typing in all the text and then going back later to add the HTML tags (rather than trying to type in the tags as you go).

2. Format the text the best you can using the tags that we've learned so far. Use the following checklist to make sure you're covering the basics. The sample résumé shown at the right is the result of hitting every item on the checklist. You don't need to match it exactly; it just shows what can be done.

___ Add structural tags

___ Add paragraphs and headings

___ Find an opportunity to include a list

___ Add inline styles

___ Play with the alignment of elements

___ Play with the `<font>` tag (change appearance of headlines; make a small copyright line)

Samantha Sample

Address: P.O. Box 10, Providence, RI 00000
Phone: 401.555.1212 | **Fax:** 401.888.1212

Summary of Skills

I have *16 years graphic design experience* in both print and web design and have a deep understanding of both media. In addition I offer strong organizational and time-management skills, the ability to learn quickly and work efficiently, great communication skills and the ability to work well in teams. I have a thorough command of most design-oriented applications.

Work Experience

Freelance designer (1987 to present)
I have been working as a freelance designer and consultant on a full-time basis since 1996. Clients include: AT&T, McDonalds, Amazon.com, MGM Studios, The Gap, and others.
Incredible Studios; Creative Director (June 1995 - June 1996)
Tasks also included producing graphics for a weekly web magazine and management and art-direction of in-house and freelance designers.
Hip Little Publishing Company; Senior Graphic Designer (Oct. 1992 - June 1995)
While at Hip Little Publishing Co., I designed book interiors, book covers, and brand collateral. I also worked as the lead designer and production manager of a unique cookbook series. Eventually, my responsibilities grew to include the design of the company's breakthrough electronic publishing ventures.
Big Old Publishing Company, Professional Division; Production Supervisor (Oct. 1988 - Oct.1992)
I was responsible for all aspects of production, from initial design through final printing. It was here that I became a power-user of Macintosh tools to design and produce book covers, develop interior designs, produce newsletters, and create technical illustrations and charts.
University Graphic Services; Graphics Assistant (1986-1987)
Aided staff designers with design and production of newsletters, logo design, posters, etc.

Test Yourself

In HTML, there is often more than one way to achieve a particular effect.
Two of the code examples listed below will center the recipe title and comments as shown in Figure 7-34; the other two will not. Which two code
examples will not work? What is wrong with them? Answers can be found in
the Appendix.

❶
```
<p align="center"><font size="+2" face="verdana, sans-serif"
color="#663399">Tapenade (Olive Spread)</font></p>
<p align="center"><i>This is a really simple dish to prepare and it's
always a huge hit at parties.</i></p>
```

❷
```
<align="center">
<p><font size="+2" face="verdana, sans-serif" color="#663399">Tapenade
(Olive Spread)</font></p>
<p><i>This is a really simple dish to prepare and it's always a huge
hit at parties.</i></p>
</align>
```

❸
```
<div align="right">
<p><font size="+2" face="verdana, sans-serif" color="#663399">Tapenade
(Olive Spread)</font></p>
<p><i>This is a really simple dish to prepare and it's always a huge
hit at parties.</i></p>
</div>
```

❹
```
<center>
<p><font size="+2" face="verdana, sans-serif" color="#663399">Tapenade
(Olive Spread)</font></p>
<p><i>This is a really simple dish to prepare and it's always a huge
hit at parties.</i></p>
</center>
```

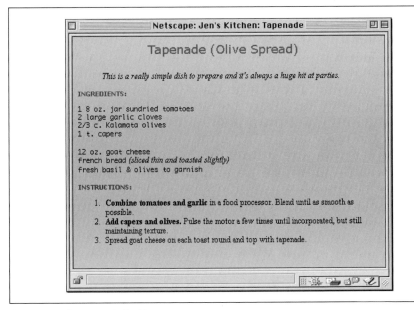

Figure 7-34. The recipe as it should appear.

HTML Review: Text-Formatting Tags

The following is a summary of the tags we covered in this chapter:

Tag and Attributes	Function
`<b>`	Bold text
`<blockquote>`	Lengthy quotation
` `	Line break
`<center>`	Centers elements on the page
`<dd>`	Definition item (in a definition list)
`<div>`	Division (used for applying styles)
`align="left|right|center"`	Horizontal alignment
`<dl>`	Definition list
`<dt>`	Term item (in a definition list)
`<em>`	Emphasized (italic) text
`<font>`	Uses attributes to specify size, font face, and color
`size="1-7"`	Text size
(or relative value)	
`face="name"`	Typeface for the enclosed text
`color="number" or "name"`	Color of the enclosed text
`<h#>`	Heading level (from 1 to 6)
`align="left|right|center"`	Horizontal alignment
`<i>`	Italic text
`<li>`	List item (in an ordered or unordered list)
`<nobr>`	"No break"; prevents line breaks in the enclosed text
`<ol>`	Ordered (numbered) list
`start="number"`	The starting number of the list
`type="1|A|a|I|i"`	Numbering style
`<p>`	Paragraph
`align="left|right|center"`	Horizontal alignment
`<pre>`	Preformatted text
`<s>`	Strikethrough text
`<strike>`	Strikethrough text
`<strong>`	Strong (bold) text
`<sub>`	Subscript
`<sup>`	Superscript
`<tt>`	Teletype (or typewriter text)
`<u>`	Underlined text
`type="disc|circle|square"`	Bullet shape
`<ul>`	Unordered (bulleted) list

Formatting Text with Style Sheets

8

As long as we're talking about text, it seems like the logical time to dig into style sheets. After all, I did sound like a broken record in Chapter 7, saying that style sheets are preferable for just about everything you'd want to do to text.

Before you get into this chapter, I want to give you the opportunity to opt out, at least temporarily. Style sheets—or Cascading Style Sheets (CSS), as they are formally known—are a somewhat advanced web-authoring technique. If you are a true beginner at writing HTML, with only as much experience as you've accumulated in the last two chapters, I recommend setting this chapter aside for now.

Once you are comfortable with HTML in general, come back and learn how style sheets can be used to fine-tune text and how they make site-wide format changes a snap. Style sheets will be less confusing once you've gotten the larger HTML picture...and we've only scratched the surface.

I also want to make clear that this chapter is just a brief introduction to style sheets. Cascading Style Sheets provide a robust set of tools that can be used to format an entire page down to the pixel. (If you want a thorough explanation of style sheets, see the resources listed in the Where to Learn More: Cascading Style Sheets sidebar.) This chapter covers the style sheet properties for basic text formatting. It should give you a good feel for how style sheets work and provide the tools you'll need to start improving the appearance and performance of your pages right away.

That said, this is the point at which you should feel free and unashamed to skip to the next chapter, where we'll learn how to add graphics to web pages. If you feel that you are ready to add style sheets to your repertoire, read on.

In this chapter

How Cascading Style Sheets work

Three ways to add styles to a document

Using HTML tags as selectors

Labeling elements with class

Creating your own elements with <div> and <span>

Style properties for text

Creating an external style sheet

If you are a beginner at writing HTML, I recommend setting this chapter aside for now.

Some Good Points, Some Bad Points

Still with me? Super. A style sheet is a set of instructions that controls the appearance of a web page. They offer more sophisticated control over typographic style and placement than HTML alone.

Style sheets have a number of advantages:

Greater typography and page layout control. With style sheets, you can specify traditional typography attributes such as font size, line spacing, indents, and margins.

Easier site maintenance. I think my favorite thing about style sheets is that you can apply one style sheet to all the pages in a site. Then if you want to change all the headings, you have to edit only one document (the style sheet) instead of each and every <h1> in the site.

Style information is kept separate from structure. In Chapter 6, I explained that HTML was intended only to mark up the structure of a document, not the way it looks. With style sheets, you can change the appearance of a page without disturbing the structure of the content.

The downside to style sheets is that they are not universally supported by all browser versions on all platforms. Fortunately, the environment continues to improve as older browser versions gradually disappear from use. Style sheets are supported to some degree by Internet Explorer Versions 3 and higher, and Netscape Versions 4 and higher. As of this writing, that accounts for approximately 95 percent of users out there.

However, even the latest browser versions don't perfectly support the style sheet specification in its entirety. Many properties and values, especially those in the later "Level 2" style sheet release, are still unsupported or are supported in buggy, unpredictable ways.

In this chapter, I introduce only the style sheet rules that can be used relatively safely, and I will make note of any exceptions. There may still be some users who won't see your page the way you intend, but as long as the HTML coding for your page is solid, they will not miss your content. Think of the styles as icing.

WHERE TO LEARN MORE

Cascading Style Sheets

The Cascading Style Sheet Specification
www.w3.org/Style/CSS/
If you're serious about style sheets, why not go right to the source and read the specification at the World Wide Web Consortium site? The document is a little dense, but it's chock-full of information.

Cascading Style Sheets: The Definitive Guide
by Eric Meyer (O'Reilly, 2000)
I learned everything I know about style sheets from Eric Meyer. This book is a thorough review of all aspects of CSS1 and a comprehensive guide to CSS implementation for both advanced and novice web authors. I recommend it highly.

How Style Sheets Work

Cascading Style Sheets work much like style sheets in any word-processing or page layout program. First, you identify the standard elements in the document and decide how you want each element to look. The style sheet stores the formatting information for all the elements.

For instance, this book uses a style sheet that makes all section headings 18-point Myriad Condensed Semibold and blue. There are separate style rules for chapter titles, body copy, figure callouts, and so on. I need to make sure that I identify each section heading consistently. That way, if I want all the headings to be black instead of blue, I can change the style sheet entry, and all the headings in the document change color at once.

Cascading Style Sheets use HTML to identify page elements. The style sheet itself is stored in the <head> of the HTML document or in a separate style sheet document. Again, one change to the style sheet changes the respective tagged elements.

Not every element in a document requires a style sheet instruction. You may decide that the browser's default rendering of paragraph text is just fine, but you want to control the appearance of headlines. Or you may have a special reoccurring text string, such as a catalog number, that you want to stand out from the surrounding copy. A style sheet is the solution.

Playing by the rules

A style sheet is made up of one or more style instructions (called rules) for how a page element should be displayed. The key to working with style sheets is to be familiar with the various parts of a rule. As you'll see, they're fairly intuitive to follow.

The following sample contains two rules. The first makes all the h1s in a document red; the second specifies that the paragraphs should be set in 12-point Verdana or some other sans-serif font:

```
h1 { color: red; }
p  { font-size: 12pt;
     font-family: Verdana, sans-serif; }
```

The two main sections of a rule are the selector (which identifies the element to be affected) and the declaration (the style instructions to be applied to that element) (Figure 8-1).

Figure 8-1. The parts of a style sheet rule.

TIP

You can write multiple rule declarations on one line, as long as they are separated by semicolons. However, stacking them, as shown in the second rule example on the previous page, makes them easier to read and edit later. Line returns within a declaration do not affect how the rule works.

Selectors

In the small style sheet above, the HTML elements <h1> and <p> are used as selectors. This is the simplest and most straightforward type of selector. The properties we defined for each will apply to all the <h1>s and <p>s in the document. Later in this chapter, we'll learn more sophisticated ways to select elements for formatting.

Declarations

The declaration is made up of a property and a value (similar to an attribute in an HTML tag) and appears within curly braces. You can list several properties in a single declaration, separated by semicolons (as shown in the second rule in the sample code above). Technically, the last declaration in a string does not require a semicolon, but web developers usually include it to make it easier to add more declarations later.

The real meat of style sheets lies in the collection of standard properties that can be applied to selected elements. The complete CSS specification includes dozens of properties; however, in this chapter, we'll look at the most common and best supported.

Values are dependent on the property. Some properties take length measurements, some take color names, and others have a predefined list of accepted values.

Applying style rules

There are three ways in which style sheet rules can be applied to an HTML document. We'll cover each type in more detail later, but it is helpful to be familiar with the terminology right away.

External style sheets. External style sheets save the rules in a separate style sheet document (named with the suffix, *.css*). The *.css* document is then linked to one or more HTML documents. In this way, all the files in a web site may share the same style sheet.

Embedded style sheets. Embedded style sheets are placed in the <head> of the HTML document using the <style> tag. Rules in an embedded style sheet apply only to that HTML document.

Inline styles. Style sheet properties can be applied to a single page element using the style= attribute right within its opening HTML tag. Inline styles apply only to that element.

Conflicting style sheets: The cascade

Have you wondered why style sheets are called "cascading"? It's time I explained. Because you can apply several style sheets to the same document, there are bound to be conflicts. The folks who wrote the style sheet specification anticipated this problem and assigned different weights to each type of style sheet (called a "cascading" order). Styles applied at the more specific level have more weight and override more general style sheets.

For instance, an HTML document may be linked to an external style sheet that applies to the whole site but might also have an embedded style sheet of its own. If the style sheets include conflicting rules for the appearance of <h1>s, the embedded style sheet will win. Inline styles override all other style sheet information. The sidebar Style Sheet Hierarchy lists the style sheet cascading order from general to specific.

Inheritance

Another important feature of style sheets is the concept of inheritance, in which properties are passed down from an element (the parent) to any elements contained within it (the children). An element is said to inherit properties applied to elements higher in the HTML hierarchy.

For example, if you set the text color for a <ul> list, this color is inherited by every list item (<li>) within that list. If you specify that the <body> of a document should be red, all text elements contained within the body of the document will be red (unless specified otherwise).

Styles applied to specific elements override settings higher in the hierarchy. With planning, inheritance can be used to make style specification more efficient. For example, if you'd like all the text on the page to be blue except for list items, set the color property for the <body> to apply to the whole document, then use another rule to make <li>s a different color. The more specific rules override more general rules.

Style Sheet Hierarchy

Style information can come from various sources, listed here from general to specific. Items lower in the list will override items above them:

- Browser default settings
- User style settings (set in a browser as a "reader style sheet")
- Linked external style sheet (added with the <link> tag)
- Imported style sheets (added with the @import function)
- Embedded style sheets (added with the <style> tag)
- Inline style information (added with the style= attribute in an HTML tag)

Creating a Simple Style Sheet

There's no better way to learn a new trick than to jump in and try it yourself. In the following activity, we'll write a very simple embedded style sheet.

Our style sheet will use three text properties that replace the controversial `<font>` tag. Let's get familiar with each one before we begin.

font-family

Values: typeface-name (or several separated by commas)

This property specifies a typeface or a list of typefaces similar to the `face` attribute in the `<font>` tag.

font-size

Values: length, percentage, relative-size, or absolute-size (see sidebar)

Just as it sounds, this property specifies the size of the font. `font-size` allows you to set specific font sizes in a variety of units (see the Font Size Values sidebar). It is much more useful than the `size` attribute in the `<font>` tag that only describes size relative to the default text size.

color

Values: color-name or RGB-value

This property changes the color of the text using either a color name or the color's numeric description. The system for specifying color in HTML is described in detail in Chapter 13. For now, we'll use intuitive standard color names.

The exercise that follows puts these properties to work in cleaning up a résumé web page. It also demonstrates how to use the `<style>` tag for embedding a style sheet, and it looks at several types of selectors. So even if you're not working along, please read each step in the activity carefully, as it will be covering new ground.

Font Size Values

There are four ways to specify font sizes using the `font-size` property.

Length values

Style sheets allow you to specify text in the following specific units:

px	pixels
pt	points
pc	picas
em	em (a relative unit that roughly equals the width of a capital letter "M" in the current font)
ex	ex (a relative unit that roughly equals the width of a lowercase "x" in the current font)
cm	centimeters
in	inches
mm	millimeters

Percentage

n%	specifies font size as a percentage of the inherited size

Relative sizes

These values change the size of the text relative to the parent object:

```
larger
smaller
```

Absolute size values

The following values roughly correspond to the 1–7 size system in HTML. These values are not well-supported and are best avoided.

```
xx-small
x-small
small
medium
large
x-large
xx-large
```

Exercise 8-1: Your First Style Sheet

In this first exercise, we'll give a well-structured résumé document a nicer appearance without resorting to the `<font>` tag. The HTML document for this exercise is provided on the CD and online at *www.learningwebdesign.com/materials/ch08/*.

1. Copy the directory *chap08* to your hard drive. Open the file *ex8-1_resume.html* (shown below) in an HTML editor such as Notepad, Homesite, or BBEdit. It has been formatted using the HTML tags we've learned so far. Try opening it in your web browser to see how it looks...not too pretty.

```html
<html>
<head>
<title>Samantha Sample Resume</title>
</head>

<body>
<p>Samantha Sample</p>

<h1>Contact Information</h1>
<p><b>Address:</b> P.O. Box 10, Providence, RI 00000<br>
<b>Phone:</b> 401.555.1212 | <b>Fax:</b> 401.888.1212</p>

<h1>Summary of Skills</h1>
<p>I have <b>16 years graphic design experience</b> in both print and web design
  and have a deep understanding of both media. In addition I offer strong organizational
  and time-management skills, the ability to learn quickly and work efficiently,
  great communication skills and the ability to work well in teams. I have a thorough
  command of most design-oriented applications.</p>

<h1>Work Experience</h1>
<dl>
  <dt><b>Freelance designer</b> (1987 to present)</dt>
  <dd>I have been working as a freelance designer and consultant on a full-time
    basis since 1996. Clients include: AT&amp;T, McDonalds, Amazon.com, MGM Studios,
    The Gap, and others.</dd>
  <dt><b>Incredible Studios;</b> Creative Director (June 1995 - June 1996)</dt>
  <dd>Tasks also included producing g
    and art-direction of in-house and
  <dt><b>Hip Little Publishing Compar
    - June 1995)</dt>
  <dd>While at Hip Little Publishing
    and brand collateral. I also wor
    of a unique cookbook series. Eve
    the design of the company's breal
  <dt><B>Big Old Publishing Company,
    (Oct. 1988 - Oct.1992)</dt>
  <dd>I was responsible for all aspe
    final printing. It was here that
    to design and produce book cover
    and create technical illustratior
  <dt><b>University Graphic Services;
  <dd>Aided staff designers with des
    posters, etc.</dd>
</dl>
</body>
</html>
```

Exercise 8-1 *(continued)*

2. Our style sheet rules will go in an embedded style sheet. In the <head> of the document, type in the <style> and </style> tags.

   The <style> element requires two bits of information. The type attribute tells the browser that we're using a Cascading Style Sheet (text/css). In addition, all the style rules must go within comment tags (<!-- ... -->). Browsers do not display any content contained in a comment. In this instance, we are using a comment to hide the style information from browsers that do not support the <style> tag.

   Your code should match this sample. All of the style rules we write in this exercise will go between the comment tags:

   ```
   <html>
   <head>
   <title>Samantha Sample Resume</title>
   <style type="text/css">
   <!--

   -->
   </style>
   </head>
   ```

3. Now we can add some style rules. First, we'll specify that all headings, paragraphs, and the definition list appear in the Verdana typeface. There are several ways to do this. One way is to write a rule for each element using the HTML tags as selectors (also known as "type" selectors), like this:

   ```
   <style type="text/css">
   <!--
   h1 { font-family: Verdana; }
   p { font-family: Verdana; }
   dl { font-family: Verdana; }
   -->
   </style>
   ```

   A more efficent way is to group the selectors so a single declaration applies to all of them. Grouped type selectors are written as a list separated by commas:

   ```
   <style type="text/css">
   <!--
   h1, p, dl { font-family: Verdana; }
   -->
   </style>
   ```

Take a moment to add this style rule to your style sheet. If you want to see the results, save the document and open it in the browser. Remember, you must save before you can see your changes.

Note that we don't need to specify the font for the terms (<dt>) or definitions (<dd>) because they will inherit the style rule from their parent element (<dl>).

4. Next, let's make the first-level headings 18 points in size (using the font-size property) and change their color. Because these instructions apply only to headings, we'll add a new rule just for <h1>s.

   ```
   <style type="text/css">
   <!--
   h1, p, dl { font-family: Verdana; }
   h1 { font-size: 18pt;
        color: orange }
   -->
   </style>
   ```

   Save your document and take a look at it in the browser. Feel free to play around with your own size and color values.

5. Next, we'll change the color of the company names in the Work Experience section. Right now, each name is formatted in bold text, so we can use the <b> tag as the selector for the rule. But we've used the <b> tag elsewhere on the page, and we only want to change the color of <b> text in the <dl> element. There's a way to do this using a contextual selector:

   ```
   dl b { color: purple; }
   ```

   In a contextual selector, the selectors are separated by a character space (no commas). The rule above says make <b> text purple only when it appears in the context of a <dl>. Add this new rule to your style sheet and take a look. The bold text in the definition list turns purple, but all the other bold text stays black.

Exercise 8-1 (continued)

6. One last change, then we're done for now. Samantha's name is formatted as a paragraph, and it looks a little weak. Let's change the appearance of just that paragraph. We can do this using an inline style on that paragraph. Inline styles are added using the style attribute right in the HTML tag. The value of the attribute is a style sheet delaration (or several declarations). Look closely at this example and add the new code to your file:

```
<p style="font-size: 16pt; color: green">Samantha
Sample</p>
```

Inline styles are a convenient way to make style changes, but avoid overusing them. Because they tie style information to a single content element, you have to hunt them down individually if you want to make changes later. In that regard, they aren't much better than the <font> tag.

We're done for now. Check your resulting style sheet against the code shown below. The screenshot shows how the résumé looks in my browser (it may look a little different for you because of your browser preferences).

```
<html>
<head>
<style type="text/css">
<!--
h1, p, dl { font-family: Verdana; }
h1 { font-size: 18pt;
     color: orange; }
dl b { color: purple; }
-->
</style>
</head>

<body bgcolor="#FFFFFF" text="#000000">
<p style="font-size: 18pt; color: green;">Samantha
Sample</p>
...
```

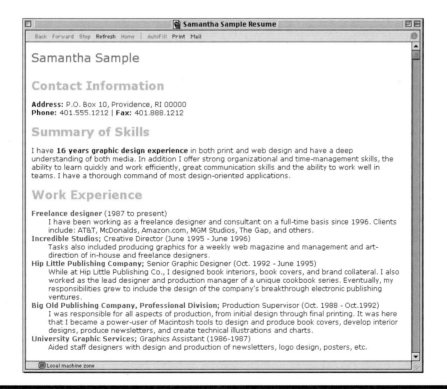

Special Selectors

So far, we've been using HTML tags as selectors. While contextual and grouped type selectors are useful, the style sheet specification provides more versatile ways to select elements on the page.

The class attribute selector

HTML does not provide for much differentiation of content. In the real world, there are usually several types of paragraphs in a document. For instance, paragraphs of article text are not the same as a list of links. It would be nice if each had a distinct and appropriate look. However, in HTML, they're all just formatted with <p>s.

Fortunately, the same HTML tag can be treated differently using the class attribute within the tag. The class attribute gives the element a label. You can then apply a style to all the elements that share the same label. To distinguish paragraphs from list entries, I label every paragraph in the article:

```
<p class="article">Mission of Burma played their first live show...</P>
```

The list entry paragraphs are labeled as well:

```
<p class="list">Billboard Review of NYC show</P>
```

In the style sheet, each class of paragraph gets its own style rule. The class selector is indicated by a period.

```
p.article { font-size: 12pt; }
p.list   { font-size: 9pt; font-family: Trebuchet MS;}
```

Figure 8-2 shows the results of the style changes (they're subtle). As we learn more text properties, we'll be able to fine-tune the appearance even more.

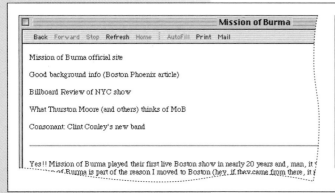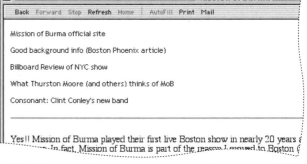

Figure 8-2. All the text in this document was formatted with paragraph tags (<p>). In the example on the right, the class attribute was used to give the list item paragraphs a different look from the paragraphs that follow.

The class selector can also be used to identify a number of different HTML elements as part of a conceptual group, allowing you to apply the same formatting to all the elements at once. For example, in the following code, certain headings and paragraphs are identified as "important":

```
<h2 class="important">Attention</h2>
<p class="important">Your account is past due.</p>
```

This style sheet makes all elements labeled as "important" appear in red:

```
h2.important { color: red; }
p.important  { color: red; }
```

If you are applying a property to all the elements in the same class (as in the previous example), you can omit the tag names. Be sure to leave the period—it's the character that indicates a class. The following rule has the same effect as the ones above:

```
.important { color: red; }
```

ID attribute selector

The id attribute is similar to class, except it can only be used to identify a single element rather than a group. In other words, two elements in the same document may not have the same id name.

In this example, a paragraph is given a specific id (the value must always begin with a letter):

```
<p id="j010703">New item today</p>
```

In the style sheet, id selectors are indicated by the hash (#) symbol. The HTML tag may be omitted, as shown in the second example:

```
p#j010703 { color: blue }
#j010703 { color: blue }
```

The id attribute is used to identify a unique element in a document.

<div> and <span> type selectors

Wouldn't it be cool if you had an HTML tag that could be used any way you want? The good news is you've got two of them. The <div> and <span> tags indicate generic page elements that you can name and format as you please. <div> creates a generic block element called a division. A <span> is a generic inline element. Neither has display properties on its own; they rely on style sheets for formatting.

Divisions

A division can contain just about any other HTML block element. You can wrap <div> tags around any part of a document, even a whole page. The formatting you apply to the division will be applied to all the elements it contains (thanks to inheritance). We looked at the <div> tag briefly in the text alignment section of Chapter 7, but it is most powerful when used with style sheets.

Here is a simple example that makes the introduction to an article blue (Figure 8-3). I've shortened the content to save space.

```
<style type="text/css">
<!--
.intro { color: blue; }
-->
</style>
<div class="intro">
<h1>Mission of Burma, LIVE!</h1>
<blockquote>Yes!! Mission of Burma played...</blockquote>
<p>For those who don't know, Mission of Burma was ...</p>
</div>
<p>Anyway! The show! Roger Miller, Peter Prescott, and...</p>
<p>First, the band sounded AMAZING! I'm fairly certain ...</p>
...
```

<div> creates a generic block element.

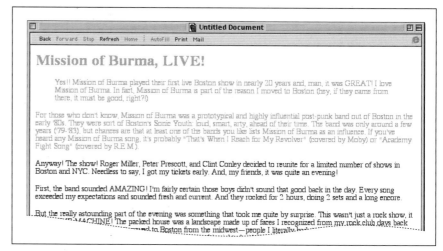

Figure 8-3. The introduction to this article is set in blue using the <div> tag and style sheets.

Back in Figure 8-2, we used the class attribute in multiple paragraph tags to label list entries. A quicker way to do this is to enclose all the list paragraphs in a labeled division.

```
<style type="text/css">
<!--
.list { font-size: 9pt; font-family: Trebuchet MS; }
-->
</style>
<div class="list">
<p>List entry 1</p>
<p>List entry 2</p>
<p>Another list entry</p>
</div>
```

<div> can also be used with inline styles as shown in the following code; however, it makes it more difficult to make changes on a global level later:

```
<div style="font-size: 9pt; font-family: Trebuchet MS;">
```

Spans

Spans work the same way as divisions, but you use them within the flow of text. They are the best substitute for text that might otherwise be formatted with that pesky `<font>` tag, but spans are much more versatile.

The `<span>` tag is best used in conjunction with the `class` selector so you can update them all with a single style sheet rule change. Inline styles are appropriate if you need to format a single span here or there.

The following code formats the account name differently from the usernames using `<span>` and `class`. The style sheet rule makes the account number text small and gray (Figure 8-4).

```
<style type="text/css">
<!--
.account { font-size: smaller;
           color: gray; }
-->
</style>
Becky Sixteen <span class="account">(#7331225)</span>
Pat Lacey <span class="account">(#1231237)</span>
Deuce Loosely <span class="account">(#7894568)</span>
```

Becky Sixteen (#7331225)

Pat Lacey (#1231237)

Deuce Loosely (#7894568)

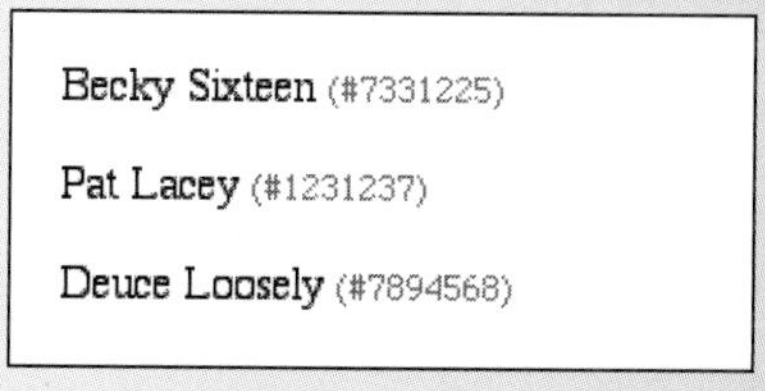

Figure 8-4. Using the `<span>` tag and style sheets to style inline elements.

Using the generic `<div>` and `<span>` elements with `class` identifiers, it is easy to customize your document for fine-tuned formatting.

Pseudo-selectors

There's one last type of selector that you should be familiar with. So far, we've looked at using parts of the HTML document as the selectors. There are other aspects of the document that the browser keeps track of behind the scenes, such as the first line of each paragraph, the first letter in a line, and whether a link is active or has been visited.

These things aren't written in the HTML code—the browser just knows about them. They are known as pseudo-elements and pseudo-classes. These pseudo-selectors are indicated by the colon character (:). Two pseudo-elements are `first-line` and `first-letter`, which can be used to apply formatting to the first line or letter of a paragraph:

```
p:first-line { font-size: larger; }
p:first-letter { font-size: 24px; color: orange; }
```

Unfortunately, the pseudo-elements are supported by Internet Explorer 5 and later, and Netscape 6 and later, making them somewhat risky to use.

There are three pseudo-classes in the first release of the style sheet specification, which apply exclusively to the

AT A GLANCE

Selector Summary

Type selector
The HTML element tag

Example: `h1 {property: value;}`

Grouped type selectors
String of HTML elements separated by commas

Example: `h1, h2, p {property: value;}`

Contextual type selectors
HTML elements separated by a space (the higher-level element goes first)

Example: `p em {property: value;}`

CLASS attribute selector
Indicated by the period character

Example: `p.news {property: value;}`
`.news {property: value;}`

ID attribute selector
Indicated by the hash symbol

Example: `p#first {property: value;}`
`#first {property: value;}`

Pseudo-selectors
Indicated by the colon symbol

Example: `a:link {property: value;}`
`a:visited {property: value;}`
`a:active {property: value;}`

anchor tag (<a>) used for linking. You can use style sheets to change the appearance of links, visited links, and active links (those in the process of being clicked) by including rules for the pseudo-classes in the style sheet:

```
a:link   { color: red; }
a:visited { color: maroon; }
a:active { color: orange; }
```

In Chapter 13, we'll learn how to control link colors using the <body> tag, which is a safer way to go due to the spotty browser support for pseudo selectors. Before we move on, let's try formatting another résumé using the special selectors we covered in this section.

TRY IT

Exercise 8-2: Customizing a Style Sheet

In this exercise, you can try out <div>, <span>, class, and id. The HTML document for this exercise is provided on the CD and online in the *chap08* directory.

1. Open the document *ex8-2_resume.html*. You will see that an embedded style sheet has been started for you.

It uses the <body> tag as a selector to apply a font to the entire document. This is a good trick for applying a format to everything on the page at once; you can always override it with more specific styles. The style sheet also includes a rule for the first-level headings.

```
<html>
<head>
<title>Rubicks Cube Resume</title>
<style type="text/css">
<!--
body { font-family: Verdana, Arial; }
h1 { font-size: 12pt; color: orange; }

-->
</style>
</head>

<body>
<p>Rubicks Cube</p>
<p><b>Address:</b> P.O. Box 434, Santa Rosa, CA 00000<b><br>
  Phone:</b> 555.1212 | <b>Fax:</b> 888.1212</p>

<h1>Employment Objective</h1>
<p>I am looking for the opportunity to use my various music-creation skills
  in a challenging and creative environment.</p>

<h1>Skills</h1>
<p>I have 13 years experience writing original music and playing in bands.In
  addition to playing traditional instruments (piano, guitar, drums), I have a
  deep understanding of digital audio technologies. I have worked as a producer,
  recording and mixing music entirely in a digital format. </p>

<h1>Work Experience</h1>
<dl>
  <dt><b>Producer</b> (1994 to present)</dt>
  <dd>I have been recording and producing bands in my home studio. Clients include:
      The Rolling Stones, U2, The Pixies, The Cars, Lemon Jelly, and others.</dd>
...
  <dt><b>Freelance Designer</b> (Oct. 1988 - Oct.1992)</dt>
  <dd>In my early career, I took advantage of my skills in visual design while
      pursuing a musical career.</dd>
</dl>
</body>
</html>
```

Exercise 8-2 *(continued)*

2. First, let's make the contact information at the beginning purple. The best way to apply a style to a group of block elements is to contain them in a `<div>` tag. The `class` attribute allows us to call it from the style sheet later. Add this code to your document:

```
<div class="contact">
<p>Rubicks Cube</p>
<p><b>Address:</b> P.O. Box 434, Santa Rosa,
   CA 00000<b><br>
   Phone:</b> 555.1212 | <b>Fax:</b> 888.1212</p>
</div>
```

Now add the rule to the style sheet:

```
div.contact { color: purple; }
```

Save the document and view it in the browser after each step. It is helpful to see the effects of your changes in small increments.

3. Next, change the font of all the descriptive text to 10-point Georgia. The best way to apply a style to different items scattered throughout the page is to give them all the same class name. Label all the paragraphs (`<p>`) and definitions (`<dd>`) containing descriptive text with the following class label:

```
class="description"
```

Now add the rule to the style sheet. We can omit the element tags and just use the period as a class indicator:

```
.description { font-family: Georgia;
               font-size: 10pt; }
```

4. Because the employment dates are less important than the job titles, let's make them a little smaller and gray. The best way to make changes in the flow of a text line is to put the text in a `<span>`. Wrap `<span>` tags around each of the dates and give them the class name date:

```
<dt><b>Producer</b> <span class="date">(1994
   to present)</span></dt>
```

Once again, add the appropriate rule for our new date class to the style sheet:

```
.date { font-size: 9pt; color: gray; }
```

5. One more little thing: let's take care of the name. Because there is only one instance of a name on the page, we can use the id selector:

```
<p id="name">Rubicks Cube</P>
```

and give it a rule in the style sheet:

```
#name { font-size: 16pt; font-family: Georgia }
```

And we're done! Since we're playing with only three style properties, this page still isn't that exciting, but you should feel comfortable with the various ways of applying styles to a document. If you feel like you got lost along the way, compare your code to the final version (next page).

Before

Rubicks Cube

Address: P.O. Box 434, Santa Rosa, CA 00000
Phone: 555.1212 | **Fax:** 888.1212

Employment Objective

I am looking for the opportunity to use my various music-creat
creative environment.

Skills

I have 13 years experience writing original music and playing in
traditional instruments (piano, guitar, drums), I have a deep un
technologies. I have worked as a producer, recording and mixin
format.

Work Experience

Producer (1994 to present)
    I have been recording and producing bands in my home st
    Rolling Stones, U2, The Pixies, The Cars, Lemon Jelly, and
Songwriter and Composer (1987 to present)
    I have been writing songs as long as I can remember. Late
    atmospheric textures for commercial use.
Hip Little Publishing Company (1990 - 1995)
    While at Hip Little Publishing Co., I managed the computer
    command of all software and hardware. I kept the systems
Freelance Designer (Oct. 1988 - Oct.1992)
    In my early career, I took advantage of my skills in visual d
    career.

After

Rubicks Cube

Address: P.O. Box 434, Santa Rosa, CA 00000
Phone: 555.1212 | **Fax:** 888.1212

Employment Objective

I am looking for the opportunity to use my various music-creation skills in a challenging and creative environment.

Skills

I have 13 years experience writing original music and playing in bands.In addition to playing traditional instruments (piano, guitar, drums), I have a deep understanding of digital audio technologies. I have worked as a producer, recording and mixing music entirely in a digital format.

Work Experience

Producer (1994 to present)
    I have been recording and producing bands in my home studio. Clients include: The Rolling Stones, U2,
    The Pixies, The Cars, Lemon Jelly, and others.
Songwriter and Composer (1987 to present)
    I have been writing songs as long as I can remember. Lately, I have been specializing in atmospheric
    textures for commercial use.
Hip Little Publishing Company (1990 - 1995)
    While at Hip Little Publishing Co., I managed the computer network, gaining a thorough command of all
    software and hardware. I kept the systems on the cutting-edge.
Freelance Designer (Oct. 1988 - Oct.1992)
    In my early career, I took advantage of my skills in visual design while pursuing a musical career.

Exercise 8-2 *(continued)*

Final code

```
<html>
<head>
<title>Rubicks Cube Resume</title>
<style type="text/css">
<!--
body { font-family: Verdana, Arial; }
h1 { font-size: 12pt; color: orange; }
div.contact { color: purple; }
.description { font-family: Georgia; font-size: 10pt; }
.date { font-size: 9pt; color: gray; }
#name { font-size: 16pt; font-family: Georgia }
-->
</style>
</head>

<body bgcolor="#FFFFFF">

<div class="contact">
<p id="name">Rubicks Cube</p>
<p><b>Address:</b> P.O. Box 434, Santa Rosa, CA 00000<b><br>
  Phone:</b> 555.1212 | <b>Fax:</b> 888.1212</p>
</div>

<h1>Employment Objective</h1>
<p class="description">I am looking for the opportunity to use my various music-creation skills in
  a challenging and creative environment.</p>

<h1>Skills</h1>
<p class="description">I have 13 years experience writing original music and playing in bands.In
  addition to playing traditional instruments (piano, guitar, drums), I have a
  deep understanding of digital audio technologies. I have worked as a producer,
  recording and mixing music entirely in a digital format. </p>

<h1>Work Experience</h1>
<dl>
  <dt><b>Producer</b> <span class="date">(1994 to present)</span></dt>
  <dd class="description">I have been recording and producing bands in my home
    studio. Clients include: The Rolling Stones, U2, The Pixies, The Cars, Lemon
    Jelly, and others.</dd>
  <dt><b>Songwriter and Composer</b> <span class="date">(1987 to present)</span></dt>
  <dd class="description">I have been writing songs as long as I can remember. Lately, I have been
    specializing in atmospheric textures for commercial use.</dd>
  <dt><b>Hip Little Publishing Company</b> <span class="date">(1990 - 1995)</span></dt>
  <dd class="description">While at Hip Little Publishing Co., I managed the computer network, gaining
    a thorough command of all software and hardware. I kept the systems on the
    cutting-edge. </dd>
  <dt><b>Freelance Designer</b> <span class="date">(Oct. 1988 - Oct.1992)</span></dt>
  <dd class="description">In my early career, I took advantage of my skills in visual design while
    pursuing a musical career.</dd>
</dl>
</body>
</html>
```

More Text Properties

Now that you're getting the hang of style sheets, let's add more properties to your arsenal.

Text style

We've been using the font-size, font-family, and color properties exclusively. The following is a list of other styles you can apply to text. They are used in the same way as the properties you've learned so far.[*]

font-style

Values: normal|italic|oblique

Use this style to make text italic (Figure 8-5). Oblique text is just a slanted version of the normal face. For most fonts, particularly those commonly available for web pages, oblique and italic will appear the same. (Note that bold is part of font-weight, not font-style.)

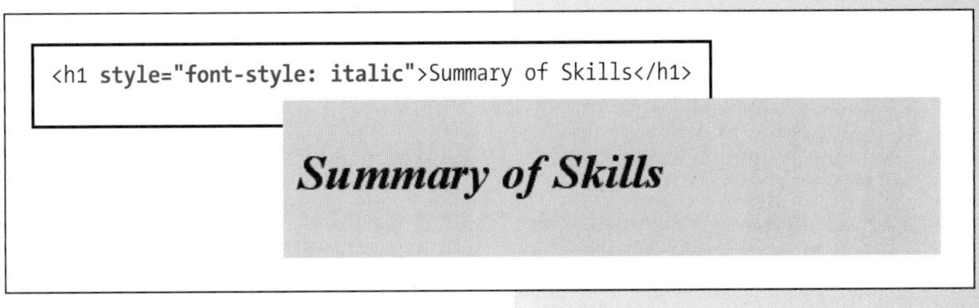

```
<h1 style="font-style: italic">Summary of Skills</h1>
```

Summary of Skills

Figure 8-5. The font-style property is used to make text italic.

font-weight

Values: normal|bold|bolder|lighter|100, 200, 300,...900

This style specifies the boldness of type (Figure 8-6). It can be specified with a descriptive term (e.g., bold, bolder) or with a numeric value from 100 to 900. Normal text corresponds to 400 on the numeric chart. The numeric chart is an interesting idea, but since there aren't many fonts with that range of weights and because browser support is spotty, they are best ignored. In practical terms, the only useful value is bold. Due to limited font weights, bolder usually displays the same as bold text, while lighter displays the same as normal text.

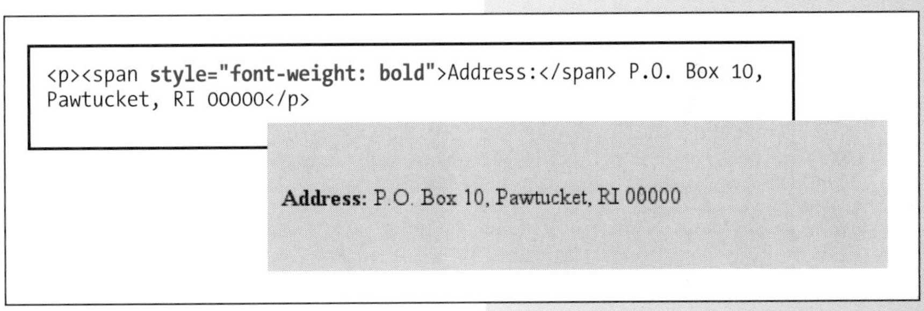

```
<p><span style="font-weight: bold">Address:</span> P.O. Box 10,
Pawtucket, RI 00000</p>
```

Address: P.O. Box 10, Pawtucket, RI 00000

Figure 8-6. The font-weight property is used to control the boldness of a font.

---

[*] All the figures in this section show the properties used as inline styles for compactness, but of course, you can use them in embedded or external style sheet rules as well.

```
<p><span style="font-variant: smallcaps">Freelance Designer</span>
(1987 to present)</p>
```

FREELANCE DESIGNER (1987 to present)

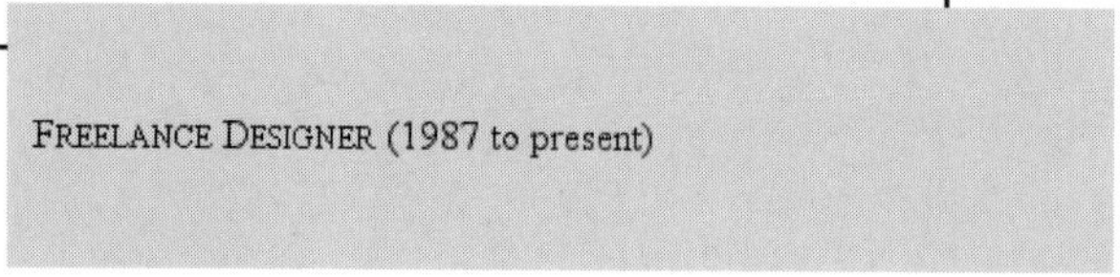

Figure 8-7. The font-variant property allows you to display type in small capitals, but it is only marginally supported.

```
<p style="font: bold italic smallcaps 16pt Verdana,Arial">Work
Experience</p>
```

WORK EXPERIENCE

Figure 8-8. The font property is shorthand to allow you to specify all properties on a single line.

```
<p style="text-transform: capitalize">Freelance Designer,
   Sixteen years experience</p>
<p style="text-transform: lowercase">Freelance Designer,
   Sixteen years experience</p>
<p style="text-transform: uppercase">Freelance Designer,
   Sixteen years experience</p>
```

Freelance Designer, Sixteen Years Experience

freelance designer, sixteen years experience

FREELANCE DESIGNER, SIXTEEN YEARS EXPERIENCE

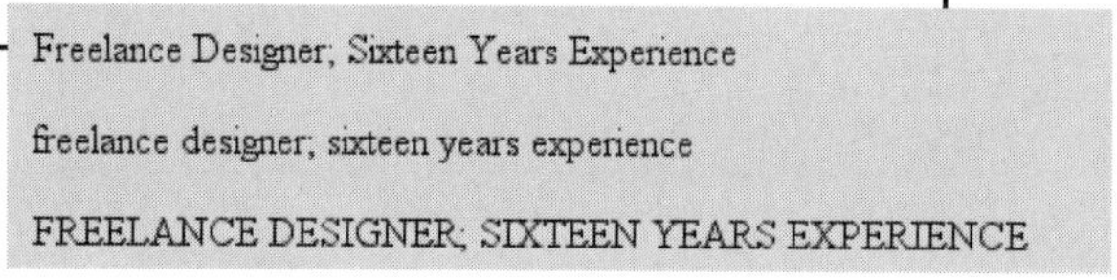

Figure 8-9. The text-transform property changes capitalization automatically.

font-variant

Values: normal|small-caps

font-variant gives you the opportunity to display text in small capital letters (Figure 8-7). It isn't very well-supported, so use it with care.

font

Values: font-style font-variant font-weight font-size/line-height font-family

The font property is a shorthand way to specify all the available font controls in a single rule. Values are separated by character spaces. In this property, the order of the values is important (although not every value needs to be present) and must be listed as follows:

```
{ font: style weight variant
  size/line-height font-family }
```

Figure 8-8 shows many properties being changed at once with the font property.

text-transform

Values: none|capitalize|lowercase| uppercase

This property changes the capitalization of text automatically, regardless of how it is typed into the HTML document (Figure 8-9). capitalize makes the first letter of every word in the sentence uppercase. lowercase and uppercase make all the characters lower- or uppercase, respectively.

text-decoration

Values: none|underline|overline|
line-through|blink

This applies a "decoration" such as an underline, overline, or a strike through the text (Figure 8-10). The line-through value should work like the <strike> inline style, but it is not well-supported. blink makes text flash on and off (but resist the urge). This tag is commonly used to turn off underlines under links by setting the value to none for the link tag.

```
<p style="text-decoration: underline">Summary of Skills</p>
<p style="text-decoration: overline">Summary of Skills</p>
<p><a href="lime.html" style="text-decoration: none">Click for more
   info</a></p>
```

Summary of Skills

Summary of Skills

Click for more info

Figure 8-10. The text-decoration property is used to underline, overline, or strike through text.

background-color

Values: color-name or RGB-value

This style changes the background color of any element. When applied to text (a block element or a span), it makes a colored rectangle around the text. In Figure 8-11, it is used to turn a span of text gray.

```
<p>Big Old Publishing Company
   <span style="background-color:gray">(Professional Div.)</span></p>
```

Big Old Publishing Company (Professional Div.)

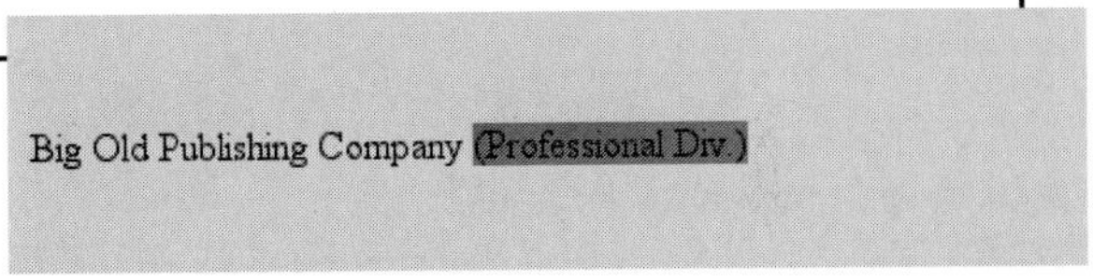

Figure 8-11. The background-color property changes the background behind a span of text.

Text alignment

In Chapter 7, we saw that HTML gives you very little control over text alignment. Fortunately, style sheets have a number of alignment properties that allow more sophisticated paragraph formatting.

text-align

Values: left|right|center|justify

Like the align attribute, this property controls the horizontal alignment of text against the margin (Figure 8-12). In addition to left, right, and center, text-align allows you to justify text, which means the margins on both sides will be neatly lined up (like the paragraphs in this book).

```
<p style="text-align: right">I was responsible for...</p>

<p style="text-align: center">I was responsible for...</p>

<p style="text-align: justify">I was responsible for...</p>
```

I was responsible for all aspects of production, from initial design through final printing. It was here that I became a power-user of Macintosh tools to design and produce book covers, develop interior designs, and create illustrations.

I was responsible for all aspects of production, from initial design through final printing. It was here that I became a power-user of Macintosh tools to design and produce book covers, develop interior designs, and create illustrations.

I was responsible for all aspects of production, from initial design through final printing. It was here that I became a power-user of Macintosh tools to design and produce book covers, develop interior designs, and create illustrations.

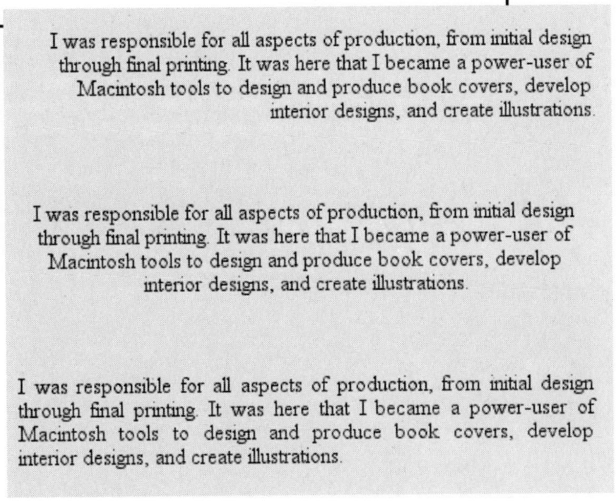

Figure 8-12. The text-align property controls the alignment of text against the margin.

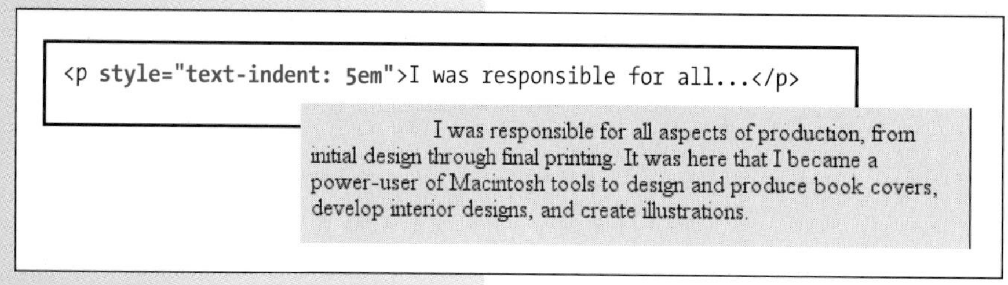

```
<p style="text-indent: 5em">I was responsible for all...</p>
```

I was responsible for all aspects of production, from initial design through final printing. It was here that I became a power-user of Macintosh tools to design and produce book covers, develop interior designs, and create illustrations.

Figure 8-13. The `text-indent` property assigns the indent for the first line of a paragraph.

```
<p style="margin-left: .5in; margin-right: 1in">I was responsible...</p>

<h1 style="font-size: 12pt; font-family: Verdana">Work Experience</h1>
<p style="margin-top: 4pc">I was responsible for all aspects of...</p>
```

I was responsible for all aspects of production, from initial design through final printing. It was here that I became a power-user of Macintosh tools to design and produce book covers, develop interior designs, and create illustrations.

Work Experience

I was responsible for all aspects of production, from initial design through final printing. It was here that I became a power-user of Macintosh tools to design and produce book covers, develop interior designs, and create illustrations.

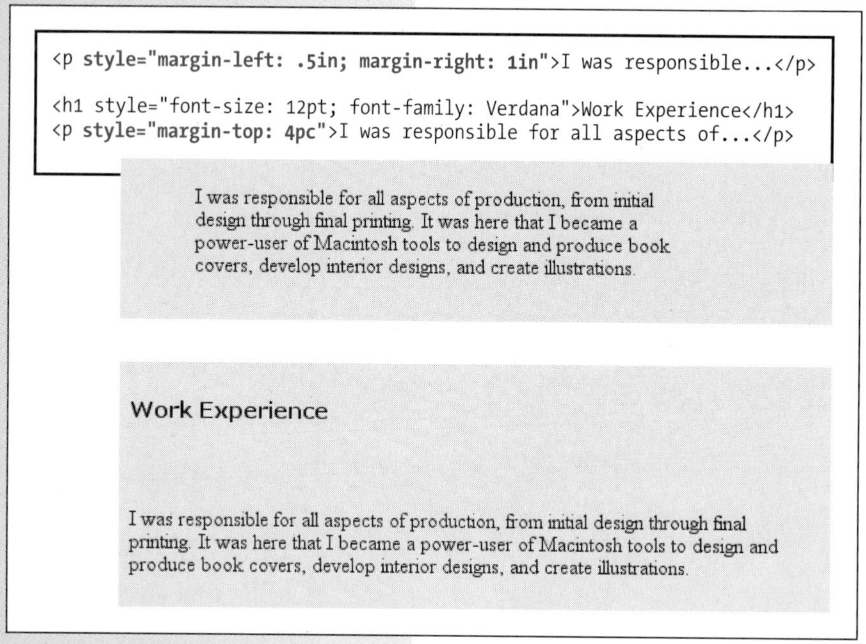

Figure 8-14. The four `margin` properties set margin widths around text elements.

text-indent

Values: length-measurement | percentage

Use the `text-indent` property to indent the first line of text in a paragraph or other element (Figure 8-13). In most cases, you'll use a specific measurement for the indent (see the sidebar Length Values on the facing page for the acceptable units of length), although you can also specify a percentage of the overall line width for the indent.

margin-left, margin-right, margin-top, margin-bottom

Values: length-measurement | percentage

With style sheets, it is possible to set specific margin widths around text elements. It is useful to know that style sheets treat every text element as though it were in a rectangular box. When you apply a margin to an element, the browser adds the specified amount of space between the page (or parent element) margin and the edge of the box. The properties listed above adjust the margins of the left, right, top, and bottom edges (just like they sound).

Margin properties can be applied to images and tables as well, but for now, we'll just look at text elements. The first example in Figure 8-14 specifies space on the left and right margins of the paragraph. In the second example, extra space is added above the paragraph to give the headline more visual space.

margin

Values: `margin-top margin-right margin-bottom margin-left`

This is a shorthand property for specifying the margins on all four sides of an object. The order is important, and they must be specified in a clockwise order as follows:

```
{ margin: top right bottom left }
```

If you specify only two values, the first value is applied to the top and bottom, and the second is applied to the left and right:

```
{ margin: top/bottom right/left}
```

In the samples in Figure 8-15, the margin values have the same effect, adding one pica above and below the paragraph and three picas on the left and right.

```
<p style="font-size: 12pt; font-family: Verdana; font-weight: bold;">
    Summary of Skills</p>
<p style="margin: 1pc 3pc 1pc 3pc">I have sixteen years graphic...</p>

<p style="font-size: 12pt; font-family: Verdana; font-weight: bold;">
    Summary of Skills</p>
<p style="margin: 1pc 3pc">I have sixteen years graphic design...</p>
```

Summary of Skills

I have sixteen years graphic design experience in both print and web design and have a deep understanding of both media. In addition, I offer strong organizational and time-management skills, the ability to learn quickly and work efficiently, and great communication skills.

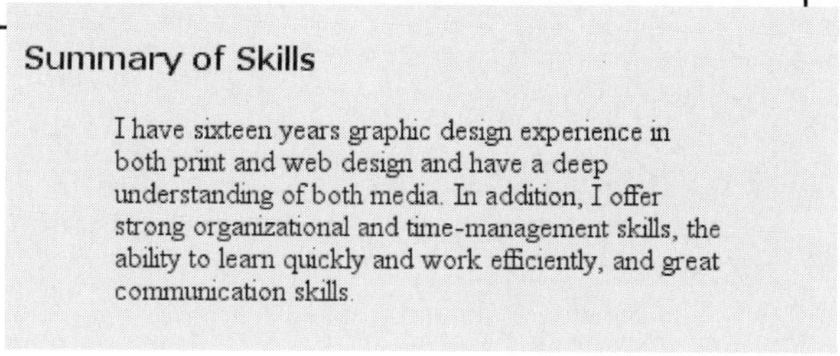

Figure 8-15. The `margin` property is shorthand for specifying all four margins at once.

line-height

Values: `length-measurement|percentage`

The `line-height` property specifies the amount of space between lines as measured from baseline to baseline (Figure 8-16). It is similar to leading in traditional print design. Graphic designers *love* this property.

```
<p style="line-height: 24pt">I have sixteen years...</p>
```

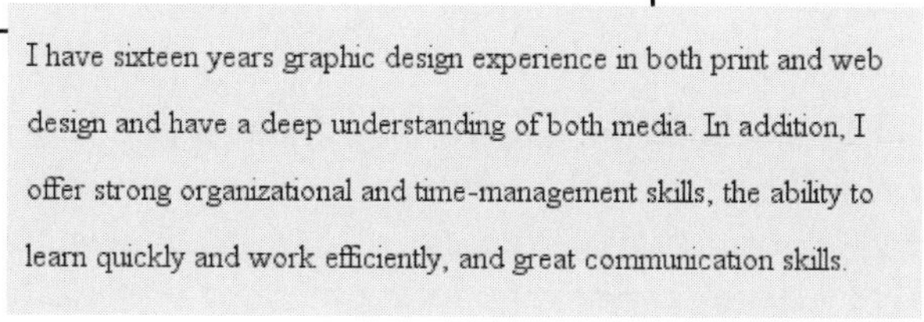

I have sixteen years graphic design experience in both print and web design and have a deep understanding of both media. In addition, I offer strong organizational and time-management skills, the ability to learn quickly and work efficiently, and great communication skills.

Figure 8-16. The `line-height` property sets the space between lines.

Length Values

Use these abbreviations when a value calls for a measurement:

cm	centimeters
in	inches
mm	millimeters
pc	picas
pt	points
px	pixels

Importing Style Sheets

The Cascading Style Sheets specification provides an alternative method for linking external sheets using the `<style>` tag with the `@import` function, as shown in this example:

```
<!--
<style="type/css">
  @import url(jennifer.css);
</style>
-->
```

Due to quirky support by the major browsers, the `@import` method is not a sure-fire way to go, so it is less popular than `<link>`.

TIP

It is possible to apply two style sheets to the same document by adding two `<link>` tags. If there are conflicts in the style sheets, the commands from the last file listed will override style sheets higher in the list.

External Style Sheets

All of the style sheets we've used so far have been either embedded or inline. While these applications have their uses, the most powerful way to apply style information is with an external style sheet.

With an external style sheet, all of the style rules are stored in a separate text-only document with the suffix *.css*. That style sheet document is then linked to one or more HTML documents, allowing them to share the same style information. The advantage is that with one change to the master style sheet, all the web pages that are linked to it are updated instantly.

Figure 8-17 shows the contents of the style sheet document *jennifer.css*. The style sheet is *not* an HTML document, therefore it may not contain HTML tags. It contains only a list of style sheet rules, as shown here.

```
.entries { font-family: Verdana, Arial, sans-serif;
          font-size: 9px;
          line-height: 10px;
          margin-top: 5px;
          margin-left: 4px; }
.body {   font-family: Verdana, Arial, sans-serif;
          font-size: 11px;
          line-height: 14px;
          text-align: justify; }
.title {  font-family: Verdana, Arial, sans-serif;
          font-size: 14px;
          font-weight: bold;
          color: #336633; }
.label {  font-family: Verdana, Arial, sans-serif;
          font-size: 9px;
          text-align: center; }
```

Figure 8-17. The contents of an external style sheet document (*.css*).

The preferred way to link a style sheet to a document is to point to it with the `<link>` tag in the `<head>` of the document. (See the Importing Style Sheets sidebar for information on an alternative method.) The code below shows the code for linking to the *jennifer.css* style sheet from an HTML document:

```
...
<head>
<link rel="stylesheet" href="jennifer.css" type="text/css">
</head>
...
```

`<link>` is a standalone tag that has three required attributes. The `rel` attribute tells the browser the relationship of the linked document to the current HTML document. For style sheets, the value is always set to `stylesheet`. The `href` attribute provides the location of the *.css* file by specifying its URL. Finally, the `type` attribute describes the type of document that is being linked; it should always be set to `text/css`.

Style Sheets

Here's how you access the style sheet controls in three of the more popular authoring programs.

Creating style sheets requires more steps than can be shown here, so see the documentation that came with your program for detailed instructions.

Dreamweaver MX

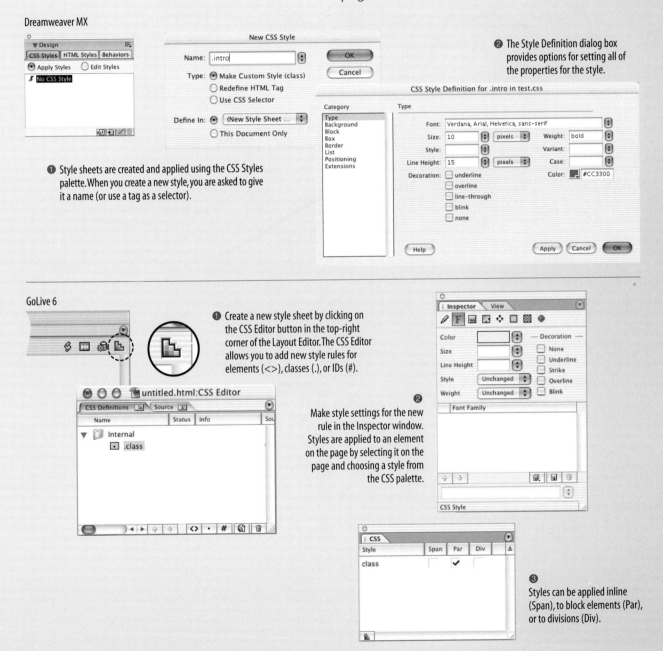

❶ Style sheets are created and applied using the CSS Styles palette. When you create a new style, you are asked to give it a name (or use a tag as a selector).

❷ The Style Definition dialog box provides options for setting all of the properties for the style.

GoLive 6

❶ Create a new style sheet by clicking on the CSS Editor button in the top-right corner of the Layout Editor. The CSS Editor allows you to add new style rules for elements (<>), classes (.), or IDs (#).

❷ Make style settings for the new rule in the Inspector window. Styles are applied to an element on the page by selecting it on the page and choosing a style from the CSS palette.

❸ Styles can be applied inline (Span), to block elements (Par), or to divisions (Div).

Style Sheets *(continued)*

FrontPage 2002

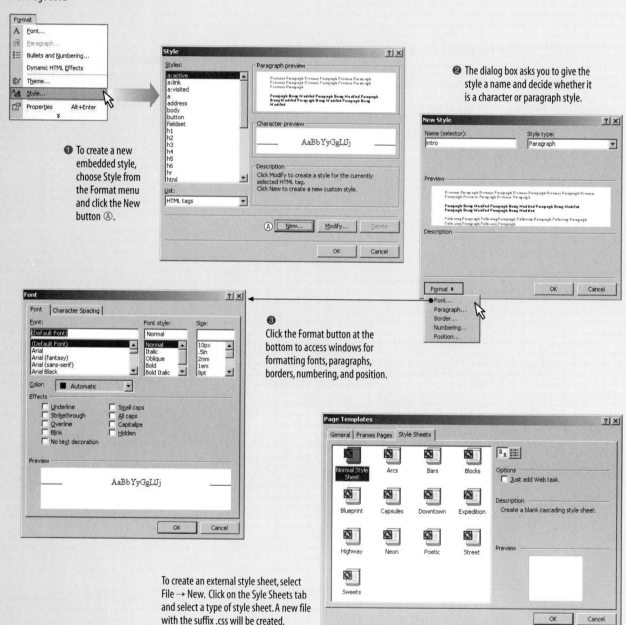

❶ To create a new embedded style, choose Style from the Format menu and click the New button ⒶA.

❷ The dialog box asks you to give the style a name and decide whether it is a character or paragraph style.

❸ Click the Format button at the bottom to access windows for formatting fonts, paragraphs, borders, numbering, and position.

To create an external style sheet, select File → New. Click on the Syle Sheets tab and select a type of style sheet. A new file with the suffix .css will be created.

Test Yourself

We've covered a lot of new ground in this chapter. You've learned how to write style sheet rules using a variety of selectors and a slew of text style properties. Now it is time to put it all together and see what you can do.

Once again, we'll use style sheets to improve the appearance of a simple résumé document. Start with the document *test_resume.html* that is provided in the *chap08* directory on the CD or online. Your assignment is to write style sheet rules as described below. Although the page is already marked up with HTML tags, in most cases you will need to add additional code specific to style sheet formatting. You will not need to retype content.

Remember to save your work and check your progress often. In the end, your page should look something the sample shown in Figure 8-18, following page. The resulting code is found in the Appendix.

1. Insert an embedded style sheet in the head of the document.

2. Make all of the text in the document Verdana. If Verdana isn't available, specify Arial or a generic sans-serif font insead.

3. Make the first-level headings 12-point, green type.

4. Use an inline style to override the formatting for Laura's name. Make the name 14-point, purple type.

5. Use class to label the first paragraph (starting "Seeking a full-time...") as intro. Write a style sheet rule that makes it italic and indents 0.5 inches on the left and right margins.

6. Use a division with an inline style rule to center the name, contact information, and intro paragraph.

7. The remainder of the résumé is made up of descriptive paragraphs and paragraphs that contain lists of projects. Use class to label all the descriptive paragraphs as text. Write a rule that makes text paragraphs 10-point type on a 14-point line height and justified with a 0.5-inch indent on the left and right margins.

8. Label the list paragraphs as list, then write a rule that makes them 10-point type on a 11-point line height with a 1-inch left margin.

9. Make the span of capitalized text at the beginning of text paragraphs purple and bold using a class label named course.

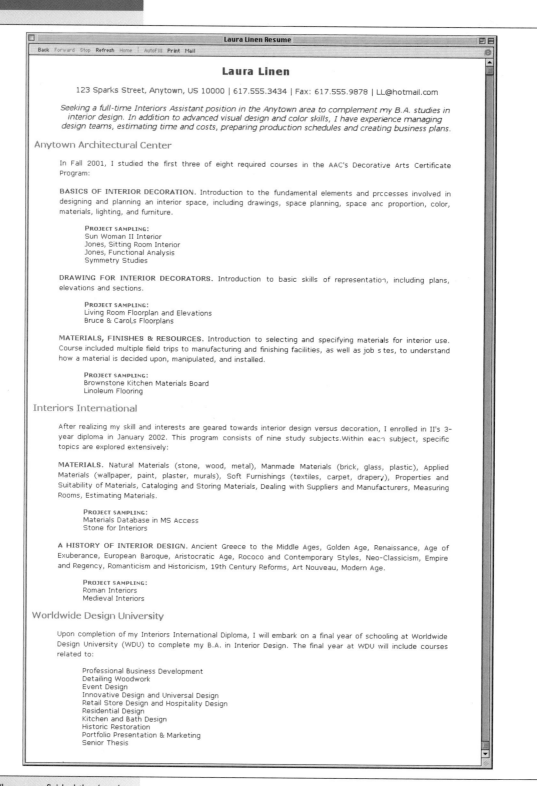

Figure 8-18. When you are finished, the résumé file should look something like this, allowing for variations in browser preferences.

10. Finally, make all "strong" text (the heading "Project sampling" throughout) small caps and purple.

11. Change the embedded style sheet to a linked external style sheet. Save the style sheet as *resume.css* in the same directory as the résumé document. (Be sure to remove the `<style>` element.) Link the external style sheet to the document.

HTML Review: Style Sheet–Related Tags

The following is a summary of the HTML tags we covered in this chapter:

Tag	Function
`<div>`	A generic block element
`<link>`	Links a document (such as a style sheet) to the current document
`<span>`	A generic inline element
`<style>`	An embedded style sheet

AT A GLANCE

Style Sheet Summary

Inline style
   Added with the style attribute:

```
<h1 style="property: value;">
```

Embedded style sheet
   Added with the `<style>` element in the head of the document:

```
<head>
  <style type="text/css">
  <!--
    (rules go here)
  -->
  </style>
</head>
```

Linked external style sheet
   Added with the `<link>` element in the head of the document:

```
<head>
  <link rel="stylesheet"
  href="pathname/file.css"
  type="text/css">
</head>
```

Imported external style sheet
   Added with the `@import` function in the `<style>` element:

```
<style="type/css">
  @import url(jennifer.css);
</style>
```

Style Property Review

The following is a summary of the text-formatting properties we covered in this chapter:

Property	Function
background-color	Sets the background color of the element
color	Sets the text color
font	A shortcut for indicating font style, weight variant, size, line height, and font family
font-family	Specifies the typeface
font-size	Specifies the text size
font-style	Makes text italic
font-variant	Makes text small caps
font-weight	Makes text bold
line-height	Specifies the space between lines (i.e., leading)
margin	A shortcut for indicating top, right, bottom, and left margins (in that order)
margin-bottom	Specfies the bottom margin
margin-left	Specfies the left margin
margin-right	Specfies the right margin
margin-top	Specfies the top margin
text-align	Sets horizontal alignment
text-decoration	Sets underlines, overlines, line-throughs, and blink
text-indent	Sets length of first-line indent
text-transform	Changes capitalization of the text

Adding Graphic Elements

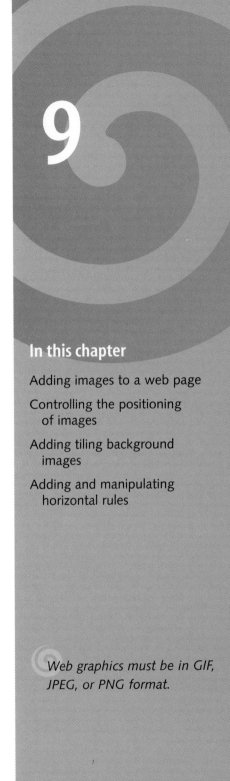

A web page with all text and no pictures isn't much fun. The Web's explosion into mass popularity is due in part to the fact that there are images on the page. Before the Web, the Internet was a text-only tundra.

Images are used in obvious and subtle ways. For instance, it may be apparent that photographs, icons, and buttons are graphics, but graphics can also be used as backgrounds, spacing devices, or for creating visual effects such as rounded corners on boxes (these tricks are discussed in Chapter 19).

In this chapter, we'll take a detailed look at the tags used for adding graphics to a page, both in the flow of text and as background images. We'll also look at that handy little page-divider, the horizontal rule.

Adding Inline Images

Most graphics on the Web are used as inline images, graphics that are part of the flow of the HTML content. These include all the illustrations, banner headlines, navigational toolbars, advertisements, etc. that you see on web pages. In other words, if it's not a background tiling image, it's an inline image. All inline images are placed in the HTML document using the `<img>` tag.

In order to be displayed in the browser, the graphics must be in the GIF, JPEG, or PNG file format (see Chapter 14 if you are not familiar with these formats). Furthermore, graphic files need to be named with the proper suffixes—.*gif*, .*jpg* (or .*jpeg*), and .*png*, respectively—in order to be recognized by the browser. Simply being in the right format is not enough.

Other popular graphics formats, such as TIFF, BMP, or EPS, will not display inline on a web page. If you have a graphic in one of these formats to display, you have two options. First, you can use an image-editing tool to convert it to GIF, JPEG, or PNG. Second, instead of putting it on the web page itself, you can make it an external image by creating a link to it with the `<a>` tag (the same way you would link to another HTML document). The browser uses special helper software to display media it does not support itself. External

In this chapter

Adding images to a web page

Controlling the positioning of images

Adding tiling background images

Adding and manipulating horizontal rules

Web graphics must be in GIF, JPEG, or PNG format.

Pointing to Graphics

It takes some practice to master pointing to graphics with the src attribute. Graphics can be tricky to keep track of and trickier to specify if you aren't familiar with URL conventions. These tips can help make image placement go smoothly:

- Be familiar with how directories and subdirectories work on computers. PCs provide a number of ways to view directories. Pick the one that best helps you envision where a file "lives" so you can find it and describe how to get to it later.

- It is common to store all the graphics in their own directory (usually called *images* or *graphics*). You can make one images directory to store all the graphics for the whole site or create an images directory in each subdirectory (subsection) of the site.

- Once you have your directory structure in place, be careful that you save your graphics in the proper directory every time. Also be sure that the graphics are in the proper format and named with the *.gif*, *.jpg*, or *.png* suffix.

- The next trick is writing the URL correctly in the src attribute. Pathnames in the <img> tag work the same as those in link tags. They are discussed in more detail in Chapter 10.

  In short, if the graphic is in the same directory as the HTML file, you can just specify the filename of the graphic. If it's in another directory, you need to provide the pathname to the graphic so the browser can find it.

images may open in a separate application window or within the browser window if the helper application is a plug-in, such as the QuickTime plug-in.

Let's take a look at the <img> tag and all its attributes that give you control over the placement and appearance of graphics.

The image tag

`<img src="`*filename or URL*`">`
Adds an image to the page

This is the basic tag that tells the browser, "Place a graphic here." There are a number of useful attributes that can be used to manipulate the image (we'll get to those next). The src attribute (short for "source") is required because it tells the browser which graphic to use.

The value of the src attribute is the URL of the graphic. If the graphic file is in the same directory as the HTML file, you can just use its filename. If the graphic is in another directory on the server, you need to provide the relative pathname to the graphic. A pathname is a list of directories and subdirectories the graphic is in, separated by forward slashes (/). It describes the location of the graphic relative to the current HTML file.

URLs and relative pathnames are covered in Chapter 10. Take a moment to read the sidebar Pointing to Graphics, which explains what it takes to successfully point to a graphic file from an <img> tag. In this chapter, I'll be keeping the URLs deliberately simple so we can focus on the tags and attributes themselves.

The image tag (<img>) is placed in the flow of HTML text at the point you want the graphic to appear (Figure 9-1). By default, graphics are displayed with their bottom edges lined up with the baseline of the surrounding text. Text will not automatically wrap around a graphic unless this is specified with the align attribute, which is described later in this chapter.

```
This is a really simple dish to prepare and it's always a huge
hit at parties.<br>
Combine tomatoes and garlic. <img src="tomato.gif"> Blend until
as smooth as possible.<br>
Add capers and olives. Pulse the motor a few times until
incorporated, but still maintaining texture.<br>
```

Figure 9-1. By default, the <img> tag aligns the bottom edge of the graphic with the text baseline.

Adding Images

Here's how you add images to a web page in three of the more popular authoring programs.

Dreamweaver MX

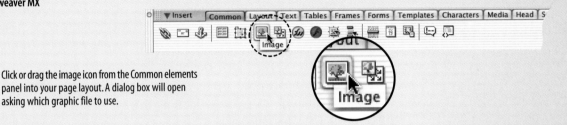

Click or drag the image icon from the Common elements panel into your page layout. A dialog box will open asking which graphic file to use.

GoLive 6

Drag the Image object icon from the palette into place in the document layout window.

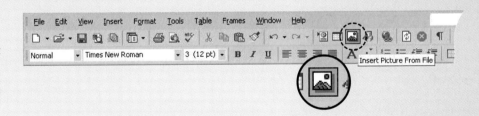

FrontPage 2002

To add an image, click the Insert Image icon. A window will pop up; browse to the picture you want from your local file system and select the file.

Alternative text

alt="*text*"
Alternative text

The alt attribute allows you to provide a brief text description of your image for instances when the graphic cannot be displayed in the browser. In the HTML specification, alt is listed as a required attribute. The alternative text you provide appears next to or within the generic graphic icon if the image is missing or if the user has graphics turned off in the browser for faster downloading (which many people do). For nongraphical browsers, such as Lynx, the text appears in brackets in place of the graphic.

Too often, I see home pages with graphical button links to sections of the site without alternative text. When the graphics are not available, these home pages become dead ends (Figure 9-2). Taking the time to add alternative text—especially to graphics that serve as navigational links—can save the day.

> *The alternative text will appear next to or within the generic graphic icon if the image doesn't display.*

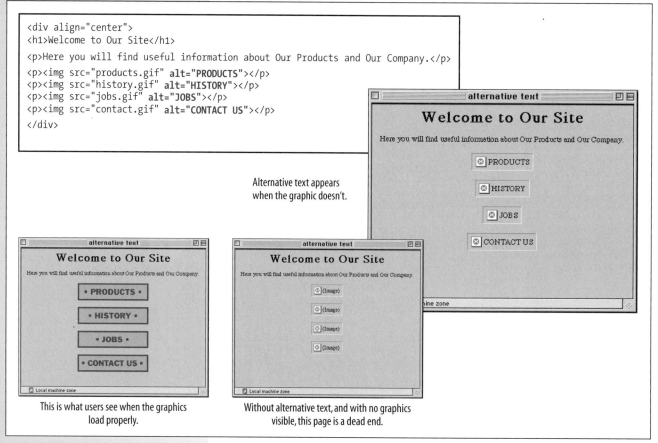

```
<div align="center">
<h1>Welcome to Our Site</h1>
<p>Here you will find useful information about Our Products and Our Company.</p>
<p><img src="products.gif" alt="PRODUCTS"></p>
<p><img src="history.gif" alt="HISTORY"></p>
<p><img src="jobs.gif" alt="JOBS"></p>
<p><img src="contact.gif" alt="CONTACT US"></p>
</div>
```

Alternative text appears when the graphic doesn't.

This is what users see when the graphics load properly.

Without alternative text, and with no graphics visible, this page is a dead end.

Figure 9-2. Alternative text is important for navigation, especially when graphics are used as links.

Image size

`width="`*number*`"`
Image width in pixels or percentage

`height="`*number*`"`
Image height in pixels or percentage

The `width` and `height` attributes indicate the dimensions of the graphic in pixels. Sounds mundane, but these attributes are your best friends because they speed up the time it takes to display the final page.

When the browser knows the dimensions of the graphics on the page, it can busy itself laying out the page while the graphics themselves are downloading. Without width and height values, the page is laid out immediately, and then reassembled each time a graphic arrives. Telling the browser how much space to hold for each graphic can speed up the final page display by seconds.

Web-authoring programs include `width` and `height` attributes for every graphic, and you should as well if you are writing HTML by hand.

It's important to note, however, that if the pixel values differ from the actual dimensions of your image, the browser will resize your image to match the specified values (Figure 9-3).

Although it may be tempting to resize images in this manner, the image usually gets blurry and deformed. In fact, if your graphics ever look blurry when viewed in a browser, the first thing to check is that your width and height values match the dimensions of the image exactly.

> ─── **T I P** ───
>
> *Don't resize very large graphics (such as high-resolution photo files) down to web-page size with the `<img>` tag. Even though the image may appear small on the page, the large image with its corresponding huge file size still needs to download. You shouldn't force a big, long download on a user when all you want is a small image on your page. It is much better to take the time to resize the graphic itself in an image editing program, then place it as actual size on the page.*
>
> *Also, if you've resized a graphic in an image-editing program, be sure also to update its dimensions in the HTML file.*

The width and height attributes can speed up the display of your page.

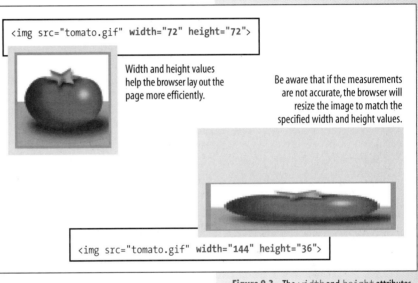

```
<img src="tomato.gif" width="72" height="72">
```

Width and height values help the browser lay out the page more efficiently.

Be aware that if the measurements are not accurate, the browser will resize the image to match the specified width and height values.

```
<img src="tomato.gif" width="144" height="36">
```

Figure 9-3. The `width` and `height` attributes determine the size at which an image displays.

Exercise 9-1: Add a Graphic

The attributes we've covered so far (src, alt, width, and height) are the ones you should include for every inline image on your site. It's time to try out the <img> tag for yourself. (The materials for this exercise are provided on the CD and online at *www.learningwebdesign.com/ materials/chap09*.)

1. Copy the directory *chap09* to your hard drive. You will find a document called *kitchenhome.html* and a directory called *graphics* that contains the five graphics used in this exercise (plus a few more we'll use shortly).

2. Open *kitchenhome.html* in an HTML editor (Notepad, BBEdit, or Homesite). It has some basic formatting, but we're going to replace some of the text headlines with graphics that have more character.

3. First, delete the first line of text ("Jen's Kitchen") and replace it with an image tag that points to the *kitchen.gif* graphic **A**. Because this graphic file is in the *graphics* directory, we need to include "graphics" in the pathname. The resulting code with a basic image tag looks like this:

   ```
   <p><img src="graphics/kitchen.gif"></p>
   ```

4. Every graphic should have alternative text in case it doesn't appear in the browser. Add alternative text to the <img> tag. It should be descriptive and adequately take the place of the graphic—for example, "Jen's Kitchen," not "header graphic."

   ```
   <p><img src="graphics/kitchen.gif"
      alt="Jen's Kitchen"></p>
   ```

5. It is also important to include the width and height of the graphic for faster downloads. The *kitchen.gif* graphic is 459 pixels wide by 68 pixels high. Add the attributes to the <img> tag.

   ```
   <p><img src="graphics/kitchen.gif"
      alt="Jen's Kitchen" width="459" height="68"></p>
   ```

6. Repeat these steps to replace the following text with their respective graphics (try to do it without peeking at the facing page!). The width and height measurements of each graphic are provided.

   - Replace the "W" in "Welcome" with *W.gif* **B** (53 pixels wide by 38 pixels high).
   - Replace "From Jen's Cookbook" with *fromjensbook.gif* **C** (200 pixels wide by 28 pixels high).
   - Replace "Good Stuff 'Out There'" with *outthere.gif* **D** (217 pixels wide by 30 pixels high).

7. One last graphic and we're done. Here's a neat trick for adding a divider rule to a web page. We're going to add the graphic *1px-orange.gif*, which is a graphic that is only 1-pixel square, and size it with the width attribute so that it stretches across the page. If we set the value to 100%, it will fill the width of the browser window regardless of how it's sized. Set the height to however thick you want the rule (I like a fine 1-pixel thick rule). A graphic that is 1-pixel square is only a few bytes, so it's a quick download.

   Just after the intro paragraph, add a new paragraph containing the 1-pixel graphic, as shown here:

   ```
   <p><img src="graphics/1px-orange.gif" width="100%"
      height="1" alt="(divider)"></p>
   ```

A *kitchen.gif*

B *w.gif*

C *fromjensbook.gif*

D *outthere.gif*

Exercise 9-1 *(continued)*

8. Save the file and look at it in a browser (you were probably doing that along the way). The final code and the resulting page are shown here:

```
<html>
<head>
  <title>Welcome to Jen's Kitchen</title>
</head>
<body>
<font face="Trebuchet MS, Arial, sans-serif">

<div align="center">
<p><img src="graphics/kitchen.gif" width="459"
  height="68" alt="Jen's Kitchen"></p>
</div>

<p><img src="graphics/W.gif" width="53" height="38"
  alt="W">elcome to my kitchen! People who know me
  know that I love to cook. I've created this site
  to share some of my favorite recipes and online
  food resources. The recipes listed here are ones
  that I have developed myself. In some cases, I
  started with a recipe found in a cookbook or
  magazine, but over time, I've adapted it enough
  to call it my own. <i>Bon Appetit!</i></p>

<p><img src="graphics/1px-orange.gif"
  alt="(divider)" width="100%" height="1"></p>

<div align="center">
<p><img
src="graphics/fromjensbook.gif"
alt="From Jen's Cookbook"
width="200" height="28"></p>
<p>tapenade (olive spread)<br>
garlic salmon<br>
wild mushroom risotto<br>
asian dishes </p>

<p><img
src="graphics/outthere.gif"
alt="Good Stuff 'Out There'"
width="217" height="30"></p>
<p>The Food Network<br>
Epicurious </p>
</div>

</font>
</body>
</html>
```

Having trouble?

If the graphics are not showing up in the browser, it is probably because the URL is not correct. Try these troubleshooting actions:

- Make sure you copied the *chap09* directory over intact.
- Make sure that you've been saving the file *kitchenhome.html* in the same directory from which it started (it should be in the same directory as the *graphics* subdirectory). You should have been overwriting with each save.
- Make sure that the pathnames in your HTML code are correct. Check for other code problems, such as missing close quotes or brackets.

Jen's Kitchen

Welcome to my kitchen! People who know me know that I love to cook. I've created this site to share some of my favorite recipes and online food resources. The recipes listed here are ones that I have developed myself. In some cases, I started with a recipe found in a cookbook or magazine, but over time, I've adapted it enough to call it my own. *Bon Appetit!*

FROM JEN'S COOKBOOK

tapenade (olive spread)
garlic salmon
wild mushroom risotto
asian dishes

GOOD STUFF "OUT THERE"

The Food Network
Epicurious

Image borders

```
border="number"
```
Border thickness in pixels

The border attribute adds a border around a graphic that is a specified number of pixels thick (Figure 9-4). The color of the border matches the text color of the page. If the graphic is a link, the border color will be the same as linked text (dark blue by default). (See Chapter 10 for how to link a graphic.)

Linked graphics get a 1-pixel-wide border by default. The border attribute is most often used to turn off that default border by setting the value to 0 pixels. You can also make it extra thick by specifying a higher pixel value .

If you want a nonlinked graphic to have a border, you're better off adding it in the image itself with an image-editing program, rather than relying on HTML.

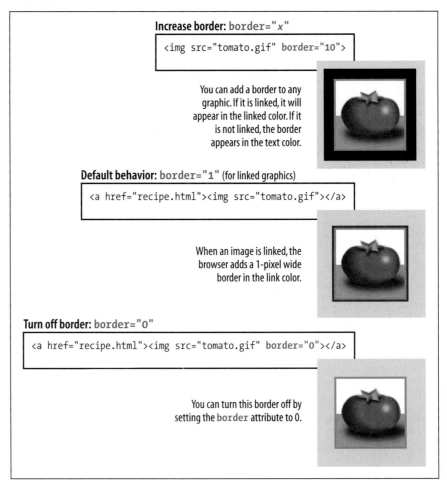

Increase border: border="x"

```
<img src="tomato.gif" border="10">
```

You can add a border to any graphic. If it is linked, it will appear in the linked color. If it is not linked, the border appears in the text color.

Default behavior: border="1" (for linked graphics)

```
<a href="recipe.html"><img src="tomato.gif"></a>
```

When an image is linked, the browser adds a 1-pixel wide border in the link color.

Turn off border: border="0"

```
<a href="recipe.html"><img src="tomato.gif" border="0"></a>
```

You can turn this border off by setting the border attribute to 0.

Figure 9-4. The border attribute and its effects.

Positioning graphics

The `align` attribute tells the browser how to align the graphic, horizontally or vertically, relative to the neighboring lines of text. The values `top`, `middle`, and `bottom` affect the vertical alignment of a graphic in relation to a neighboring single line of text (such as a label). The values `left` and `right` affect the horizontal alignment of the graphic (i.e., the margin the graphic is placed against). Let's look at how they work.

Vertical alignment

align="top|middle|bottom"
Vertical alignment relative to neighboring text line

By setting the value of the `align` attribute to `top`, `middle`, or `bottom`, you affect the positioning of the graphic in relation to the neighboring line of text. By default (that is, if you don't specify anything), the neighboring text line will align with the bottom of the image. This is the same as specifying `align="bottom"`. If you want the text baseline to line up with the middle of the graphic, set the value to `middle`; `top` aligns the text with the top edge of the image (Figure 9-5).

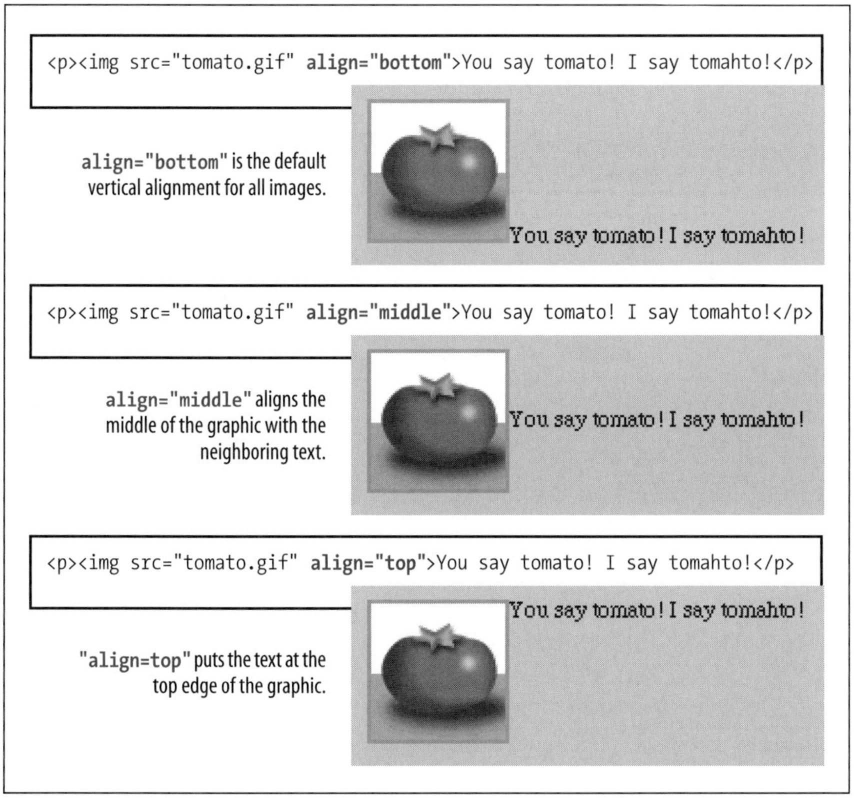

Figure 9-5. The `align` attribute determines the relationship between the graphic and surrounding text.

The *align* attribute is used to position graphics vertically and horizontally, depending on the value you specify.

Wrapping text around a graphic

`align="left|right"`
Horizontal alignment with text wrap

The `align` attribute also adjusts the horizontal positioning of the graphic when you set the value to `left` (against the left margin) or `right` (against the right margin).

This attribute is a favorite of mine because, in addition to specifying whether the graphic should appear against the left or right margin, it makes the text wrap around the graphic (Figure 9-6). As we've seen in earlier examples, without horizontal alignment values, the space next to the graphic is held blank.

Look carefully at the `<img>` tag placement in the file and the resulting location of the image on the page.

Notice in the second example that although the tag is placed before the word "Drain," the graphic ends up next to other words in the paragraph after being repositioned on the right margin of the page.

```
<p>
<b>SAUCE:</b><br>
Cut prosciutto into 1/2" chunks and fry with chopped onion in olive oil
over low heat, until fat is rendered and meat is crisp. Remove meat and
set aside.<br>

<img src="tomato.gif" align="left"> Drain the tomatoes, finely chop them
and add to the onion in the pan. Season with red pepper flakes and salt
and pepper. Simmer 20 minutes, stirring occasionally.<br>
<b>TO SERVE:</b><br>
Cook pasta according to directions on package. Drain well.<br>

Transfer sauce to large skillet over medium-high heat. Add the pasta and
reserved meat and cook for 30 seconds. Remove the skillet from heat. Add
cheese.
</p>
```

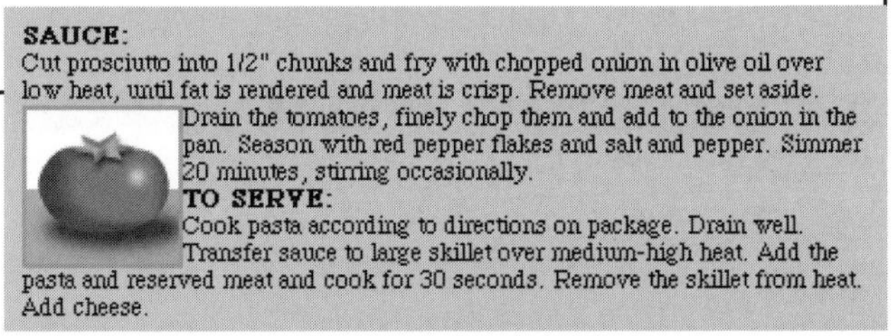

SAUCE:
Cut prosciutto into 1/2" chunks and fry with chopped onion in olive oil over low heat, until fat is rendered and meat is crisp. Remove meat and set aside. Drain the tomatoes, finely chop them and add to the onion in the pan. Season with red pepper flakes and salt and pepper. Simmer 20 minutes, stirring occasionally.
TO SERVE:
Cook pasta according to directions on package. Drain well. Transfer sauce to large skillet over medium-high heat. Add the pasta and reserved meat and cook for 30 seconds. Remove the skillet from heat. Add cheese.

```
<img src="tomato.gif" align="right"> Drain the tomatoes, finely chop them
and add to the onion in the pan. Season with red pepper flakes and salt
and pepper. Simmer 20 minutes, stirring occasionally.<br>
```

SAUCE:
Cut prosciutto into 1/2" chunks and fry with chopped onion in olive oil over low heat, until fat is rendered and meat is crisp. Remove meat and set aside. Drain the tomatoes, finely chop them and add to the onion in the pan. Season with red pepper flakes and salt and pepper. Simmer 20 minutes, stirring occasionally.
TO SERVE:
Cook pasta according to directions on package. Drain well. Transfer sauce to large skillet over medium-high heat. Add the pasta and reserved meat and cook for 30 seconds. Remove the skillet from heat. Add cheese.

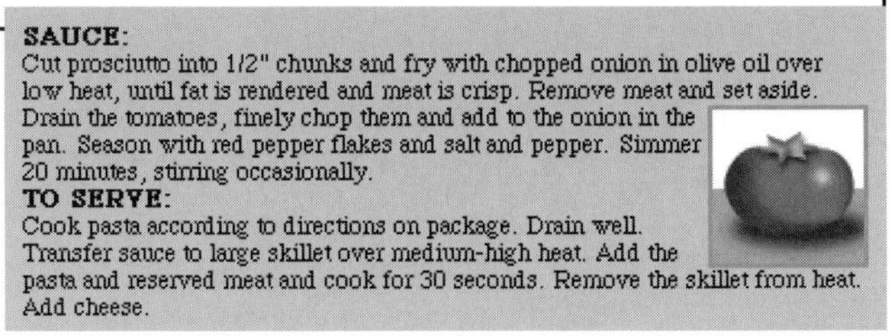

Figure 9-6. Aligning an image left or right makes the text wrap around the graphic.

hspace="*number*"
Horizontal space

vspace="*number*"
Vertical space

Use the hspace attribute to specify an amount of space (in pixels) to be held clear on the left and right of the image (Figure 9-7). Similarly, vspace holds a specified amount of space above and below. Compare Figure 9-7 to Figure 9-6.

The hspace and vspace attributes can be used in conjunction with the align="left" and align="right" settings to add a little space around the graphic. Without them, the browser runs the wrapped text right up to the edge of the graphic. I find that 6 to 12 pixels usually does the trick.

```
<img src="tomato.gif" align="left" hspace="12" vspace="12"> Drain
the tomatoes, finely chop them and add to the onion in the pan.
Season with red pepper flakes and salt and pepper. Simmer 20 minutes,
stirring occasionally.<br>
```

SAUCE:
Cut prosciutto into 1/2" chunks and fry with chopped onion in olive oil over low heat, until fat is rendered and meat is crisp. Remove meat and set aside.
Drain the tomatoes, finely chop them and add to the onion in the pan. Season with red pepper flakes and salt and pepper. Simmer 20 minutes, stirring occasionally.
TO SERVE:
Cook pasta according to directions on package. Drain well.
Transfer sauce to large skillet over medium-high heat. Add the pasta and reserved meat and cook for 30 seconds. Remove the skillet from heat. Add cheese.

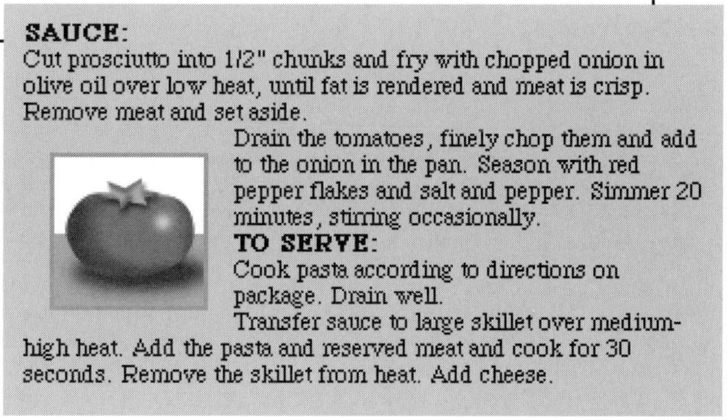

Figure 9-7. Using our same example, I've added hspace to the <img> tag to insert 12 pixels of space to the left and right of the graphic and vspace to add 12 pixels above and below.

TIP

Right Alignment, No Wrap

If you want to position a graphic on the right edge of the page without text wrap, put the image tag in a paragraph (<p>), then align the paragraph to the right:

```
<p align="right"><img src="tomato.gif"></p>
<p>Drain the tomatoes, finely chop them and add to
the onion in the pan. Season with red pepper flakes and salt
and pepper. Simmer 20 minutes, stirring occasionally.</p>
```

Drain the tomatoes, finely chop them and add to the onion in the pan. Season with red pepper flakes and salt and pepper. Simmer 20 minutes, stirring occasionally.

Stopping the text wrap

`<br clear="all|left|right">`
Insert line break; start next line below the graphic

You may decide you don't want all the text to wrap around a graphic—for instance, you have a headline or some other text that you want to start against the margin.

To "turn off" the text wrap, insert a line break (`<br>`) enhanced with the `clear` attribute, which instructs the browser to start the next line of text below the image when the margin is clear (Figure 9-8).

The `clear` attribute has three possible values: `left`, `right`, and `all`. Use `left` only when you want to start the next line below a graphic that is against the left margin; use `right` when you want to start the next line below a graphic on the right margin. The `all` value starts the next line below graphics on either or both sides, so it'll do the job for most cases (I use it almost exclusively).

> *To turn off the text wrap, insert a <br clear="all"> just before the line that you want to start under the graphic.*

> The line break with the `clear` attribute starts the next line against the margin, not next to the graphic.

```
<img src="tomato.gif" hspace="12" vspace="12" align="left">
Drain the tomatoes, finely chop them and add to the onion in
the pan. Season with red pepper flakes and salt and pepper.
Simmer 20 minutes, stirring occasionally.<br clear="all">

<b>TO SERVE:</b><br>
Cook pasta according to directions on package. Drain well.<br>
```

SAUCE:
Cut prosciutto into 1/2" chunks and fry with chopped onion in olive oil over low heat, until fat is rendered and meat is crisp. Remove meat and set aside.

Drain the tomatoes, finely chop them and add to the onion in the pan. Season with red pepper flakes and salt and pepper. Simmer 20 minutes, stirring occasionally.

TO SERVE:
Cook pasta according to directions on package. Drain well. Transfer sauce to large skillet over medium-high heat. Add the pasta and reserved meat and cook for 30 seconds. Remove the skillet from heat. Add cheese.

Figure 9-8. The `clear=all` attribute tells the browser to add a line break and position the next line when all margins are "clear" (i.e., when there are no graphics). Now the "To Serve" section starts below the graphic.

Exercise 9-2: Graphic Positioning

This exercise gives you a chance to play with the `align`, `vspace`, and `clear` attributes.

1. Open the *kitchenhome.html* file you created in Exercise 9-1. Save the file as *kitchenhome2.html* so you can always go back to a fresh file.

2. First, we'll give the header graphic a little more visual space at the top of the page. Add 12 pixels of space above and below the graphic using the `vspace` attribute (see following code). Save your document and view it in the browser. Try different amounts of space, saving and refreshing in the browser after each change.

   ```
   <p><img src="graphics/kitchen.gif" width="459"
       height="68" alt="Jen's  Kitchen" vspace="12"></p>
   ```

3. Let's change the "W" in Welcome into a drop-cap (a capital letter that drops into the lines of text). To get the text to wrap around the *W.gif* graphic, set the `align` attribute to `left`:

   ```
   <p><img src="graphics/W.gif" width="53" height="38"
       alt="W" align="left">elcome to my kitchen! ...
   ```

4. Finally, we'll start the second sentence under the W instead of wrapping around it. Do this by inserting a `<br>` tag with the `clear="all"` attribute at the end of the first sentence:

   ```
   <p><img src="graphics/W.gif"
   width="53" height="38"
   alt="W" align="left">elcome
   to my kitchen! People who
   know me know that I love to
   cook. <br clear="all"> I've
   created this site to share
   some of my favorite recipes
   and online food...
   ```

   Save and view the file. It should look something like the screenshot at the right.

Want more practice?

This exercise is complete, but if you want to get more practice with the attributes in this section, you can use the pieces in this document to play around and see what happens. Try the following:

- Align the W graphic on the right margin (ignore the fact that this doesn't make sense).

- Add a little space to the left and right of the W graphic with the `hspace` attribute. Add a *lot* of space to the left and right of the W graphic. (Again, this doesn't make sense because the W should be as close as possible to the rest of the word, but this is just practice.)

- Insert the W graphic somewhere else in the intro text and move it to the left and right to get a feel for what happens.

- Try breaking the text in different places. Write up some more text if you want more to play with.

W elcome to my kitchen! People who know me know that I love to cook.

I've created this site to share some of my favorite recipes and online food resources. The recipes listed here are ones that I have developed myself. In some cases, I started with a recipe found in a cookbook or magazine, but over time, I've adapted it enough to call it my own. *Bon Appetit!*

FROM JEN'S COOKBOOK

tapenade (olive spread)
garlic salmon
wild mushroom risotto
asian dishes

GOOD STUFF "OUT THERE"

The Food Network
Epicurious

Setting Image Attributes

Here's how you access image attribute controls in three of the more popular authoring programs.

Dreamweaver MX

With the image selected (handles will be visible), all the settings for the image are available on the Properties palette.

GoLive 6

With the graphic selected, you can set all of the image attributes using the Basic and More palettes in the Image Inspector.

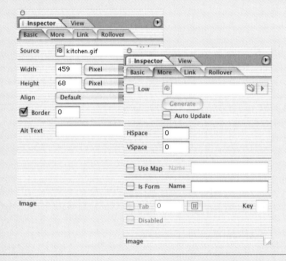

FrontPage 2002

Right-click the graphic to bring up Picture Properties on the shortcut menu. Then click the Appearance tab to see the attributes for the graphic within the layout.

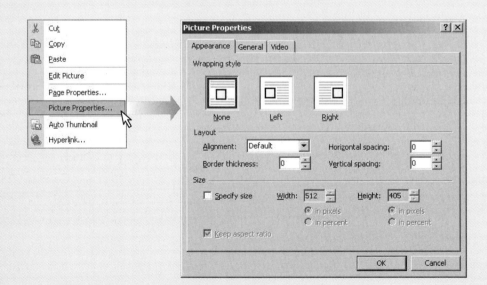

Background Tiles

The other way graphics can be used is as tiled background patterns behind the page. This is easy to do.

`<body background="`*filename or URL*`">`
Adds tiled background image

Tiled backgrounds are added using the `background` attribute within the `<body>` tag. We've used the `<body>` tag earlier as the structural tag that defines the visible part of the web document. It can also be used for certain settings that affect the whole page, such as background tiles and color settings. (Using the `<body>` tag to change color settings is discussed in Chapter 13.)

In Figure 9-9, I've specified that the graphic *tile1.gif* be used as a tiled background. The graphic pattern starts in the upper-left corner of the page and is repeated automatically.

The key to successful tiling backgrounds is *subtlety*. Nothing can ruin a web page faster than a tiled background that is bold and busy, making the text virtually unreadable. So, please, tile with care.

Solid Background Colors

The `<body>` tag is also used to make the background a solid color using the `bgcolor` attribute as shown in this example:

`<body bgcolor="`*color-name*`"`
`    or "`*number*`">`

The system for specifying colors in HTML is discussed in detail in Chapter 13.

I often use the `bgcolor` and `background` attributes at the same time. The `bgcolor` attribute loads a solid color that is the same as the dominant color of the background tile. That way, the tone for the page is set immediately while the background tile graphic is still downloading.

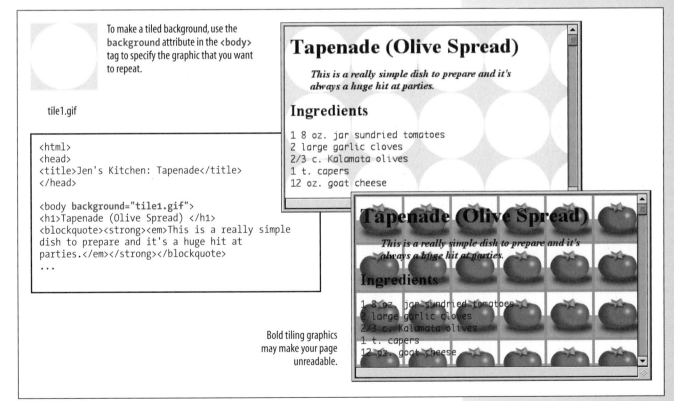

To make a tiled background, use the **background** attribute in the `<body>` tag to specify the graphic that you want to repeat.

tile1.gif

```
<html>
<head>
<title>Jen's Kitchen: Tapenade</title>
</head>

<body background="tile1.gif">
<h1>Tapenade (Olive Spread) </h1>
<blockquote><strong><em>This is a really simple
dish to prepare and it's a huge hit at
parties.</em></strong></blockquote>
...
```

Bold tiling graphics may make your page unreadable.

Figure 9-9. Design tiles so they do not compete with the text in front of them. Flat colors with little or no texture work best.

Exercise 9-3: Adding a Tiled Background

In this exercise, we'll try adding a number of background tiles to the Jen's Kitchen home page. A variety of background tiles have been provided for you in the *graphics* subdirectory in the *chap09* materials directory.

1. Start by opening your recently saved homepage document, *kitchenhome2.html*. Save the file as *kitchenhome3.html* so you have a fresh copy available.

2. Make the file *tile1.gif* Ⓐ a tiled background using the code below (note that the *graphics* directory name needs to appear in the pathname so the browser knows to look there for *tile1.gif*):

   ```
   <body background="graphics/tile1.gif">
   ```

   Save the document and look at it in the browser. The graphic is a square with a circle in it, so it is easy to see how it repeats in rows and columns.

3. Let's try another one. Replace *tile1.gif* with *tile2.gif* Ⓑ. Save the file and take a look in the browser. This tile is tall and skinny, but it still repeats in rows and columns.

4. Replace *tile2.gif* with *tile3.gif* Ⓒ. Save the file and have a look. This graphic is very wide and only a few pixels tall. It repeats in rows and columns like the others, but the seams are less apparent. In fact, the colored pixels on the left stack up and give the impression of vertical stripes. If the graphic were wider, the stripes would be farther apart.

5. Now replace *tile3.gif* with *kitchentile.gif* Ⓓ (the graphic that was actually designed for this page):

   ```
   <body background="graphics/kitchentile.gif">
   ```

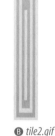

Ⓐ *tile1.gif*   Ⓑ *tile2.gif*

Ⓒ *tile3.gif*

Ⓓ *kitchentile.gif*

kitchentile.gif is an extremely tall and narrow graphic. It still repeats in rows and columns, but it is so tall you can't see the next row. The result is a band of color across the top of the page. Now you know a little web designer trick to get a stripe of color on the left or top of the window by using long, narrow graphics with two colored areas.

The final result is shown here and in the gallery Ⓖ.

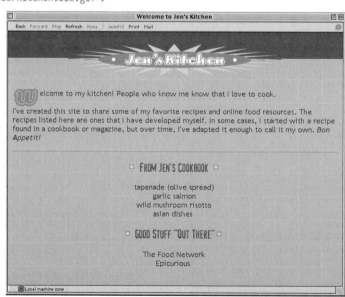

The finished product Ⓖ

Adding Tiled Backgrounds

Here's how you add tiled background graphics in three of the more popular authoring programs.

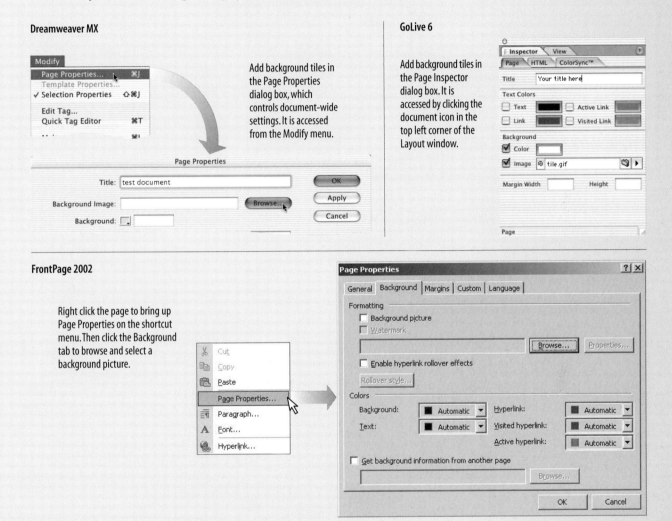

Dreamweaver MX

Add background tiles in the Page Properties dialog box, which controls document-wide settings. It is accessed from the Modify menu.

GoLive 6

Add background tiles in the Page Inspector dialog box. It is accessed by clicking the document icon in the top left corner of the Layout window.

FrontPage 2002

Right click the page to bring up Page Properties on the shortcut menu. Then click the Background tab to browse and select a background picture.

Nontiled Backgrounds

When you place a graphic in the background using the `<body>` tag, it will automatically repeat in rows and columns to fill the screen. If you want an image to appear just once in the top-left corner, you have two options.

Giant Background Graphic

First, you can make the graphic really big—that is, wider and taller than most browsers can open even if they were to fill the whole monitor. To account for high-resolution monitors, this means making a background graphic that is around 1500 x 1200 pixels. The drawback to this technique, of course, is that an image that large is going to come with a big file size and a long download time. Filling the majority of the graphic with flat color and saving it as a GIF helps keep file sizes down, but it's still a risky move.

Style Sheet Rule

The other method is to use a style sheet rule to specify a background graphic and prevent it from tiling. In this technique, you do *not* use the `background` attribute.

In the style sheet, add the following rule:

```
body {background-image: url(graphic.gif);
      background-repeat: no-repeat}
```

The `background-repeat` property is what allows the image to appear only once in the background.

Style sheet rules are explained in detail in Chapter 8.

Horizontal Rules

If you need to break up a long flow of text into more manageable chunks, you can use an HTML horizontal rule. ("Rule" is another term for a line.)

`<hr>`

Horizontal rule

Horizontal rules are plopped on the page with the `<hr>` tag. When the browser sees the `<hr>` tag alone, it draws an "embossed" shaded line across the full available width of the page (Figure 9-10). Rules are block elements, so some space will be added above and below. This means you can't place a rule on the same line as text.

There are a number of attributes that allow you to create different effects with horizontal rules. Let's take a look.

```
<hr>
<b>SAUCE:</b><br>
Cut prosciutto into 1/2" chunks and fry with chopped onion in olive oil
over low heat, until fat is rendered and meat is crisp. Remove meat and
set aside. Drain the tomatoes, finely chop them and add to the onion in
the pan. Season with red pepper flakes and salt and pepper. Simmer 20
minutes, stirring occasionally.<br>

<hr>
<b>TO SERVE:</b><br>
Cook pasta according to directions on package. Drain well.<br>

Transfer sauce to large skillet over medium-high heat. Add the pasta and
reserved meat and cook for 30 seconds. Remove the skillet from heat. Add
cheese.
<hr>
```

SAUCE:
Cut prosciutto into 1/2" chunks and fry with chopped onion in olive oil over low heat, until fat is rendered and meat is crisp. Remove meat and set aside. Drain the tomatoes, finely chop them and add to the onion in the pan. Season with red pepper flakes and salt and pepper. Simmer 20 minutes, stirring occasionally.

TO SERVE:
Cook pasta according to directions on package. Drain well.
Transfer sauce to large skillet over medium-high heat. Add the pasta and reserved meat and cook for 30 seconds. Remove the skillet from heat. Add cheese.

Figure 9-10. The default horizontal rule is a "beveled" line that fills the width of the browser window.

size="number"

Rule thickness

This attribute specifies the thickness of the rule in pixels (Figure 9-11).

width="number or %"

Rule width

width determines how long the rule should be (in other words, its width across the page). You can specify a pixel measurement or a percentage of the available page width (Figure 9-12).

align="left|right|center"

Horizontal alignment

You can specify where you'd like the rule positioned across the page with this attribute (Figure 9-13). Rules are centered by default.

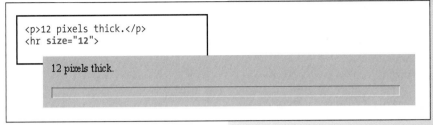

Figure 9-11. The size attribute affects the thickness of the rule.

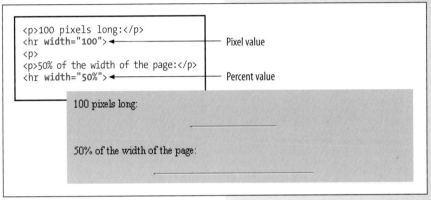

Figure 9-12. The width attribute affects the length of the rule.

```
<p>100 pixel wide rule positioned on the right margin:</p>
<hr width="100" align="right">
```

100 pixel wide rule positioned on the right margin:

Figure 9-13. Use the align attribute to position the rule horizontally on the page.

TIP

How Do I Make a Vertical Rule?

While adding a horizontal rule is easy with the <hr> tag, there is no similar tag for adding a vertical rule to a web page. However, there are a number of ways you can fake it using tables and graphics, as demonstrated in Chapter 19.

```
<p>Rule with "no shade" attribute:</p>
<hr noshade>
```

Rule with "no shade" attribute:

Figure 9-14 The noshade attribute creates a solid black or gray line (rather than beveled).

```
<p>A square rule created by a combination of attributes:</p>
<hr size="24" width="24" noshade>
```

A square rule created by a combination of attributes:

Figure 9-15. You can combine attributes to radically change the way a rule looks.

noshade
Turns off shading

If you don't like the shaded bar effect, add this attribute to the <hr> tag to make the rule a solid line (Figure 9-14). This attribute is just an instruction; it doesn't take a value.

Remember that attributes can be used in combination in a single tag, so feel free to get creative. In Figure 9-15, the rule has been manipulated to form a small square centered on the page.

TRY IT

Exercise 9-4: Adding a Horizontal Rule

Adding horizontal rules to a page is pretty simple. Here are a few activities that will give you some practice:

1. Open your recent document, *kitchenhome3.html*, and save it as *kitchenhome4.html* (make sure you save it in the same directory as the others so the graphic links still work).

2. Add a horizontal rule above "Good Stuff 'Out There'." Save the file and look at it in the browser.

   ```
   ...
   asian dishes </p>
   <hr>
   <p><img src="graphics/outthere.gif"
        width="217" height="30"></p>
   ```

3. Play with the size attribute. Set it to 3 pixels, save, and take a look. Try it at 24 pixels. Set it to something that looks good to you.

4. Play with the width attribute. Set it to a specific pixel value and see how it looks. Try setting it to a percentage value (e.g., 75%). When you view it in a browser, resize the window and see how the rule reacts. (PC users will need to minimize the window to resize it.)

5. With the width set to something less than 100%, use the align attribute to move the rule against the left margin, and then against the right margin.

Adding Horizontal Rules

Here's how you add horizontal rules in three of the more popular authoring programs.

Dreamweaver MX

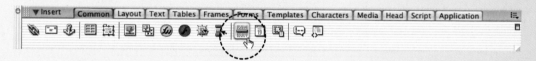

Drag the rule icon from the list of common elements on the Objects palette into place in your document.

GoLive 6

❶ Drag the rule icon from the Palette window into place in your document.

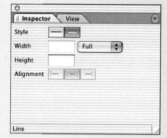

❷ When the rule is selected, you can change its attributes in the Line Inspector.

FrontPage 2002

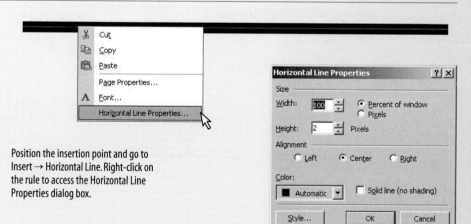

Position the insertion point and go to Insert → Horizontal Line. Right-click on the rule to access the Horizontal Line Properties dialog box.

Test Yourself

Images are a big part of the web experience. Answer these questions to see how well you've absorbed the key concepts of this chapter. The correct answers can be found in the Appendix.

1. Which attribute in the `<img>` tag can you absolutely not do without?

2. How do you write the code for adding an image called *furry.jpg* that is in the same directory as the HTML file?

3. Why is it important to include alternative text?

4. What is the advantage to including `width` and `height` attributes for every graphic on the page?

5. What might be going wrong if your images don't appear when you view the page in a browser? There are three key explanations.

6. How do you get rid of the blue line around linked graphics?

HTML Review: Graphic Element Tags

The following is a summary of the tags we covered in this chapter:

Tag and attributes	Function
`<body>`	Body of the document; can contain attributes that affect document appearance
`background="url"`	Tiling background graphic
`bgcolor="number" or "name"`	Background color
`<br clear="all|left|right">`	Inserts a line break and starts next line below the graphic
`<img>`	Inserts an inline image
`src="url"`	The graphic file to use
`alt="text"`	Alternative text
`width="number"`	Width of the graphic
`height="number"`	Height of the graphic
`border="number"`	Thickness of border when graphic is linked
`align="left|right"`	Horizontal alignment
`align="top|middle|bottom"`	Vertical alignment
`hspace="number"`	Space held to the left and right of a graphic
`vspace="number"`	Space held above and below a graphic
`<hr>`	Inserts a horizontal rule (a line)
`size="number"`	Adjusts the thickness of the rule
`width="number"`	Adjusts the length of the rule
`align="left|right|center"`	Horizontal positioning
`noshade`	Turns off 3-D bevel

Adding Links

10

If you're creating a page for the Web, chances are you'll want it to point to other web pages, whether to another section of your own site or to someone else's. You can even link to another spot on the same page. Linking, after all, is what the Web is all about.

In this chapter, we'll look at the HTML that makes linking work: to other sites, to your own site, and within a page. In addition, we'll cover imagemaps, which are single images that contain a number of links.

If you've used the Web at all, you should be familiar with the highlighted text and graphics that indicate "click here." There is one tag that makes linking possible, the anchor tag (<a>). The anchor tag is a container tag; it has start and end tags that you wrap around a span of text. The href attribute in the tag provides the URL of the linked page.

To use the anchor tag, just wrap it around the text you want linked, like this:

```
<a href="http://www.oreilly.com">Go to O'Reilly.com</a>
```

To make a graphic a link, simply place the anchor tag around the entire image tag, as shown here:

```
<a href="http://www.oreilly.com"><img src="ora.gif"></a>
```

T I P

Anchor Tag Syntax

The simplified structure (or syntax) for the anchor tag is:

```
<a href="url">linked text or image</a>
```

Changing Link Colors

Tired of your links always being that default bright blue? Change them. Special attributes in the `<body>` tag apply link colors for the whole document. In addition to ordinary links, you can specify the color of links that have already been clicked ("visited links") and the color that links appear as while they are being clicked ("active links"):

`link="color-name"` or `"number"`
> Sets the link color (blue by default)

`vlink="color-name"` or `"number"`
> Sets the color of visited links (purple by default)

`alink="color-name"` or `"number"`
> Sets the color of active links

Of course, you can use all of these attributes in a single `<body>` tag, as follows:

```
<body link="aqua" vlink="teal"
alink="red">
```

The system for specifying colors in HTML is covered in detail in Chapter 13.

One word of caution, however: if you do choose to change your link colors, it is recommended that you keep them consistent throughout your site so as not to confuse your users. For a more thorough discussion, see the section Color coding in Chapter 20.

When viewed in a browser, the marked text is blue and underlined (by default) and the linked graphic appears with a blue outline (unless you turn it off; see Chapter 9). When a user clicks on the linked text or graphic, the page you specify in the anchor tag will load in the browser window. The code listed previously would look like Figure 10-1.

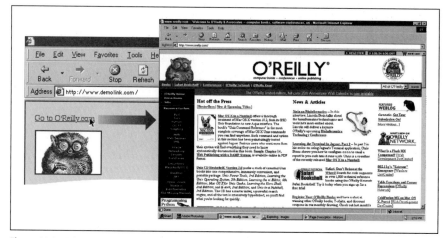

Figure 10-1. When a user clicks on the linked text or graphic, the page you specify in the anchor tag will load in the browser window.

The Anchor Tag Dissected

The anchor tag is an ordinary container tag with attributes, so you should already have a good idea of how it works. Let's look at the parts of the tag.

`<a>...</a>`
Anchor tag

Text or graphics within the anchor container tag will display as a link in the browser. By default, links appear as blue underlined text or as blue outlined graphics in most browsers. You can change the color of links as described in the sidebar, Changing Link Colors.

`href="url"`
The location of the linked file

You'll need to tell the browser which document to link to, right? `href` (hypertext reference) is the attribute that provides the URL of the page (its address) to the browser. Most of the time you'll point to other web pages; however, you can also point to other web resources, such as images, audio, and video files.

Since there's not much to slapping an anchor tag around some text, the real art of linking comes in getting the URL correct.

There are two ways to specify the URL:

Absolute URLs provide the full URL for the document, including *http://*, the domain name, and the pathname as necessary. You need to use an absolute URL when pointing to a document out on the Web.

Example: *http://www.oreilly.com/*

Relative URLs describe the pathname to the linked file *relative* to the current document. It doesn't require the protocol or domain name—just the pathname. Relative URLs can be used when you are linking to another document on your own site (i.e., on your own server).

Example: *recipes/index.html*

Both absolute and relative URLs are discussed in this chapter. Absolute URLs are easy, so let's get them out of the way first.

Linking to Pages on the Web

Many times, you'll want to create a link to a page that you've found on the Web. This is known as an "external" link because it is going to a page outside of your own server or site.

To make an external link, you need to provide the absolute URL, beginning with the *http://* part (the protocol). This tells the browser, "Go out on the Web and get the following document." For more information on the parts of a URL, go back to our URL dissection example in Chapter 2.

I've added some external links to popular cooking sites to the bottom of my cooking home page (Figure 10-2).

Opening a Link in a
New Window

At times, you may want to open a linked page in a new browser window so readers don't leave your site. This is done using the target attribute in the <a> tag. This technique is described in detail in Chapter 19.

Use the complete URL (including "http://") when linking to pages on the Web.

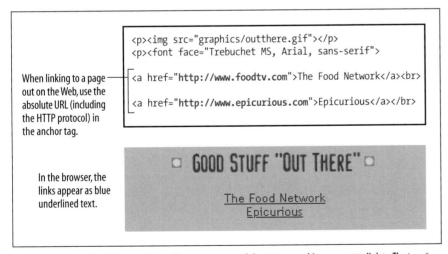

When linking to a page out on the Web, use the absolute URL (including the HTTP protocol) in the anchor tag.

```
<p><img src="graphics/outthere.gif"></p>
<p><font face="Trebuchet MS, Arial, sans-serif">
<a href="http://www.foodtv.com">The Food Network</a><br>

<a href="http://www.epicurious.com">Epicurious</a></br>
```

In the browser, the links appear as blue underlined text.

GOOD STUFF "OUT THERE"

The Food Network
Epicurious

Figure 10-2. To make a link, wrap the anchor tag <a> around the text or graphic you want to link to. The href attribute tells the browser which file to link to.

Sometimes, when the page you're linking to has a long URL pathname, the link can end up looking pretty confusing (Figure 10-3). Just keep in mind that the structure is still a simple container tag with one attribute. Don't let the pathname intimidate you.

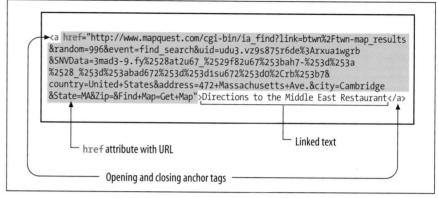

Figure 10-3. An example of a long URL. Although it may make the anchor tag look confusing, the structure is the same.

Linking Within Your Own Site

A large portion of the linking you'll do will be between pages of your own site: from the home page to section pages, from section pages to content pages, and so on. In these cases, you can use a relative URL—one that calls for a page on your own server.

Without *http://*, the browser looks on the current server for the linked document. A pathname (the notation used to point to a particular file or directory) tells the browser where to find the file. Web pathnames follow the Unix convention of separating directory and filenames with forward slashes (/). A relative pathname describes how to get to the linked document (or graphic) starting from the directory the current document is in.

Relative pathnames can get a bit tricky. In my teaching experience, nothing stumps beginners like writing relative pathnames, so we'll take it one step at a time. At the end of this chapter is an exercise that allows you to recreate the links as they are demonstrated in the figures. If you want to work as you go along, look ahead to Exercise 10-1 and follow the directions.

Important pathname don'ts

When you are writing relative pathnames, it is critical that you avoid the following common errors:

Don't use backslashes (\). Web URL pathnames use forward slashes (/) only.

Don't start with the drive name (D:, C:, etc.). Although your pages will link to each other successfully while they are on your own computer, once they are uploaded to the web server, the drive name is irrelevent and will break your links.

Don't start with file://. This indicates that the file is local. It also causes the link to break when it is on the server.

The root directory

All web sites have a root directory, which is the directory that contains all the directories and files for the site. When you diagram the structure of the directories on a server, it generally ends up looking like an inverted tree with the root directory at the top of the hierarchy. In Figure 10-4, *jenskitchen* is the root directory.

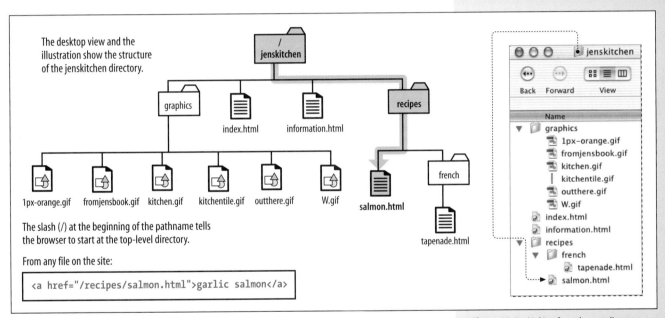

Figure 10-4. Linking from the root directory.

In the Unix pathname convention, the root directory is referred to with a forward slash (/). The relative pathname in the following link reads, "Go to the very top-level directory for this site, open the *recipes* directory, then find the *salmon.html* file":

```
<a href="/recipes/salmon.html">garlic salmon</a>
```

Note that you don't need to specify the root directory (*jenskitchen*) in the URL—the forward slash (/) at the start of the pathname stands in for it and takes the browser to the top level. From there, it's a matter of specifying the directories the browser should look in.

TIP

Relative pathnames starting with the root directory (/) are useful for content that might not always be in the same directory or for dynamically generated material. Describing pathnames from the root ensures that the relative URL in the link will work even if the document moves around.

Linking within a directory

While the root directory is a handy way to start pathnames, it is usually quicker to describe the path to the linked document starting from the current directory (rather than the top level of the site).

The easiest type of link to write is to another file within the same directory. When you are linking to a file in the same directory, you only need to provide the name of the file (its filename). Without the root directory slash, the browser starts looking for the linked document in the same directory as the current HTML file.

In my example, I want to make a link from my home page (*index.html*) to a general information page (*information.html*). Currently, both files are in the same directory (*jenskitchen*). So from my home page, I can make a link to the information page by simply providing its filename in the URL (Figure 10-5):

```
<a href="information.html">[more information]</a>
```

A link to just the filename indicates the linked file is in the same directory as the current document.

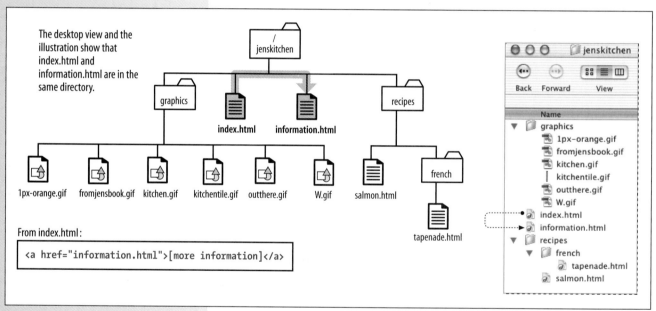

Figure 10-5. Linking within a directory.

Linking to a lower directory

But what if the files aren't in the same directory? You have to give the browser directions by including the pathname in the URL. Let's see how this works.

Getting back to our example, my recipe files are stored in a subdirectory called *recipes*. I want to make a link from *index.html* to a file in the *recipes* directory called *salmon.html*. The pathname in the URL tells the browser to look in the subdirectory called *recipes*, and then look for the file *salmon.html* (Figure 10-6):

```
<a href="recipes/salmon.html">garlic salmon</a>
```

IMPORTANT

These relative pathname examples *don't* start with a slash. You want the browser to start looking from the current directory, not the top level.

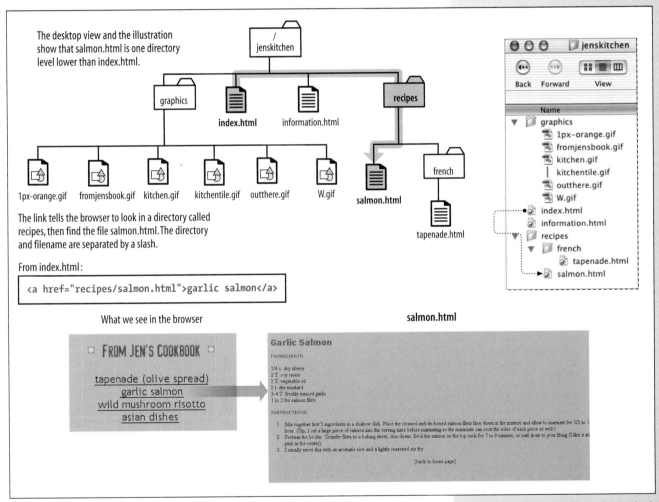

Figure 10-6. Linking to a file one directory level lower.

Now let's link down to the file called *tapenade.html*, which is located in the *french* subdirectory. All we need to do is provide the directions through two subdirectories, *recipes* and *french*, to our file (Figure 10-7):

```
<a href="recipes/french/tapenade.html">tapenade (olive spread)</a>
```

The resulting anchor tag is telling the browser, "Look in the current directory for a directory called *recipes*. There you'll find another directory called *french*, and in there is the file I'd like to link to, *tapenade.html*."

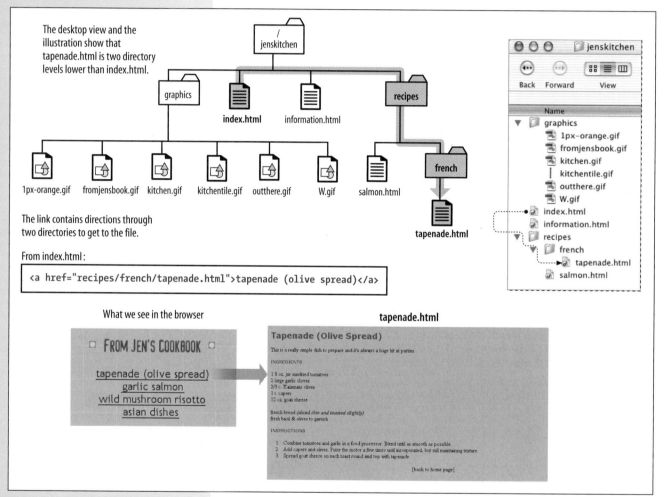

The desktop view and the illustration show that tapenade.html is two directory levels lower than index.html.

The link contains directions through two directories to get to the file.

From index.html :

```
<a href="recipes/french/tapenade.html">tapenade (olive spread)</a>
```

What we see in the browser

tapenade.html

Figure 10-7. Linking to a file that is two directories level lower.

Linking to a higher directory

So far, so good, right? Here comes the tricky part. This time we're going to go in the other direction and make a link from a recipe page back to the home page, which is one directory level up.

In Unix, there is a pathname convention just for this purpose, the "dot-dot-slash" (../). When you begin a pathname with a ../, it's the same as telling the browser "back up one directory level" and then follow the path to the specified file. If you are familiar with browsing files on your desktop with Windows Explorer, it is helpful to know that a "../" has the same effect as clicking the "Up" button.

Let's start by making a link back to the home page (*index.html*) from *salmon.html*. Because *salmon.html* is in the *recipes* subdirectory, we need to back up a level to *jenskitchen* to find *index.html*. The pathname tells the browser to "go up one level" then look for *index.html* (Figure 10-8):

```
<a href="../index.html">[back to home page]</a>
```

Each ../ at the beginning of the pathname tells the browser to go up one directory level to look for the file.

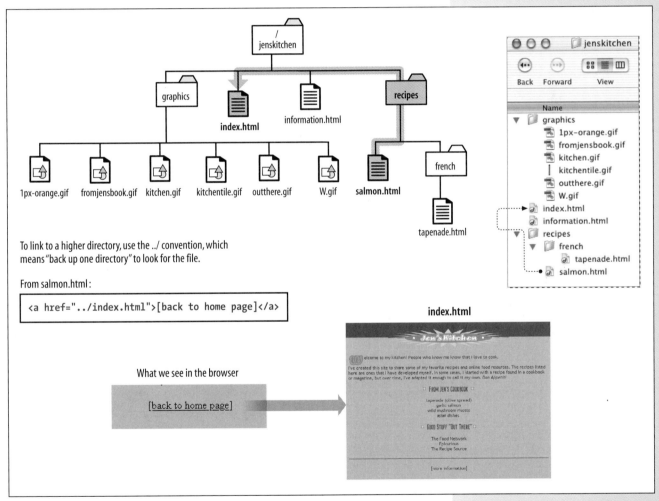

Figure 10-8. I want to create a link from *salmon.html* back to the home page, which is one level higher.

TIP

I confess to still sometimes silently chanting "go-up-a-level, go-up-a-level" for each ../ when trying to decipher a complicated relative URL. It helps me sort things out.

But how about linking back to the home page from *tapenade.html*? Can you guess how you'd back your way out of two directory levels? Simple, just use the dot-dot-slash twice (Figure 10-9)!

A link on the *tapenade.html* page back to the home page (*index.html*) would look like this:

```
<a href="../../index.html">[back to home page]</a>
```

The first ../ backs up to the *recipes* directory; the second ../ backs up to the top-level directory where *index.html* can be found.

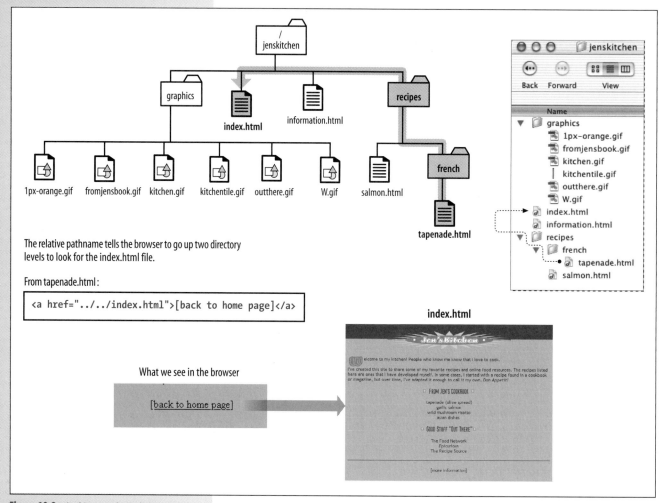

Figure 10-9. In this example, I'm linking to a document that is two directory levels higher.

It's the same for graphics

The `src` attribute in the `<img>` tag works the same as the `href` attribute in anchors when it comes to specifying URLs. Since you'll most likely be using graphics from your own server, the `src` attributes within your image tags will be set to relative URLs.

Let's look at a few examples using the same files listed in the previous figures. First, to add a graphic to the *index.html* page, the code would be:

```
<img src="graphics/kitchen.gif">
```

The URL says, "Look in this directory for the *graphics* directory; in there you will find *kitchen.gif*."

Now for the *piece de résistance*. Let's add a graphic to the file *tapenade.html*:

```
<img src="../../graphics/kitchen.gif">
```

This is a little more complicated than what we've seen so far. This pathname tells the browser to go up two directory levels to the top-level directory and, once there, look in the *graphics* directory for a graphic called *kitchen.gif*. Whew!

Don't worry!

The good news is that if you use a WYSIWYG authoring tool to create your site, the tool generates the relative URLs for you. Be sure to use one of the automated link tools (such as the Browse button or GoLive's "Point and Shoot" function) for links and graphics. Some programs, such as Macromedia Dreamweaver and Adobe GoLive, have built-in site management functions that adjust your relative URLs even if you reorganize the directory structure.

If you anticipate writing HTML by hand, you'll need to know your way around relative pathnames and other Unix conventions. There is a summary of Unix server functions and operating commands in *Web Design in a Nutshell* (O'Reilly, 2001). If you want to go even deeper, try *Unix in a Nutshell* by Arnold Robbins (O'Reilly, 1999).

Most web-authoring tools will write the relative pathnames for you when you use the "browse" or drag-and-drop function for linking documents on your site.

TIP

Still Having Trouble?

Some of my students have found it helpful to use Windows Explorer on their PCs as a teaching device for writing relative pathnames. Each click on the Explorer window translates into a section of the pathname, as follows.

Open Explorer and maneuver until you can see the current document in the righthand contents window. Now click on directories and the Up button until the linked file appears in the window. Write down each thing you click on, in order, separated by slashes:

- Each time you click on a directory name to view its contents, write that directory name in the pathname.
- Each time you click on the "Up" button, write a "../" in the pathname.

Continue until the file you are linking to is visible in the contents window. Write the filename at the end of the pathname and the URL is complete.

Exercise 10-1: Working with URLs

This is your opportunity to try creating links as we've covered throughout the chapter. After the 10 quick activities below, you should have a good feel for URLs.

The materials for this exercise are provided on the CD and online at *www.learningwebdesign.com/materials/chap10*. Copy the directory *chap10* to your hard drive to begin. The files you need are in the *10-1* subdirectory.

1. Open *index.html*. This file is very similar to the one we've been building in previous chapters. Add the external links to the entries in the "Good Stuff" section as shown in Figure 10-2. Similarly, link "The Recipe Source" to *www.recipesource.com*. Save the document and try out the links in a browser (you'll need to be connected to the Internet).

2. In the file *index.html*, link "More information" to *information.html*. (See Figure 10-5 for an example.) Save the file and test your link in the browser. Be careful to save it in the same directory where it started. If you accidentally save it to another directory, the link won't work as written. You don't need to be on the Internet to view files on your own computer.

3. In the file *index.html*, link "garlic salmon" to *salmon.html* in the *recipes* directory. (See Figure 10-6 for an example.) Save and test the link.

4. In the file *index.html*, link "tapenade (olive spread)" to *tapenade.html* in the *french* subdirectory of the *recipes* directory. (See Figure 10-7 for an example.) Save and test.

5. Open the file *information.html*. Make the text "[home page]" link back to the home page (*index.html*). (Hint: they are in the same directory.) Save and test.

6. In the file *information.html*, add the graphic *1px-orange.gif* with the width set to 100% to make a rule above the home page link. (Hint: you have to tell the browser to look in the *graphics* directory first). Save and view the file to make sure the graphic shows up.

7. Open the file *salmon.html*. Make the text "[home page]" link back to the home page (*index.html*). (See Figure 10-8 for an example.)

8. Add the *1px-orange.gif* graphic with the width set to 100% in the *salmon.html* document (above the home page link). Remember to back up one directory to find the *graphics* directory. Save and view the file to make sure the graphic is there.

9. Open the file *tapenade.html*. Make the text "[home page]" link back to the home page (*index.htm*). (See Figure 10-9 for an example.) Save and test the link.

10. Finally, add the *1px-orange.gif* rule above the home page link on *tapenade.html*, as you've done for the others. Save and make sure the graphic shows up in the browser.

Adding Links

Here's how you add links to a page in three of the more popular authoring programs.

Dreamweaver MX

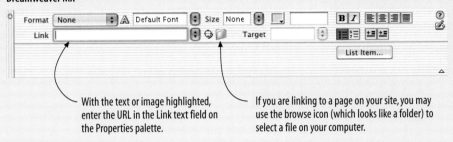

With the text or image highlighted, enter the URL in the Link text field on the Properties palette.

If you are linking to a page on your site, you may use the browse icon (which looks like a folder) to select a file on your computer.

GoLive 6

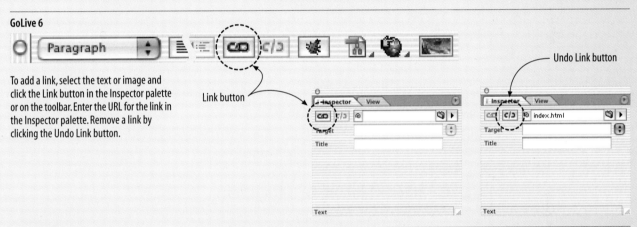

To add a link, select the text or image and click the Link button in the Inspector palette or on the toolbar. Enter the URL for the link in the Inspector palette. Remove a link by clicking the Undo Link button.

Link button

Undo Link button

FrontPage 2002

Selected text can be linked from the toolbar, using Insert → Hyperlink. The URL can be typed or the file, if local, can be selected from the Finder.

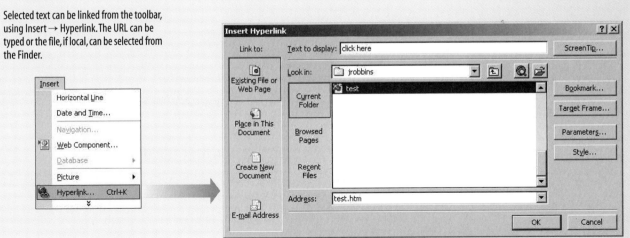

Linking Within a Page

Did you know you can link to a specific point in a web page? This is useful for providing shortcuts to information at the bottom of a long scrolling page or for getting back to the top of a page with just one click.

Linking to a fragment within a page is a two-part process. First, you need to give the fragment a name, and then you make a link to it. In the following example, I create an alphabetical index at the top of the page that links down to each alphabetical section of my glossary page (Figure 10-10). When users click on the letter "C", they'll jump down on the page to the first term starting with C.

Step 1: Naming a fragment

`<a name="text">`
Named anchor

The anchor tag (`<a>`) with the `name` attribute is used to give a section of the page a name that can be referenced elsewhere. It's like putting a marker or a flag in the file so you can get back to it easily. You can wrap the anchor tag around text as shown in the example, or just insert an empty anchor element before the text:

```
<a name="startC"></a>CGI
```

❶ I've added a named anchor at "CGI" (my first term starting with C), and I've given it the name `startC`.

Step 2: Linking to a fragment

`<a href="#text">`
Link to a fragment (a "named anchor")

Next, at the top of the page, I'll create a link down to the named anchor. The link is an ordinary link (using the `href` attribute), but it includes a hash (#) symbol before the name to indicate that we're linking to a fragment.

❷ I've linked the letter "C" in my alphabetical index to the fragment labeled `startC`. And we're done! Now, if you click on the C, you are transported to the first C term.

Linking to a fragment in another document

You can link to a fragment in another document by adding the fragment name to the end of the URL (absolute or relative), as shown here:

```
<a href="http://www.oreilly.com/niederst.htm#fragment">
<a href="content/glossary.htm#fragment">
```

❶ Add the named anchor.

```
<dt><a name="startC">CGI</a></dt>
<dd>Common Gateway Interface; the mechanism for communication between the
web server and other programs (CGI scripts) running on the server.</dd>
<p>
<dt>character entities</dt>
<dd>Strings of characters used to specify characters not found in the
normal alphanumeric character set in HTML documents.</dd>
<p>
<dt>character set</dt>
<dd>An organization of characters (units of a written language system)
in which each character is assigned a specific number.</dd>
```

❷ Create a link to the anchor.

```
<html>
<head>
        <title>Named Anchor</title>
</head>
<body>

<pre>A B <a href="#startC">C</a> D E F G H I J K L M N O P Q R S T U V W
X Y Z</pre>
```

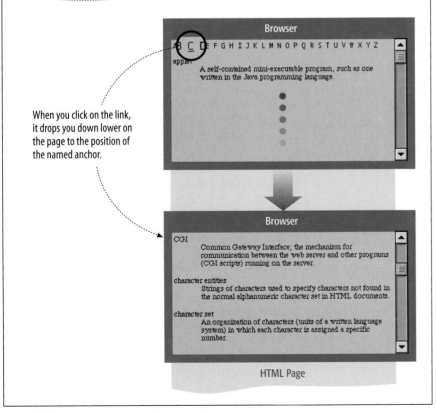

When you click on the link, it drops you down lower on the page to the position of the named anchor.

Figure 10-10. A glossary page illustrating links within a single page.

TRY IT

Exercise 10-2: Linking Within a File

Want some practice at linking to named anchors? Open the file *glossary.html* in the *chap10* materials directory. It looks just like the file in Figure 10-10.

1. Place a named anchor called startA just before the first "a" entry in the list:

   ```
   <a name="startA">
     absolute pathname</a>
   ```

   or:

   ```
   <a name="startA"></a>
     absolute pathname
   ```

2. Make the letter "A" at the top of the page a link to the named anchor:

   ```
   <a href="#startA">A</a>
   ```

   Repeat steps 1 and 2 for every letter across the top of the page until you really know what you are doing (or until you can't stand it anymore).

3. Place a named anchor called top at the very top of the page (just before the <h1>).

   ```
   <a name="top"></a>
   ```

4. Type "[TOP]" at the end of the first glossary definition. Link that word to the top anchor:

   ```
   [<a href="#top">TOP</a>]
   ```

   Copy and paste this code to the end of every glossary definition. Now your readers can get back to the top of the page from each definition.

Adding Named Anchors

Here's how you add named anchors to a page in three of the more popular authoring programs.

Dreamweaver MX

Double click the Anchor icon on the Common elements palette, or drag it into place on the page. A dialog box will open to ask you to name the anchor.

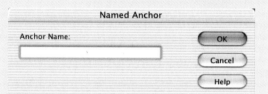

GoLive 6

Drag the Anchor object icon from the Palette into place in the document window. With the anchor selected, enter the name in the Anchor Inspector.

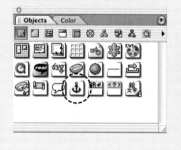

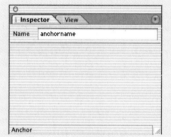

FrontPage 2002

A "bookmark" (anchor), can be added to the page with Insert → Bookmark. The dialog box will prompt you for a unique name.

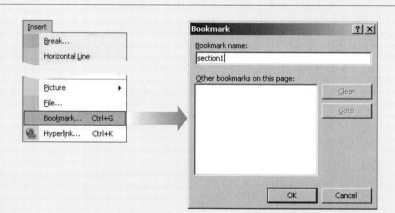

Several Links in One Graphic (Imagemaps)

In your web travels, I'm sure you've run across a single graphic that has multiple "hot spots," or links, within it (Figure 10-11). These graphics are called imagemaps.

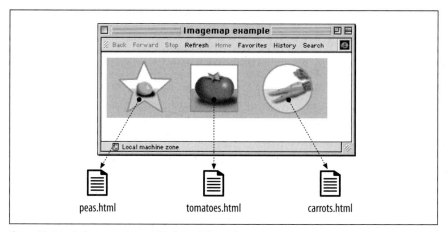

Figure 10-11. An imagemap has multiple links within one image.

Putting the links in one graphic has nothing to do with the graphic itself; it's just an ordinary graphic. Rather, the graphic merely serves as the frontend to the mechanisms that match a particular mouse-click to a URL.

The real work is done by a map in the HTML document that matches sets of pixel coordinates to their respective link information. When the user clicks somewhere within the image, the browser passes the pixel coordinates of the pointer to the map, which in turn generates the appropriate link. If the cursor passes over a hot spot, the cursor changes to let the user know that the hot spot is a link and the URL appears in the browser's status bar.

We'll be focusing on client-side imagemaps in our example, which puts the map directly in the HTML file. The mouse-clicks and URLs are matched up by the browser on the user's machine (thus, client-side). See the sidebar The Other Imagemap for more information on server-side imagemaps.

Client-side imagemaps have three components:

- An ordinary graphic file (.gif, .jpg/.jpeg, or .png)

- The usemap attribute within that graphic's <img> tag that identifies which map to use

- A map file (identified with the <map> element tag) located within the HTML document

> *An imagemap is a single graphic file that contains a number of links, or hot spots.*

The Other Imagemap

Before client-side imagemaps, all imagemaps were processed on the server. For server-side imagemaps, the map is a separate file (named with the .map suffix) that lives on the server. It relies on a CGI script to interpret the .map file and send the correct URL back to the browser. The whole graphic is linked to the .map file via a regular anchor tag, as shown here:

```
<a href="/cgi-bin/veggie.map">
  <img src="veggie.gif" ismap></a>
```

In addition, the <img> tag uses the ismap attribute to indicate it is an imagemap.

There isn't much reason to use a server-side imagemap these days. Client-side imagemaps aren't supported in Netscape Navigator 1.0 and Internet Explorer 2.0, but those browser versions are virtually extinct, as is the server-side imagemap.

Imagemap Tools

There are a few imagemap tools available as shareware and freeware for both Windows systems and Mac. Try MapEdit by Tom Boutell, available at *www.boutell.com/mapedit/*. There is a recommended $10 shareware fee. You can also do a search for "imagemap" at CNET's Download.com for additional options.

Creating the map

Fortunately, there are tools that generate maps so you don't have to write out the map by hand. Adobe ImageReady and nearly all web-authoring tools have built-in imagemap generators. You could also download shareware imagemap programs (see the sidebar Imagemap Tools).

The process for creating the map is essentially the same for all imagemap tools:

1. Open the graphic in the imagemap program (or place it on the page in a web-authoring tool).

2. Define areas that will be "clickable" by using the appropriate shape tools: rectangle, circle, or polygon (for tracing irregular shapes).

3. While the shape is still highlighted, enter a URL for that area in the text entry field provided.

4. Continue adding shapes and their respective URLs for each clickable area in the image.

5. Select the type of imagemap you want to create (we're focusing on client-side in this example). If you choose server-side, you will also have to define a default URL, which is the page that will display if users click outside one of the defined areas.

6. Give the map a name and add the map to the HTML file. Web-authoring tools insert the map automatically. If you are using ImageReady or Fireworks, you need to export the map code and insert it into the HTML file.

7. Save the HTML document and open it in your browser.

TRY IT

Exercise 10-3: Making an Imagemap

The graphic (*veggies.gif*) shown in this section is available in the *chap10* materials subdirectory, *10-3*.

If you have Adobe ImageReady, you can use Figure 10-11 to help make your own imagemap.

The general steps for making an imagemap are outlined above, but you'll need to consult the documentation for a detailed explanation of how to use your program.

veggies.gif

Using ImageReady

Let's see these steps in action using Adobe ImageReady (Figure 10-12):

1. Open the graphic (*veggies.gif*) and make sure the Image Map window is visible (Window → View Image Map). The imagemap tools are located on the Tools window. Click and hold to access the full tool set (rectangle, circle, polygon, and select tools).

2. To create the map, draw shapes over the areas of the image you want clickable. I've used the rectangle tool to click and drag a "hot spot" over the square tomato icon.

3. While the shape is highlighted (its corner and side handles available), give the area a name and enter the URL you want it to link to. Alternative text (optional) shows up when the user mouses over the area. Specify a target if you want the link to open in a different browser window (targeting windows is discussed in Chapters 12 and 19).

4. Repeat steps 1–3 for each area of the imagemap. Use the circle tool to draw over round areas. Use the polygon tool to trace irregular shapes. If you need to edit a shape afterward (move, resize, or reshape it), select it with the Image Map Select Tool arrow.

5. When you're done, select Save Optimized As from the File menu. From the Format pop-up menu, select HTML only and give the document a name. When you click Save, ImageReady creates an HTML file containing the proper `<img>` tag and the `<map>`. By default, the map file is client-side and placed at the bottom of the HTML file. You can change the settings by selecting Other from the Settings menu.

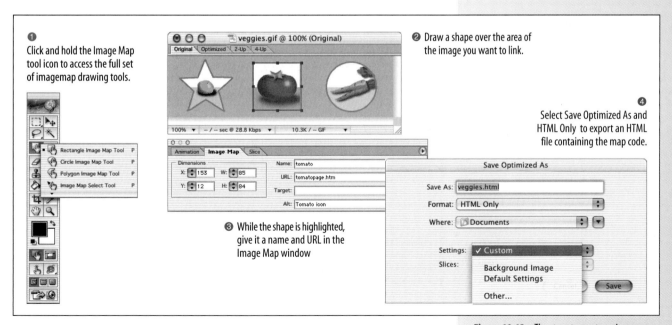

Figure 10-12. The steps to create an imagemap in ImageReady.

Now let's look at the HMTL file ImageReady generated:

```
<html>
<head>
<title>veggies</title>
</head>
<body bgcolor="#FFFFFF">
```

❶ `<!-- ImageReady Slices (veggies.gif) -->`

❷ `<map name="veggies_Map">`
❸
Ⓐ `<area shape="rect" alt="This is the tomato area" coords="152,11,239,99" href="tomato.htm">`

Ⓑ `<area shape="circle" alt="This is the carrot area" coords="327,56,46" href="carrot.htm">`

Ⓒ `<area shape="poly" alt="This is the pea area" coords="68,7, 53,38, 22,38, 47,62, 35,100, 68,77, 104,100, 91,61, 117,38, 81,37" href="pea.html">`

```
</map>
```

❹ `<img src="veggies.gif" width="400" height="109" border="0" usemap="#veggies_Map">`
`<!-- End ImageReady Slices -->`

```
</body>
</html>
```

You can include several imagemapped graphics and their respective maps in a single HTML document.

❶ Anything between comment tags (`<!--...-->`) will not be displayed in the browser. ImageReady uses comments as a convenience to point out a section of code in a document.

❷ This marks the beginning of the map. The map is named `veggies_Map` (the program named it automatically). Within the `<map>` tag there are `<area>` tags for each hot spot in the image.

❸ Each `<area>` tag contains the shape identifier (`shape`), pixel coordinates (`coords`), the URL for the link (`href`), and alternative text (`alt`). In this map there are three areas corresponding to the rectangle, circle, and polygon that I drew over my image:

Ⓐ The x,y pixel coordinates for the rectangle (`rect`) identify the top-left, and bottom-right corners of the area.

Ⓑ The pixel coordinates for the circle (`circle`) identify the center point and the length of the radius.

Ⓒ The list of x,y coordinates for the polygon (`poly`) identifies each of the points along the path.

❹ The `<img>` tag now sports the `usemap` attribute, which tells the browser which map to use (`veggies_Map`). You can include several imagemapped graphics and their respective maps in a single HTML document.

TIP

Once you've exported the code, you can easily copy and paste it into an existing HTML document. The `<map>` can go at the top or the bottom of the document; just make sure to keep it together. Then make sure that the `<img>` tags point to the correct map name.

Mail Links

Here's a nifty little linking trick: the `mailto` link. By using the `mailto` protocol in a link, you can link to an email address. When the user clicks on a `mailto` link, the browser opens a new mail message in a designated mail program. The browser has to be configured to launch a mail program, so the effect won't work for 100% of your audience, but it reaches enough people to be a worthwhile shortcut.

Figure 10-13 shows the structure of a `mailto` link and what happens when you click on it in a browser.

> **TIP**
>
> *If you use the email address itself as the linked text, nobody will be left out if the* `mailto` *function does not work.*

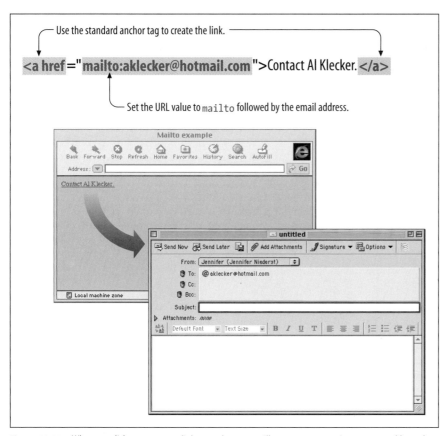

Figure 10-13. When you click on a `mailto` link, many browsers will open a new outgoing message addressed to the specified email address. The browser needs to be configured with a helper email program for the `mailto` protocol.

Test Yourself

The most important lesson in this chapter is how to write URLs for links and graphics. Here's another chance to brush up on your pathname skills.

Using the directory hierarchy shown in Figure 10-14, write the code for the following links and graphics. I filled in the first one for you as an example. The answers are located in the Appendix.

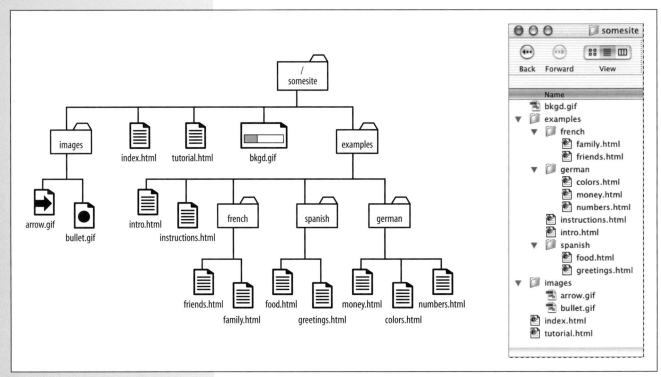

Figure 10-14. The test directory hierarchy.

This diagram should provide you with enough information to answer the questions. If you need hands-on work to figure them out, the directory structure is available in the test directory in the *chap10* materials directory. The HTML documents are just dummy files and contain no content.

1. In *index.html* (the site's home page), write the code for a link to *tutorial.html*.

    <a href="tutorial.html">...</a>

2. In *index.html*, write the code for a link to the page *instructions.html*.

3. Create a link to *family.html* from the page *tutorial.html*.

4. Create a link back to the home page (*index.html*) from the page *instructions.html*.

5. To place the graphic *arrow.gif* on the page *intro.html*, the tag is:

6. Create a link to *instructions.html* from the page *greetings.html*.

TIP

The ../ (or multiples of them) always appears at the beginning of the pathname and never in the middle. If the pathnames you write have ../ in the middle, you've done something wrong.

7. Create a link back to the home page (*index.html*) from *money.html*.

8. To place the graphic *bullet.gif* on the *friends.html* page, the tag is:

9. On the *friends.html* page, make the bullet graphic a link to *numbers.html*.

10. Create a link to *numbers.html* from the *family.html* page, but this time, start with the root directory.

11. In *index.html*, include the graphic *bkgd.gif* as a background image (see Chapter 9 if you need a refresher).

12. In the file *intro.html*, create a link to the web site for this book (*www.learningwebdesign.com*).

HTML Review: Link Tags

The following is a summary of the tags covered in this chapter:

Tag and attributes	Function
`<a>`	Anchor tag
`href="url"`	Location of the target file
`name="text"`	Name for a fragment in the page
`<map>`	Map information for an imagemap
`name="text"`	Name for the map
`<area>`	Link information in an imagemap
`shape="rect|circle|poly"`	Shape of the linked area
`coords="numbers"`	Pixel coordinates for the linked area
`href="url"`	Target file for the link

Tables

11

Tables are the web designer's best friend and worst enemy. While they offer much welcomed control over text alignment and page layout, the HTML code behind them is not especially intuitive and is prone to going haywire.

You'll be much better off relying on a web-authoring tool to create tables rather than writing them out by hand (although it's not *that* difficult, once you get used to it). Web tools, such as Macromedia Dreamweaver and Adobe GoLive, have built-in tricks that anticipate some common table problems, and they'll save you a lot of time. However, even with the tools, it's beneficial to understand how tables work and to be familiar with table terminology.

We'll start this chapter by looking at the basic structure of an HTML table. Once you have the general idea, we'll jump right into designing a complex table to give you the big picture of table-planning strategy. Finally, we'll dig into the nitty-gritty of all the specific HTML tags for controlling the appearance of tables and the cells within them. The chapter closes with some design and troubleshooting tips.

How Tables Are Used

Although originally intended for the display of rows and columns of data, tables were quickly coopted to serve many purposes. In each of the examples below, the table border has been turned on to reveal the structure of the table and its cells. With the borders turned off, these pages would be seamless and clean. Some uses for tables, illustrated in Figure 11-1, include:

For data display. Ah, the beauty of the table used as it was originally intended—rows and columns full of data (❶). Very tidy and useful.

For better text alignment. As we saw in Chapter 7, HTML alone offers little control over how text is aligned. Putting text in tables allows you to format indents and columns and add whitespace to a page (❷).

For overall page structure. One common use of tables is to divide a page into major sections. In this example, the column on the left is for navigational items and the main column is for content (❸).

For holding together a multipart (sliced) image. Tables can be used to hold together an image that has been divided up to accommodate animations, rollovers, etc. (❹). The best way to create these tables is to use a web image program such as Macromedia Fireworks or Adobe ImageReady. With the tool, you just drag guides where you want the image to be sliced, and the tool divides up the image and writes all the code for the table. Multipart images are covered in Chapter 20.

Values That Make Up the Web Palette		
Decimal	Hexadecimal	Percentage
0	00	0%
51	33	20%
102	66	40%
153	99	60%
204	CC	80%
255	FF	100%

❶ Data display

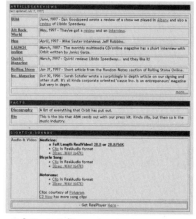
❷ Better text alignment

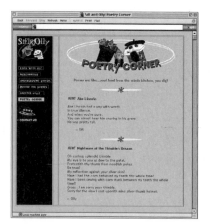
❸ Overall page structure

❹ Holding together "sliced" images

Figure 11-1. These screenshots illustrate some of the common uses of tables.

Basic Table Structure

Let's take a look at a simple table to see what it's made of. At their most basic, tables are made up of cells arranged into rows and columns (Figure 11-2).

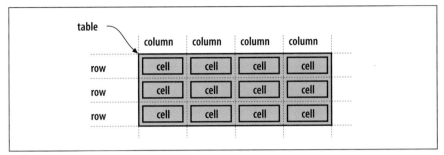

Figure 11-2. Tables are divided into rows and columns. Cells are the containers for content.

Simple enough, right? Let's look at how the table elements translate into HTML.

It's a cell thing

As shown in Figure 11-3, there are tags that identify the table (`<table>`), rows (`<tr>`, for "table row"), and cells (`<td>`, for "table data"). Cells are the heart of the table, since that's where the actual content goes. The other tags just hold things together.

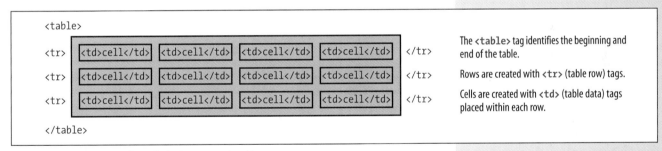

Figure 11-3. The tags that make up the basic structure of a table.

What we don't see are tags for columns. The number of columns in a table is determined by the number of table cells in each row. This is one of the things that make HTML tables tricky to deal with. Rows are easy—if you want the table to have three rows, just use three `<tr>` tags. Columns are different. For a table with four columns, you need to make sure that every row has four sets of `<td>` tags; the columns are implied.

Stacking the `<td>` cells in the HTML file makes table code easier to manage, although it may be less intuitive at a glance.

The resulting table as it appears in the browser window is shown below.

cell	cell	cell	cell
cell	cell	cell	cell
cell	cell	cell	cell

```
<table>

<tr>
<td>cell</td>
<td>cell</td>
<td>cell</td>
<td>cell</td>
</tr>

<tr>
<td>cell</td>
<td>cell</td>
<td>cell</td>
<td>cell</td>
</tr>

<tr>
<td>cell</td>
<td>cell</td>
<td>cell</td>
<td>cell</td>
</tr>

</table>
```

Figure 11-4. The previous table's HTML source and how it might be rendered in a browser.

Figure 11-4 shows how the table from Figure 11-3 is more likely to look in a real HTML document and in the browser window. It is common to stack the `<td>`s in order to make them easier to find in the code, and does not affect how they are rendered by the browser.

The following is the source code for another table as it might appear in an HTML document. Can you tell how many rows and columns it will have when it is displayed in a browser?

```
<table>
<tr>
  <td>Elliott Smith</td>
  <td>Enon</td>
  <td>Spoon</td>
</tr>
<tr>
  <td>The Shins</TD>
  <td>The Magnetic Fields</td>
  <td>Well</td>
</tr>
</table>
```

If you guessed that it's a table with two rows and three columns, you're right. Two `<tr>` tags create two rows; three `<td>`s in each row create three columns.

Remember, all content for a table must go in cells; that is, within `<td>` tags. You can put any HTML content in a cell: text, a graphic, even another table. `<table>` tags are used to identify the beginning and end of the table. The only thing that can go between `<tr>` tags is some number of `<td>`s.

In addition to forming the overall structure of the table, the `<table>`, `<tr>`, and `<td>` tags have attributes that you can use to adjust the formatting and appearance of the table. We will examine all of these attributes in detail later in this chapter.

TIP

Be sure to close your table tags! Some browsers will not display the table at all if the end tag (`</table>`) is missing.

TRY IT

Exercise 11-1: Making a Simple Table

Try writing the code for the table shown here. You can open an HTML editor or just write it down on paper. The code is provided in the Appendix.

cell 1	cell 2
cell 3	cell 4
cell 5	cell 6
cell 7	cell 8
cell 9	cell 10

Spanning cells

One fundamental feature of table structure is cell spanning, which is the stretching of a cell to cover several rows or columns. The ability to span cells gives you more flexibility when designing tables; however, it can also make the code a little more difficult to keep track of.

Column spans

Column spans, created with the colspan attribute in the <td> tag, stretch a cell to the right to span over the subsequent columns (Figure 11-5). Notice in the code that the <td> cell for the column that was spanned over is no longer in the HTML code; the cell with the colspan stands in for it. Be careful with colspan values; if you specify a number that exceeds the number of columns in the table, most browsers will add columns to the existing table, which will screw things up.

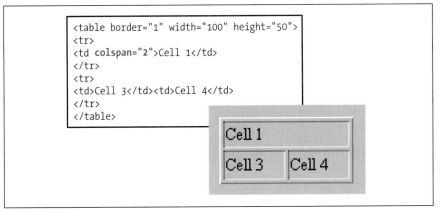

```
<table border="1" width="100" height="50">
<tr>
<td colspan="2">Cell 1</td>
</tr>
<tr>
<td>Cell 3</td><td>Cell 4</td>
</tr>
</table>
```

Figure 11-5. The colspan attribute stretches a cell to span the specified number of columns. Note how there is now only one <td> tag in the first row.

> *The colspan attribute stretches a cell to the right and replaces the cells next to it.*

Advanced Table Tags

The HTML 4.0 specification introduced a number of table tags that allow you to group columns and rows for faster table rendering. The <thead>, <tfoot>, and <tbody> tags determine whether rows are part of the header, footer, or body of the table, respectively. Column groups are identified with the <colgroup> tag. Only the most recent browser versions support the new table enhancements. They are beyond the scope of this book, but you may want to do more research if you anticipate working with data-heavy tables.

TRY IT

Exercise 11-2: Column Spans

Try writing the code for the table shown below. You can open an HTML editor or just write it down on paper. If you're working in an HTML editor, don't worry if your table is much wider than the one shown here. The code is provided in the Appendix.

cell 1		
cell 2	cell 3	cell 4
cell 5	cell 6	

Some hints:

- The second row shows you that the table has a total of three columns.
- When a cell is spanned over, its <td> tag does not appear in the table.

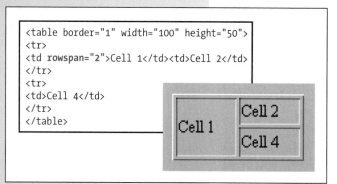

```
<table border="1" width="100" height="50">
<tr>
<td rowspan="2">Cell 1</td><td>Cell 2</td>
</tr>
<tr>
<td>Cell 4</td>
</tr>
</table>
```

Figure 11-6. The rowspan attribute extends a cell down to span a specified number of rows. Note how there is now only one <td> in the second row, accounted for by the spanned cell.

Row spans

A row span, created with the rowspan attribute in the <td> tag, causes the cell to stretch downward to span across several rows (Figure 11-6). Again, the <td> that was spanned over does not appear in the HTML code.

TRY IT

Exercise 11-3: Row Spans

Try writing the code for the table shown below. If you're working in an HTML editor, don't worry that if table is much wider than the one shown here. The code is provided in the Appendix.

cell 1	cell 2	cell 3
cell 4		cell 5
cell 6		

Some hints:

- Rows always span down, so cell 2 is part of the first row.
- Cells that are spanned over do not appear in the table code.

Nesting tables

One last thing that's good to know about tables is that you can nest one table inside the cell of another. You do this by putting all of the table's code between <td> tags, as shown in Figure 11-7.

```
<table>
<tr>
<td>
    <table>
      <tr><td>cell</td><td>cell</td></tr>
      <tr><td>cell</td><td>cell</td></tr>
    </table>
</td>
<td>cell</td>
</tr>
</table>
```

cell	cell	cell
cell	cell	

Figure 11-7. Nest one table inside another by putting its code inside a table cell <td>.

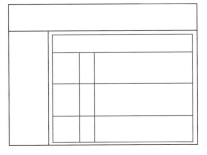

The Finished Product

The table demonstration in this section walks you through the creation of an online order form. You can see a color version in this book's gallery Ⓖ.

Designing Tables

Now that you see how tables are built, I want to give you a flavor of the table design process. When it comes to creating tables, especially complicated ones, I highly recommend WYSIWYG web-authoring tools over writing out the HTML by hand. With web-authoring software, you fill out the dialog boxes, and the tool keeps track of the code.

But even with a good tool, designing tables requires some planning and strategy. Of course, every designer has his own approach, but the process I'll outline covers some of the key issues you'll face. Again, don't worry about the specific tags right now; it's the process that's important.

We'll start with good old pencil and paper.

Step 1: Sketch it!

One key to preventing an avalanche of `<tr>`s and `<td>`s is to plan your table in advance. Even if you are using a web-authoring program, you'll need to know how many rows and columns your table has, and sometimes that's not evident, especially if there are overlapping spanned cells.

I start with a sketch of the page I want to make. I often use Photoshop to make a mock-up of a page; however, this time I'm using pencil and paper to sketch out my page quickly.

In this example, I'm designing an order form (the completed form is shown in the sidebar The Finished Product). I've sketched out the basic structure of the page and the information I need to include with each entry (Figure 11-8).

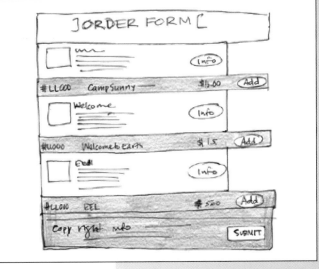

Figure 11-8. A rough sketch of the merchandise interface.

Step 2: Find the grid

Next, draw a grid over the sketch, making sure there is a line at each significant division of information. I find it easiest to start by drawing the lines between every row. Then I turn my ruler vertically and drag it left to right across the page, drawing a vertical line at every point where there should be a column break in any of the rows. Even if only one or two rows require a column at a certain point, the column line is drawn across the whole table.

This exercise reveals the total number of rows and columns in the table. It is also a good opportunity to assign pixel measurements to the columns and rows if you intend to restrict the size of the table. In this case, I want to control the column widths, but I'm allowing the heights of the rows to resize automatically (Figure 11-9).

Step 3: Plan the spans

Once I have my master grid, I start knocking out cells with column and row spans until the grid resembles the structure of my sketch (Figure 11-10). This step can be done in a web-authoring tool as well, but I find it useful to draw shaded boxes on the sketch itself (either on paper or with guides and layers in Photoshop).

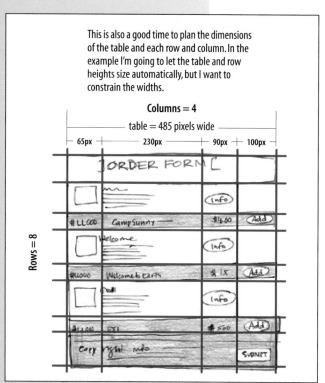

Figure 11-9. I draw a grid over my sketch to figure out the total number of rows and columns. (Believe me, it's not always evident just by looking, especially if there are a lot of spanned cells.)

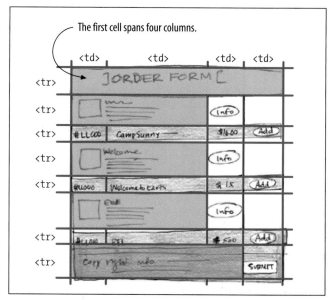

Figure 11-10. Blocking out the main areas of the table helps me plan the row spans and column spans (although there are no row spans in this example).

Step 4: Start building

When all the planning is done, building the table should be a breeze. You can write out the HTML by hand (it wouldn't hurt to try a few to get a feel for it) or get some help from a web-authoring tool such as Macromedia Dreamweaver. In this demonstration, we'll get started by writing out the HTML by hand.

> **TIP**
>
> *If you are working with a web authoring tool (such as Dreamweaver), you can start laying out the table at this point. Insert a table object and specify the total number of rows and columns. From there, it is easy to knock out cells with row and column spans. You can also specify column widths and other attributes such as color. Adding the contents of each cell is easier, too, when you can see what it looks like as you go along.*

Creating the structure in HTML

There are many ways to approach table construction in HTML, depending on the complexity of the table and your style of working. I'm going to build the table framework first (working from my grid layout).

I usually start designing with the border turned on (`border="1"`) so I can see if the table is structured the way I want it. Once the table is working properly, I turn off the border (`border="0"`) and add all the content.

DESIGN TIP

Use Comments to Label Your Document

The code for tables can get complicated, particularly for complex tables or tables nested within other tables.

This is a good opportunity to use comment tags to leave notes for yourself in the document. Anything you put between comment tags (`<!-- -->`) will not show in the browser and will not have any effect on the rest of the HTML page.

For instance, if you have a table holding your navigation system together, you might insert the following comments to make it easier to find in the HTML source code:

```
<!-- Start nav. table -->
<table>
...
</table>
<!-- end nav. table -->
```

I find it useful to write the row and cell tags right on my sketch. This helps me get the right number of <td>s in each row and set the spans correctly. Using the marked-up sketch as a map, it's simple to write out the actual HTML file (Figure 11-11).

I've also inserted the column widths in one of the rows (one row is enough to set the widths for the whole table) and specified varying colors to set apart certain cells and rows. (Don't worry if the color values look strange—we will discuss colors in Chapter 13.)

> The code in this example uses some attributes we haven't talked about yet, but they are fairly self-explanatory; we'll discuss them further in the next section.

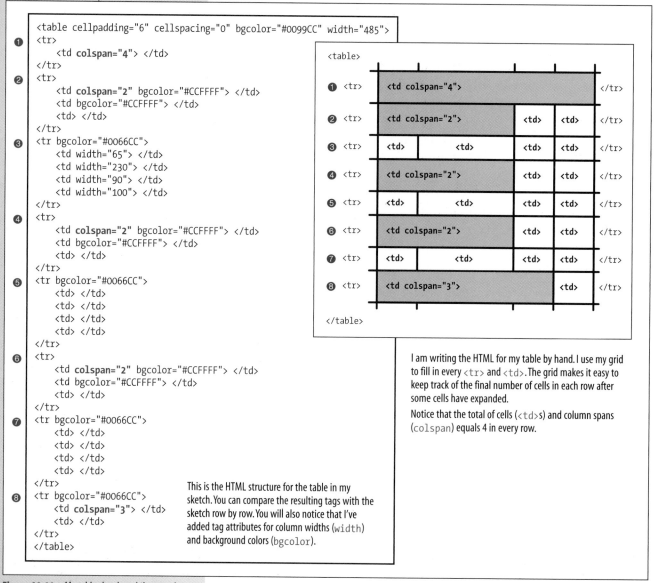

```
<table cellpadding="6" cellspacing="0" bgcolor="#0099CC" width="485">
❶  <tr>
        <td colspan="4"> </td>
    </tr>
❷  <tr>
        <td colspan="2" bgcolor="#CCFFFF"> </td>
        <td bgcolor="#CCFFFF"> </td>
        <td> </td>
    </tr>
❸  <tr bgcolor="#0066CC">
        <td width="65"> </td>
        <td width="230"> </td>
        <td width="90"> </td>
        <td width="100"> </td>
    </tr>
❹  <tr>
        <td colspan="2" bgcolor="#CCFFFF"> </td>
        <td bgcolor="#CCFFFF"> </td>
        <td> </td>
    </tr>
❺  <tr bgcolor="#0066CC">
        <td> </td>
        <td> </td>
        <td> </td>
        <td> </td>
    </tr>
❻  <tr>
        <td colspan="2" bgcolor="#CCFFFF"> </td>
        <td bgcolor="#CCFFFF"> </td>
        <td> </td>
    </tr>
❼  <tr bgcolor="#0066CC">
        <td> </td>
        <td> </td>
        <td> </td>
        <td> </td>
    </tr>
❽  <tr bgcolor="#0066CC">
        <td colspan="3"> </td>
        <td> </td>
    </tr>
    </table>
```

This is the HTML structure for the table in my sketch. You can compare the resulting tags with the sketch row by row. You will also notice that I've added tag attributes for column widths (width) and background colors (bgcolor).

I am writing the HTML for my table by hand. I use my grid to fill in every <tr> and <td>. The grid makes it easy to keep track of the final number of cells in each row after some cells have expanded.

Notice that the total of cells (<td>s) and column spans (colspan) equals 4 in every row.

Figure 11-11. My table sketch and the actual HTML source.

Put content in the cells

Now that the table structure is established, I can write in the content for each cell. Because the final file is quite lengthy, I'll show just a portion of it here, as well as a shot of the table as it's viewed in a browser (Figure 11-12). In reality, I made many trips to the browser to check my progress as I went along, tweaking the HTML code and viewing it again until I got something I liked.

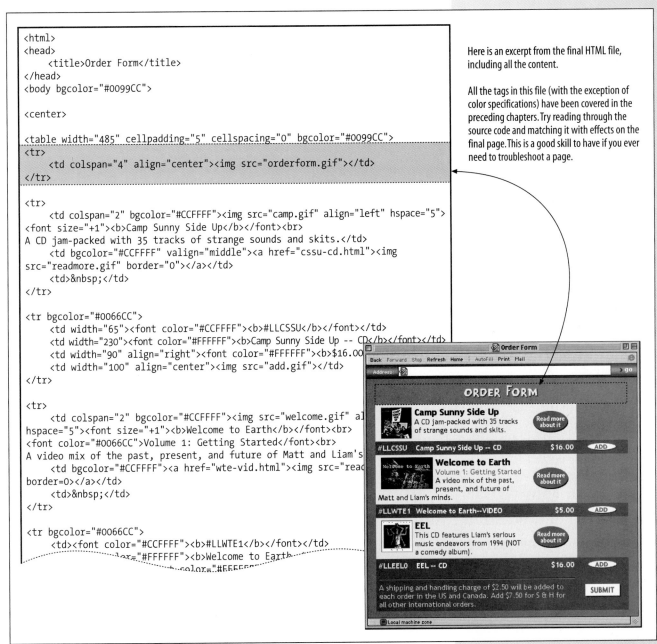

```
<html>
<head>
    <title>Order Form</title>
</head>
<body bgcolor="#0099CC">

<center>

<table width="485" cellpadding="5" cellspacing="0" bgcolor="#0099CC">
<tr>
    <td colspan="4" align="center"><img src="orderform.gif"></td>
</tr>


<tr>
    <td colspan="2" bgcolor="#CCFFFF"><img src="camp.gif" align="left" hspace="5">
<font size="+1"><b>Camp Sunny Side Up</b></font><br>
A CD jam-packed with 35 tracks of strange sounds and skits.</td>
    <td bgcolor="#CCFFFF" valign="middle"><a href="cssu-cd.html"><img
src="readmore.gif" border="0"></a></td>
    <td> </td>
</tr>


<tr bgcolor="#0066CC">
    <td width="65"><font color="#CCFFFF"><b>#LLCSSU</b></font></td>
    <td width="230"><font color="#FFFFFF"><b>Camp Sunny Side Up -- CD</b></font></td>
    <td width="90" align="right"><font color="#FFFFFF"><b>$16.00
    <td width="100" align="center"><img src="add.gif"></td>
</tr>


<tr>
    <td colspan="2" bgcolor="#CCFFFF"><img src="welcome.gif" al
hspace="5"><font size="+1"><b>Welcome to Earth</b></font><br>
<font color="#0066CC">Volume 1: Getting Started</font><br>
A video mix of the past, present, and future of Matt and Liam's
    <td bgcolor="#CCFFFF"><a href="wte-vid.html"><img src="read
border=0></a></td>
    <td> </td>
</tr>


<tr bgcolor="#0066CC">
    <td><font color="#CCFFFF"><b>#LLWTE1</b></font></td>
        lor="#FFFFFF"><b>Welcome to Earth
                  color="#FFFFF
```

Here is an excerpt from the final HTML file, including all the content.

All the tags in this file (with the exception of color specifications) have been covered in the preceding chapters. Try reading through the source code and matching it with effects on the final page. This is a good skill to have if you ever need to troubleshoot a page.

Figure 11-12. My table with content added.

Exercise 11-4: Finding the Table Structure

Imagine you work in the production department of a small web design firm. The graphic designer just handed you this Photoshop sketch, and now it's your job to build the page in HTML.

Using the techniques we just covered, see if you can find the table structure for this web page and write the HTML code.

Don't worry about the content; just leave the cells empty (or fill them in with a character space,). Also, don't

worry about setting cell dimensions or adding any attributes to control appearance; just work on the table's skeleton.

You can draw lines right on this page or make photocopies if you want to try more than once. Tracing paper is a good tool if you have it because once you trace the rows and columns, it is easier to see your markup on the plain paper than if it is written right on the sketch.

The code for this page is provided in the Appendix.

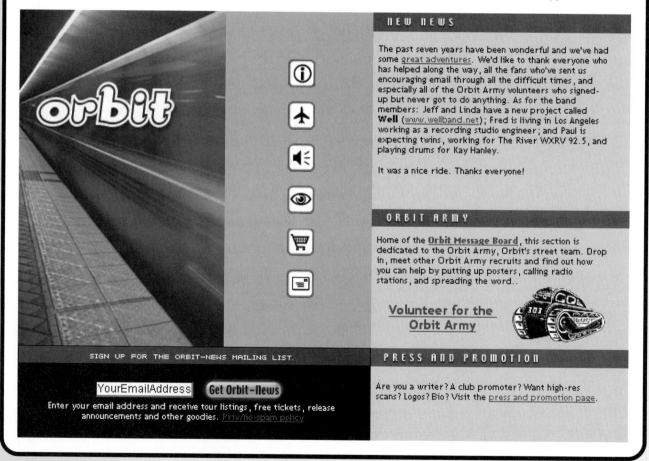

HTML for Tables

Now that you have a feel for how tables are put together, we'll look at all the specific table tags and how they work. Even if you're using an authoring tool, knowing the terminology will help you use it more efficiently.

Like so many other web elements, the real power lies in the attributes. We'll start with the settings that apply to the whole table, then we'll move on to those that affect individual cells.

Formatting the whole table

At the table level (that is, using attributes in the `<table>` tag), you can change the following aspects of the whole table:

- Thickness of the border around the table
- Dimensions of the table
- Amount of space within and between table cells
- Background color for the table

Let's look at each of these `<table>` attributes.

`<table border="number">`

Border thickness

The `border` attribute indicates the thickness (in pixels) of the border around the outside edge of the table (Figure 11-13). The most popular setting for this attribute is 0, which removes the cell borders. Using the attribute `border` alone, without a value, will result in the default 1-pixel border. If you omit the `border` attribute, most browsers will display the table without a border, but it's best to set the border to 0 to be on the safe side.

```
<table border="0">
<tr>
<td>Cell 1</td><td>Cell 2</td>
</tr>
<tr>
<td>Cell 3</td><td>Cell 4</td>
</tr>
</table>
```

To be sure the border is not visible, set the `border` value to 0.

```
<table border="15">
<tr>
<td>Cell 1</td><td>Cell 2</td>
</tr>
<tr>
<td>Cell 3</td><td>Cell 4</td>
</tr>
</table>
```

You can make the border as wide as you like. Notice that it affects only the outside edge of the table.

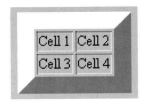

Figure 11-13. The `border` attribute of a table at work.

One of the difficult parts of writing table code is remembering which elements you control at the table level and which you control at the cell level.

Border Colors

Internet Explorer recognizes a few `<table>` tag attributes for specifying the colors of borders.

`bordercolor="color"`
: Specifies the color of the whole border.

`bordercolorlight="color"`
: Specifies the highlight color on a beveled table border.

`bordercolordark="color"`
: Specifies the shadow color on a beveled table border.

These nonstandard attributes are not universally supported and should be used with caution.

```
<table width="pixels or %"
       height="pixels or %">
```
Table width and height

These attributes are used to specify the dimensions of the whole table (Figure 11-14). You can specify either a pixel dimension or a percentage. For instance, if you set the width to 100%, the table will fill the entire available width of the page. By default, the table will expand to be just wide enough to fit the contents within it.

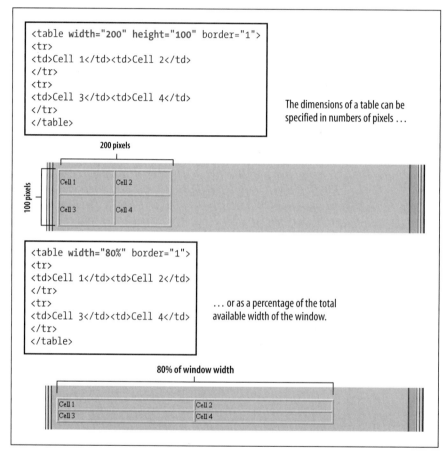

Figure 11-14. The width and height attributes of a table can be absolute pixel measurements or percentages.

`<table cellpadding="number">`

Margins around cell content

Cell padding is the amount of space held between the contents of the cell and the cell border (Figure 11-15). Think of it as a margin held within a cell. Because it is specified only at the table level, this setting will apply to all the cells in the table. In other words, you can't specify different amounts of padding for individual cells. If you don't specify anything, the cells will have the default value of one pixel of padding.

TIP

To get a different amount of cell padding in a single cell within a table, put a nested table in that cell with its own cellpadding *setting. This is useful, for instance, when you want a few pixels of padding within a cell with text while the rest of the table has a* cellpadding *of zero.*

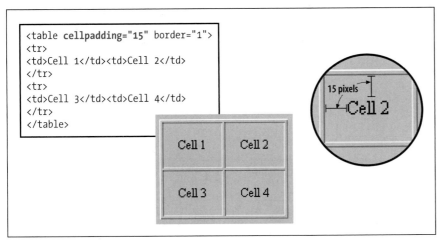

```
<table cellpadding="15" border="1">
<tr>
<td>Cell 1</td><td>Cell 2</td>
</tr>
<tr>
<td>Cell 3</td><td>Cell 4</td>
</tr>
</table>
```

Figure 11-15. Cell padding specifies the margin of space within each cell (between the contents and the cell border).

`<table cellspacing="number">`

Space between cells

Cell spacing is the amount of space held between cells, specified in number of pixels (Figure 11-16). If you don't specify anything, the browser will use the default value of two pixels of space between cells.

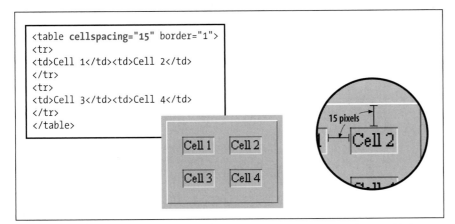

```
<table cellspacing="15" border="1">
<tr>
<td>Cell 1</td><td>Cell 2</td>
</tr>
<tr>
<td>Cell 3</td><td>Cell 4</td>
</tr>
</table>
```

Figure 11-16. Cell spacing is the space between cells. When the border is turned on (as in this example), the spacing is rendered as a raised border.

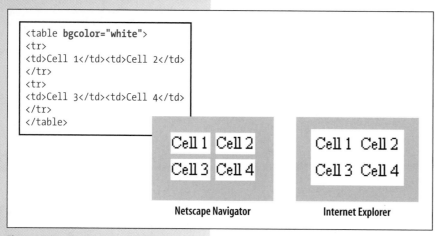

```
<table bgcolor="white">
<tr>
<td>Cell 1</td><td>Cell 2</td>
</tr>
<tr>
<td>Cell 3</td><td>Cell 4</td>
</tr>
</table>
```

Netscape Navigator | Internet Explorer

Figure 11-17. The bgcolor attribute assigns a color that fills all the cells in the table. This attribute is implemented differently in Navigator and Internet Explorer and is not supported at all by pre-4.0 browsers.

`<table bgcolor="color">`
Table background color

Use the bgcolor attribute to specify the background color applied to the whole table (Figure 11-17). Unfortunately, this will work only in Version 4.0 browsers and higher, so be careful how you implement it. The value is a color name or its numerical equivalent. Specifying colors in HTML is covered in Chapter 13.

HTML TIP

Background Patterns

You can also use a tiled image as the background for a table using the background attribute in the `<table>` tag:

```
<table background="image.gif">
```

While recent versions of Internet Explorer handle this nonstandard attribute fairly well, other browsers display the tiled image in unpredictable ways. Use this one with caution.

Combining table attributes

Of course, it's likely that you'll be using a combination of these settings in a single table, as shown in Figure 11-18.

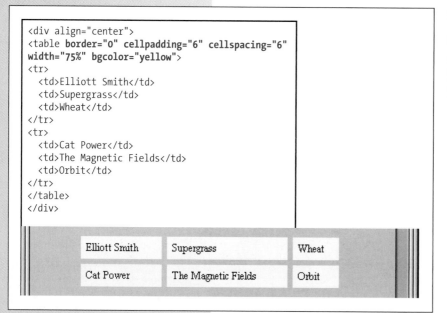

```
<div align="center">
<table border="0" cellpadding="6" cellspacing="6"
width="75%" bgcolor="yellow">
<tr>
  <td>Elliott Smith</td>
  <td>Supergrass</td>
  <td>Wheat</td>
</tr>
<tr>
  <td>Cat Power</td>
  <td>The Magnetic Fields</td>
  <td>Orbit</td>
</tr>
</table>
</div>
```

| Elliott Smith | Supergrass | Wheat |
| Cat Power | The Magnetic Fields | Orbit |

Figure 11-18. In most cases, these attributes are used in combination.

Adding Tables

Here's how you add a table and adjust all table-level settings in three of the more popular authoring programs.

Dreamweaver MX

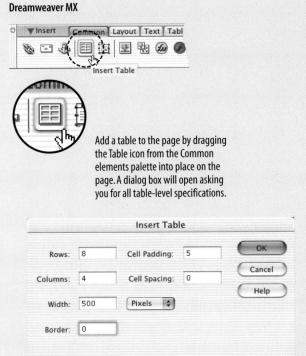

Add a table to the page by dragging the Table icon from the Common elements palette into place on the page. A dialog box will open asking you for all table-level specifications.

GoLive 6

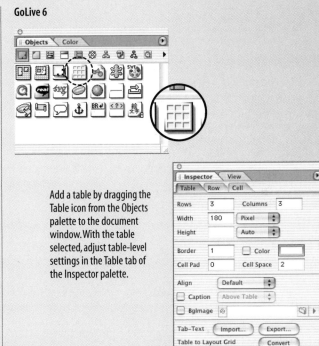

Add a table by dragging the Table icon from the Objects palette to the document window. With the table selected, adjust table-level settings in the Table tab of the Inspector palette.

FrontPage 2002

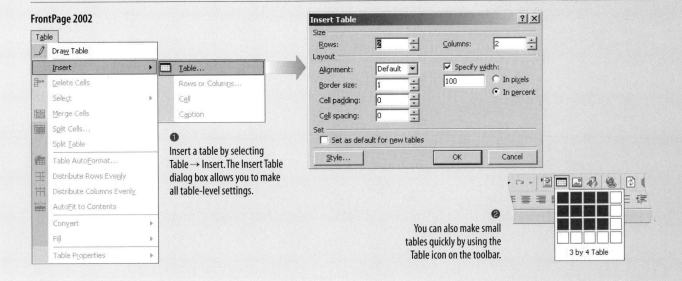

❶ Insert a table by selecting Table → Insert. The Insert Table dialog box allows you to make all table-level settings.

❷ You can also make small tables quickly by using the Table icon on the toolbar.

Header Cells

There is a table cell tag used especially for the headings above each column. These cells are called "headers" and are indicated with `<th>` tags. They follow the same rules as `<td>`s, only they display text within them as bold and centered by default:

```
<table cellpadding="6"
       border="1">
<tr>
  <th>Name</th>
  <th>Occupation</th>
  <th>Location</th>
</tr>
  <td>Jennifer Niederst</td>
  <td>Web Designer</td>
  <td>Boston, MA</td>
</tr>
</table>
```

Name	Occupation	Location
Jennifer Niederst	Web Designer	Boston, MA

Controlling individual cells

Some of the more interesting table settings are controlled at the cell level. These include:

- Column and row spanning
- Cell dimensions
- Alignment of cell contents
- Background color for the cell

All of these aspects are controlled using attributes within the `<td>` tag. The following is a description of each.

`<td colspan="number">`
Column span

`<td rowspan="number">`
Row span

Column span and row span are examples of cell-level settings since they control the behavior of a single cell. Earlier in this chapter, we looked at how `colspan` causes a cell to stretch to the right a specified number of columns (Figure 11-5). Similarly, `rowspan` causes a cell to to stretch down to span a specified number of rows (Figure 11-6).

It is also possible to specify both a `colspan` and `rowspan` within a single cell to make it knock out a whole block of cells, as shown in Figure 11-19.

```
<table width="200" border="1" cellpadding="3">
<tr>
  <td>one</td>
  <td colspan="3" rowspan="2">two</td>
</tr>
<tr>
  <td>three</td>
</tr>
<tr>
  <td>four</td>
  <td>five</td>
  <td>six</td>
  <td>seven</td>
</tr>
</table>
```

one	two		
three			
four	five	six	seven

Figure 11-19. Using both the `colspan` and `rowspan` attributes with a single cell.

```
<td width="pixels or %"
    height="pixels or %">
```
Cell width and height

The width and height attributes are used to specify the dimensions of a particular cell (Figure 11-20). You can specify a pixel measurement or a percentage of the overall size of the table.

When you specify the width of a cell, you establish the width of the entire column. Likewise, setting the height of a cell affects the height of all the cells in that row. Be careful you don't have conflicting cell widths within a column (or conflicting heights within a row). The best way to avoid this is to set the widths only once in the table, using a row that has all its cells intact (i.e., no column spans).

Also, when using specific pixel measurements, make sure that the total of your cell measurements is the same as the dimensions set in the <table> tag.

Table sizes are unpredictable even when specified. If the content requires more space, the cell will generally resize to accommodate, so cell and table size specifications should be considered minimum values.

When you specify the width of a cell, you establish the width of the entire column. Likewise, setting the height of a cell affects the height of the entire row.

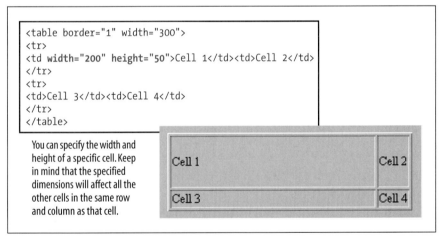

```
<table border="1" width="300">
<tr>
<td width="200" height="50">Cell 1</td><td>Cell 2</td>
</tr>
<tr>
<td>Cell 3</td><td>Cell 4</td>
</tr>
</table>
```

You can specify the width and height of a specific cell. Keep in mind that the specified dimensions will affect all the other cells in the same row and column as that cell.

Figure 11-20. Setting cell size with the width and height attributes. The dimensions in Cell 1 determine the height of the first row and the width of the first column.

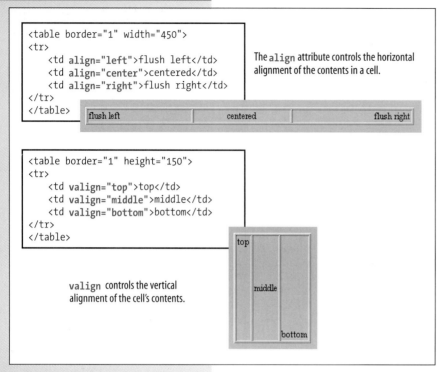

```
<table border="1" width="450">
<tr>
    <td align="left">flush left</td>
    <td align="center">centered</td>
    <td align="right">flush right</td>
</tr>
</table>
```

The `align` attribute controls the horizontal alignment of the contents in a cell.

```
<table border="1" height="150">
<tr>
    <td valign="top">top</td>
    <td valign="middle">middle</td>
    <td valign="bottom">bottom</td>
</tr>
</table>
```

`valign` controls the vertical alignment of the cell's contents.

Figure 11-21. The `align` and `valign` attributes control the horizontal and vertical alignment of a cell's content.

```
<table bgcolor="white" border="1" cellpadding="5" >
<tr>
    <td bgcolor="black"><font color="white">Cell 1</font></td>
    <td>Cell 2</td>
</tr>
<tr>
    <td>Cell 3</td>
    <td>Cell 4</td>
</tr>
</table>
```

Figure 11-22. You can set the background color of a cell by using the `bgcolor` attribute in the `<td>` tag. Color settings at the cell level will override table color settings.

`<td align="left|right|center" valign="top|center|bottom">`
Cell content alignment

The `align` and `valign` attributes control the alignment of elements within cells. By default, the text (or any element) placed in a cell will be positioned flush left and centered vertically within the available height of the cell. Use the `align` attribute to position elements horizontally in a cell. Its values are `left`, `right`, or `center`. `valign` positions elements vertically in the cell. Its values are `top`, `center`, or `bottom` (Figure 11-21)

`<td bgcolor="color">`
Cell background color

This specifies the background color to be used in the table cell (Figure 11-22). Cell color settings override any colors set at the table or row level.

DESIGN TIP

Row Row Row

You can use the `align`, `valign`, and `bgcolor` attributes in the `<tr>` tag to make settings that affect all cells in a table row:

```
<table bgcolor="white">
<tr align="right" valign="top"
bgcolor="gray">
    <td>Cell 1</td>
    <td>Cell 2</td>
    <td>Cell 3</td>
</tr>
<tr>
    <td>Cell 4</td>
    <td>Cell 5</td>
    <td>Cell 6</td>
</tr>
</table>
```

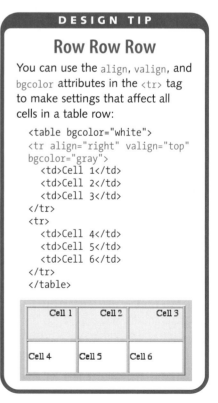

Formatting Table Cells

Here's how you adjust cell-level settings in three of the more popular authoring programs.

Dreamweaver MX

When your cursor is in a cell, all cell-level settings can be adjusted in the Properties window (make sure it is fully opened). You can apply settings to several cells at once by dragging and selecting groups of cells.

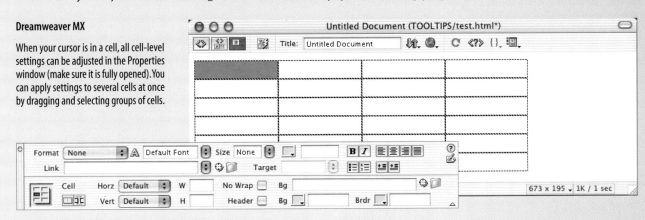

GoLive 6

To make cell settings, select the cell border with the pointer and enter attribute values in the Cell palette of the Table Inspector. You can apply the same settings to several selected cells at once. Use the Row palette (not shown) to control the cells in the current row.

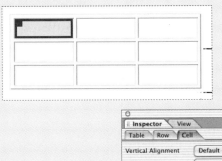

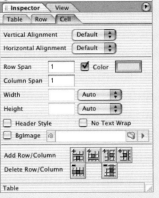

FrontPage 2002

Cell settings can be made when the cursor is in the desired cell(s). Go to the menubar, Table → Properties → Cell. A dialog box to specify cell attributes will appear.

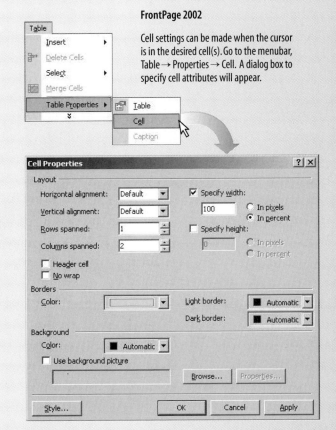

Exercise 11-5: Building a Table

In this exercise, we'll work together to build a table very similar to the one shown in Exercise 11-4. We'll use many of the table and cell attributes as well as tags from previous chapters by the time we're finished. The materials for this exercise are provided in the *chap11* materials folder on the CD and online at *www.learningwebdesign.com/ materials/ch11/*.

1. Start by opening the document *ex11-5_start.html*. This is the same table code you should have ended up with in Exercise 11-4, only it has nonbreaking spaces ( ) in each cell, so it's not entirely empty.

2. First, we'll make table-level settings. Make the table 650 pixels wide and 450 pixels tall. Set the border to 1-pixel thick so it is easy to see the table structure while we build it. Also, add four pixels of padding in the cells so the contents don't bump up against the edges of the cells. The code should look like this:

```
<table width="650" height="450" border="1"
    cellpadding="4">
```

Save the file and take a look at it in the browser. You can see that the table is now our specified size. By default, the browser makes the columns equal width and the rows equal height, as shown here:

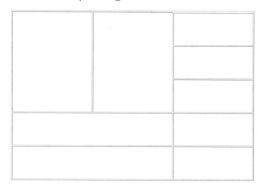

3. Next, set the widths of the columns. We'll do this in the first row because that row has all three cells intact (no column spans). Make the columns 225, 175, and 250 pixels wide, in that order.

```
<tr>
<td rowspan="4" width="225"> </td>
<td rowspan="4" width="175"> </td>
<td width="250"> </td>
</tr>
```

4. Now we'll set the row heights. We'll use the third column (the last <TD> in each row), because all the rows are intact. Starting from the top, make the rows 20, 200, 20, 120, 20, and 70 pixels high.

To make the next steps in this exercise easier to follow, I've assigned numbers to the cells of our table. Refer to the following diagram when implementing steps 5 and 6:

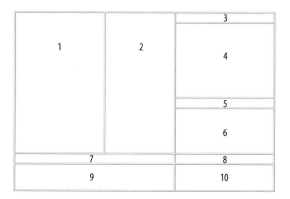

5. Now we'll jazz things up a bit by assigning colors to the cells. I've used Photoshop to pick some colors for the table. The colors are provided in their numeric RGB equivalents, which may look strange to you at this point. Numeric color values are explained in Chapter 13, but for now, just copy the color values into each cell as assigned below. The attribute for changing the background color looks like this:

```
bgcolor="003300"
```

Cell 1	#003300 (dark green)
Cell 2	#99CC66 (light green)
Cell 3	#669900 (green)
Cell 4	#FFFFCC (light yellow)
Cell 5	#669900 (green)
Cell 6	#FFFFCC (light yellow)
Cell 7	#FF0033 (red)
Cell 8	#669900 (green)
Cell 9	#000000 (black)
Cell 10	#FFFFCC (light yellow)

Feel free to save the file at this point and look at it in the browser.

Exercise 11-5 *(continued)*

6. All that's left now is to replace the nonbreaking spaces ( ) with real content and adjust the cell alignment as needed. Follow the instructions and see if your table looks like the final version shown below and in the color gallery Ⓖ. The code that defines this table can be found in the Appendix.

   If you want more practice when you're done, try customizing the table with your own table and cell settings.

   CELL 1: Add the graphic *redbottles.jpg* from the *images* folder. Be careful not to have any extra spaces or returns in the <td> tag (see the "Avoiding Extra Whitespace" sidebar at the end of the chapter). The graphic is 217 × 351 pixels. Remember to provide alternative text for all graphics.

   CELL 2: Add the graphic *buttons.gif* from the *images* folder (81 x 267 pixels). Center the graphic in the cell with the align and valign attributes.

   CELL 3: Add the graphic *about.gif* from the *images* folder (66 x 12 pixels).

   CELL 4: Write a brief description of yourself. If you write something that is too long, it will stretch the cell and break the table design. Use the valign attribute to position the text at the top of the cell.

   CELL 5: Add the graphic *contact.gif* from the *images* folder (150 x 12 pixels).

   CELL 6: Type your name, address, and phone number on three lines, separated by
s.

   CELL 7: Leave this as it is.

   CELL 8: Add the graphic *link.gif* from the *images* folder (108 x 12 pixels).

   CELL 9: Type in the following text:

   All contents copyright © 2003 [*your name*].

   Use a character entity for the copyright symbol. Set the text to "gray." Use the align attribute to center all of the content in the cell.

   CELL 10: Write the name of a web page you like and make it a link to that page.

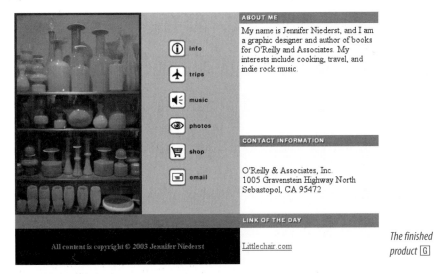

The finished product Ⓖ

```
<html>
<head><title>Centered object</title></head>
<body>

<table width="100%" height="100%" border="0">
<tr>
    <td align="center" valign="middle"><img src="tomato.gif"></td>
</tr>
</table>

</body>
</html>
```

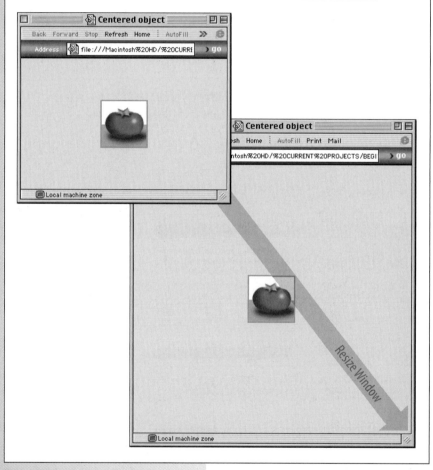

Figure 11-23. With this one-celled table, you can keep any object centered in the browser window, regardless of how it is resized.

Using Tables for Alignment

As I said earlier in this chapter, tables were *originally* intended to display rows and columns of data. But designers quickly found creative ways to use them to control the display of the page. Here are couple of popular tricks you can do with tables.

Centering in the window

Here's a trick that uses a table to keep a page element centered in the browser window. You simply make a one-celled table (one row and one column) and set the width and height to 100%. Next, set the alignment to center and the vertical alignment to middle. And *voila*! Your object will be the center of attention regardless of how the window is resized (Figure 11-23).

Page structure

Many sites use a two-column table to lay out the structure of the page. One common layout is to have a narrow column for links and use the remainder of the page for content.

You have a choice of fixing the width of your table to precise pixel measurements, letting the widths resize relative to the width of the window, or a combination of both (Figure 11-24). The code for each page layout is simple.

Fixed width

In this example, the width of the table and the widths of each column are set to specific pixel measurements.

```
<html>
<head>
<title>Page Formatting</title>
</head>
<body>
<table border="1" width="600" height="100%">
<tr>
    <td width="150">left column</td>
    <td width="450">right column contents here</td>
</tr>
</table>

</body>
</html>
```

The columns and table will remain the same width regardless of the size of the browser window.

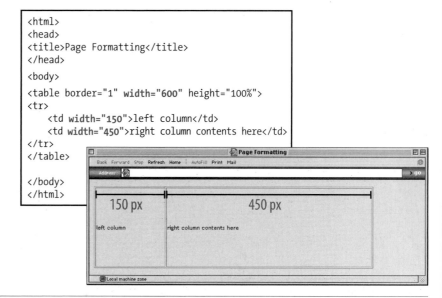

Relative width

Here, the table always fills the width of the page (its width is set to 100%), and each column is a specified percentage of that width.

```
<table border="1" width="100%" height="100%">
<tr>
    <td width="15%">left column</td>
    <td width="85%">right column contents here</td>
</tr>
</table>
```

This layout flexes to fill the width of the window. The columns flex too, but in proportion to each other.

Combination

In this table, the left column stays a fixed width, while the right one is allowed to flex with the page.

```
<table border="1" width="100%" height="100%">
<tr>
    <td width="150">left column</td>
    <td>right column contents here</td>
</tr>
</table>
```

This table fills the window (its width is set to 100%). Cells with a pixel measurement stay put (this one is at 150 pixels), and cells with no measurement expand to fill the remaining space.

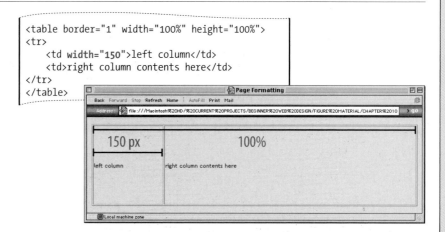

Figure 11-24. Fixed-width versus relative-width layouts.

Tables can easily go haywire if everything isn't perfectly in place.

Where Tables Go Wrong

Tables are known to cause headaches, partly because of the potential for complex code, and partly because of the quirky and inconsistent ways browsers interpret that code. This is especially troublesome for tables that require precise cell dimensions to hold the page or graphics together.

Although not every problem can be anticipated, here are a few of the places tables tend to go awry. More table idiosyncrasies are discussed in detail in my big book of web design, *Web Design in a Nutshell* (O'Reilly, 2001).

Expanding text in cells

Remember that text size varies from user to user. If you are using text in a cell, the cell will expand to accommodate your text, potentially breaking apart a carefully constructed table (Figure 11-25). Make sure there is ample room in the cell for the text or allow the height of your cell to be flexible.

TIP

Be careful putting text in cells with critical pixel dimensions. Design with room for the text to expand.

```
<table border="0" cellpadding="0" cellspacing="0">
<tr>
    <td colspan="3"><img src="top.gif"></td>
</tr>
<tr>
    <td width="28" height="144"><img src="left.gif"></td>
    <td width="94" height="144" bgcolor="white">Roses are red, <br>Violets
are Blue<br>Sugar is Sweet<br>And So Are You!</td>
    <td width="28" height="144"><img src="right.gif"></td>
</tr>
<tr>
    <td colspan="3"><img src="bottom.gif"></td>
</tr>
</table>
```

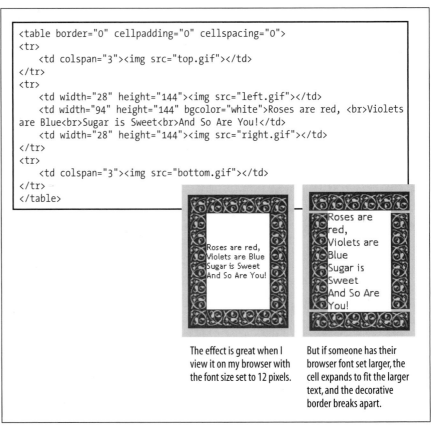

The effect is great when I view it on my browser with the font size set to 12 pixels.

But if someone has their browser font set larger, the cell expands to fit the larger text, and the decorative border breaks apart.

Figure 11-25. I've created a decorative border using four graphics held together by a table with specific cell measurements. However, spacing can create problems.

Collapsing cells

Netscape Navigator (all versions) has an annoying habit of collapsing any cell that doesn't contain content: the cell disappears and its cell background color is not displayed (Figure 11-26). If the table border is turned on, the cell will be filled in with a solid "raised" area that is the same color as the page background. For this reason, it is a good idea to make sure there is some minimal content between every set of `<td>` tags.

At a minimum, you can hold open the cell with a `<br>` tag or nonbreaking space (` `). Neither will display in the browser, but it will hold the cell open. If precise cell sizing is an issue, try using a transparent graphic that is only 1 pixel square, then use the `width` and `height` attributes in the `<img>` tag to size the graphic to the target cell size.

A `<br>` tag, nonbreaking space (` `), or 1-pixel transparent GIF will prevent a table cell from collapsing in Netscape.

Figure 11-26. Empty cells collapse in Navigator.

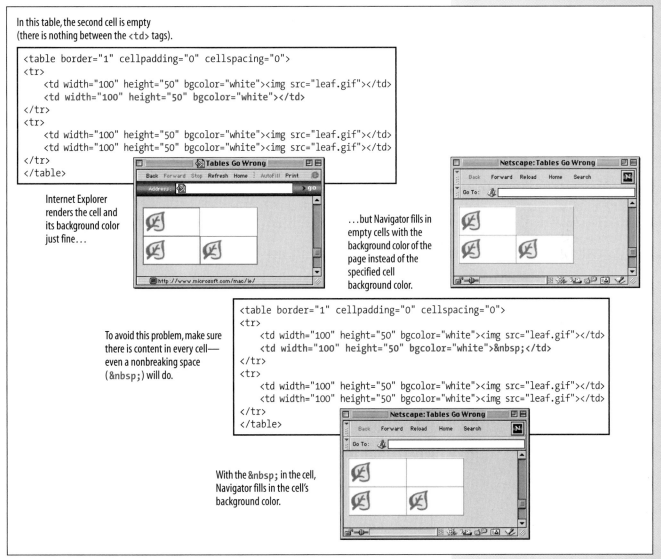

In this table, the second cell is empty (there is nothing between the `<td>` tags).

```
<table border="1" cellpadding="0" cellspacing="0">
<tr>
    <td width="100" height="50" bgcolor="white"><img src="leaf.gif"></td>
    <td width="100" height="50" bgcolor="white"></td>
</tr>
<tr>
    <td width="100" height="50" bgcolor="white"><img src="leaf.gif"></td>
    <td width="100" height="50" bgcolor="white"><img src="leaf.gif"></td>
</tr>
</table>
```

Internet Explorer renders the cell and its background color just fine...

...but Navigator fills in empty cells with the background color of the page instead of the specified cell background color.

To avoid this problem, make sure there is content in every cell— even a nonbreaking space (` `) will do.

```
<table border="1" cellpadding="0" cellspacing="0">
<tr>
    <td width="100" height="50" bgcolor="white"><img src="leaf.gif"></td>
    <td width="100" height="50" bgcolor="white"> </td>
</tr>
<tr>
    <td width="100" height="50" bgcolor="white"><img src="leaf.gif"></td>
    <td width="100" height="50" bgcolor="white"><img src="leaf.gif"></td>
</tr>
</table>
```

With the ` ` in the cell, Navigator fills in the cell's background color.

Shifting columns

Lots of column spans in a table can make your careful column width specifications go haywire. I once wrote the HTML for a table that looked perfect in the source code, but completely fell apart once it hit the browser (Figure 11-27). What I hadn't noticed was that my column spans had left the specific widths of some of my columns unaccounted for. The browser does its best to render the table based on the code you give it.

The trick to getting column widths to behave is to enter the width values in a row that has all its cells intact, with no colspan settings. If there are no intact rows, create a control row at the top or bottom of the table that has its height set to 0, yet contains all the proper widths for each cell (and therefore, column). The control row doesn't render in the browser, but it keeps the table in shape, even after lots of spanning.

Many authoring tools build this control row in automatically, which is why their table code tends to be more reliable across different browsers.

Figure 11-27. Using a control row can prevent column shifting.

```
<table border="0" cellpadding="0" cellspacing="0" width="250">
<tr>
    <td colspan="2"><img src="sweetpea-1.gif" width="200"></td>
    <td><img src="sweetpea-2.gif" width="50"></td>
</tr>
<tr>
    <td><img src="sweetpea-3.gif" width="50"></td>
    <td colspan="2"><img src="sweetpea-4.gif" width="200"></td>
</tr>
</table>
```

This table source code does not contain enough information for the browser to render the table correctly. Both rows span the required center column, so the widths of the columns are never clearly defined.

```
<table border="0" cellpadding="0" cellspacing="0" width="250">
<tr>
    <td width="50" height="0"></td>
    <td width="150" height="0"></td>
    <td width="50" height="0"></td>
</tr>
<tr>
    <td colspan="2"><img src="sweetpea-1.gif" width="200"></td>
    <td><img src="sweetpea-2.gif" width="50"></td>
</tr>
<tr>
    <td><img src="sweetpea-3.gif" width="50"></td>
    <td colspan="2"><img src="sweetpea-4.gif" width="200"></td>
</tr>
</table>
```

To correct the problem, add a control row that explicitly defines the widths for all three columns. Because the cells are empty and the height is set to "0", the row will not display in the browser.

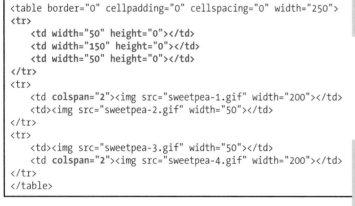

Avoiding extra whitespace

Extra space between cells is unacceptable when using a table to hold an image together, yet it is very easy for whitespace to creep in.

The problem most often lies within the cell tag (<td>). Some browsers render any extra space or carriage return within a <td> tag as whitespace in a table. Both of these code examples could result in extra space:

```
<td><img src="topleft.gif"> </td>

<td>
<img src="topleft.gif">
</td>
```

If you want a seamless table, begin with the border, cellpadding, and cellspacing all set to 0 in the <table> tag. Be sure that the enclosing <td> and </td> tags are flush against the content of the cell with no extra spaces or returns. The safest approach is to keep your cell tags and their contents all on one line, like this:

```
<td><img src="topleft.gif"></td>
```

If you must break the line of code, do so within a tag. It won't hurt the tag, and it won't introduce any extra space to the cell. For example:

```
<td><img
src="topleft.gif"></td>
```

It is worthwhile to note that because <table> and <tr> tags contain only other tags, not actual content for the table, spaces and returns within these tags are ignored. If you are getting pesky whitespace in your tables, check those <td> tags.

Test Yourself

The answers to these questions are in the Appendix.

1. What are the parts of an HTML table? What tags define them?

2. What attribute adds space between table cells? Where is it placed?

3. What attribute would you use to position text at the bottom of of a cell? Where does that attribute go?

4. How do you change the background color of a cell? What happens if there is alread a background color set for the table?

5. Write the code for the table shown in Figure 11-28. Be sure to consider how the text is aligned in each cell. Additional instructions are provided in the figure.

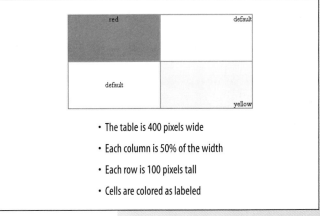

- The table is 400 pixels wide
- Each column is 50% of the width
- Each row is 100 pixels tall
- Cells are colored as labeled

Figure 11-28. Test your table-writing skills.

HTML Review: Table Tags

The following is a summary of the tags we covered in this chapter:

Tag and attributes	Function
`<table>`	Establishes beginning and end of a table
`bgcolor="number"` or `"name"`	Background color for the whole table
`border="number"`	Thickness of the border around the table
`cellpadding="number"`	Space within cells
`cellspacing="number"`	Space between cells
`height="number"`	Table height (in pixels or percentage)
`width="number"`	Table width (in pixels or percentage)
`<td>`	Establishes a cell within a table row
`align="left|right|center"`	Horizontal alignment of cell contents
`bgcolor="number"` or `"name"`	Background color for the cell
`colspan="number"`	Number of columns the cell should span
`height="number"`	Cell height (in pixels or percentage)
`rowspan="number"`	Number of rows the cell should span
`valign="top|middle|bottom|baseline"`	Vertical alignment of cell contents
`width="number"`	Width (in pixels or percentage)
`<th>`	Table head
(attributes are the same as the `<td>` tag)	
`<tr>`	Establishes a row within a table
`align="left|right|center"`	Horizontal alignment of cell contents for an entire row
`bgcolor="number"` or `"name"`	Background color for the entire row
`valign="top|middle|bottom|baseline"`	Vertical alignment of cell contents for the entire row

Frames 12

Have you ever seen a web page with content that scrolls while the navigation toolbar or an ad stays in the same place? Pages like these are created using a web design feature called frames. Frames divide the browser window into mini-windows, each displaying a different HTML document (Figure 12-1).

The primary advantage of frames is the ability to have one portion of the window always visible while others scroll through longer content. Frames open up navigational possibilities, and they can be used to unify information from several sites onto one page.

However, frames have been controversial since their introduction in Netscape Navigator 2.0. They cause as many navigational problems as they solve, since some users find it difficult to click through them. It is also difficult for content in frames to be bookmarked or found by search engines. And since each framed page is comprised of several HTML documents, this means more work for developers and a heavier load for the server.

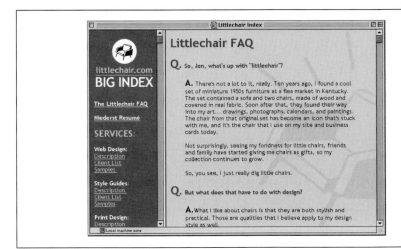

Figure 12-1. Frames divide the browser into separate windows, each displaying its own web page. The windows can scroll independently.

As a result of their numerous disadvantages, frames have become an unspoken "no-no" for big commercial sites. Don't be surprised if your client declares "no frames" at the very first meeting. But like most things, frames are neither all good nor all bad, so feel free to play around with them and decide for yourself. If you do use frames, make sure that you think the navigation and site structure through and don't let the frame structure get too complicated.

How Frames Work

When you view a framed page in a browser, you are actually looking at several HTML documents at once (Figure 12-2). The key to making the page display in frames is the frameset document, which is an HTML document that contains instructions for how each frame is drawn and which HTML document is displayed in each frame.

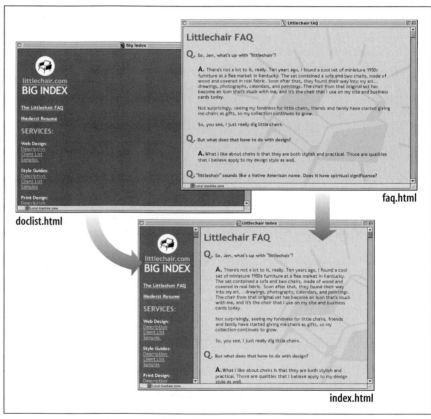

Figure 12-2. This framed document is actually displaying two separate external documents at the same time.

The primary function of the frameset document is to set up a structure for the page. Let's take a peek at the HTML source for our example framed page (Figure 12-3).

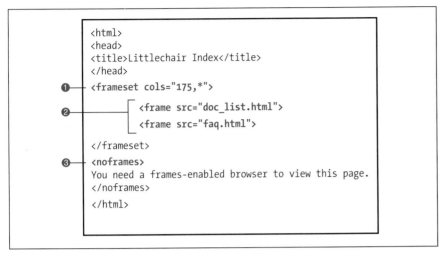

Figure 12-3. This is the HTML source for the frameset document *index.html* in our example.

❶ `<frameset>`

We'll talk about creating frameset documents in more detail in the next section, but for now I want to highlight a few points of interest. First, notice that the frameset document uses the `<head>` structural element, but it does *not* have a `<body>`. It uses the `<frameset>` structural tag instead. This sets framesets apart from all other web pages.

The `cols` attribute in the frameset tag divides the window into two frame columns, one 175 pixels wide and the second filling whatever space is remaining (indicated by the asterisk).

❷ `<frame>`

Within the `<frameset>` container tags, we see a `<frame>` tag for each frame on the page. The primary job of the `<frame>` tag is to specify which HTML document to display; however, you can control other features of a frame, as we'll see later in this chapter.

❸ `<noframes>`

Finally, there's some minimal content within the `<noframes>` tag. This is what will display if the frames do not work (for instance, if the user is using an ancient browser). It is similar to the alternative text provided in image tags. We'll talk more about "noframes" content at the end of this chapter.

When the browser sees that this is a frameset document, it draws out the frames as instructed in the document and then pulls the separate HTML documents into the page.

Setting Up a Frameset Document

I'm going to create a framed interface for the cookbook section of the recipe site I started earlier. In this section, I'll walk you step by step through the process of writing the HTML for framed documents.

As with any HTML document, the first step is to create the document structure. Let's do that for our new framed document; remember that it will use the <frameset> tag instead of <body> (Figure 12-4).

The Finished Product

The frame demonstration in this section walks you through the creation of this three-framed "Jen's Kitchen" page, shown here and in color in the gallery Ⓖ.

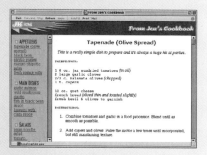

```
<html>
<head>
<title>From Jen's Cookbook</title>
</head>

<frameset>



</frameset>

</html>
```

Frameset documents use a <frameset> tag instead of <body>.

Figure 12-4. I begin by adding basic structural tags to a new document using the <frameset> tag.

Now we can decide how many rows and/or columns we want the page to have and what size each should be. These settings are all made within the <frameset> tag.

TRY IT

Exercise 12-1: Setting Up a Framed Page

All of the HTML and graphics files that appear in the figures throughout this chapter are provided on the CD and online at *www.learningwebdesign.com/ materials*. Copy the directory *chap12* to your hard drive to begin.

The step-by-step nature of the chapter will make it easy to follow along. Look for the "Try It" sidebars at critical points in the frameset development.

STEP 1: Open a new document in an HTML editor or Notepad. Type the structure of the frameset as shown in Figure 12-4. Name the document *frameset.html* and make sure that you save it in the *chap12* directory with the other files to ensure the pathnames are correct.

If you want to divide the page into vertical frames (columns), use the `cols` attribute and specify the width measurement for each column, separated by commas (Figure 12-5, left). The number of measurements you provide specifies the number of vertical frames you'll create. Similarly, if you want to create horizontal frames (rows), use the `rows` attribute, followed by the height measurement for each row (Figure 12-5, right).

The number of measurements you provide specifies the number of frames you'll create.

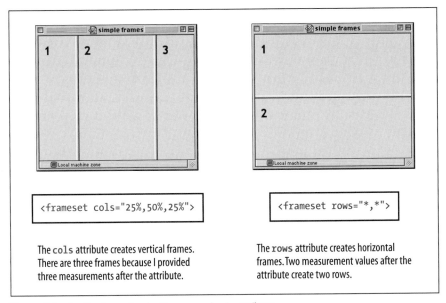

```
<frameset cols="25%,50%,25%">
```

The `cols` attribute creates vertical frames. There are three frames because I provided three measurements after the attribute.

```
<frameset rows="*,*">
```

The `rows` attribute creates horizontal frames. Two measurement values after the attribute create two rows.

Figure 12-5. Creating framesets using the `rows` and `cols` attributes.

When it comes to specifying the measurements, you have some options, as the next section explains.

HTML TIP

Gridlock

You can combine rows and columns to make a grid of frames. The frames will be filled from left to right, top to bottom. This method gives you less flexibility than others described in this chapter.

```
<frameset rows="*,*"
          cols="25%,50%,25%">
   <frame src="1.html">
   <frame src="2.html">
   <frame src="3.html">
   <frame src="4.html">
   <frame src="5.html">
   <frame src="6.html">
</frameset>
```

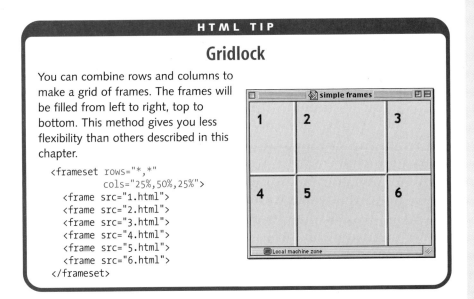

Frame measurements

There are three ways to specify sizes for frames:

Frame measurements can be specified in pixels, percentages, or relative values.

Absolute pixel values. To make a frame a specific pixel size, enter the number of pixels after the `rows` or `cols` attribute. The frameset `<frameset rows="100,400">` creates two horizontal frames, one exactly 100 pixels high, the other exactly 400 pixels high. If the browser window is larger than the combined 500 pixels high, it will enlarge each frame proportionally to fill the window.

Percentages. You can also specify sizes as percentages of the browser window. The frameset `<frameset cols="25%,50%,25%">` creates three columns: the left and right columns always take up 25% of the browser width, and the middle column takes up 50%, regardless of how the window is resized.

Relative values. There's another system that uses asterisks to specify relative values. The best way to explain this is with an example. The frameset `<frameset cols="100,*">` creates two columns: the left column is exactly 100 pixels wide, and the right column fills whatever portion of the window is left. This combination of fixed width and flexible width is one of my personal favorites.

You can also specify relative values in multiples, as in `<frameset cols="100,2*,*">`, which creates a 100-pixel-wide column on the left of the page, then the remainder of the page is divided into two frames; the middle column is always twice the width of the right column.

That said, let's start designing the frames for our new page. I'm going to start with two frames, a narrow one at the top for a banner and the remainder of the page for my content (Figure 12-6).

Figure 12-6. I'm designing my cookbook page to have two rows, a narrow one at the top (50 pixels high) for top-level navigation, and a frame that fills the remainder of the window for content.

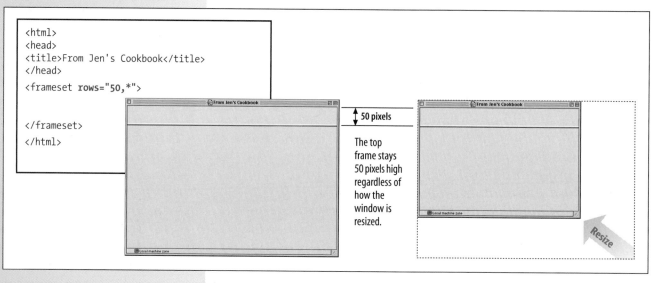

```
<html>
<head>
<title>From Jen's Cookbook</title>
</head>
<frameset rows="50,*">


</frameset>
</html>
```

50 pixels

The top frame stays 50 pixels high regardless of how the window is resized.

Resize

Adding and nesting frames

Now I need to enter the frame information for each row. Frames are added by inserting <frame> tags within the <frameset> tags (Figure 12-7). Within each <frame> tag, the src attribute specifies the URL of the document to load into that frame.

```
<html>
<head>
<title>From Jen's Cookbook</title>
</head>
<frameset rows="50,*">
          <frame src="header.html">
          <frame src="tapenade.html">
</frameset>
</html>
```

Figure 12-7. For each frame, I've added a <frame> tag that tells the browser which HTML document to display in that frame.

TRY IT

Exercise 12-1 (continued)

STEP 2: Add two rows to the frameset as shown in Figure 12-7. Save the file and take a look in a browser. If pages aren't showing up, make sure that the frameset document is saved in the same directory as the other files.

Wait, I just had an idea. I'd like to take that large bottom frame and divide it into two vertical frames. I can do this by nesting a second frameset inside my current frameset. Nesting is done by replacing a <frame> tag with a complete frameset (a <frameset> tag with its <frame> tags).

In Figure 12-8, I've swapped out my bottom <frame> for a <frameset> containing two vertical frames.

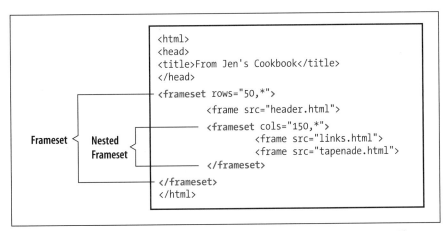

Figure 12-8. To nest frames (fill one frame with another frameset), simply replace the <frame> tag with a complete <frameset>. You can do this as many levels deep as you like. Just make sure you close your <frameset> tags properly.

TRY IT

Exercise 12-1 (continued)

STEP 3: Replace the bottom frame with a two-column frameset as shown in Figure 12-8. Save and view the frameset in a browser.

I've already created the HTML documents (*header.html*, *links.html*, and *tapenade.html*) that will be displayed in each frame. Let's take a look at my framed cookbook page in a browser, as it stands so far (Figure 12-9).

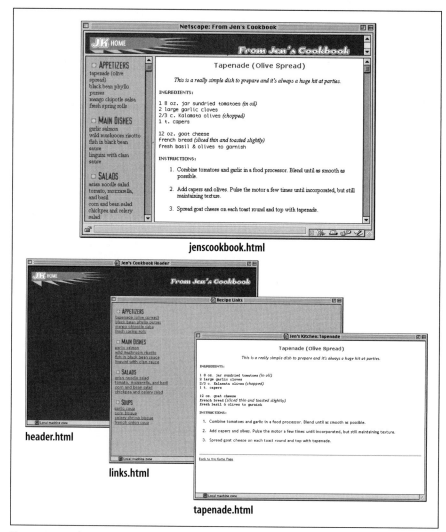

Figure 12-9. My framed cookbook page as it looks in the browser. Below you can see the separate HTML documents that are held together by the frameset.

This is a good start, but I can perform some adjustments to make the page less clunky.

Borders

The last decision I can make at the frameset level (i.e, within the <frameset> tag) is whether I want borders to appear around my frames. If you don't specify otherwise, frames will be divided by thick 3-D bars (as shown in Figure 12-9). To control borders for the entire frameset, use the frameborder and border attributes in the <frameset> tag.*

To turn off the borders completely, making a smooth transition between frames, simply set the border attribute to 0. This works for Netscape Navigator and Microsoft Internet Explorer, Versions 4 and higher. If you want to support Navigator 3 and IE 3, set the frameborder attribute to 0 as well.

You might want to control just the thickness of the borders. If this is the case, set frameborder to 1 ("on") and use the border attribute to specify a pixel thickness.

I definitely don't want borders around my frames, so I'm turning them off at the frameset level (Figure 12-10).

We've done everything we can do with the whole frameset. Now let's see the kinds of things we can tweak within each frame.

You can choose whether to have 3-D borders display around your frames.

TRY IT

Exercise 12-1 *(continued)*
STEP 4: Turn off the borders for the frameset using the border attribute. Save and view.

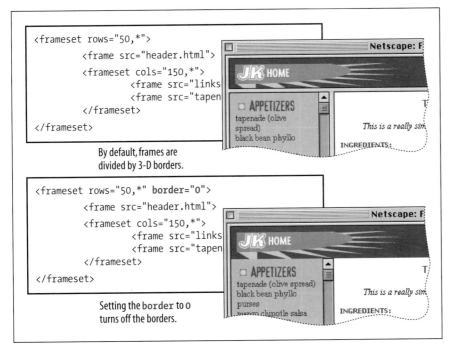

Figure 12-10. Adjusting borders at the frameset level.

---

* The border attribute is not part of the standard HTML specification, but it works fine in the current versions of the major browsers.

Creating a Frameset

Here's how you create a new frameset in three of the more popular authoring programs.

Dreamweaver MX

① One way to create a frameset document is to add a frame to the current document with the Modify → Frameset menu.

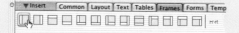

② Alternatively, you can click on a predefined frame icon from the Frames panel of the Object window.

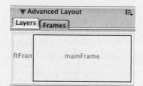

③ The Frames window (accessed from the Windows menu) is used to manage the frameset and its settings.

④ When you select the whole frameset in the Frames window, you can make frame-level settings in the Properties window.

GoLive 6

Frames tab

① First, select the Frame Editor tab at the top of the document window to switch to the Frames Editor view. This view is used to set up and organize the framed document.

② From the Frames tab of the Palette, drag a frame configuration into your document window.

③ Select the frameset by clicking on any border (you can drag the border to resize the frame) and make your frameset settings in the Inspector palette.

FrontPage 2002

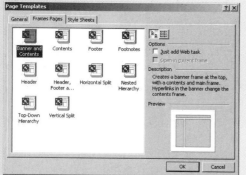

① Create a new document and select the Frames Pages tab. There are a variety of frame templates, each with a short description of suggested use. Choose the frameset closest to the layout you want.

② Pages can then be set or created for each frame. The frames can be modified by moving the frame borders.

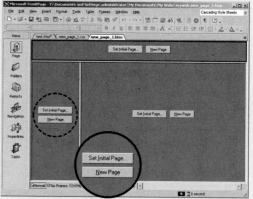

Frame Appearance and Function

At the frame level (that is, within each `<frame>` tag), you can specify three attributes for the frame: whether it has a scrollbar, the margin width, and whether users can resize the frame.

This doesn't seem like much, but remember, everything you see in the frame—the background color or text alignment, for example—is part of the HTML document that is filling the frame. The frameset document itself only has instructions for the frame layout and functionality.

Scrolling

You control whether the frame has a scrollbar with the `scrolling` attribute in the `<frame>` tag. There are three options:

- The default value is `auto`, which means that scrollbars will appear only if the content of the frame is too big to entirely fit in the window.

- If you want to make sure that a scrollbar is always available, regardless of the content, set the `scrolling` value to `yes`.

- If you want to make sure that scrollbars never appear to clutter up your frameset, set the value to `no`. Be careful with this one, particularly if your frame contains text. If the fonts are set too large on a viewer's browser, there will be no way for her to access content that runs out of the frame without a scrollbar.

On my frameset, I'd like the top frame to never scroll, since I'm just using it for a banner (Figure 12-11). Since my other frames contain content that could potentially run out of the user's available browser space, I'll allow them to have scrollbars on an as-needed basis. Because scrolling is set to `auto` by default, I don't need to add any code to achieve this effect.

Figure 12-11. I've removed the scrollbar from my top frame by setting the `scrolling` attribute to `no` in the `<frame>` tag for that frame.

DESIGN TIP

Space for Scrollbars

When scrollbars are visible, they take up some of the width of the frame. So be sure to figure in the width of a scrollbar when calculating frame sizes in precise pixel measurements. On a Macintosh, scrollbars are 15 pixels wide; on a PC, they're 12 pixels wide.

TRY IT

Exercise 12-1 *(continued)*

STEP 5: Turn off scrolling in the top frame as shown in Figure 12-11. Save and view.

Setting margins

Browsers automatically add a little space between the edge of the frame and its contents, just as they do for a web page in the browser. You can control the margin amount inside each frame by adding extra space or setting the contents flush to the frame's edge.

The `marginheight` attribute controls the pixel width of the margin at the top and bottom edges of the frame. The `marginwidth` attribute controls the space on the left and right edges. Figure 12-12 shows examples of these attributes.

BUG ALERT

Margins Bug in Navigator

There's a weird bug in Netscape Navigator Versions 4.0 and earlier that leaves a 1-pixel margin even if the `marginheight` and `marginwidth` attributes are set to 0. There's not much you can do except camouflage it with a matching background color or image. Netscape 6.0 seems to have corrected the problem.

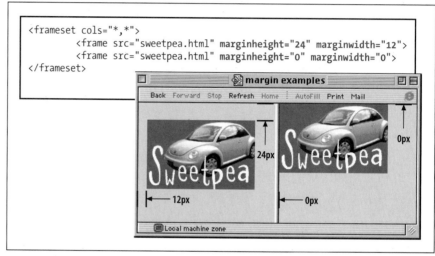

```
<frameset cols="*,*">
        <frame src="sweetpea.html" marginheight="24" marginwidth="12">
        <frame src="sweetpea.html" marginheight="0" marginwidth="0">
</frameset>
```

Figure 12-12. The `marginheight` attribute controls the amount of space between the top and bottom edges of the frame and its contents. `marginwidth` controls the space on the left and right edges.

I'm going to set both margins to 0 in my top frame, to nestle my banner graphic as close as possible into the top-left corner (Figure 12-13).

TRY IT

Exercise 12-1 (continued)

STEP 6: Set the margins to 0 in the top frame as shown in Figure 12-13. Save and view.

```
<frame src="header.html" scrolling="no" marginheight="0" marginwidth="0">
```

Figure 12-13. With `marginwidth` and `marginheight` set to 0, my graphic is positioned flush to the top-left corner of the frame, with no extra space.

Frame resizing

By default, users can resize your frames, overriding your careful size settings, simply by clicking on and dragging the border between frames. You can prevent them from doing this by plopping the noresize attribute in the <frame> tag. I'd like to make that top frame stay put, so I will add the noresize attribute there (Figure 12-14). (I had to temporarily turn on my frame borders to demonstrate the noresize trick; I'll turn them off again for the final product.)

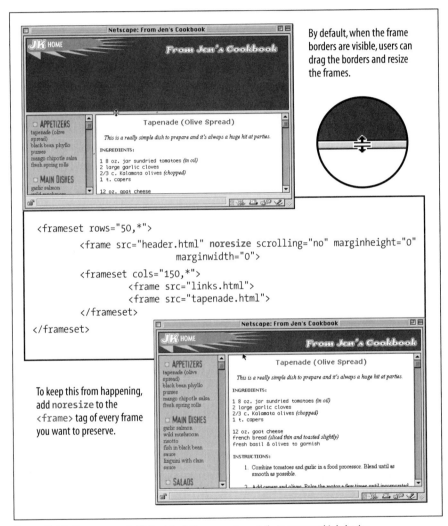

By default, when the frame borders are visible, users can drag the borders and resize the frames.

```
<frameset rows="50,*">
        <frame src="header.html" noresize scrolling="no" marginheight="0"
                        marginwidth="0">
        <frameset cols="150,*">
                <frame src="links.html">
                <frame src="tapenade.html">
        </frameset>
</frameset>
```

To keep this from happening, add noresize to the <frame> tag of every frame you want to preserve.

TRY IT

Exercise 12-1 *(continued)*

STEP 7: Add the noresize attribute to the top frame as shown in Figure 12-14. Save and view.

Figure 12-14. Frames are resizable by default. The noresize attribute prevents this behavior.

Before you go setting all your frames to noresize, consider whether there might be a good reason to allow resizing (such as to view more text in the screen). In my example, users aren't gaining anything by resizing that top frame, so I restricted the ability to change it.

Formatting Frames

Here's how you format individual frames in three of the more popular authoring programs.

Dreamweaver MX

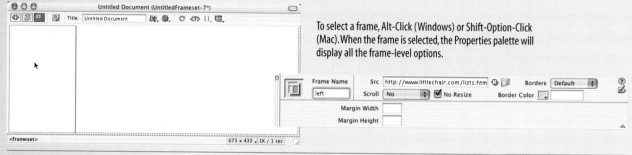

To select a frame, Alt-Click (Windows) or Shift-Option-Click (Mac). When the frame is selected, the Properties palette will display all the frame-level options.

GoLive 6

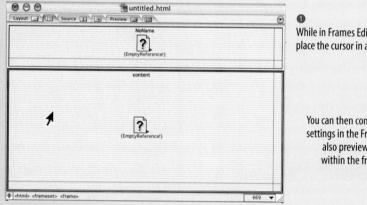

❶ While in Frames Editor view, place the cursor in a frame.

❷ You can then control all the frame-level settings in the Frame Inspector. You can also preview your HTML document within the frame by clicking on the Preview button.

FrontPage 2002

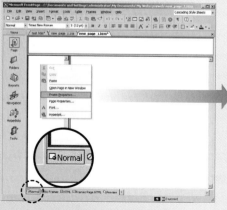

❶ Open the frames page you want to modify, and click the Normal tab.

❷ Place the cursor in the frame to be modified and right-click to bring up a shortcut menu. Go to Frame Properties and specify the settings to control the look of the frame.

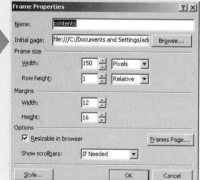

❸ To set the border, click the Frames Page button (this window can also be accessed from File → Properties → Frames tab).

Targeting Frames

Now that you've gotten the hang of setting up framed documents, it's time to tackle one last aspect of frames: making sure linked documents load into the correct frame.

When you click on a link in an ordinary browser window, the new page replaces the current one in the browser window. The same thing happens by default within a frame. When you click on a link in a frame, the linked document will load in that same frame (after all, a frame is just a mini–browser window).

In many cases, however, you want the linked document to load in a different frame, such as when you have a list of links in one frame and your content in another. In these instances, you need to tell the link which frame to use—in other words, you need to target a specific frame.

Naming the frame

Before you can target a frame, you need to give it a name using the name attribute in the <frame> tag ❶ (Figure 12-15, following page). I'd like to load my content documents into the main frame on the page, so I've given that frame the name "main".

```
<frame src="salmon.html" name="main">
```

Targeting the frame

Now I can point to that frame from any link ❷. My left frame contains a document (*links.html*) with a list of links. Within *links.html*, I add the target attribute to each of my links and set the value to "main". When someone clicks on that link, the browser will load the new document in the frame called "main":

```
<a href="risotto.html" target="main">wild mushroom risotto</a><br>
```

Reserved target names

There are four standardized target names for specific targeting actions. Note that they all begin with an underscore (_). You should avoid giving frames names that begin with an underscore because they will be ignored by the browser. The reserved target names are:

_top

> When you set the target to _top, the new document is loaded in the top level of the browser window, replacing all the frames with a single window. A document that is linked using target="_top" breaks out of its frameset and is displayed in the full browser window.

Setting the Target for a Whole Document

If you want all the links on a page to point to the same window, you can specify the target in the header of the document using the <base> tag, as follows:

```
<head>
<base target="main">
</head>
```

With this specification in the head of the document, all the links on that page will automatically load in the "main" frame (unless specified otherwise in the link). This technique saves extra typing and keeps the file size down.

```
<frameset rows="50,*" border="0">
        <frame src="header.html" scrolling="no" marginheight="0" marginwidth="0">
        <frameset cols="150,*">
                <frame src="links.html" name="links" >
                <frame src="salmon.html" name="main" >
        </frameset>
</frameset>
```

jenscookbook.html

❶ First, give the frame a name
so you can refer to it later.

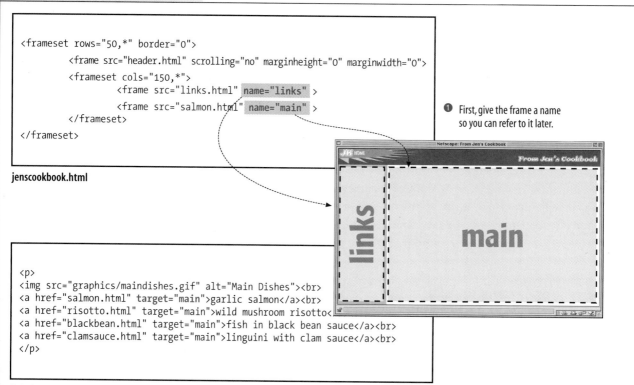

```
<p>
<img src="graphics/maindishes.gif" alt="Main Dishes"><br>
<a href="salmon.html" target="main">garlic salmon</a><br>
<a href="risotto.html" target="main">wild mushroom risotto<
<a href="blackbean.html" target="main">fish in black bean sauce</a><br>
<a href="clamsauce.html" target="main">linguini with clam sauce</a><br>
</p>
```

links.html

❷ Then, in the html document that
contains the link, use the target
attribute in the anchor tag (<a>)
to call the frame by name.

Now, when a user clicks on that link,
the linked document will open in
the specified frame.

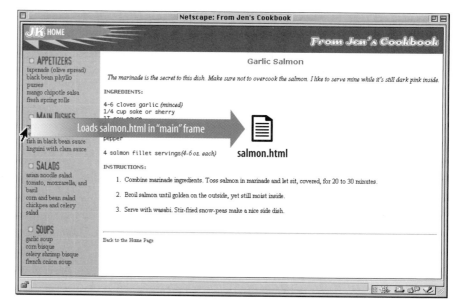

Figure 12-15. Naming a frame allows you to
target your links to a specific frame.

_parent

> This target name causes the linked document to load into the parent frame (the frameset that is one step up in the nested frame hierarchy). This causes some breaking out as well, but only to the next frame level.

_self

> This causes the document to load in the same frame. Since this action is the default for all frames, you generally don't need to specify it. However, it might be useful if you need to override a target set with the `<base>` tag introduced earlier.

_blank

> A link with `target="_blank"` opens a new browser window to display the linked document. This is not necessarily a frame-related value—you can use it from any web page. Bear in mind, however, that each time a link that targets _blank is clicked, the browser launches a new window, potentially leaving the user with a mess of open browser windows. By contrast, when a target window is given a specific name (such as `sample` or `new`), it will be reused by all links that specify that name.

I'm going to need to take advantage of the _top value in my documents. The top frame contains a graphic link to the home page. If I leave it as it is, the home page will load in that little sliver of a frame. To break out of the frames and get back to a normal browser window, I'll target the top level in that link (Figure 12-16).

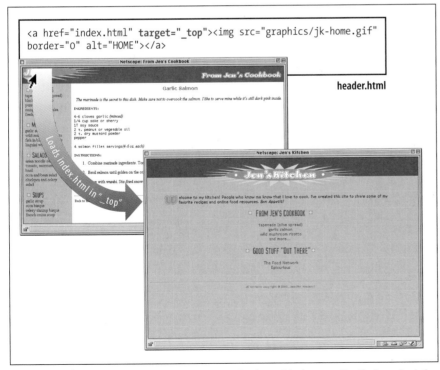

```
<a href="index.html" target="_top"><img src="graphics/jk-home.gif"
border="0" alt="HOME"></a>
```

header.html

Figure 12-16. The _top target value makes the home page break out of the frames and load in the top level of the browser window.

TRY IT

Exercise 12-1 *(continued)*

STEP 8: Name each of the frames as shown in Figure 12-15.

STEP 9: Set the appropriate targets for the links so the frameset functions properly:

- In *header.html*, make sure that the home graphic links to the top level of the browser window (Figure 12-16).

- In *links.html*, use the `<base>` element in the `<head>` of the document to make all of the links on the page link to the `main` window.

Save and view the frameset in the browser. Test the links to be sure that they load in the proper frames (a few recipe files have been provided for testing). Be sure the links back to the home page on each recipe page load in the top frame.

Note that this is only an exercise and not a fully designed and functioning site. In the files provided there is no way to get back to the frameset from the sample home page document.

Content for Users Without Frames

The last thing you should add to your frameset document is some content that will display for users without frames-enabled browsers. This benefits users who have older browsers (or text-only browsers) that don't support frames, as well as users who have turned off frames support in their browser preferences. You place your alternative content between <noframes> tags.

Many people simply use a message such as "You need a frames-enabled browser to view this page." While this is acceptable, it is preferable to put a full page of content, including links to deeper pages of your site, within the <noframes> tags. For one thing, this provides actual content and navigation to users who are using non-frames-enabled browsers (they may be using them for a good reason). In addition, it gives major search engines something to index on your page as well as access to content linked to that page. If there are only frameset and frame tags on the page, the page will be ignored.

Between the <noframes> tags, add everything you would put in an ordinary non-framed document. This includes the <body> tag with its attributes for setting background tiles and colors. Figure 12-17 shows the <noframes> content I've provided for my "From Jen's Cookbook" frameset.

noframes content prevents your framed document from becoming a dead end to search engines and users without frames-enabled browsers.

TRY IT

Exercise 12-1 *(continued)*

STEP 10: Add minimal <noframes> content to the frameset document. Make sure that it is useful for users who don't have frames.

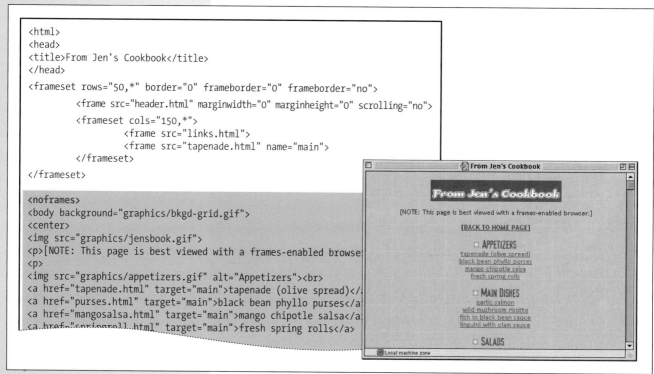

Figure 12-17. The content I've provided within <noframes> tags will appear in any browser that does not support frames. My "noframes" content provides similar functionality and a similar look to the framed document.

Test Yourself

Answers to these frames questions can be found in the Appendix.

1. What makes frameset documents different from all other HTML documents?

2. What are the disadvantages of frames that have made them unpopular in the the industry?

3. In the space on the right, sketch the frameset that results from the following code:

    a. `<frameset cols="*,*,*">`

    b. `<frameset rows="*,3*">`

    c. `<frameset rows="*,*" cols="50%,50%">`

4. How do you make a linked document appear in the top level of the browser, instead of within the frame?

5. Write the code for the frameset shown in Figure 12-18. Place a document called *empty.html* in each frame. Your column and row measurements can be approximate.

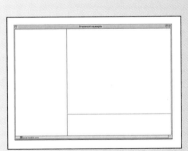

Figure 12-18. A simple frameset.

HTML Review: Frame Tags

The following is a summary of the tags we covered in this chapter:

Tag and attributes	Function
`<frameset>`	Indicates the body of a framed document
`border="number"`	Border thickness in pixels when border is on
`cols="measurements"`	Number of columns (vertical frames)
`frameborder="1|0"`	Specifies whether borders appear between the frames (1 is yes; 0 is no)
`rows="measurements"`	Number of rows (horizontal frames)
`<frame>`	Adds a frame to a framed document
`marginwidth="number"`	Pixel space held on the left edge of the frame
`marginheight="number"`	Pixel space held on the top edge of the frame
`name="text"`	Name of the frame (for targeting)
`scrolling="yes|no|auto"`	Specifies whether scrollbars appear in the frame
`src="url"`	Name of the file to load in the frame
`<noframes>`	Content that will display in a non-frames browser

Color on the Web

In past chapters, we've come across several opportunities to specify colors in our HTML code. There are two methods for doing this: by name or by numeric value. Not surprisingly, both methods are quirky. Let's start with the least complicated.

Specifying Colors by Name

You can specify a color using one of 140 standard color names. Some names are normal ("red," "brown," "white"), while many are sort of silly (my favorites are "burlywood" and "papayawhip"). The set of names was originally developed for a Unix windowing system and was adopted early on by the creators of the Web.

To use a color name, insert it as the value for any attribute that calls for a color specification (Figure 13-1).

Table 13-1 (next page) lists the complete color name list by hue. To view a sample of each color, see the chart on the web page for this book at *www.learningwebdesign.com/colornames.html*.

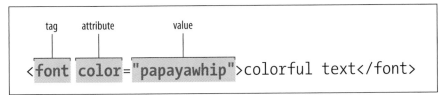

```
          tag     attribute          value

       <font color="papayawhip">colorful text</font>
```

Figure 13-1. Use a color name as the value of any color setting attribute.

Table 13-1. Web color names by hue

black
white

Cool neutrals
darkgray
darkslategray
dimgray
gainsboro
ghostwhite
gray
lightgray
lightslategray
silver
slategray
snow
whitesmoke

Warm neutrals
antiquewhite
cornsilk
floralwhite
ivory
linen
oldlace
papayawhip
seashell

Browns/tans
beige
bisque
blanchedalmond
brown
burlywood
chocolate
khaki
moccasin
navahowhite
peru
rosybrown
saddlebrown
sandybrown
sienna
tan
wheat

Oranges
darkorange
orange
orangered
peachpuff

Yellows
darkgoldenrod
gold
goldenrod
lemonchiffon
lightgoldenrodyellow
lightyellow
palegoldenrod
yellow

Greens
aquamarine
chartreuse
darkgreen
darkkhaki
darkolivegreen
darkseagreen
forestgreen
green
greenyellow
honeydew
lawngreen
lightgreen
lime
limegreen
mediumseagreen
mediumspringgreen
mintcream
olive
olivedrab
palegreen
seagreen
springgreen
yellowgreen

Blue-greens
aqua
cyan
darkcyan
darkturquoise
lightcyan
lightseagreen
mediumaquamarine
mediumturquoise
paleturquoise
teal
turquoise

Blues
aliceblue
azure
blue
cadetblue
cornflowerblue
darkblue
darkslateblue
deepskyblue
dodgerblue
indigo
lightblue
lightskyblue
lightsteelblue
mediumblue
mediumslateblue
midnightblue
navy
powderblue
royalblue
skyblue
slateblue
steelblue

Purples
blueviolet
darkmagenta
darkorchid
darkviolet
fuchsia
lavender
lavenderblush
mediumorchid
mediumpurple
mediumvioletred
orchid
palevioletred
plum
purple
thistle
violet

Pinks
coral
darksalmon
deeppink
hotpink
lightcoral
lightpink
lightsalmon
magenta
mistyrose
pink
salmon

Reds
crimson
darkred
firebrick
indianred
maroon
red
tomato

Specifying Colors by Number

The more precise way to specify color is to provide the numeric description of the color. For those who are not familiar with how computers deal with color, I'll start with the basics before jumping into the HTML.

A word about RGB color

Computers create the colors you see on a monitor by combining three colors of light: red, green, and blue. This color model is known as RGB color. When you mix full intensities of the three colors, they blend together to create white (Figure 13-2 G).

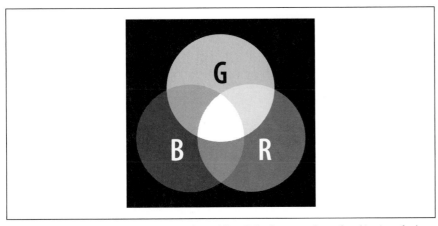

Figure 13-2. Computer monitors use the RGB color model in which colors are made up of combinations of red, green, and blue light. RGB color is additive. For example, if you mix all three colors at full intensity you get white. G

You can provide recipes (of sorts) for colors by telling the computer how much of each color to mix in. The amount of light in each color "channel" is described on a scale from 0 (none) to 255 (full-blast). The closer the three values get to 255, the closer the resulting color gets to white.

So, any color you see on your monitor can be described by a series of three numbers: the red value, the green value, and the blue value. With the RGB color system, a pleasant lavender can be described as 200, 178, 230.

This is one of the ways that image editors (such as Adobe Photoshop or Macromedia Fireworks) keep track of colors. Every pixel in an image is described in terms of its RGB color values. You can use an image editor to find the RGB values for the colors you want to use.

> *Computers create colors by combining red, green, and blue light (thus "RGB color"). The amount of light in each color "channel" is given a value from 1 to 255. You can specify any RGB color by providing its numeric values.*

Let's say I want to match elements on my web page to a certain yellow-orange that appears in one of my graphics. Using Adobe Photoshop, I can find out the RGB values of any color in my image by positioning the pointer over my chosen color and reading the RGB values in the Info palette (Figure 13-3 G).

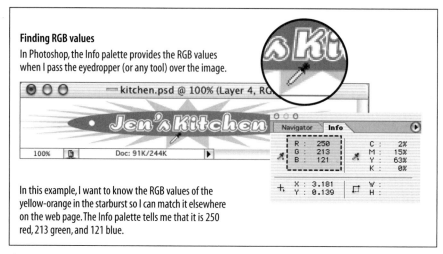

Finding RGB values

In Photoshop, the Info palette provides the RGB values when I pass the eyedropper (or any tool) over the image.

In this example, I want to know the RGB values of the yellow-orange in the starburst so I can match it elsewhere on the web page. The Info palette tells me that it is 250 red, 213 green, and 121 blue.

Figure 13-3. Photoshop has a tool to allow you to find the RGB values of a color. G

Hexadecimal values

Now that I know the RGB values for my yellow-orange color, I should be able to plug them right into my HTML, right? Unfortunately, it's not that straightforward.

Browsers want their RGB number values as hexadecimal, not decimal, numbers. The hexadecimal numbering system is base-16 instead of base-10 (base-10 is the decimal system we're used to). Hexadecimal uses 16 digits (0–9 and A–F) to make up numbers. Figure 13-4 shows how this works.

Figure 13-4. The hexadecimal numbering system is base-16. It uses the characters 0–9 and A–F (for representing the quantities 10–15).

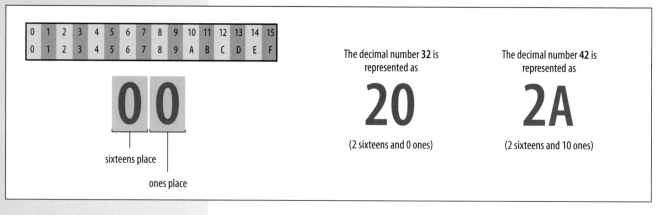

The decimal number **32** is represented as

20

(2 sixteens and 0 ones)

The decimal number **42** is represented as

2A

(2 sixteens and 10 ones)

The hexadecimal system is used widely in computing to reduce the space it takes to store certain information. For instance, our RGB values are reduced from three to two characters once they are converted to hexadecimal ("hex" for short) values.

The easiest way to find out the hex color values for your selected color is to get them from the Color Picker in Photoshop (Versions 5.5 and higher), as shown in Figure 13-5. Most graphics and web development software today provide easy access to hexadecimal color values.

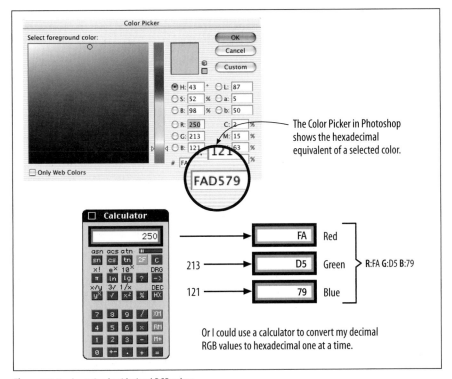

Figure 13-5. Accessing hexidecimal RGB values.

If that is not an option for you, you can use a calculator to convert each RGB value to hexadecimal (see the Hexadecimal Calculators sidebar). For your convenience, a decimal-to-hexadecimal chart has been provided in Table 13-2 (following page).

Using either method, I can determine that the hex value for my orange-yellow color is FAD579 (R:250=FA, G:213=D5, B:121=79).

Hexadecimal Calculators

In Windows, the standard calculator has a hexadecimal converter in the Scientific view. Mac users can download a copy of Calculator II (*ftp://ftp.amug.org/pub/ mirrors/info-mac/sci/calc/ calculator-ii-15.hqx*).

Just enter the decimal number for each color value and hit the HEX conversion button. Make a note of the resulting 2-digit hex value.

Of course, you could calculate a hex value yourself by dividing your number by 16 to get the first number, and then using the remainder for the second number. So, 200 equals C8 because 200=(16 × 12) + 8. That's {12,8} in base-16, or C8 in hexadecimal. Whew! I think I'll be sticking with my color picker.

Table 13-2. Decimal to hexadecimal equivalents

dec = hex	dec = hex	dec = hex	dec = hex	dec = hex	dec = hex
0 = 00	51 = 33	102 = 66	153 = 99	204 = CC	255 = FF
1 = 01	52 = 34	103 = 67	154 = 9A	205 = CD	
2 = 02	53 = 35	104 = 68	155 = 9B	206 = CE	
3 = 03	54 = 36	105 = 69	156 = 9C	207 = CF	
4 = 04	55 = 37	106 = 6A	157 = 9D	208 = D0	
5 = 05	56 = 38	107 = 6B	158 = 9E	209 = D1	
6 = 06	57 = 39	108 = 6C	159 = 9F	210 = D2	
7 = 07	58 = 3A	109 = 6D	160 = A0	211 = D3	
8 = 08	59 = 3B	110 = 6E	161 = A1	212 = D4	
9 = 09	60 = 3C	111 = 6F	162 = A2	213 = D5	
10 = 0A	61 = 3D	112 = 70	163 = A3	214 = D6	
11 = 0B	62 = 3E	113 = 71	164 = A4	215 = D7	
12 = 0C	63 = 3F	114 = 72	165 = A5	216 = D8	
13 = 0D	64 = 40	115 = 73	166 = A6	217 = D9	
14 = 0E	65 = 41	116 = 74	167 = A7	218 = DA	
15 = 0F	66 = 42	117 = 75	168 = A8	219 = DB	
16 = 10	67 = 43	118 = 76	169 = A9	220 = DC	
17 = 11	68 = 44	119 = 77	170 = AA	221 = DD	
18 = 12	69 = 45	120 = 78	171 = AB	222 = DE	
19 = 13	70 = 46	121 = 79	172 = AC	223 = DF	
20 = 14	71 = 47	122 = 7A	173 = AD	224 = E0	
21 = 15	72 = 48	123 = 7B	174 = AE	225 = E1	
22 = 16	73 = 49	124 = 7C	175 = AF	226 = E2	
23 = 17	74 = 4A	125 = 7D	176 = B0	227 = E3	
24 = 18	75 = 4B	126 = 7E	177 = B1	228 = E4	
25 = 19	76 = 4C	127 = 7F	178 = B2	229 = E5	
26 = 1A	77 = 4D	128 = 80	179 = B3	230 = E6	
27 = 1B	78 = 4E	129 = 81	180 = B4	231 = E7	
28 = 1C	79 = 4F	130 = 82	181 = B5	232 = E8	
29 = 1D	80 = 50	131 = 83	182 = B6	233 = E9	
30 = 1E	81 = 51	132 = 84	183 = B7	234 = EA	
31 = 1F	82 = 52	133 = 85	184 = B8	235 = EB	
32 = 20	83 = 53	134 = 86	185 = B9	236 = EC	
33 = 21	84 = 54	135 = 87	186 = BA	237 = ED	
34 = 22	85 = 55	136 = 88	187 = BB	238 = EE	
35 = 23	86 = 56	137 = 89	188 = BC	239 = EF	
36 = 24	87 = 57	138 = 8A	189 = BD	240 = F0	
37 = 25	88 = 58	139 = 8B	190 = BE	241 = F1	
38 = 26	89 = 59	140 = 8C	191 = BF	242 = F2	
39 = 27	90 = 5A	141 = 8D	192 = C0	243 = F3	
40 = 28	91 = 5B	142 = 8E	193 = C1	244 = F4	
41 = 29	92 = 5C	143 = 8F	194 = C2	245 = F5	
42 = 2A	93 = 5D	144 = 90	195 = C3	246 = F6	
43 = 2B	94 = 5E	145 = 91	196 = C4	247 = F7	
44 = 2C	95 = 5F	146 = 92	197 = C5	248 = F8	
45 = 2D	96 = 60	147 = 93	198 = C6	249 = F9	
46 = 2E	97 = 61	148 = 94	199 = C7	250 = FA	
47 = 2F	98 = 62	149 = 95	200 = C8	251 = FB	
48 = 30	99 = 63	150 = 96	201 = C9	252 = FC	
49 = 31	100 = 64	151 = 97	202 = CA	253 = FD	
50 = 32	101 = 65	152 = 98	203 = CB	254 = FE	

Using RGB values in HTML

Now we are ready to insert the hexadecimal RGB value in our HTML code. Color values are written into HTML in the following syntax: "#RRGGBB" (Figure 13-6).

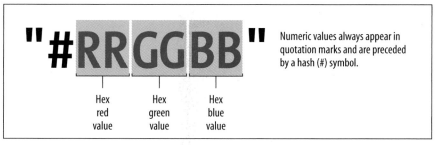

Numeric values always appear in quotation marks and are preceded by a hash (#) symbol.

Hex red value   Hex green value   Hex blue value

Figure 13-6. Putting color values into HTML.

For example, if I want to make a table cell the same yellow-orange as my banner graphic, I use the hexadecimal values I calculated in Figure 13-5 after the bgcolor attribute, as shown in Figure 13-7.

```
<td bgcolor="#FAD579">
```

Figure 13-7. The tag needed to use my yellow-orange as the background color in a table cell.

Quick summary

It took us a few pages to get here, but the process is actually easy: find the RGB values of the color you want to use (your image-editing tool may even provide the hex values), convert each value to hexadecimal if you need to, and put them in the tag. Be sure to include the hash (#) mark at the beginning.

HTML TIP

Handy Hex Values

White = #FFFFFF
(the equivalent of 255,255,255)

Black = #000000
(the equivalent of 0,0,0)

Elements You Can Color with HTML

Now that you know *how* to set colors in HTML, let's look at all the things you *can* color. We've run across them in past HTML chapters, but it is useful to look at the big picture.

Document-wide color settings

The `<body>` tag is used to structure the document, but it also has attributes that apply color settings for the entire document. You can use any number and combination of the following attributes in a single `<body>` tag:

`<body bgcolor="`*color-name or number*`">`
> Sets a solid background color for the entire document.

`<body text="`*color-name or number*`">`
> Specifies the default text color for the entire document. The default color is black. You can override the default color of any text using the `<font color>` tag (or the `color` style sheet property).

`<body link="`*color-name or number*`">`
> Specifies the color used for all links in the document. In most browsers, the default color is bright blue. (See the sidebar Coloring Individual Links for information on how to override the global link color setting.)

`<body vlink="`*color-name or number*`">`
> Sets the color of all visited links. A visited link is one that has already been clicked on and followed. The default color is purple.

`<body alink="`*color-name or number*`">`
> Sets the color of all active links. The active link color shows up only as the link is in the process of being clicked—so it is a fleeting color, but it does provide useful visual feedback to the user.

> Remember, you can use either color names or hexadecimal color descriptions as the values for any of these attributes.

Coloring Individual Links

Setting the link color in the `<body>` tag changes the color of all the links in the document. If you want a link to be different from the global link color, use the `<font>` tag with the `color` attribute. In order for it to work, the opening and closing `<font>` tags need to be entirely enclosed within the anchor (`<a>`) tags, as shown here:

```
<a href="foo.html"><font
color="seagreen">Click
here!</font></a>
```

A better method is to use Cascading Style Sheets. Give the links you want to override a `class` name, then change their color with the style sheet rule:

```
<a href="foo.html"
class="special">Click here!</a>
<style>
a.special {color: red}
</style>
```

Be aware that consistent link colors are important to good site usability, so use caution when changing the color of individual links. It should only be done for good reason.

AT A GLANCE

Color-Ready

The following tags and attributes accept color values:

`<body bgcolor>`	`<body vlink>`	`<tr bgcolor>`
`<body text>`	`<font color>`	`<td bgcolor>`
`<body link>`	`<basefont color>`	`<th bgcolor>`
`<body alink>`	`<table bgcolor>`	

Coloring text

You can specify colors for any text selection using the `color` attribute in the `<font>` tag (see Chapter 7 for more information about the `<font>` and `<basefont>` tags):

`<font color="`*color-name or number*`">`
> Changes the color of content between the container tags. Text color set with the `<font>` tag overrides color settings in the `<body>` tag.

`<basefont color="`*color-name or number*`">`
> Changes the color of all the text following the tag (except if it is in a table). `basefont` can also be used to adjust the size of following text with the `size` attribute.

> Although the `color` attribute is in the HTML specification and supported by Internet Explorer Version 3 and higher, Netscape Navigator does not support it in the `<basefont>` tag. For this reason, setting text colors with this method is unreliable.

Table backgrounds

You can color the backgrounds of cells and tables using the `bgcolor` attribute in the standard table tags (see Chapter 10 for more information on these tags):

`<table bgcolor="`*color-name or number*`">`
> Applies a background color to all the cells in a table. This attribute is implemented differently across browsers. Microsoft Internet Explorer makes the table a solid block of color, while some browsers (such as Netscape Navigator 4.7 and earlier) only fill the cell space with color, leaving the border and any cell spacing the same color as the background of the page, which results in a checkered look.

`<tr bgcolor="`*color-name or number*`">`
> Applies a background color to every cell in that row. Settings in the row tag override color settings in the `<table>` tag.

`<td bgcolor="`*color-name or number*`">`
> Specifies the background color of an individual cell. Color settings in the cell tag override color settings at the row and table level.

`<th bgcolor="`*color-name or number*`">`
> Specifies the background color of header cells. Like `<td>` settings, settings in the header override row- and table-level settings.

`<table bordercolor="`*color name or number*`">`
`<table bordercolorlight="`*color name or number*`">`
`<table bordercolordark="`*color name or number*`">`
> These nonstandard attributes specify the colors of the border around a table, its highlight color, and its shadow color, respectively. They are supported by Internet Explorer only.

Coloring Elements with Style Sheets

Similarly, color can be applied to elements on a web page using Cascading Style Sheet properties. Style sheet properties are explained in Chapter 8.

The following properties can be applied to just about any object on a page, including blocks of text, spans of text, table elements, even images:

color: "*color-name or number*"
> Sets the foreground color of a given element. When applied to text elements, it sets the text color.

background-color: "*color-name or number*"
> Sets the background color of a given element. Every element is treated as though it is in a rectangular box; setting the background color fills this bounding box with color.

border-color: "*color-name or number*"
> Sets the color of the overall border of an element.

The Web Palette

If you spend any time at all in the web biz, you will surely hear the term "web palette" sooner or later. It also goes by the names "web-safe colors," "the Netscape palette," and "the browser-safe palette," just to name a few. As a web designer, it is important to understand the web palette concept and its applications.

What it is

Before we launch into the web palette, let's talk a little about palettes in general. A palette is just a set of colors. Palettes come in handy for computers that can display only a limited number of colors, such as 8-bit monitors that can display a maximum of 256 colors at a time. PCs with 8-bit color have a palette of 256 system colors that they use to display images on the screen. Macs have a similar system palette.

The web palette is the specific set of 216 colors that will stay solid and consistent when viewed in a browser on Macs or PCs. The major browsers use colors from this built-in web palette only when they are running on computers with 8-bit (256 colors) monitors. Because the palette is part of the browser software, this is a way of ensuring that the graphics will look more or less the same on all platforms.

The web palette in its natural habitat can be seen on the web page for this book at *www.learningwebdesign.com/webpalette.html*. You can also access the web palette easily in web-authoring tools, usually from a pop-up window of color choices (see the Tool Tip at the end of this chapter).

TIP

Chapter 15 has more information about the web palette as it relates to graphic production, including how to access the web palette swatches in Adobe Photoshop and Macromedia Fireworks.

The web palette is a set of 216 predefined colors that will not dither on Macs or PCs.

You'll probably notice the large percentage of fluorescent shades and otherwise unpleasant colors. Unfortunately, because the colors in the web palette were selected mathematically, not aesthetically, many of the colors wouldn't be your first choice.

How it works

On monitors with millions (24-bit) or thousands (16-bit) of colors, browsers don't need to refer to a palette to render colors accurately. But on 8-bit monitors with only 256 colors available, many colors from the full visual range must be approximated using the colors on hand.

Browsers are stuck using just the 216 colors from the web palette to do this approximating. Most will fill in the extra 40 colors of the possible 256 from the user's system palette.

When a color from the full color space (millions of RGB colors) is rendered on an 8-bit monitor, the browser does the best it can to represent the color using colors from the web palette. Depending on the color, it may be shifted to the nearest web-safe equivalent or be approximated by blending two colors from the web palette in a process called dithering (Figure 13-8). The results can be unpredictable and are most undesirable in text and areas of flat color. In continuous tone images, such as photographs, dithering is not as big of a problem; in fact, it can even be beneficial.

The web palette only comes into play on 8-bit monitors.

What Makes Colors "Safe"

The 216 web palette colors are the colors shared by the Windows and Mac system palettes. This means that colors chosen from the web palette will render accurately on Mac or PC displays without shifting or dithering. That's why they're called web-"safe" colors—they stay true on both platforms. (Unfortunately, the Unix operating system was left out of this equation.)

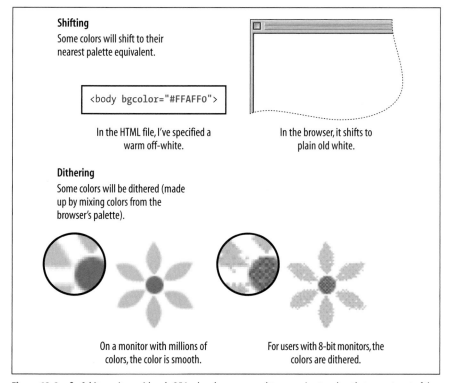

Shifting
Some colors will shift to their nearest palette equivalent.

`<body bgcolor="#FFAFF0">`

In the HTML file, I've specified a warm off-white.

In the browser, it shifts to plain old white.

Dithering
Some colors will be dithered (made up by mixing colors from the browser's palette).

On a monitor with millions of colors, the color is smooth.

For users with 8-bit monitors, the colors are dithered.

Figure 13-8. On 8-bit monitors with only 256 colors, browsers need to approximate colors that are not part of the web palette.

Is the Web Palette Obsolete?

Browsers resort to the web palette only when they are running on 8-bit monitors (256 colors). In the early days of the Web, that accounted for the majority of color monitors out there.

But things have changed since 1994. As of this writing, users with 8-bit monitors make up only 2–5% of total web traffic. More than half of web browsing is done on monitors with thousands of colors (16-bit, also known as high color), and the remaining 40 percent or so use 24- or 32-bit moniors that support the true color space (millions of colors).

In my opinion, it is time to stop worrying about a browser palette that is irrelevent to as much as 98% of your audience. Those 8-bit users are accustomed to things not looking so slick anyway.

However, at this time, the web development industry still takes the web palette pretty seriously. Companies make sure to specify web-safe equivalents for their corporate colors and may insist that the rest of their site be web-safe as well. So, for the time being, you still need to know about the web palette and how to use it.

For a more detailed and technical explanation of these issues, read "Death of the Websafe Color Palette?" by David Lehn and Hadley Stern on Webmonkey (*hotwired.lycos.com/webmonkey/00/37/index2a.html*). The article was written in 2000 but is even more relevent today.

The web palette in numbers

An important way to look at the web palette is by its numeric values. The palette recognizes six shades of red, six shades of green, and six shades of blue, resulting in 216 possible color values (6 × 6 × 6 = 216). That is why it is sometimes called the "6 × 6 × 6 color cube."

Those six shades in decimal values are 0, 51, 102, 153, 204, and 255. These translate to 00, 33, 66, 99, CC, and FF in hexadecimal. It's easy to recognize a web-safe color in HTML code because it is a combination of these six hex values: #6699FF and #0033CC are web-safe, #FAD579 is not.

Table 13-3 shows the decimal, hexadecimal, and percentage values for each of the six component values in the web palette.

Table 13-3. Numerical values for web palette colors

Decimal	Hexadecimal	Percentage
0 (darkest)	00	0%
51	33	20%
102	66	40%
153	99	60%
204	CC	80%
255 (lightest)	FF	100%

Web-safe color names

Of the 140 standard color names, only 10 are from the web palette. They are:

aqua	black	blue	cyan	fuchsia
lime	magenta	red	white	yellow

What this means to you

Now you know that when browsers are running on 8-bit monitors, they use colors from their built-in palette of 216 web-safe colors to approximate the colors on the page. How can this help you?

Since you know *exactly* which color values will not dither, you can use the web palette to your advantage by designing with those colors in the first place. You'll beat the browser to the task. This way, you can ensure that your colors and your graphics look the same to the maximum number of users. You can prevent the color shifts and blotchy dithering that result when the browser remaps colors to the web palette.

In addition, you will find that many web design firms and their clients require designers to use colors from the web palette for consistency in quality. The web palette applies to all colors on the page, whether specified in HTML or as part of a graphic. We'll discuss designing graphics with the web palette in Chapter 15.

Accessing the Web Palette

With so much emphasis placed on the web-safe palette, it is becoming a standard feature of web-authoring software tools. The tools provide an easy visual interface to select web-safe colors for your web page elements, and they take care of filling in the HTML code for you.

Here's how you access the web palette in three of the more popular authoring programs.

Dreamweaver MX

Clicking on the Palette icon ( ) in the Properties window or any dialog box pops up a web-safe color palette. Choose a color by clicking on it with the eyedropper pointer (it will even show you the hex values as you pass the cursor over the squares).

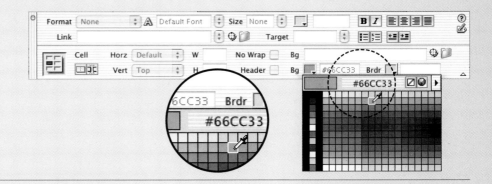

GoLive 6

All colors are managed by the Color Palette.

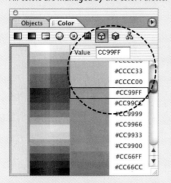

If you choose the Real Web Colors tab ( ), you can select colors from the complete web palette. Simply drag the color from the Color Palette to the highlighted object or field to apply the color.

FrontPage 2002

Color can be applied from the Properties window or most dialog boxes. A few web-safe choices are typically given, with access to a complete web-safe palette. Choose a color by clicking on it with the eyedropper pointer. The hex value will appear as the eyedropper moves over each color.

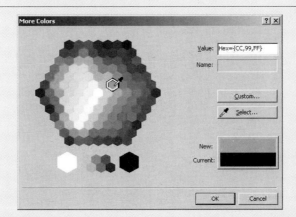

Test Yourself

Take some time to answer these questions about using color in HTML. The answers are in the Appendix.

1. Where did the 140 standard color names come from?

2. What does RGB stand for?

3. What color is R: 255, G: 255, B: 255 (or FFFFFF in hexadecimal)?

4. Where do the colors in the web palette come from? Why is the web palette useful? Why might might it not be useful one day?

5. What is the HTML code that makes the background color of a table a light green with the values of R:277, G:249, and B:187? (Use Table 13-2 for conversions.)

6. Which of the following hex color values is web-safe?

   a. B5B5B5
   b. CCFF33
   c. 78A2CF
   d. 33DD00

Creating Web Graphics

III

For me—a graphic designer by trade—making the graphics is the fun part of web design. But in the beginning, I needed to learn to adapt my style and process to make graphics that are appropriate for web delivery. The chapters in Part III review the formats and techniques that are part of the web designer's bag of tricks.

The following chapters include step-by-step demonstrations on how to create web graphics in a number of popular graphics programs (Adobe Photoshop 7, Macromedia Fireworks MX, and JASC Paint Shop Pro 7). The examples assume that you have a basic understanding of how to use your image-editing program to create graphics. If you are new to making graphics, I recommend you spend time with the manual or other books about your graphics software. This book focuses on how to make your graphics web-friendly.

All About Web Graphics

Here's what you need to know about web graphics:

> Web graphics need to be low-resolution graphics saved in GIF, JPEG, or PNG format.

This tidy sentence basically says it all. Although simple, it touches on some major issues that I'll explore in this and the following chapters. I'll use the above statement as a starting point for discussing the nuts and bolts of web graphics. In addition, I'll share some tips on getting images and creating web graphics.

File Formats

The Web has its own alphabet soup of graphics file formats. Graphics formats that make it on the Internet are those that are easily ported from platform to platform over a network.

Nearly all of the graphics you see on the Web are in one of two formats: GIF (pronounced "jif") and JPEG ("jay-peg"). There is a third format, PNG ("ping"), but it has been slow to catch on. What follows is a brief introduction to each of these formats.

The ubiquitous GIF

The GIF (Graphic Interchange Format) file is the traditional favorite of the Internet. GIF files are compressed files that can contain a maximum of 8-bit color information. *Compressed* means that in turning your graphic into a GIF file, you are running it through a process that squeezes the color information into the smallest file size possible. *8-bit color* means that the graphic can contain a maximum of 256 different pixel colors, although it may contain fewer.

Figure 14-1. The GIF file format is best for images with sharp lines and areas of flat color. ⒢

Figure 14-2. The JPEG file format works best for images with gradient colors, such as photos or paintings. ⒢

The GIF format is most appropriate for images with areas of flat color, such as logos, cartoon-like illustrations, icons, and line art (Figure 14-1 ⒢). GIFs are not efficient at saving photographic images.

GIFs also have other advantages. You can make parts of a GIF file transparent, allowing your background image or color to show through. They can also contain simple animation effects right in the file. The vast majority of animated ad banners you see on the Web are animated GIFs.

The GIF file format is discussed in detail in Chapter 15, and animation is covered in Chapter 17.

The photogenic JPEG

The second most popular graphics format on the Web is JPEG. JPEGs are 24-bit color images; they can contain millions of colors. Unlike the GIF format, JPEGs use a compression scheme that loves gradient and blended colors and doesn't work especially well on flat colors or images with hard edges. JPEG's full-color capacity and compression scheme make it the ideal choice for photographic images (Figure 14-2 ⒢).

Although the compression scheme is "lossy" (meaning some detail in the image is thrown out to achieve better compression), JPEGs still offer excellent image quality packed into smaller files.

JPEGs are discussed in detail in Chapter 16.

The amazing PNG

The PNG format was created specificallly with the Web in mind. However, despite the fact that it has some excellent features, it hasn't made much of an impact on the Web due to lackluster browser and tools support.

The unique thing about a PNG is that it can be 8-bit indexed color (working just like a GIF), or full-color 24-bit (so it can do the job of a JPEG). Theoretically, the format can compress files smaller than the competition for either file type; however, with the tools currently available, it is difficult to make any given image smaller in PNG format. 24-bit PNGs, in particular, tend to be significantly larger than their JPEG counterparts.

PNG has some other nifty features, such as multiple levels of transparency so you can make soft shadows over patterned backgrounds (Figure 14-3 Ⓖ). It also has an interlacing option, built-in Gamma correction, and the ability to embed text (such as copyright information) into the file.

The PNG format supported to some degree by brower versions 4 and higher, but its advanced features (such as multiple levels of transparency) are not reliably supported. Because PNGs are not in widespread use, this book focuses on the more popular GIF and JPEG formats. However, you can generally apply the rules for making GIFs when creating 8-bit PNGs and the JPEG tricks when making 24-bit PNGs.

Figure 14-3. The PNG graphic format supports multiple levels of transparency. Ⓖ

Choosing the best file format

Part of the trick to making quality web graphics that download quickly is choosing the right file format for the job. Table 14-1 provides a good starting point.

Table 14-1. Choosing the best file format

If your image...	use...	because...
is graphical, with flat colors	GIF	it will compress more efficiently and keep colors flat and crisp, resulting in higher quality images at smaller file sizes.
is photographic or contains gradations of colors, such as a watercolor painting	JPEG	the JPEG compression works best on images with blends of colors, and it can portray images with millions of colors, resulting in better image quality at smaller file sizes.
is a combination of flat and photographic art, such as a banner with text on a flat background and a small photographic image	GIF	in most cases, it is better to preserve your flat colors and crisp edges and to tolerate a little dithering in the photographic edges than to turn the whole image over to JPEG compression.
is a postage stamp– or icon-sized photograph	GIF or JPEG	although JPEG is better suited for photographic images, I have found that when the image dimensions are really small, GIF usually creates smaller file sizes with acceptable image quality. It is advisable to try both and find the one that works best for your particular image.
includes a transparent area	GIF	it's the only file format that supports transparency.
needs to be animated	GIF	it's the only format that supports native animation.

Fortunately, the web graphics tools available today allow you to preview your image (and the resulting file sizes) as it would appear in different file formats. You can even view them side by side to choose the format that works the best for your image (Figure 14-4).

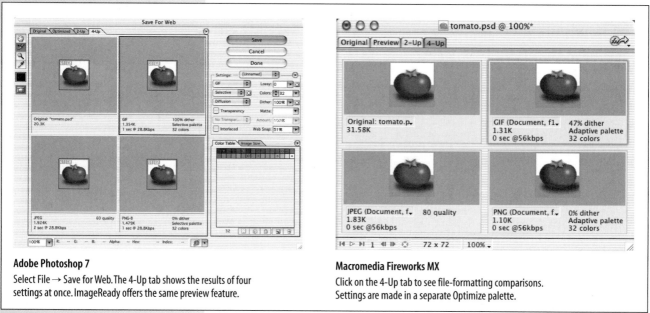

Adobe Photoshop 7

Select File → Save for Web. The 4-Up tab shows the results of four settings at once. ImageReady offers the same preview feature.

Macromedia Fireworks MX

Click on the 4-Up tab to see file-formatting comparisons. Settings are made in a separate Optimize palette.

Figure 14-4. Photoshop (and ImageReady) and Fireworks allow you to preview image quality and resulting file sizes for different file formats and settings. This is helpful in choosing the best file format for an image.

Image Resolution

Both GIFs and JPEGs are pixel-based, or bitmapped (also called raster) images. When you zoom in, you can see that the image is like a mosaic made up of many pixels (tiny, single-colored squares). These are different from vector graphics that are made up of smooth lines and filled areas, all based on mathematical formulas (Figure 14-5).

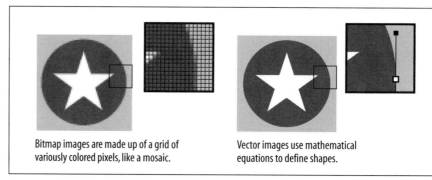

Bitmap images are made up of a grid of variously colored pixels, like a mosaic.

Vector images use mathematical equations to define shapes.

Figure 14-5. Bitmap versus vector graphics.

Goodbye inches, hello pixels!

If you have been using pixel-based images such as TIFFs in print design, you are familiar with the term resolution, the number of pixels per inch. For print, an image typically has a resolution of 300 dots per inch (or dpi).

On the Web, images need to be created at much lower resolutions; 72 dpi has become the *de facto* standard, but in reality the whole notion of "inches" and even "dots per inch" becomes irrelevant in the web environment. In the end, the only meaningful measurement of a web graphic is its actual number of pixels.

When a graphic is displayed on a web page, the pixels map one-to-one with the display resolution of the monitor. Because the monitor resolution varies by platform and user, the image will appear larger or smaller depending on the configuration, as the following example demonstrates.

I have created a graphic that is 72 pixels square (Figure 14-6). Since I set the resolution to be 72 dpi in my image-editing program, I expect the graphic to appear about one inch square when I view it on my monitor. And sure enough, on my Mac, that's about right.

But what happens when that same graphic is displayed on another person's monitor—one with a much higher resolution setting? Let's take another look at my "one inch" graphic.

Suddenly, my inch-square graphic is less than a three-quarter-inch square because the same 72 pixels are mapping one-to-one across a resolution that is closer to 100 pixels per inch. For this reason, it is useless to think of "inches" on the Web. It's all relative. And without inches, the whole notion of pixels per inch is basically thrown out the window as well. The only thing we know for sure is that the graphic is 72 pixels across, and it will be twice as wide as a graphic that is 36 pixels across, for instance.

Web graphics need to be low-resolution (typically 72 dpi).

Measuring Resolution

Because web graphics exist solely on the screen, it is technically correct to measure their resolutions in pixels per inch (ppi). Another resolution measurement, dpi (dots per inch), refers to the resolution of a printed page, dependent on the resolution of the printing device.

In practice, the terms dpi and ppi are used interchangeably (albeit incorrectly so). It is generally accepted practice to refer to web graphic resolution in terms of dpi.

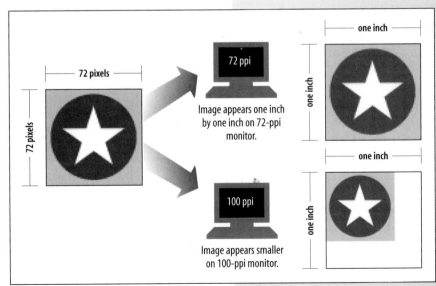

Figure 14-6. The size of an image is dependent on the monitor resolution.

High-resolution graphics (e.g., 300 dpi) are inappropriate for the Web.

After this example, it should be fairly clear why graphics scanned in or created at higher resolutions (such as 300 dpi) are inappropriate for the Web. At higher resolutions, it's typical for images to be several thousand pixels across. With browser windows as small as 600 pixels wide, all those pixels are unnecessary and will result in graphics that are *huge* once shown in the browser window (Figure 14-7).

This 3-inch square image fits nicely in the browser window at 72 dpi...

...but at 300 dpi, most of the image falls outside the visible area of the browser window.

Figure 14-7. At high resolutions, images are too large for the Web.

Working in low resolution

Despite the fact that resolution is irrelevant, nearly everyone creates web graphics at 72 dpi because it gets them in the ballpark for the correct number of pixels. The drawback to working at such a low resolution is that the image quality is lower because there is not as much image information in a given space. This tends to make the image look more grainy or pixelated and, unfortunately, that's just the nature of the Web. On the upside, image edits that are noticable in high-resolution graphics (such as retouching or cloning) are virtually seamless at low resolution.

File Size Matters

A web page is published over a network, and it will need to zip through the lines as little packets of data in order to reach the end user. It is fairly intuitive, then, that larger amounts of data will require a longer time to arrive. And guess which part of a web page is the greatest hog of bandwidth—that's right, the graphics. Simply put, large graphics mean longer download times.

Thus is born the love/hate relationship with graphics on the Web. On one hand, graphics can make a web page look more interesting than a page with text alone. The ability to display graphics is one of the factors that made the Web the first segment of the Internet to explode into mass popularity. On the other hand, graphics can also try the patience of the eager surfer waiting for the pictures to download and display on the screen.

The user has three choices: hang in there and wait, turn the graphics-downloading function of the browser off and read the text-only page, or click the "Back" button and surf somewhere else.

Despite the emergence of high-bandwidth connections in the household (such as DSL and cable modems), the 56 Kbps dial-up modem connection is not yet a thing of the past. The golden rule of web design remains "Keep download times as short as possible."

In fact, many corporate clients will set a kilobyte limit (sometimes referred to as the K-limit) that the sum of all the files on a page cannot exceed. I know of one corporate site that set its limit to a scant 15 KB per page (that includes the HTML file and all the graphics combined!). Similarly, many sites insist that advertising banners be no larger than 6 or 7 KB. Even if keeping files small is not a priority for you, it may be for your clients.

It is up to web designers to be sensitive to this issue in general, and to mind the graphics files in particular. Here are a few strategies.

Design for compression

One of the key ways to make your files as small as possible is to take full advantage of their compression schemes. For instance, since we know that GIF compression likes flat colors, don't design GIF images with gradient color blends when a flat color will suffice. And since we know that JPEGs like soft transitions and no hard edges, you can try strategically blurring images that will be saved in JPEG format. These techniques are discussed in the Optimizing sections of Chapters 15 and 16.

How Long Does It Take?

It's impossible to say exactly how long a graphic will take to download over the Web. It depends on many factors, including the speed of the user's connection, the speed of the user's computer, the amount of activity on the web server, and the general amount of traffic on the Internet itself.

The general rule of thumb is to figure that a graphic will take 1 second per kilobyte (KB) under worst-case conditions (say, over a 28.8 Kbps modem connection). That would mean that a 30 KB graphic would take 30 seconds to download, a long time for a user to be staring at the screen of a computer.

Even over faster connections, display times are dependent on unpredictable factors such as general web traffic and the speed of the user's computer.

Use the 1 sec/KB guideline only to get a ballpark estimate for the lowest common denominator. Actual times may be a lot better, or a lot worse.

Limit the dimensions

Though fairly obvious, the easiest way to keep file size down is to limit the dimensions of the graphic itself. There aren't any magic numbers; just don't make graphics any larger than they need to be. By simply eliminating extra space on the graphic in Figure 14-8, I was able to reduce the file size by 3 KB.

600 x 200 pixels (**13 KB**)

500 x 136 pixels (**10 KB**)

Figure 14-8. You can reduce the size of your files simply by cropping out extra space.

Reuse and recycle

A good way to limit download times is to take advantage of your browser's cache and reuse your graphics. Here's how it works.

When browsing the Web, it's typical to move back and forth between documents, often returning to the same document repeatedly. It doesn't make sense for the browser to ask a server for the same document over and over again; instead, the browser retains a copy of the most recently accessed documents, keeping it handy in the event you return. This is called caching (pronounced "cash-ing"), and the place these files are temporarily stored is called the cache (pronounced "cash").

You can take advantage of the browser's cache by reusing graphics whenever possible on your site. That way, each graphic will need to download only once, which speeds up the display of subsequent pages (Figure 14-9).

The only trick is that each instance of the graphic must have the exact same URL in its <img> tag; that is, it must be a single graphic in a single directory. If you make copies of a graphic and put it in different directories, even though the file has the same name, the browser will do a fresh download when it sees the new pathname.

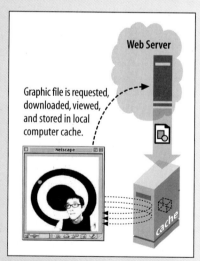

Figure 14-9. You can speed up page display by reusing graphics. The browser downloads the graphic only once and relies on the cache for subsequent instances.

Tools of the Trade

Web graphics tools have come a long way since I started making web graphics in 1993. In those days, we had to make do with tools designed for print graphics, and we relied on one-trick-pony utilities to add web-specific features, such as transparency.

But with the explosion of the Web and the demands it puts on designers, software developers responded quickly and competitively to cater to the specific requirements of web designers.

What follows is a brief introduction to the most popular graphics tools among professional web designers. It is by no means an exhaustive list. There are many worthy graphics programs that crank out GIF and JPEG files; if you've found one that works for you, that's great.

Adobe Photoshop/ImageReady. Without question, the industry standard for web graphics creation is Adobe Photoshop. It's the tool of choice of every graphic designer I've ever met. Starting with Version 5.5, Photoshop includes many web-specific features such as a "Save to Web" option that shows previews of your graphic in different file formats and at different compression rates.

Adobe's ImageReady, which comes with Photoshop, does special web tricks such as animation and rollover effects. ImageReady also provides sophisticated tools for optimizing image file size.

Some web development shops require their designers and freelancers to create their graphics using Photoshop and ImageReady. If you are interested in making web graphics professionally, I recommend getting up to speed with Photoshop right away.

JASC Paint Shop Pro. If you work on a PC and are on a budget, you might want to try out Paint Shop Pro, which has many of the same features as Photoshop, but at a much lower cost (U.S. $99 as of this printing). It comes with Animation Shop for creating animated GIFs.

Macromedia Fireworks. This is one of the first graphics programs designed from the ground up to address the special requirements of web graphics. It has tools for creating both vector (line-based) and raster (pixel-based) images. Its features include side-by-side export previews, animation and rollover tools, advanced image-slicing tools, great file optimization, and more. It is also well integrated with Macromedia Dreamweaver, the industry standard web-authoring tool.

The learning curve for Fireworks is a little steep (particularly if you are accustomed to Adobe's interface). Once I got used to it, I found that I could use it for almost all of my web graphics (although, I must admit that it didn't make Photoshop completely obsolete).

Demo Software

For more information and free downloadable trial versions of the software mentioned here, check these companies' web sites:

Adobe Systems, Inc.
www.adobe.com

Macromedia, Inc.
www.macromedia.com

JASC Software
www.jasc.com

The CD included with this book contains trial versions of Adobe Photoshop 7 and Macromedia Fireworks MX.

Adobe Illustrator; Macromedia Freehand. I list these programs together because they are popular vector-drawing programs. Many web designers start their designs in a drawing program because the tools are ideal for creating the flat, graphical images that are well-suited for web delivery. Although these programs have the ability to save directly to GIF format, designers usually open their drawings in a web graphics tool for final processing.

The program you use is a matter of preference; however, it is not uncommon for a client to insist their designers and freelancers use a specific tool (usually Photoshop) to ensure consistency in graphic quality across the site.

Image Sources

We know about the various graphics formats, and we've seen some of the tools used to make them, but where do we begin? Where do these graphics come from?

Acquiring images to use in web graphics is much the same as finding them for print, with a few extra considerations. Let's look at some possible sources for artwork to jazz up your pages.

Scanning

Scanning is a great way to collect source material for web graphics. You can scan almost anything, from flat art to actual 3-D objects. Beware, however, the temptation to scan and use found images. Keep in mind that most images you find are probably copyright-protected and may not be used without permission, even if you modify them considerably. Remember that millions of people have access to the Web, and using images you do not have permission for can put you and your client at risk.

Digital cameras

You can capture the world around you and pipe it right into an image-editing program with a digital camera. Since the Web is a low-resolution environment, you don't need a fancy high-resolution camera to get the job done. Be aware, however, that digital cameras compress the images (usually using JPEG compression), so you'll be starting out with slightly lower-quality originals. Each time you apply JPEG compression to an image, quality suffers.

Scanning Tips

If you are scanning images for use on the Web, these tips will help you get better-quality images:

- Your final images should be at a resolution of 72 dpi. For most images, you can scan directly at 72 dpi. Scanning at a slightly higher resolution (say, 100 dpi) may give you more flexibility for resizing (particularly for very small images) because you'll have more pixels to work with. In the end, however, it's the number of pixels that count, and 72 dpi is the standard resolution.

- I recommend scanning black and white images in grayscale (8-bit) mode, not in black-and-white (2-bit, or bitmap) mode. This enables you to make adjustments in the midtone areas once you have sized the image to its final dimensions and resolution. If you really want just black and white pixels, convert the image as the last step.

- If you are scanning an image that has been printed, you will need to eliminate the dot pattern that results from the printing process. The best way to do this is to apply a slight blur to the image (in Photoshop, use the Gaussian Blur filter), resize the image slighly smaller, then apply a sharpening filter. This will eliminate the pesky dots.

Electronic illustration

In many cases, you can create your images from scratch in a graphics program such as Illustrator, Fireworks, or Photoshop. Since I enjoy illustrating, I often create my own images in a drawing program using a drawing tablet and stylus.

Although there are basic vector tools in Photoshop and Fireworks, I turn to my trusty Adobe Illustrator or Macromedia Freehand to do serious vector drawing or get effects such as text placed on a curve. When I'm finished, I bring the EPS file into Photoshop to create the low-resolution web versions. The advantage to starting with a vector drawing is that it is scaleable, which gives me lots of flexibility.

Photo archives and clip-art

If you don't want to generate images from scratch, that's okay, too. There are plenty of collections of ready-made photos, illustrations, and buttons available. Nowadays, there are whole clip-art collections available specifically for web use. A trip to your local software retail store or a browse through the pages of a software catalog will no doubt turn up royalty-free image collections, many boasting more than 100,000 pieces of art.

There are also a number of great resources online, and the good news is that some of these sites are giving graphics away for *free*. Others charge a small membership fee ($10 to $20 per year). The drawback is that a lot of them are poor quality or kind of hokey (but then, "hokey" is in the eye of the beholder).

The following sites are good starting points for accessing thousands of free icons, backgrounds, buttons, animations, and more. If you need more, look in the Yahoo directory under Computers and Internet → Graphics → Clip Art.

ClipArt.com *www.clipart.com*	Web Clip-Art Links Page at About.com *webclipart.about.com*
Original Free Clip Art *www.free-clip-art.net*	#1 Free Clip Art *www.1clipart.com*

If you are doing professional work with a professional budget, you should consider these top-notch online resources for photographs and illustrations. The majority of the images they offer are rights-protected, which means you'll need to pay a licensing fee based on use. But the quality is first-rate.

Getty Images *www.gettyimages.com*	Photonica *www.photonica.com*
PictureQuest *www.picturequest.com*	Wonderfile (royalty-free) *www.wonderfile.com*

Stealing Isn't Nice

It's poor form (not to mention illegal) to use copyrighted images that you do not own or have not paid to license. Don't "borrow" graphics from other people's web sites or scan found images and call them your own.

Even if you've bought a photo or clip-art CD collection, be sure to read the licensing information carefully to see if there are additional charges for commercial use.

If you're looking for free image material, use the appropriate resources and look for the magic words "unrestricted" and "royalty-free."

Graphics Production Tips

I've picked up a few basic tricks for producing web graphics over the years that apply to all file formats. I'll share these with you now. Other format-specific techniques can be found in Chapters 15, 16, and 17.

Work in RGB mode

You should always do your image-editing work in RGB mode (grayscale is fine for non-color images) regardless of the final format of the file. JPEG and 24-bit PNG files compress the RGB color image directly. For GIFs and 8-bit PNGs, you must convert to Indexed Color first before saving it (we'll discuss this more in Chapter 15). If you have experience creating graphics for print, you may be accustomed to working in CMYK mode (printed colors are made up of Cyan, Magenta, Yellow, and blacK ink), but ink—and CMYK mode—is irrelevant and inappropriate in web design.

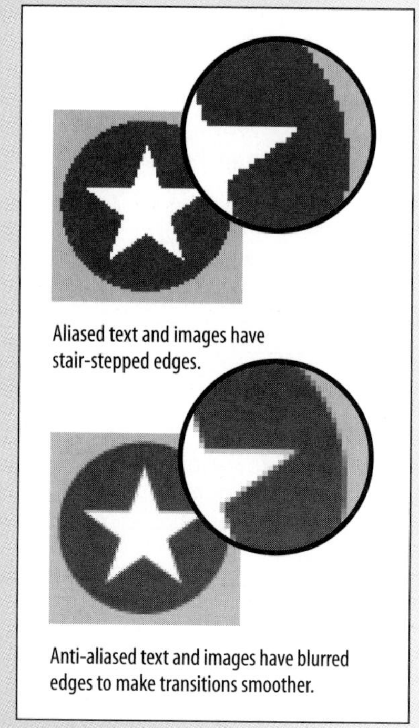

Use anti-aliased text

In general, to create professional-looking graphics for the Web, you should use anti-aliased text and objects. Anti-aliasing is the slight blur used on curved edges to make smoother transitions between colors. Aliased edges, by contrast, are blocky and stair-stepped. Figure 14-10 shows the effect of aliasing (top) and anti-aliasing (bottom). You will find a control for turning anti-aliasing on and off (or selecting a particular type of anti-aliasing, in the case of Photoshop) with the text tool in your graphics program.

The exception to this guideline is very small text (10 points or smaller), for which anti-aliased edges blur the characters to the point of illegibility. Text at small sizes may fare much better when it is aliased.

Anti-aliased edges may add a few extra bytes to the size of your file due to the extra colors, but the improved quality is usually worth it.

Save your work

Just as you would for any other desktop design, it is a good idea to save your work often. If you are creating your graphic in a layered Photoshop file, be sure to save the layered version separate from the "flattened" GIF or JPEG file. It is much easier to make those inevitable changes to the layered file.

Aliased text and images have stair-stepped edges.

Anti-aliased text and images have blurred edges to make transitions smoother.

Figure 14-10. Anti-aliased and aliased images.

Name files properly

Be sure to use the proper file extensions for your graphics files. All GIF files must be named with the suffix *.gif*. JPEG files must have either *.jpeg* or *.jpg* as a suffix. PNG files end in *.png*. Even if your files are saved in the correct format, the browser will not recognize them without the proper suffix.

Consider other end uses

One of the drawbacks to creating files at low resolution is that they look lousy in print. Normally, resolutions of 300 dpi or higher are required for smooth printing, so the measly 72 dots per inch of a web graphic will make for a blocky and blotchy printed image.

If you anticipate needing images (such as logos or important illustrations) for printed pieces as well as on your web page, it makes sense to create the high-resolution image first, save it, and then create a duplicate at a web-appropriate size. Whenever possible, try to take advantage of drawing programs for creating logos in vector format; the logos can be resized infinitely with no loss of quality, then output at the desired resolution.

WHERE TO LEARN MORE

Web Graphics Techniques

Once you've mastered the basics, you may want to continue learning about advanced graphics techniques. These books are highly recommended:

Adobe Photoshop 7.0 Classroom in a Book
by Adobe Creative Team (Adobe Press, 2002)
  If you need basic training in Photoshop, this book provides step-by-step lessons in the basic workings of the program. It also covers ImageReady and web elements such as animation and rollovers.

www.photoshop.imageready
by Greg Simsic (Que, 2001)
  This book focuses on Photoshop's web development features.

Designing Web Graphics, Fourth Edition
by Linda Weinman (New Riders Publishing, 2002)
  This is a treasure of web graphics tips and techniques and includes clear step-by-step demonstrations.

Web Graphics Highlights

Here are some of the main points from this chapter that you should keep in mind when creating web graphics:

- Save images with flat areas of color and hard edges in GIF format.

- Save photographic images in JPEG format.

- Images with a combination of flat graphic areas and photographic material are usually best saved in GIF format.

- Web graphics should be low-resolution bitmapped images.

- Web graphics should be created in RGB color mode (not CMYK).

- The only meaningful measurement for web graphics is pixels.

- Images can be created from scratch, scanned in, shot with a digital camera, or taken from a clip-art library.

- The most popular professional tools for creating web graphics are Adobe Photoshop (with ImageReady) and Macromedia Fireworks.

Test Yourself

Answer the following questions to see if you got the big picture on web graphics. The correct answers are in the Appendix.

1. What is the most popular graphic format for web graphics? What sort of images is it good for?

2. What is the difference between bitmapped and vector graphics?

3. What does ppi stand for?

4. Which graphic is more appropriate for placement on a web page: a 7-inch wide graphic at 72 dpi or a 5-inch wide graphic at 300 dpi?

5. Name three ways to reduce graphic download times.

6. What does anti-aliasing mean? What purpose does it serve?

7. Which graphic format would you use for each of the images shown in Figure 14-11 G, and why? (You should be able to make the decision just by looking at them as they're printed here.)

Figure 14-11. What are the best formats for these three images? G

Creating GIFs 15

If you want to make web pages, plan on becoming handy at making GIFs. Although creating basic GIFs is straightforward, making professional-quality GIFs requires extra attention to matters of transparency, optimization, and the web palette, as we'll see in this chapter. Fortunately, these tasks are made simple with the web-ready graphics tools we have today.

Before we jump into making GIFs, I'll give you a more detailed explanation of how GIFs work and their unique characteristics. In the process, we'll cover terminology that will make using your graphics tools easier.

All About GIFs

The vast majority of graphics you see on the Web are GIF (Graphic Interchange Format) files. Although not designed specifically for the Web, the format was quickly adopted for its versatility, small file sizes, and cross-platform compatibility. In the first graphical browsers (way back in 1993), GIF was the only choice for inline graphics.

Because the GIF compression scheme excels at compressing flat colors, it is the best file format to use for images with flat areas of color, such as logos, line art, graphics containing text, icons, etc. You can save photographs or textured images as GIFs, too, but they won't be saved as efficiently, resulting in larger file sizes. (These are best saved as JPEGs, as discussed in Chapter 16.)

Figure 15-1 [G], following page, shows a few examples of images that are well suited for the GIF format.

In this chapter

Key characteristics of the GIF
  file format

Creating a simple GIF,
  step by step

Adding transparency

Optimizing GIFs

Designing graphics with
  the web palette

Figure 15-1. The GIF format is great for graphical images comprised mainly of flat colors and hard edges. ⒢

8-bit, indexed color

Simply put, all GIFs are indexed color images with a maximum of 8-bit color information. Let's examine the parts of that sentence.

Indexed color refers to a system of storing the pixel colors from an image in a color table (also called a palette). The table serves as a numeric index (of sorts) to all the colors found in the image (Figure 15-2 ⒢).

Before you can save a graphic as a GIF, you need to convert the RGB image to Indexed Color mode (some tools do this for you automatically when you select "GIF" as the file format). Doing so assigns colors from the image to positions in the table.

> All GIFs are indexed color images with a maximum of 8-bit color information.

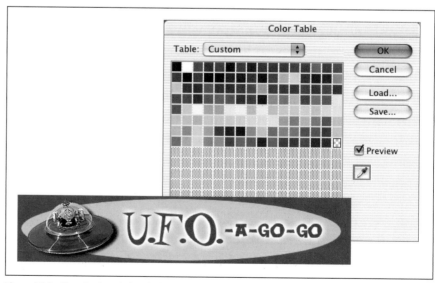

Figure 15-2. The colors in an indexed color image are stored in and referenced by a color table. The color table (also called a palette) can contain a maximum of 256 colors (8-bit). In this figure we see the color table for the U.F.O. banner graphic. ⒢

8-bit color means that the image (and its color table) can contain a maximum of 256 colors—the maximum number that 8 bits of information can define ($2^8 = 256$). GIFs can have lower bit-depths as well, resulting in fewer colors and smaller file sizes. This will be discussed in the Optimizing GIFs section of this chapter.

When creating GIFs, you often come in direct contact with the color table for that image.

GIF compression

GIF compression is easy to understand. First, it's "lossless," which means that no image information is sacrificed in order to compress the image. Second, it uses a compression scheme (called "LZW") that compresses the image row by row. When it hits a row of pixels that are the same color, it can compress that into one data description. This is why images with large areas of flat colors condense down more than images with textures.

GIFs compress images row by row. Rows of identical pixel colors condense more efficiently and result in a smaller file size.

Figure 15-3 demonstrates the general way in which GIF compression works. It is not technically accurate (the real story is more complicated, of course), but it is a good mental model to keep in mind when designing GIFs for maximum compression.

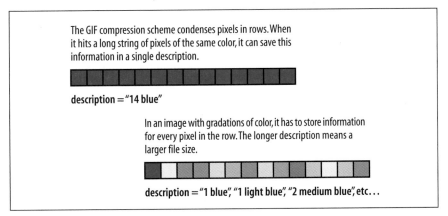

Figure 15-3. A simple demonstration of GIF compression.

This leads to some interesting design quirks for GIFs. For instance, images with horizontal stripes will be smaller than an image of the same size with vertical stripes. You can also reduce the size of an image by adding alternating rows of solid color. These techniques are discussed in the Optimizing GIFs section later in this chapter.

Figure 15-4. Transparency allows the striped background to show through the graphic. The image on the top uses transparency; the image on the bottom does not.

Transparency

One of the niftiest things about GIFs is that you can make parts of them transparent and allow the background image or color to show through. All bitmapped graphics (including GIFs) are rectangular by nature, but with transparency, you can create the illusion that your graphic has a more interesting shape (Figure 15-4). Transparency is discussed in detail in the section Adding Transparency later in this chapter.

Interlacing

Interlacing is an effect you can apply to a GIF that makes the image download in a series of passes. Each pass is clearer than the pass before until the GIF is fully rendered in the browser window (Figure 15-5). Without interlacing, some browsers may wait until the entire image is downloaded before displaying the image. Others may display the image a few rows at a time, from top to bottom, until the entire picture is complete.

Interlaced GIFs display in a series of passes, each clearer than the pass before.

Figure 15-5. The display of interlaced GIFs.

Over a fast connection, these effects (interlacing or image delays) may not even be perceptible. However, over slow modem connections, interlacing large images may be a way to provide a hint of the image to come while the entire image downloads. If the image is used as an imagemap, the user could even click on part of the image and move on before it's completely downloaded.

Whether you interlace or not is your design decision. My rule of thumb is that for small graphics, it is probably not necessary; but for large images, particularly those used as image-maps, interlacing is worthwhile.

Animation

Another feature built into the GIF file format is the ability to display simple animations (Figure 15-6). Once you create the separate frames of your animation, there are web graphics tools that make it easy to save them as a single animated GIF. We'll explore animated GIFs in Chapter 17.

Figure 15-6. All the frames in this simple animation are contained within one GIF file.

Naming GIFs

GIFs must be named with the *.gif* suffix in order to be used on a web page. Even if the graphic is in GIF format, the browser relies on the proper suffix to recognize the file as a GIF and to place it on the page.

Creating a Simple GIF, Step by Step

Now that we know what GIFs can do, let's make one. This first example is going to be very basic; we'll get to the fancy stuff such as transparency and optimization later.

Virtually every graphics program has some basic GIF-saving feature. The exercise that follows uses Adobe Photoshop because it is the industry standard. The process is nearly identical in Adobe's ImageReady software. After the exercise, we'll take a look at the GIF-making processes in Macromedia Fireworks and JASC Paint Shop Pro. Regardless of the tool you use, the process is about the same:

1. Start with a low-resolution (72 dpi) image in RGB color mode.

2. Do your image editing (resizing, cropping, color correction, etc.) while the image is still in RGB mode.

3. When you have your image looking exactly the way you want it, convert it to indexed color (you'll be asked to flatten the image first if it has layers). If you are using a web graphics tool, the image will be converted to indexed color automatically when you select "GIF" from the format options.

   You will be asked to select a palette that will be applied to the image when the colors are reduced. The sidebar Color Palettes describes the various palette options.

4. After you've selected your desired settings, save or export the GIF.

One important note: be sure to hold on to the original RGB image in case you need to make changes later. It is preferable to edit in RGB color mode and then export to GIF as the last step. Web graphics tools make this easy.

Color Palettes

All 8-bit indexed color images use a palette to define the colors in the image, and there are several standard palettes you can choose from within popular graphics programs:

Exact. Creates a custom palette out of the actual colors in the image if the image already contains fewer than 256 colors.

Adaptive. Creates a custom palette using the most frequently used pixel colors in the image.

Web. Applies the 216-color web palette (discussed later in this chapter) to the image.

Perceptual. "Creates a custom color table by giving priority to colors for which the human eye has greater sensitivity" (Photoshop manual).

Selective. "Creates a color table similar to Perceptual color table, but favoring broad areas of color and the preservation of Web colors… usually producing images with the greatest color integrity" (Photoshop manual).

Uniform. Creates a palette that contains an evenly stepped sampling of colors from the RGB spectrum.

System (Windows or Macintosh). Uses the colors in the specified system's default palette.

Exercise 15-1: Making a Basic GIF in Photoshop

This exercise takes you through the basic steps of saving an image in the GIF format. The CD that accompanies this book contains a try-out version of Photoshop 7, so you can work along.

1. Start by dragging the contents of the *chap15* directory to your hard drive. Launch Photoshop and open the file *sweetpea.tif*, which is in the *15-1* folder.

2. Make sure that the image is ready for the Web by choosing Image Size from the Image menu. The Image Size dialog box tells you the exact pixel measurements as well as the resolution of the image.

   Our *sweetpea.tif* image is way too big, so let's size it down. Making sure both the Constrain Proportions and Resample Image boxes are checked, change the resolution to 72 dpi. The resulting image should be 250 pixels wide and 160 pixels high. Click OK.

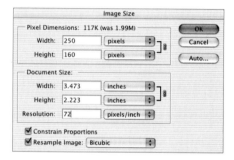

3. Now we can export a GIF version of the graphic. Select Save for Web from the File menu. When you select the Optimized tab, Photoshop gives you a preview of how the resulting GIF will look with the current settings. Selecting the 2-Up and 4-Up tabs give you multiple views so you can compare the resulting image quality and file size of your settings to the original.

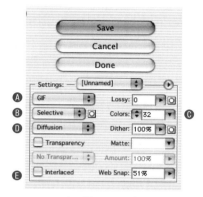

Keep your eye on the file size information in the bottom-left corner of the window and observe how it changes with your various settings.

In the Save for Web dialog box, we'll need to make a few settings:

- Choose GIF from the Format pull-down menu **A**.

- Select Selective from the Palette pull-down menu **B**. The palette options are explained in the Color Palettes sidebar on the previous page.

- Try out different numbers of colors and see how both the image quality and the file size responds **C**. Limiting the colors makes the file smaller. For this image, I think we can go as low as 64 colors without drastically degrading the image.

- Leave the dithering set to Diffusion and 100% **D**. We'll talk about the significance of these settings later in the chapter.

- Decide whether you want the image to be interlaced **E**. This image is pretty small, so I've left the box unchecked.

- Leave Transparency unchecked as well.

4. Once you have the settings where you want them, click Save and give the file a name that ends with the *.gif* suffix. (Windows users, choose GIF from the format menu to get the proper suffix.)

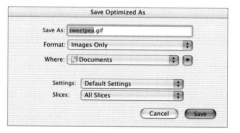

In Macromedia Fireworks MX

Because Fireworks was designed specifically for web graphics, you'll find its tools are ideal for creating optimized, high-quality GIFs. It gives you very fine-tuned control over many aspects of the image to improve compression rates (Figure 15-7).

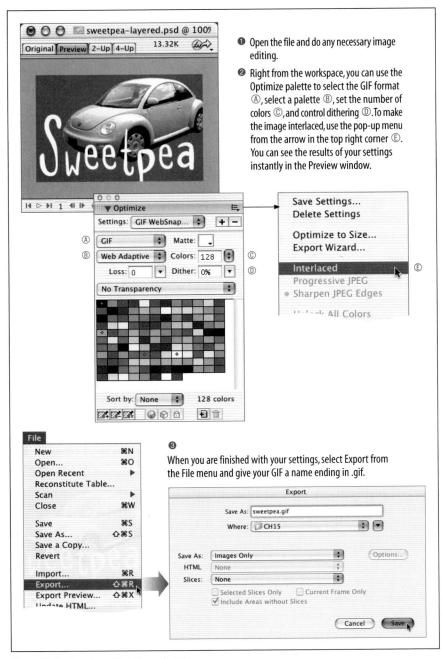

❶ Open the file and do any necessary image editing.

❷ Right from the workspace, you can use the Optimize palette to select the GIF format Ⓐ, select a palette Ⓑ, set the number of colors Ⓒ, and control dithering Ⓓ. To make the image interlaced, use the pop-up menu from the arrow in the top right corner Ⓔ. You can see the results of your settings instantly in the Preview window.

❸ When you are finished with your settings, select Export from the File menu and give your GIF a name ending in .gif.

Figure 15-7. Exporting a GIF in Fireworks MX.

WORK ALONG

The CD that accompanies this book also includes a trial version of Macromedia Fireworks MX, so you can work along with Figure 15-7, if you'd like. Use the sweetpea.tif file, found in 15-1 of the ch15 folder.

In JASC Paint Shop Pro 7

Just as with Photoshop, it is easy to create GIFs in Paint Shop Pro. A GIF-optimization tool was introduced in Version 6 (Figure 15-8).

❶
Open the file and do necessary image editing while in RGB mode. When you are ready to save the image as a GIF, choose File → Export → GIF Optimizer.

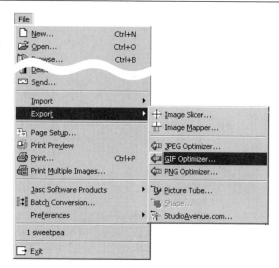

❷
Use the Transparency tab if you'd like portions of the GIF to be transparent. If you are starting with a layered image with transparent areas, select "Existing image or layer transparency". If you would like to make a specific pixel color in the image transparent, select "Areas that match this color".

❸
Use the Colors tab to set the bit depth, dither amount, and the palette for the image. The method of color selection choices refer to the palette. Use Existing if you are starting with an indexed color image. Use Standard/Web-safe to apply the web palette to the image. Optimized Median Cut reduces the image to a few colors using something similar to an adaptive palette. Use Optimized Octree if the original image has just a few colors you want.

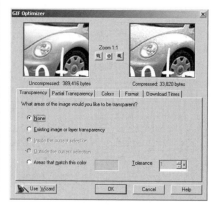

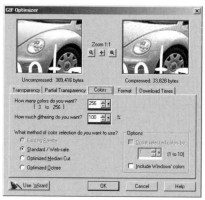

❹
Use the Format tab to select whether the GIF is interlaced. Version 89a is the best version for GIFs.

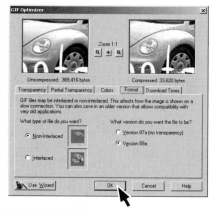

Figure 15-8. Saving a GIF file in Paint Shop Pro 6 and higher.

Adding Transparency

Another feature of the GIF format is that you can make parts of the image transparent, allowing whatever is behind the transparent area (most likely the background color or pattern) to show through.

This works by designating one slot in the indexed color table as "transparent." You select the color you'd like to turn transparent, and the tool takes care of the rest. Be aware, however, that *all* pixels of your selected color in the image will turn transparent.

The method you use to add transparency to your image depends on whether your source image is layered (in native Photoshop or Fireworks format) or flat (such as a pre-existing GIF file). Let's look at both techniques, starting with the layered file.

Preserving transparency in layered images

If you start with a layered image that already has transparent areas (you can tell because the gray and white checkerboard shows through), then keeping those areas transparent is a no-brainer with Photoshop (5.5 or higher) or Fireworks.

In both tools, when you choose Transparency from the Save for Web (Photoshop) or Optimize (Fireworks) palette, the transparent areas in the layered graphic will stay transparent in the final GIF (Figure 15-9).

Both tools allow you to specify a Matte color, which is the color that will fill in the transparent areas of your image if GIF transparency is *not* selected. The Matte color is also useful in making the edges of the image blend into the background color of the page. We'll discuss this feature in the Avoiding Halos section coming up later in the chapter.

> **WORK ALONG**
> The layered file, *tuesday.psd*, pictured in Figure 15-9 is available in the *chap15* materials folder, if you'd like to work along.

Figure 15-9. Preserving transparency in layered documents.

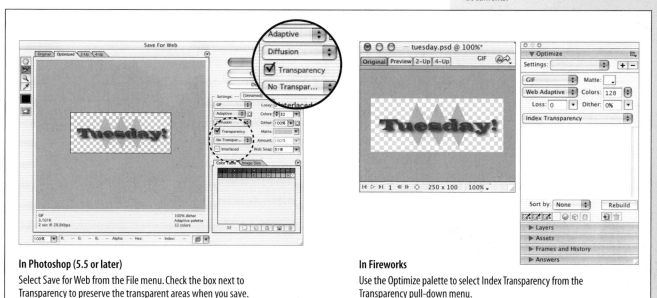

In Photoshop (5.5 or later)
Select Save for Web from the File menu. Check the box next to Transparency to preserve the transparent areas when you save.

In Fireworks
Use the Optimize palette to select Index Transparency from the Transparency pull-down menu.

Adding transparency to a flattened image

What if you are starting with an image that has already been flattened, such as a pre-existing GIF file? The good news is that adding transparent areas to an existing file is simple in Photoshop and Fireworks. The bad news is that depending on your image, you may run into problems with quality.

If the image was flattened to a background color that is different from the background color of your web page, you may see a fringy outline of pixels (called a "halo") around the transparent image when it is displayed. We will discuss halos in detail in the next section, Avoiding Halos.

In the meantime, let's add transparency to a flattened image under the best possible circumstances, in which the solid background color of the GIF matches the patterned background of the web page.

Say you've got a GIF file filled with a green that perfectly matches the green background of your page. But now, you've decided to jazz up the page by changing the solid green background to a subtle tiled pattern. That nice GIF file is suddenly a big green rectangle floating like a raft on a sea of pattern (Figure 15-10). You can fix this by making the green areas of your GIF transparent and letting the pattern show through.

Figure 15-10. The flat GIF on the top looks awkward in front of a patterned background. We can fix this by making the flat green areas transparent as shown in the bottom example.

In Adobe Photoshop (Versions 6 or 7)

There are two ways to add transparent areas to a flattened graphic.

The first is to copy the whole image to a new layered file, then use a selection tool (such as the Magic Wand) to delete the areas of the image you want to be transparent in the final image. Use the Save for Web feature and select the Transparency option to preserve the transparent areas.

To make areas transparent based on a pixel color, use the transparency eyedropper found on the Color Table dialog box as shown in Figure 15-11.

In earlier versions of Photoshop (4 and 5), the transparency eyedropper is accessed on the GIF89a Export dialog box (select File → Export → GIF89a).

In Photoshop 6 and 7

① Open the image and change it to Indexed Color mode if it isn't indexed already (Image   Mode   Indexed Color).

② Open the Color Table for the image (Image   Mode   Color Table)

③ Use the transparency eyedropper to select the color in the image that you'd like to be transparent. The checkered background will show through the transparent areas of the image.

④ When you are finished, click OK.

⑤ To save the new transparent GIF, select Save for Web and proceed as demonstrated in Figure 15-9.

In Photoshop 4 and 5

Select GIF89a from the Export menu. You will find the transparency eyedropper in the GIF89a Export dialog box. Click on the color to be transparent and proceed with the export.

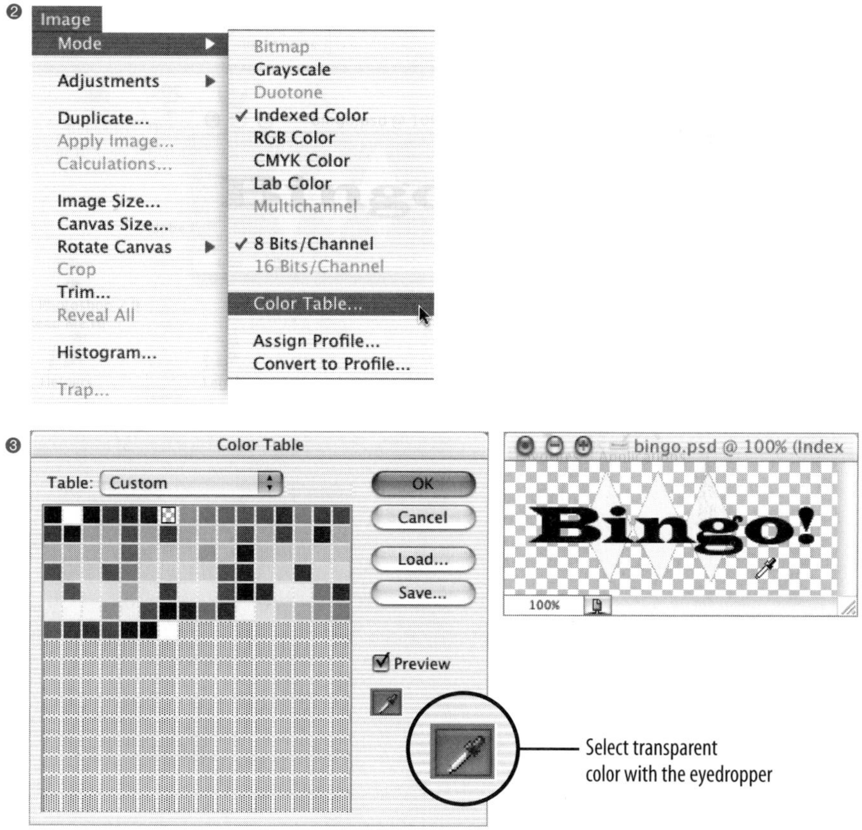

Select transparent color with the eyedropper

Figure 15-11. Adding transparency to a flattened image.

In Macromedia Fireworks MX

In Fireworks, you can make colors in a flattened graphic transparent right from the workspace using the Optimize palette, as shown in Figure 15-12.

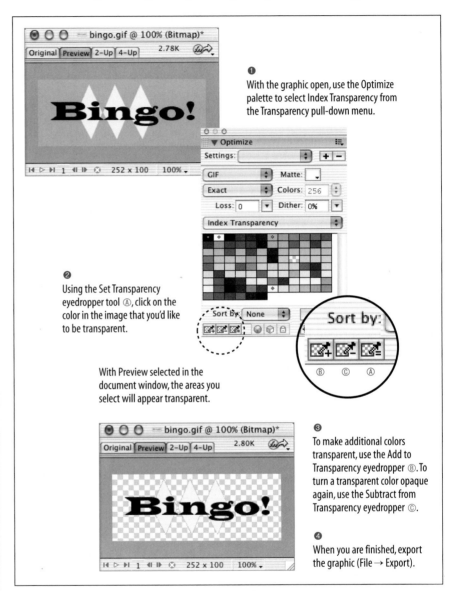

❶ With the graphic open, use the Optimize palette to select Index Transparency from the Transparency pull-down menu.

❷ Using the Set Transparency eyedropper tool Ⓐ, click on the color in the image that you'd like to be transparent.

With Preview selected in the document window, the areas you select will appear transparent.

❸ To make additional colors transparent, use the Add to Transparency eyedropper Ⓑ. To turn a transparent color opaque again, use the Subtract from Transparency eyedropper Ⓒ.

❹ When you are finished, export the graphic (File → Export).

Figure 15-12. Adding transparency to a flat graphic in Fireworks MX.

Avoiding Halos

Have you ever seen a transparent graphic that has a fringe of pixels that doesn't blend in with the background color of the page? That's what's commonly known as a halo, and it's easy to prevent, especially with the aid of the web graphics tools we've been using so far in this chapter.

Halos are the result of anti-aliased edges that have been blended with a color *other* than the background color of the page (Figure 15-13). Making the outside of a graphic transparent leaves the blur along the image edge still intact. All those shades are visible against the new background color and ruin the transparency effect.

One way to prevent halos is simply to avoid anti-aliased edges. In aliased images, there is a hard edge between colors. Unfortunately, the jagged, stair-stepped effect of aliased edges usually looks just as bad.

But in the more likely event that your image does have anti-aliased edges, there are two ways to prevent halos. The parts of your graphic must be on transparent layers without any surrounding pixels. In other words, the image must not have already been "flattened."

The best prevention for halos is to use the Matte color feature in Photoshop (5.5 or higher), ImageReady, or Fireworks. Set the Matte color to match the background color of the HTML page the graphic is going on (Figure 15-14, following page). When you export the transparent GIF, the anti-aliased edges in your image blend with the specified Matte color. No more halos!

If you are using a tool that doesn't have the Matte feature (such as earlier versions of Photoshop or Paint Shop Pro), the trick is to create a new layer at the bottom of the layer "stack" and fill it with the background color of your page (Figure 15-14, bottom). When the image is flattened (as a result of changing it to Indexed Color), the anti-aliased edges blend with the proper background color. Next, just select the background color to be transparent during export and your halo problems should be over.

Halos are the fringe that's left around a transparent image. They happen when anti-aliased edges have been blended with a color that is lighter than the page background.

Halos do not happen around aliased (stair-stepped) text and images because there is a hard edge between colors.

Figure 15-13. The halo effect.

IMAGE TIP

Fixing Halos in Flattened Images

Unfortunately, the way to fix a halo in an image that has already been flattened is to get in there and erase the anti-aliased edges, pixel by pixel. You need to get as close to the image area as possible to get rid of the blended edge, making sure not to erase parts of the image itself. Even if you get rid of all the edges, you'll be left with aliased (stair-stepped) edges, and the quality of the image will suffer.

Another technique that may work on certain images is to select the image area with a marquee that has the "feathering" set to 1 to 3 pixels. Copy the image and paste it into a new document that has a background that matches your page and re-export as a GIF.

If you're concerned with the professional appearance of your site, I'd say it's better to recreate the graphic from scratch, taking care to prevent halos, than to waste time trying to fix them. This is another good reason to always save your layered files.

TIP

If your page background is a multi-colored pattern or is otherwise difficult to match with the Matte color, opt for a color that is slightly darker than the dominant web page color.

In Photoshop (5.5 and higher)

Select Save for Web from the File menu. Click Matte to launch a color picker where you can specify the background color of your web page.

The Matte color is blended into the antil-aliased edges around the image.

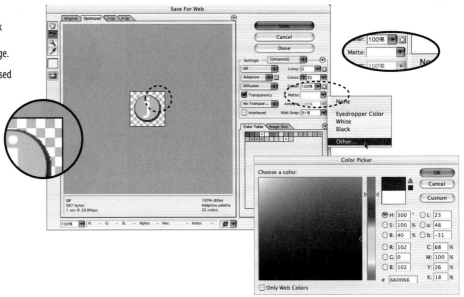

In Fireworks

The Matte option is available on the Optimize palette. Clicking it pops up a palette of web-safe colors (or you can enter your own values).

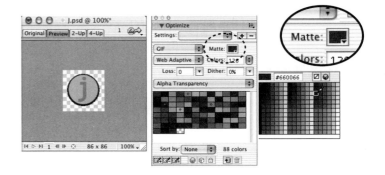

Other Tools

If your tool does not offer a Matte function, simply create a new layer behind the image and fill it with the background color of your web page. When the layers merge, the anti-aliased edges will blend with the background color when you make the remaining color transparent.

RESULT:

The anti-aliased edges blend in with the page color and the halo is gone.

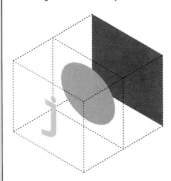

Figure 15-14. Graphics programs have tools to avoid halos around transparent graphics.

Exercise 15-2: Working with Transparency

Now is your chance to make some transparent graphics. The files are available in *15-2* in the *chap15* materials folder. The demonstration that follows uses Photoshop, but ImageReady would be fine, too.

1. Our goal is to make transparent graphics that blend in with the background graphic (*bkgd.gif*) used on *transparency.html*. Start by finding the RGB values of the predominant color in *bkgd.gif*. Use the eyedropper tool to sample the light-yellow color. Click on the color swatch (toolbar) to get the RGB values and jot them down. Click OK and close the file.

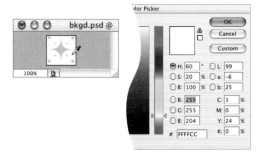

2. Now let's work on the header graphic. Open *kitchen-banner.psd*. If you look at the Layers palette (Windows → Layers), you'll see that the rule, the illustration, and type are on separate layers and there are transparent areas that we want to preserve.

   Select Save for Web from the File menu. Make sure the Transparency box is checked. Click on the Matte block and choose Other. Enter the RGB values we got from the background graphic in the Color Picker.

   Click OK and save the file as *kitchen-banner.gif*. Be sure to save it in the same directory as *transparency.html*.

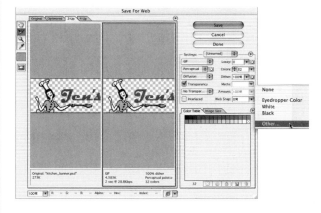

3. Next, we'll add transparency to the *foods.tif* graphic. Open the file and look at the Layers palette. You'll see that it is flattened (all on one layer). This makes it more difficult to blend with the background because the anti-aliased edges are already filled with white, and we can't change that now.

   The best we can do is make the white pixels in the image transparent. Convert the image from RGB color to Indexed Color (Image → Mode → Indexed Color). Accept the default settings and click OK. Next, view the Color Table for the image (Image → Mode → Color Table). Use the eyedropper to click on any white area. The white pixels should immediately turn transparent (a checked pattern shows through).

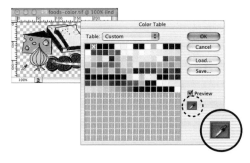

Now you can use Save for Web as before, although the Matte feature will have no effect since the anti-aliased edges are already filled with white.

4. Open *transparency.html* in a browser to see the results. The banner graphic matches the background smoothly, and because the background is a light color, the white halo in the foods image is not too visible.

5. Try replacing the background image in *transparency.html* with a darker background color (BGCOLOR="#FF9999") and resaving it. To get rid of the halos around the header graphic, you will need to export a new version of the GIF using the new background color for the Matte. Unfortunately, there's not much you can do with the food illustration because the halo is part of the image. The lesson here is that it is always preferable to start with layered originals.

Optimizing GIFs

Do you remember the Golden Rule of Web Design, "Keep your files as small as possible"? That rule applies especially to graphics files, since they are typically the biggest files on the page. For this reason, it is certainly worth the extra effort to make your GIF files as small as possible—in other words, to "optimize" them.

When optimizing GIF files, it is useful to keep in mind that GIF compression works by condensing rows of identical pixel colors. In most of the following optimization strategies, the net result is that you are creating more areas of solid color in the image for the compression to sink its teeth into.

Again, if you're using Photoshop (5.5 or higher), ImageReady, or Fireworks, you'll find a number of tools that make the job of optimization simple, such as the ability to see the effects of your settings instantly and even do side-by-side comparisons (Figure 15-15).

WORK ALONG

The source file, barn.psd, pictured in the following figures is available in the chap15 materials folder, if you'd like to try out the optimization techniques.

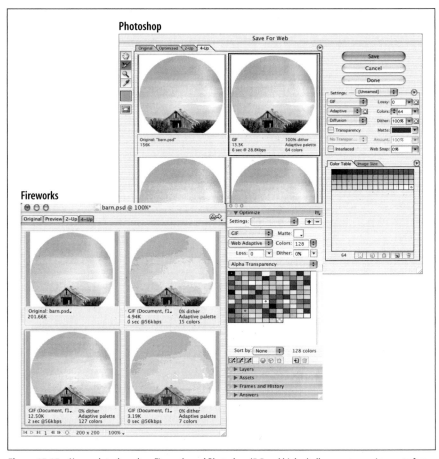

Figure 15-15. New web tools such as Fireworks and Photoshop (5.5 and higher) allow you to preview up to four variations of your image at once. This allows you to try out a number of settings to get the best image quality at the smallest file size.

Reduce the number of colors

Although GIFs can contain up to 256 colors, there's no rule that says they have to. In fact, by reducing the number of colors in the image (i.e., reducing its bit depth), you can significantly reduce its file size (Figure 15-16 Ⓖ). One reason for this is that files with lower bit depths contain less data. Another by-product of the color reduction is that more areas of flat color are created by combining similar, abutting pixel colors. More flat color, more efficient compression.

Nearly all graphics programs that allow you to save or export to GIF format will also allow you to specify the number of colors (or bit depth).

At a certain point, of course, if you reduce the number of colors too far, the image will begin to fall apart or will cease to communicate the effect you are after. For instance, in Figure 15-16, once I reduced the number of colors to eight, I lost the rainbow (which was the whole point of the image). This "meltdown" point is different from image to image.

You'll be surprised to find how many images look perfectly fine at 5-bit with only 32 pixel colors (that's usually my starting point for color reduction, and I go higher only if needed). Some image types fare better than others with reduced color palettes, but as a general rule, the fewer the colors, the smaller the file.

The real size savings kick in when there are large areas of flat color. Keep in mind that even if your image has only eight pixel colors, if it has a lot of blends and gradients, you won't see the kind of file size savings you might expect with that kind of severe color reduction.

Bit Depth

Bit depth is a way to refer to the maximum number of colors a graphic can contain. This chart shows the number of colors each bit depth can represent:

1-bit	2 colors
2-bit	4 colors
3-bit	8 colors
4-bit	16 colors
5-bit	32 colors
6-bit	64 colors
7-bit	128 colors
8-bit	256 colors
16-bit	65,536 colors
24-bit	16,777,216 colors (usually referred to as "millions")

Web tools allow you to select the number of colors when you save in GIF format. However, some tools make you choose from a list of bit depths, so it is useful to know how many colors you'll end up with for each one.

256 colors: 21 KB

64 colors: 13 KB

8 colors: 8 KB

Figure 15-16. Reducing the number of colors in an image reduces the file size. Ⓖ

Reduce dithering

When the colors in an image are reduced to a specific palette, the colors that are not in the palette are approximated by dithering. Dithering is the speckle pattern you see in images when palette colors are combined to simulate unavailable colors.

In photographic images, dithering is not a problem and can even be beneficial; however, dithering in flat areas is usually distracting and undesirable. Beyond aesthetic reasons, dithering is undesirable because the speckles disrupt otherwise smooth areas of color. Those stray speckles stand in the way of GIF compression and result in larger files.

One way to shave extra bytes off a GIF is to limit the amount of dithering. Again, nearly all GIF-creation tools allow you to turn dithering on and off. Photoshop (5.5 and higher), ImageReady, and Fireworks go one step further by allowing you to set the specific amount of dithering on a sliding scale. You can even view the results of the dither setting, so you can decide at which point the degradation in image quality is not worth the file size savings (Figure 15-17 ⒢). In images with smooth color gradients, turning dithering off results in unacceptable banding and blotches.

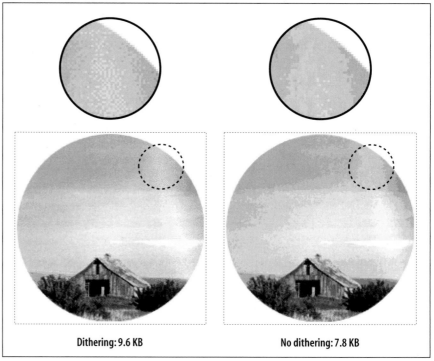

Dithering: 9.6 KB   No dithering: 7.8 KB

Figure 15-17. Turning off or reducing the amount of dithering will reduce the file size. Both images have 32 pixel colors and use an Adaptive palette. ⒢

Lossy GIFs

As we discussed earlier, GIF compression is "lossless," which means every pixel in the image is preserved during compression. But you can force some pixels to be thrown out using the Lossy setting in Photoshop or ImageReady or the Loss setting in Fireworks (Figure 15-18 G). Again, throwing out stray pixels is all in the name of maximizing solid blocks of pixel color, thus allowing the GIF compression to do its stuff. Depending on the image, you can apply a loss value of 5–30% without seriously degrading the image. This technique works best for continuous tone art (however, images that are all continuous tone should probably be saved as JPEGs anyway). You might try this on an image with a combination of flat and photographic content.

Lossy set to 0%: 13.2 KB   Lossy set to 25%: 7.5 KB

Figure 15-18. Applying a Lossy (in Photoshop) or Loss (in Fireworks) value removes pixels from the image and results in smaller file size. Both images shown here contain 64 colors and use Diffusion dither. G

Design for compression

We've looked at several ways you can use the settings in your tools to reduce the size of your GIFs. But even before you get to that point, you can be proactive about optimizing your graphics by designing them to compress well in the first place.

Finding the "Sweet Spot"

You will see that finding the best optimization for a given image requires adjusting all of these attributes (number of colors, dithering, lossiness) simultaneously until the best image quality at the smallest file size is achieved. It takes time and patience, but eventually you will find the "sweet spot" for each image. It's a Zen thing.

Keep it flat

I've found that as a web designer, I've changed my illustration style to match the medium. In instances where I might have used a gradient blend, I now opt for a flat color. In most cases, it works just as well, and it doesn't introduce unflattering banding and dithering or drive up the file size (Figure 15-19 G). You may also choose to replace areas of photos with subtle blends, such as a blue sky, with flat colors if you need to save them in GIF format (otherwise, the JPEG format may be better).

This GIF has gradient blends and 256 colors. Its file size is 19 KB.

Even when I reduce the number of colors to 8, the file size is still 7.6 KB.

When I create the same image with flat colors instead of blends, the size of the GIF file is only 3.2 KB.

Figure 15-19. You can keep file sizes small by designing in a way that takes advantage of the GIF compression scheme. G

Play with horizontal stripes

When you are designing your web graphics, keep in mind that the compression works best on horizontal bands of colors. If you want to make something striped, it's better to make the stripes horizontal than vertical (Figure 15-20). Silly, but true.

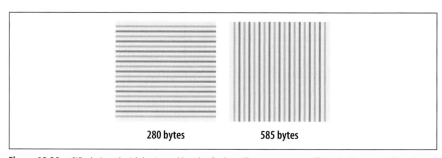
280 bytes   585 bytes

Figure 15-20. GIFs designed with horizontal bands of color will compress more efficiently than vertical bands.

One technique that is commonly used in web design is to apply 1-pixel-wide horizontal lines over a photographic image. The image still shows through the horizontal lines, but the GIF compression can work its magic on a significant portion of the image area (Figure 15-21).

Weighted optimization

Photoshop 6 and higher and ImageReady offer a "weighted optimization" feature for GIFs that allows you to apply varying amounts of optimization to different parts of the image.* This is done using an "alpha channel" (called a mask). The white areas of the mask correspond to the highest image quality, while black areas describe the lowest (gray areas are on a linear scale in between). Channels can be used to control the color reduction, dithering, and lossiness in a GIF image. To access the Modify dialog box (Figure 15-22), click the Mask button next to each of the controls on the Optimization palette. This advanced optimization technique requires solid Photoshop skills. See Photoshop's documentation for more detailed instructions.

13 KB

10 KB

Figure 15-21. Adding a 1-pixel striped pattern over a photographic image is one design technique for reducing file size.

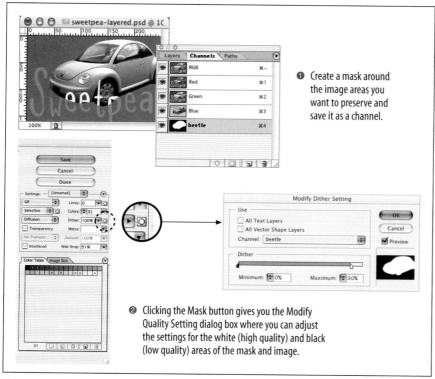

❶ Create a mask around the image areas you want to preserve and save it as a channel.

❷ Clicking the Mask button gives you the Modify Quality Setting dialog box where you can adjust the settings for the white (high quality) and black (low quality) areas of the mask and image.

Figure 15-22. Weighted optimization in Photoshop.

---

* While both Photoshop and Fireworks offer weighted optimization for JPEGS, only Photoshop offers this featue for GIFs.

Optimize to a file size

In some cases, you may know the target file size for your graphic—for example, when designing a page with a strict K-limit. Photoshop (5.5 and higher), ImageReady, and Fireworks offer an Optimize to File Size function that automatically optimizes an image to meet a specified target size. Figure 15-23 demonstrates how to access this feature in both tools.

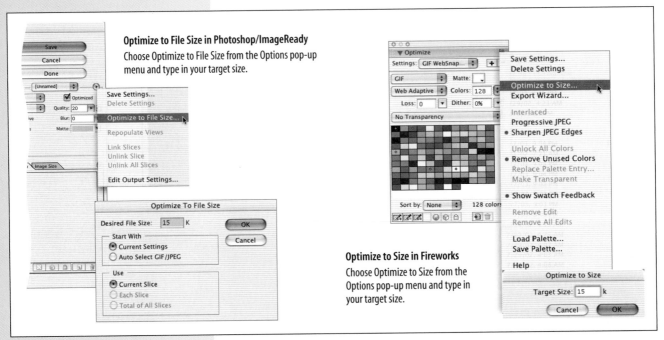

Optimize to File Size in Photoshop/ImageReady
Choose Optimize to File Size from the Options pop-up menu and type in your target size.

Optimize to Size in Fireworks
Choose Optimize to Size from the Options pop-up menu and type in your target size.

Figure 15-23. Optimizing to a file size.

TRY IT

Exercise 15-3: Optimizing GIF Files

See if you can reduce file sizes of the images below to within 1 KB of the target sizes without seriously sacrificing image quality. Take advantage of all the techniques covered in this section.

The starting images are available in *15-3* in the *chap15* materials folder on the CD and online.

You will get the best results using a web graphics tool such as Photoshop, ImageReady, or Fireworks. There are many ways to achieve the desired results, and there are no "right" answers.

1. *bunny.psd*; target < 5 KB

2. *asian.psd*; target < 4 KB

3. *info.psd*; target < 250 bytes

INFO

Designing with the Web Palette

Another big part of designing GIFs for the Web is whether and how to use the web palette. The web palette is a set of 216 colors that will not dither on PCs or Macs, and it is built into all the major browsers. When a browser is running on a computer with an 8-bit monitor (capable of displaying only 256 colors at a time), it refers to its internal web palette to make up the colors on the page. The colors in the images are remapped to the colors in the web palette.

Chapter 13 has a more technical explanation of how the web palette was devised and how it is applied in HTML documents. But the web palette comes into play when you are designing and creating GIF graphics as well. It is particularly useful for images with flat colors, since those suffer the most from unwanted dithering.

We've seen several examples already of what happens when colors are mapped to a smaller palette—shifting and dithering. But at least we have the advantage of knowing exactly which colors the browser will use, and if we use those "web-safe" colors in the first place, we can prevent unpredictable results on 8-bit monitors (Figure 15-24 G). Our graphics will look consistent from platform to platform, user to user.

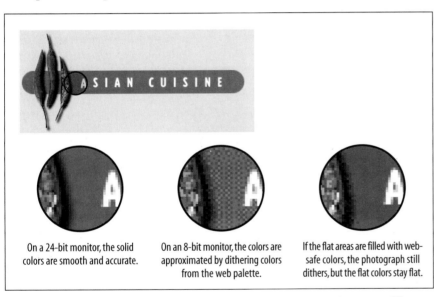

| On a 24-bit monitor, the solid colors are smooth and accurate. | On an 8-bit monitor, the colors are approximated by dithering colors from the web palette. | If the flat areas are filled with web-safe colors, the photograph still dithers, but the flat colors stay flat. |

Figure 15-24. This GIF is designed with non-web-safe colors, resulting in dithering on 8-bit monitors. G

I want to point out the distinction between dithered graphics and dithering in a monitor. Some graphics contain dithered colors right in the image file. These graphics will look dithered regardless of the monitor they are viewed on because the dither pattern is in the source. What we are concerned with in this section is the dithering that the monitor adds when it cannot reproduce a particular RGB value in an image. Even if your source image is smooth and flat, it may not end up that way when viewed on 8-bit monitors.

What Does the Web Palette Look Like?

The colors in the web palette were not chosen because of the way they look; they are just the results of combining amounts of red, green, and blue light at even 20% increments. Because web colors are light-based, it is impossible to get even a decent representation of them in print (especially the more fluorescent tones), so they are not reproduced in this book.

To see samples of all the colors in the web palette, load them into your Photoshop swatches palette (see Figure 15-25 for a demonstration) or view the web palette chart available at *www.learningwebdesign.com*.

> **TIP**
>
> *To see how your image will look in the 8-bit environment, try using Photoshop's Browser Dither preview (accessed in the Save for Web dialog box). This may help you make decisions regarding optimization.*

> **DESIGN TIP**
>
> ## When You Don't Need to Worry About the Web Palette
>
> There are some instances when you don't need to be concerned with the web palette:
>
> *If you don't care about performance on 8-bit monitors.* Remember, the web palette comes into play only on 8-bit monitors. 16- and 24-bit monitors can accurately display just about any image. So if you are not concerned with your site's performance on low-end systems, you don't need to worry about the web palette. With 8-bit monitors making up only about 5% of web traffic, you might decide it's not worth it.
>
> *If your image is primarily photographic.* First, I should say that if you're starting with a purely photographic image, you should save it in JPEG format (see Chapter 16 for more information).
>
> But say you have a photographic image that you want to save as a GIF. Because the image is going to dither somewhat anyway when you reduce its colors, and because dithering can actually be beneficial in photographic images, you do not need to apply the web palette. Selecting an adaptive or selective palette (a customized palette based on the colors most used in the image) is a better choice during the conversion process.
>
> *If your image is in JPEG format.* The web palette is irrelevant for JPEG images. For one thing, JPEGs don't use palettes to keep track of colors. But more importantly, even if you have flat areas of web-safe colors in your original image, they will shift and distort during the JPEG compression process. Designing with the web palette is a GIF-specific issue.

Starting with web-safe colors

If you are creating images from scratch, you have the perfect opportunity to use web-safe colors in your design.

If you are creating images from scratch, you have the perfect opportunity to use web-safe colors in your design. The benefit is knowing that your graphics will look the same for all users. The main drawback is that the color selection is very limited. Not only is 216 not many colors to choose from, but a good percentage of them are colors that you'd never be caught dead using for anything (the web palette was generated mathematically, not aesthetically).

The trick is to have the colors of the web palette available in a Swatches palette (or in whatever device your graphics program uses to make colors handy). Fortunately, with the great demand for web graphics, the web palette has been integrated into the majority of graphics-related programs, including, but not limited to:

> Adobe Photoshop (5.0 and higher)
> Macromedia Fireworks (1.0 and higher)
> JASC Paint Shop Pro (5 and higher)
> Adobe Illustrator (7.0 and higher)
> Corel (previously MetaCreations) Painter (6 and higher)
> Macromedia Freehand (7.0 and higher)
> Macromedia Director (5.0 and higher)
> Macintosh System Color Picker (OS 8 and higher)

The web palette may be called by one of its many names, such as the Netscape Palette, Web 216, Browser-Safe Palette, Non-Dithering Palette, the 6×6×6 Cube, and so on—but you should recognize it when you see it.

Photoshop and other graphics tools save palettes in files called CLUTs (Color Look-Up Tables). Some tools, such as Fireworks, offer the web palette by default. In others, you may need to load the appropriate web CLUT file into the program to make it available. Figure 15-25 shows how that works in Adobe Photoshop.

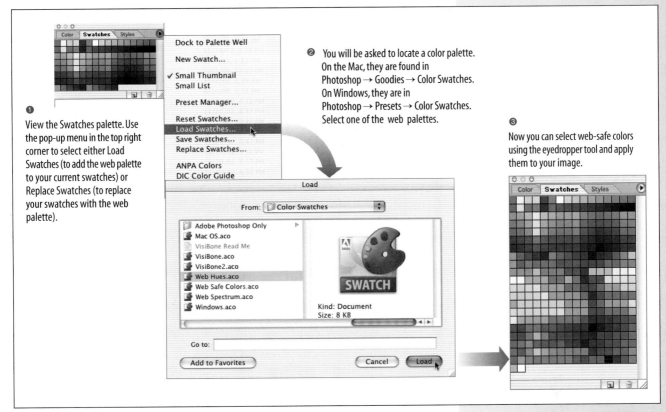

❶ View the Swatches palette. Use the pop-up menu in the top right corner to select either Load Swatches (to add the web palette to your current swatches) or Replace Swatches (to replace your swatches with the web palette).

❷ You will be asked to locate a color palette. On the Mac, they are found in Photoshop → Goodies → Color Swatches. On Windows, they are in Photoshop → Presets → Color Swatches. Select one of the web palettes.

❸ Now you can select web-safe colors using the eyedropper tool and apply them to your image.

Figure 15-25. Loading the web palette into Photoshop.

Applying the web palette

Another way to make sure your image uses web-safe colors is to apply the web palette in the conversion process from RGB to Indexed Color. In any tool, once you have chosen to make your image into a GIF or to convert it to Indexed Color, you will be asked to select a palette for the image.

The simplest and crudest method is to select the Web palette option when you are asked for the palette. The color table for the resulting GIF will contain colors from the web palette exclusively, regardless of the colors in the source image (Figure 15-26, following page).

The newer web graphics tools offer a more sophisticated method for applying and preserving web-safe colors in the conversion process. These are especially useful for images that contain a combination of full-color photographic images and flat, web-safe colors.

> **TIP**
>
> ### Shortcut to Web Colors
>
> Photoshop's Color Picker includes an Only Web Colors button that, when checked, limits the available colors in the spectrum to web-safe colors. The Color Picker is accessed by clicking on one of the color swatches in the tool palette.

The source file, ufo.psd, pictured in Figures 15-26 and 15-28, is available in the chap15 materials folder. The image was created using web-safe colors in the flat areas, but the photgraph of the toy on the left is full-color. You can see the effects of applying the Web Adaptive palette or various degrees of Web Snap for yourself.

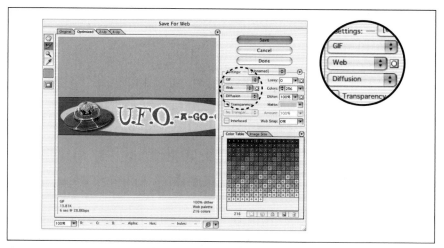

Figure 15-26. When you apply the web palette to an image, its color table will contain all the colors from the web palette, regardless of the colors that appear in the original image.

Fireworks gives you the option of saving with the Web Adaptive palette. This is an adaptive palette, so the palette will be customized for the image, but any colors that are near in value to web palette colors will "snap" to the closest web palette colors (Figure 15-27).

In Photoshop 5.5 and later, you can control how many colors shift to their nearest web-safe equivalents by selecting an adaptive palette (Adaptive, Perceptual, or Selective) and using the Web Snap slider tool (Figure 15-28). The higher you set the slider, the more colors will shift. This allows Photoshop to construct a custom color table for the image while keeping areas of the image web-safe.

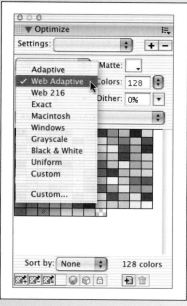

Figure 15-27. Fireworks offers a Web Adaptive palette. Some colors are shifted to web-safe equivalents while an adaptive palette is created from the original image.

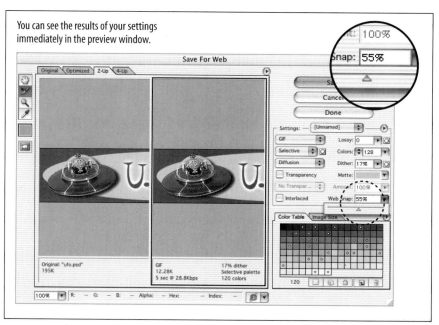

Figure 15-28. Use the Photoshop (5.5 and later) Web Snap slider to control precisely how many colors snap to their nearest web-safe equivalents. In the Color Table, the swatches with dots are web-safe.

Web palette strategies for graphics

Many beginners make the mistake of applying the web palette to every graphic they produce. After all, they're "web" graphics, right? Wrong. The web palette isn't appropriate for all image types and can actually reduce potential quality. In fact, I almost never apply the straight web palette to an image, particularly now that web graphics tools provide more sophisticated options. There are no hard and fast rules, since every image has its own requirements. The following are some basic guidelines for using—and resisting—the web palette.

The web palette isn't appropriate for all image types and can actually reduce potential quality.

Flat graphical images

GOAL: Keep flat color areas from dithering while maintaining smoothness in the anti-aliased edges.

STRATEGY: Use colors from the web palette to fill flat color areas when you are designing the image. Do not apply the simple web palette option when saving or exporting because you'll lose the gradations of color in the anti-aliasing. It is better to choose an Adaptive palette with a Web Snap option, if it is available. In Photoshop, set the amount of Web Snap with the slider scale. In Fireworks, apply the Web Adaptive palette. These options maintain the web colors in your flat areas, but allow the colors in the anti-aliasing to remain.

Photographic images

GOAL: Maintain clarity and color fidelity for the maximum number of users.

STRATEGY: First, entirely photographic images should be saved in JPEG format. Otherwise, choose an Adaptive, Perceptual, or Selective palette when converting the image to GIF format. Any time you reduce the colors in a photographic image you'll get some dithering, so choose a palette that best matches the colors in the image. That way, the image will look the best it possibly can for users with 24-bit monitors. For users with 8-bit monitors, the image will map again to the web palette, but dithering is usually not detrimental in photographic images. Applying the web palette to a continuous-tone image only ensures that it will look equally bad to everyone.

Combination images (both flat and photographic areas)

GOAL: Keep the flat areas from dithering while allowing the continuous tone areas to dither with an adaptive palette.

STRATEGY: Use web-safe colors in the flat areas when you are designing the image. When it's time to save or export to GIF format, choose an Adaptive palette with a Web Snap option if it is available. The Adaptive palette preserves the color fidelity in the photographic areas while the Web Snap option preserves the web-safe colors in the flat areas.

Some Things to Remember About GIFs

In closing, I'd like to round up some of the major points from this lengthy but important chapter:

- GIF is the best file format for images with flat areas of color, such as logos, line art, text graphics, etc. The GIF compression scheme works by finding and condensing rows of identically colored pixels.

- GIFs can be interlaced, transparent, and/or animated.

- A GIF uses a color palette that can contain up to 256 colors. When you save an image as a GIF, you need to convert it to Indexed Color and select an appropriate color palette.

- You can make parts of a GIF transparent by preserving the transparent areas in a layered document (in Photoshop and Fireworks) or by selecting a color in a flattened image with the proper transparency tool.

- Halos occur when an image is anti-aliased to a color other than the background color of the page, causing a fringe of pixels around the image. Halos are easier to prevent than correct.

- Some strategies for keeping GIF file sizes small are: design with flat areas of colors, reduce the number of colors when converting to Indexed Color, limit dithering, and take advantage of lossy GIF compression if it is available.

- The web palette is a set of 216 colors that will not dither in browsers on 8-bit monitors. Choosing colors from the web palette when designing GIF images prevents flat areas of color from dithering.

Test Yourself

Take some time to answer these questions about creating and optimizing GIF files. Answers are provided in the Appendix.

1. What is "indexed color"?

2. How many colors are in the index color table for an 8-bit graphic? For a 5-bit graphic?

3. Name two things you can do with a GIF that you can't do with a JPEG.

4. What is an "adaptive" palette?

5. How does reducing the amount of dithering affect the size of the file?

6. What is the advantage of designing graphics with the web palette?

Creating JPEGs

If you have a photograph or any other image with blended color (such as a painting or realistic digital illustration), JPEG is the file format to use. It's perfect for compressing continuous-tone color and even grayscale images (Figure 16-1 Ⓖ).

In this chapter

Characteristics of JPEG compression

Making JPEGs, step by step

Optimizing JPEGs

Figure 16-1. The JPEG file format is ideal for photographs (color or grayscale) or any image with subtle color gradations. Ⓖ

Compared to GIFs, saving images in JPEG format is a walk in the park. Before we get into the JPEG creation process, there are a few things you should know about the file format that will help you decide when to use JPEG and how to make the best possible JPEG images.

More About JPEGs

JPEG (Joint Photographic Experts Group, the standards body that created it) is a compression algorithm developed especially for photographic images. By understanding JPEG terminology and the nature of JPEG compression, you'll be able to use your graphics tools efficiently to make the highest-quality JPEGs at the smallest sizes.

24-bit color

The nice thing about JPEGs is that they contain 24-bit RGB color information; that's millions of colors. This is one aspect that makes them ideal for photographs—they have all the colors you'll ever need. With JPEGs, you don't have to worry about color palettes or limiting yourself to 256 colors the way you do with GIFs. JPEGs are much more straightforward.

Lossy compression

The JPEG compression scheme is lossy, which means that some of the image information is thrown out in the compression process. Fortunately, this loss is not discernable for most images at most compression levels. When an image is compressed with high levels of JPEG compression, you begin to see color blotches and squares (usually referred to as "artifacts") that result from the way the compression scheme samples the image (Figure 16-2 ⓖ).

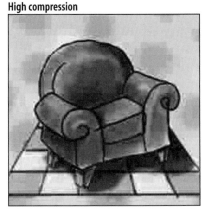

Figure 16-2. JPEG compression discards image detail to achieve smaller file sizes. At high compression rates, image quality suffers, as shown in the image on the right. ⓖ

What About the Web Palette?

When you're working with JPEGs, you don't need to worry about the web palette. JPEGs don't have color tables like GIFs; they just try to stay true to the original RGB colors in the image.

When a JPEG appears on an 8-bit monitor, the browser applies its internal web palette to the image and, as a result, the image dithers. Fortunately, while dithering is distracting on areas of flat color, it is usually not a problem in photographic images.

As an added bonus, you get to control how aggressively you want the image to be compressed. This involves a trade-off between compression level and quality. The more you compress the image (for a smaller file size), the more the image suffers. Conversely, when you maximize quality, you also end up with larger files. The best compression level is based on the particular image and your objectives for the site. We'll talk more about this in the Optimizing JPEGs section later in this chapter.

JPEGs love smooth colors

JPEGs compress areas of smooth, blended colors much more efficiently than areas with high contrast and sharp detail (Figure 16-3 ⓖ). In fact, the blurrier your image, the smaller the resulting JPEG. Later in this chapter, we'll look at how you can use this to your advantage when optimizing JPEGs.

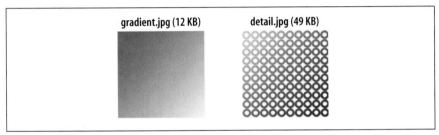

Figure 16-3. JPEG compression works better on smooth images than images with hard edges and detail. Compare the file sizes of these examples. ⓖ

Totally flat colors don't do well in JPEG format because the colors may shift and get mottled (Figure 16-4 ⓖ), particularly at higher rates of compression. In general, flat graphical images should be saved as GIFs.

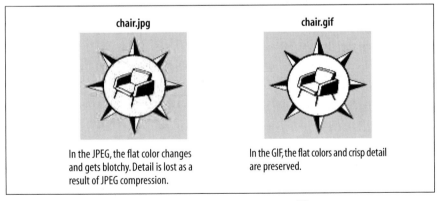

Figure 16-4. The same flat graphical image saved as both a JPEG and a GIF. ⓖ

In GIF files, you have total control over the colors that appear in the image, making it easy to match colors in adjoining GIFs, or in an inline GIF and a tiled background image.

Unfortunately, flat colors shift around and get somewhat blotchy with JPEG compression, so there is no way to control the colors precisely. Even pure white can be distorted in a JPEG.

This makes it nearly impossible to create a perfect, seamless match between a JPEG and a GIF with its pure flat colors. If you want to match a graphic in the foreground to a tiling background graphic, don't mix formats. You will have the best results in matching GIF to GIF because of the unpredictability of JPEG color.

Progressive JPEGs

Progressive JPEGs are just ordinary JPEGs that display in a series of passes (like interlaced GIFs), starting with a low-resolution version that gets clearer with each pass (Figure 16-5 Ⓖ). In some graphics programs, you can specify the number of passes it takes to fill in the final image (3, 4, or 5).

The advantage of using progressive JPEGs is that viewers can get an idea of the image before it downloads completely. Also, making a JPEG progressive usually reduces its file size slightly. The disadvantages are that they take more processing power to display and are not supported in very early browser versions.

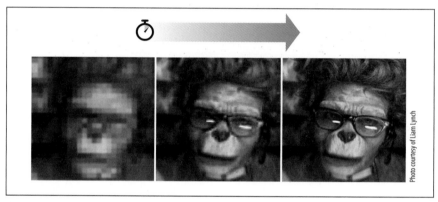

Figure 16-5. Progressive JPEGs render in a series of passes. The image detail and quality is improved with each pass. Ⓖ

Decompression

JPEGs need to be decompressed before they can be displayed; therefore, it takes a browser longer to decode and assemble a JPEG than a GIF of the same file size. It's not a big difference, though, and is not a reason to avoid the JPEG format.

Naming JPEGs

JPEGs must be named with the *.jpg* or *.jpeg* suffix in order to be used on a web page. Even if the graphic is in JPEG format, the browser relies on the proper suffix to recognize the file as a JPEG and to place it on the page.

Making JPEGs, Step by Step

Regardless of the tool you use, the process of creating a JPEG is about the same. You'll begin by opening your image in an image editing program and performing any necessary edits such as resizing, cropping, color adjustments, etc. Always save your original in case you need to make changes to the image later.

In the process of saving or exporting the JPEG, you will be asked to make the following decisions:

Image quality. The quality setting tells the program how aggressively to compress the image. Image quality is generally tracked on a scale from 1–10 or from 0–100%. Higher numbers correspond to better image quality and therefore, larger file sizes. Lower numbers correspond to worse image quality with smaller file sizes. In most cases, "medium," or approximately 50%, produces an acceptable JPEG image; however, you may be able to go even lower.

Progressive. Decide whether you want the JPEG to be progressive (see the section Progressive JPEGs earlier in this chapter).

Optimized. Decide whether you want the JPEG to be optimized. This usually results in a slightly smaller JPEG, but it may not display in early browser versions. Photoshop 7 does not allow you to optimize progressive JPEGs.

Matte. If you are working with a layered image or one that contains transparent areas, the matte color you specify will be used to fill in the transparent areas of the image. Generally, you'd want to select a color that matches the background color of the page to simulate transparency (JPEGs can't have real transparent areas like GIFs.)

Blur or smoothing. Some tools let you blur your image slightly to improve the compression and reduce file size. If you choose to do this, it is important to preview your image to make sure the image quality is still acceptable. The setting, of course, will depend on your image.

Once you have made all your settings, export or save the file as a JPEG. Be sure to name it with the *.jpg* or *.jpeg* suffix.

The exercise that follows walks you through the JPEG creation process step by step using Adobe Photoshop 7, but the technique works in Versions 5.5 and higher. The sections following the exercise demonstrate how JPEGs are made in Macromedia Fireworks and JASC Paint Shop Pro.

IMPORTANT

Be sure that your image is in RGB or grayscale color mode (not CMYK) and that the resolution is set at 72 dpi.

WARNING

Some really old browsers (Version 2 and earlier) do not support optimized and progressive JPEGs, so if you are concerned with 100% browser support, choose Baseline (Standard) and avoid the special options. Fortunately, Version 1 and 2 browsers are virtually extinct as of this writing.

Exercise 16-1: Making a Basic JPEG in Photoshop

This exercise takes you through the basic steps of saving an image in the JPEG format using Photoshop's Save for Web feature. Similar tools are available in ImageReady.

1. Start by dragging the contents of the *chap16* directory to your harddrive. Launch Photoshop and open the file *stmartin.psd*.

2. Make sure that the image is in RGB format and at low resolution (in other words, ready for the Web). Check the format by selecting Image → Mode ①. This image is RGB, so we're good to go.

   Choose Image Size from the Image menu. The dialog box tells you the exact pixel measurements as well as the resolution of the image ②. Our image is 450 x 325 pixels, which is just fine for a web page. Click OK.

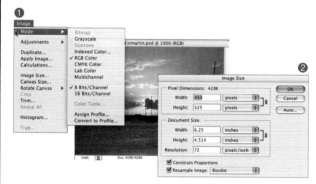

3. Now we can export a JPEG version of the graphic. Select Save for Web from the File menu ③. Click the 2-Up tab so you can see a before-and-after view of your settings. Again, pay attention to how the file size (listed in the bottom-left corner) changes as a result of your settings.

   Let's make a few settings in the dialog box:

   • Choose JPEG from the Format pulldown menu Ⓐ.

   • Select Optimized and see what happens to the file size Ⓑ. It reduces the size, so we'll leave it checked.

   • The most important setting is the quality Ⓒ. The pop-up menu jumps to general quality settings (low, medium, high), but I find it more useful to play with specific number settings. See what happens to the image and the file size at extremely low and high settings. For this image, my opinion is that the 30–40 range results in the best balance of quality and file size. Choose a setting that suits you.

   • Checking the box next to Progressive makes the JPEG display in a series of passes Ⓓ. Because we've opted to optimize this JPEG, leave this unchecked.

   • For now, we'll keep Blur set to 0 Ⓔ. The ICC Profile Ⓕ contains precise color information for the file, but it usually results in unacceptably large file sizes. Leave it unchecked. Because we have no transparent pixels in the image, the Matte feature is not necessary Ⓖ.

   • There are two palettes under the settings. The Color Table will be empty because JPEGs don't use palettes Ⓗ. The Image Size palette Ⓘ lets you resize the exported image (your original says the same). Let's leave the size alone. If you do use this feature, be sure to click Apply before you click Save.

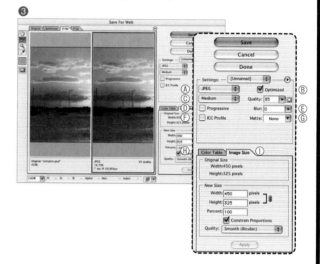

4. Once you have the settings where you want them, click Save and give the file a name that ends with *.jpg* or *.jpeg*. In Windows, save as type Images Only (*.jpg*). Click Save to save the file.

In Macromedia Fireworks

It's easy to make JPEGs in Fireworks because you can do all your compression settings right in the workspace using the Optimize palette and the Preview option in the document window. You also have access to the same settings during the export process when you select File → Export Preview. Figure 16-6 shows the JPEG controls in Fireworks MX, but the technique is the same for all versions.

❶
Open the image and do any necessary image editing (cropping, resizing, etc.) to prepare it for the Web.

❷
When you are ready, choose JPEG on the Optimize panel. If you select the 2-Up tab, you will be able to see the effects of your settings compared to the original image.

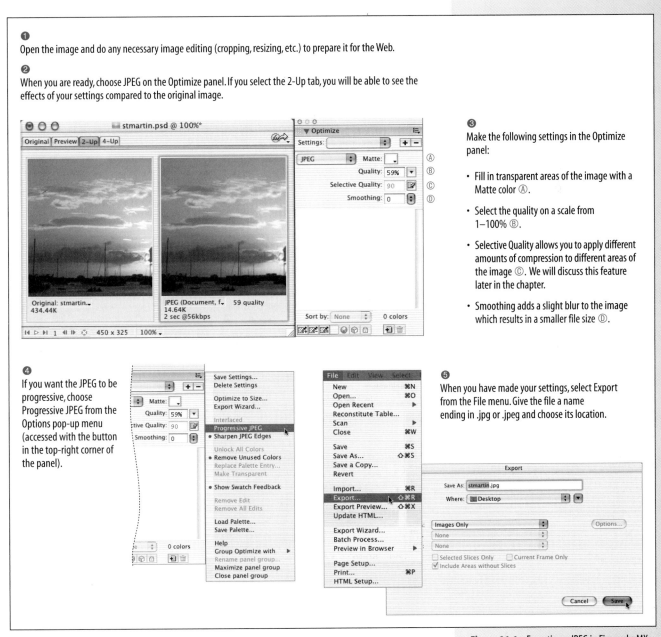

❸
Make the following settings in the Optimize panel:

- Fill in transparent areas of the image with a Matte color Ⓐ.

- Select the quality on a scale from 1–100% Ⓑ.

- Selective Quality allows you to apply different amounts of compression to different areas of the image Ⓒ. We will discuss this feature later in the chapter.

- Smoothing adds a slight blur to the image which results in a smaller file size Ⓓ.

❹
If you want the JPEG to be progressive, choose Progressive JPEG from the Options pop-up menu (accessed with the button in the top-right corner of the panel).

❺
When you have made your settings, select Export from the File menu. Give the file a name ending in .jpg or .jpeg and choose its location.

Figure 16-6. Exporting a JPEG in Fireworks MX.

In JASC Paint Shop Pro 7

Paint Shop Pro works similarly to early versions of Photoshop, but is a less expensive alternative. The downside is that it works only on the Windows operating system, so you Mac users are out of luck. Figure 16-7 shows the steps for saving a graphic as a JPEG in Paint Shop Pro 7.

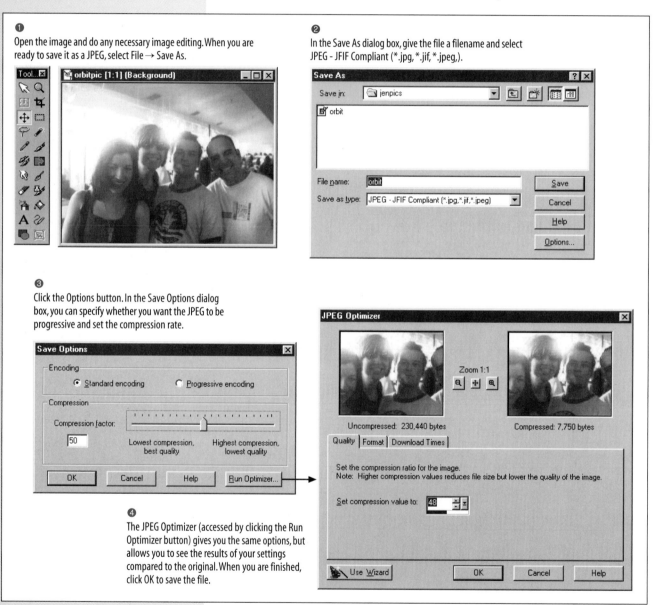

❶
Open the image and do any necessary image editing. When you are ready to save it as a JPEG, select File → Save As.

❷
In the Save As dialog box, give the file a filename and select JPEG - JFIF Compliant (*.jpg, *.jif, *.jpeg,).

❸
Click the Options button. In the Save Options dialog box, you can specify whether you want the JPEG to be progressive and set the compression rate.

❹
The JPEG Optimizer (accessed by clicking the Run Optimizer button) gives you the same options, but allows you to see the results of your settings compared to the original. When you are finished, click OK to save the file.

Figure 16-7. Saving a JPEG in JASC Paint Shop Pro 7.

Optimizing JPEGs

I've said it before and I'll say it again: when you're producing graphics for the Web, it is crucial to keep file sizes as small as possible. Using the tools and settings we've already seen, there are basic strategies you can take to make sure your JPEGs are lean and mean.

Be aggressive with compression

The easiest and most straightforward way to reduce the file size of a JPEG is to opt for a higher compression rate. Of course, this comes with the sacrifice of some image quality, but you'll be surprised how far you can compress a JPEG while maintaining an acceptable image. Figure 16-8 G, following page, shows the results of different quality (compression) rates as applied in Macromedia Fireworks and Adobe Photoshop.

Notice that the image holds up reasonably well, even at very low-quality (high-compression) rates. Every image is different, so where you draw the line between file size and image quality will vary. But unless you are publishing works of art or other types of images in which detail is important, feel free to be aggressive with compression.

Try different tools

Another interesting aspect of Figure 16-8 is that the same settings in each program produce different results. This is because the quality rating scale is not objective—it varies from program to program. For instance, a quality of 0% in Photoshop is similar to 30% in Fireworks and other programs. JPEG compression can actually go further than Photoshop allows, but you probably don't want to go there. (Take a look at the mess that happens at the 1% rating in Fireworks!) It's better to go by the way the image looks rather than a specific number setting.

There are third-party JPEG plug-ins that work within Photoshop and other image-editing programs that make the smallest JPEGs of all. See the sidebar JPEG Optimization Tools for details.

Choose optimized

Optimized JPEGs have slightly smaller file sizes and better color fidelity than standard JPEGs. For this reason, you might select the Optimized option if your image software offers it.

The drawback is that the optimized JPEG format is not supported in some older browsers (Versions 2 and earlier), but since these make up a tiny fraction of a percent of browser use, it is generally not a problem. In Photoshop 7, you cannot optimize a progressive JPEG, but the file savings you get from the progressive formatting is comparable to optimizing.

JPEG Optimization Tools

If you are really concerned with making the smallest JPEGs possible while maximizing image quality, I recommend checking out third-party compression tools. These tools have been programmed specifically to work with JPEGs, so they've got fancy algorithms that can work magic:

ProJPEG by BoxTop Software
www.boxtopsoft.com

JPEG Cruncher Pro by Spinwave
www.spinwave.com

Photoshop 7 (and ImageReady)

Photoshop 100% (42.4 KB)   Photoshop 80% (22.3 KB)   Photoshop 60% (13.6 KB)

Photoshop 40% (8.8 KB)   Photoshop 20% (6.3 KB)   Photoshop 0% (3.6 KB)

Fireworks MX

Fireworks 100% (51.5 KB)   Fireworks 80% (12.3 KB)   Fireworks 60% (7.7 KB)

Fireworks 40% (5 KB)   Fireworks 20% (1.8 KB)   Fireworks 1% (1.2 KB)

Figure 16-8. A comparison of various compression levels in Photoshop 7 and Fireworks MX. [G]

W O R K   A L O N G

This file, flower.psd, *is included in the* chap16 *materials folder on the CD and online, if you'd like to try these settings yourself.*

Soften the image

The JPEG compression scheme loves images with subtle gradations, few details, and no hard edges. One way you can take advantage of that compression is to start by softening the image prior to compression.

Photoshop (5.5 and higher) and Fireworks allow you to soften the image as part of the optimization process. In Photoshop, the tool is called Blur; in Fireworks, it's Smoothing. The blur makes the JPEG compression work better, resulting in a smaller file (Figure 16-9 [G]). If you don't have these tools, you can soften the whole image yourself by applying a slight blur to the image with the Gaussian Blur filter (or similar) and then exporting to JPEG format.

You can help JPEG compression by applying a slight blur to your image or parts of it.

Quality: 20 Blur: 0 (8.7 KB)

This JPEG was saved at low quality (20 in Photoshop) with no blurring applied.

Quality: 20 Blur: .5 (6.9 KB)

In this JPEG, I applied a slight blur to the image (.5 in Photoshop) before exporting it. Although it has the same quality setting (20), the file size is 20% smaller.

In Fireworks, use the Smoothing setting to apply a blur.

Figure 16-9. Blurring the image slightly before exporting as a JPEG will result in smaller file sizes. [G]

Weighted optimization

Weighted optimization (or selective optimization) is a method for applying different amounts of JPEG compression to different parts of the image. The advantage is that you can retain detail in the important parts of the image (such as the woman's face in Figure 16-9 above), while sacrificing quality in other areas to keep the file size as small as possible.

Both Photoshop (Versions 6 and higher) and Fireworks (4 and higher) offer weighted JPEG compression. If you don't have these tools, you can apply a blur to areas of your image manually before exporting them as JPEGs.

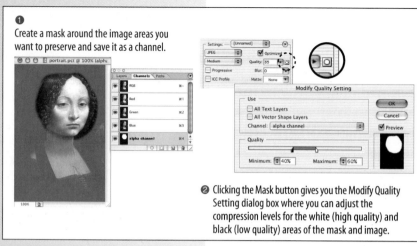

❶ Create a mask around the image areas you want to preserve and save it as a channel.

❷ Clicking the Mask button gives you the Modify Quality Setting dialog box where you can adjust the compression levels for the white (high quality) and black (low quality) areas of the mask and image.

Figure 16-10. Weighted optimization in Photoshop.

Photoshop and ImageReady use masks, generated manually with a selection or automatically for text and shape layers, to control weighted optimization. The white areas of the mask correspond to the highest image quality; black corresponds to the lowest. Clicking on the Mask button next to Quality in the Optimizaton panel opens a dialog box where you can enter compression settings for each area (Figure 16-10). See the Photoshop documentation for detailed instructions.

Fireworks has specific tools for creating what they call "selective JPEGs." Use a marquee tool to select the areas of the image you want to preserve, then select Modify → Selective JPEG → Save Selection as JPEG Mask. Then, in the Optimize panel, the Selective Quality setting applies to your selected area and the regular Quality setting applies to everything else (Figure 16-11). Again, see Fireworks' documentation for further details.

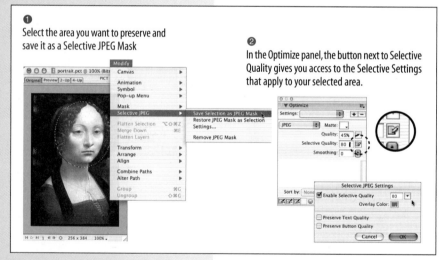

❶ Select the area you want to preserve and save it as a Selective JPEG Mask

❷ In the Optimize panel, the button next to Selective Quality gives you access to the Selective Settings that apply to your selected area.

Figure 16-11. Selective JPEGs in Fireworks.

Optimize to file size

This setting allows you to set your target file size and let the program figure out the best way to get there. This is a nifty time-saving feature if there are specific K-limits on the graphics you produce. You'll find this feature in Photoshop, ImageReady, and Fireworks (Figure 16-12). It is pretty straightforward to use.

Some Things to Remember About JPEGs

JPEGs are simpler to use than their GIF counterparts. Still, there are a few points from this chapter you might want to keep in mind:

- JPEG compression works best on continuous-tone images such as photographs or illustrations with smooth colors (such as a watercolor). It loves smooth colors and blurry areas. It doesn't like hard edges and fine detail.

- JPEGs can contain millions of colors (24-bit color).

- JPEG is a "lossy" compression scheme, meaning small parts of the image are actually thrown away upon compression.

- Each time you open and resave a JPEG, you throw away more data. The loss in image quality is cumulative. For this reason, it is best to save the originals of your images and do fresh exports when you need to make changes.

- You can be fairly aggressive with the quality setting for JPEGs in order to reduce file size.

- Another way to reduce the file size of JPEGs is to apply a slight blur to all or part of the image.

Test Yourself

Ready to test yourself on the finer points of JPEGs? Answers to these questions appear in the Appendix.

1. What does JPEG stand for?

2. What sort of palette do JPEGs use?

Optimize to File Size in Photoshop/ImageReady

Choose Optimize to File Size from the Options pop-up menu and type in your target size. The tool adjusts the Optimization settings to achieve the file size at the best image quality. It will even choose the best file format for you.

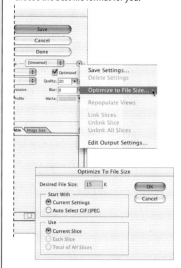

Optimize to Size in Fireworks

Choose Optimize to Size from the Options pop-up menu and type in your target size. Fireworks adjusts the Optimization settings to achieve the file size at the best image quality.

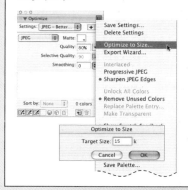

Figure 16-12. Optimizing to a specified file size can help you maintain page size quotas.

3. JPEG compression is cumulative. What does that mean? Why is it important to know?

4. What is the difference between a progressive and an optimized JPEG?

5. Name at least three techniques for reducing the size of a JPEG.

Animated GIFs

When you see a web graphic spinning, blinking, fading in and out, or otherwise putting on a little show, chances are it's an animated GIF. These days, they're *everywhere*—most notably in the advertising banners that crown nearly every page on the Web.

This chapter provides a basic introduction to how animated GIFs work and how to create them. Like so many web techniques, it's not difficult to start making simple animations, but it takes time and dedication to really master the art. This chapter is the first step.

Animated GIFs have a lot going for them: they're easy to make, and because they are just ordinary GIF files, they will work on virtually any browser without the need for plug-ins. Adding simple animation to a web page is an effective way to attract attention (advertisers are no dummies).

However, be forewarned that it's easy to end up with too much of a good thing. Many users complain that animation is distracting and even downright annoying, especially when trying to read content on the page. So if you choose to use it, use it wisely (see the sidebar Responsible Animation on the following page).

How They Work

Basic animation is one of the features built into the GIF89a graphic file format. It allows one graphic to contain a number of animation "frames," which are separate images that, when viewed quickly together, give the illusion of motion or change over time (Figure 17-1 [G], following page). All of those images are stored within a single GIF file, along with settings that describe how they should be played in the browser window.

Within the GIF, you can control whether and how many times the sequence repeats, how long each frame stays visible (frame delay), the manner in which one frame replaces another (disposal method), whether the image is transparent, and whether it is interlaced. We'll discuss each of these settings later in this chapter.

Each frame is similar to a page in a child's flipbook.

Figure 17-1. This animated GIF contains all of the images shown above. The images play back in sequence, creating a motion effect. When this GIF is viewed in a browser, the chick pops up, takes a look around, and then goes back in its shell. [G]

Responsible Animation

If you don't want to annoy your audience, follow these recommendations for animation moderation:

- Avoid more than one animation on a page.

- Use the animation to communicate something in a clever way (not just gratuitous flashing lights).

- Avoid animation on text-heavy pages that require concentration to read.

- Consider whether the extra bandwidth to make a graphic "spin" is really adding value to your page.

- Decide if your animation really needs to loop continuously.

- Experiment with timing. Sometimes a long pause between loops can make an animation less distracting.

GIF Animation Tools

To make an animated GIF, all you need is an animated GIF–making tool. These tools fall roughly into two categories.

Animation utilities are built into web graphics tools such as Adobe Image-Ready and Macromedia Fireworks. If you already have one of these tools, you won't need additional software to make animations. The nice thing about built-in tools is that they allow you to create and save your animations all in one place. Another advantage is that they have advanced features that can do automatic frame generation.

If you don't have the big guns, you can still make animations using stand-alone GIF-animation utilities. These take a pre-existing group of GIF files (one for each frame in the animation sequence) and turn them into a single animated GIF. They provide a simple interface for entering the animation settings (speed, looping, etc.). Some also provide excellent optimization options and even transition effects. The good news is that animation utilities are inexpensive (even free) and available for download (see the sidebar Animated GIF Utilities, facing page).

Animation Settings

All GIF animation tools provide an interface for adding new frames to the animation and for viewing the frames in sequence. They also allow you to make standard animation settings that affect the behavior of the animation. These are the real heart of GIF animation. Some settings will be familiar and intuitive; some you will be encountering for the first time. The location of these settings may vary from tool to tool, but they'll be there.

Soon, we'll go through the GIF animation process step by step, but first, let's take a look at each setting and pick up some important terminology that we'll need to use our tools later.

Frame delay

Also called "interframe delay," this setting adjusts the amount of time between frames. Frame delays are usually measured in 1/100ths of a second. Theoretically, a setting of 100 would create a one-second delay, but in reality, this is a loose estimate and depends on the processor speed of the user's computer.

You can apply a uniform delay across all the frames or apply delay amounts to individual frames. Use custom frame delays to create pauses and other timing effects. You can set the frame delay to 0 (or "as fast as possible"), but I find that a setting of 10 (that's 10/100ths), or 0.1 second, usually results in smoother continuous-motion animations.

Transparency

Like their static cousins, animated GIFs can contain areas of transparency. You can set transparency for each frame within an animation. Previous frames will show through the transparent area of a later frame. If the background frame is made transparent, the browser background color will show through. You need to properly coordinate frame transparency with the disposal method.

Don't be surprised if the transparent areas you specified in your original GIFs are made opaque when you open the files in a GIF animation utility. You may need to reset the transparency in the animation package.

Transparent areas can be generated from black or white pixels, "first color" (the top-left pixel color), or a color chosen from the image with an eyedropper tool.

Looping

You can specify the number of times an animation repeats: "none," "forever," or a specific number. Early browsers do not consistently support a specific number of loops. Some will show the first frame, others the last. One workaround is to build the looping into the file by repeating the frame sequence a number of times. Of course, this increases the file size.

Color palette

Animated GIFs use a palette of up to 256 colors that are used in the image. Although each frame can have its own palette, it is recommended that you use a global palette for the whole animation for smoother display (especially on older browsers).

Interlacing

Like ordinary GIFs, animated GIFs can be interlaced, which causes them to display in a series of passes (starting blocky, finishing clear). It is recommended that you leave the interlacing option set to "no" or "off" because each frame is on the screen for a short amount of time.

Animated GIF Utilities

These tools are inexpensive, and useful for creating animated GIFs. Searching CNET's Download.com will turn up other options.

GIFmation
(Mac and Windows)
This commercial software from BoxTop Software comes highly recommended by web developers for its visual interface, efficient compression methods, and sophisticated palette handling. GIFmation costs $49.95 (as of this writing). It is available at *www.boxtopsoft.com*.

GifBuilder 0.5
(Mac only)
GifBuilder, developed by Yves Piguet, is the old Mac standby for creating animated GIFs. It's freeware that is easy and intuitive to use. It is available for download at *www.mac.org/graphics/gifbuilder/*.

JASC Animation Shop 3
(Windows only)
This inexpensive GIF animation tool also comes bundled with JASC Paint Shop Pro ($39.95).

Disposal method

The disposal method gives instructions on what to do with the previous frame once a new frame is displayed (Figure 17-2). The options are:

Unspecified (Nothing). Use this option to replace one full-size, nontransparent frame with another.

Do Not Dispose (Leave As Is). With this option, any pixels not covered by the next frame continue to display. Use this method if you are using transparency within frames.

Restore to Background. The background color or background tile shows through the transparent pixels of the new frame (replacing the image areas of the previous frame).

Restore to Previous. This option restores to the state of the previous, undisposed frame. This method is not well supported and is best avoided.

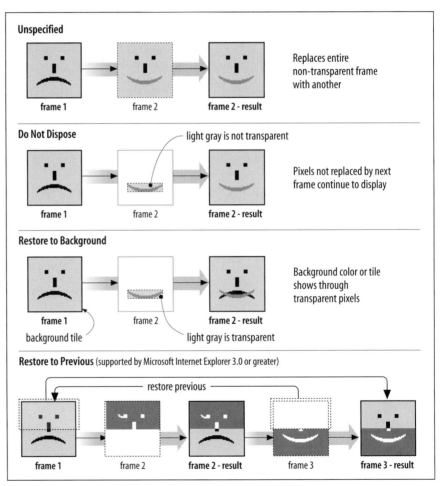

Figure 17-2. Animated GIF disposal methods.

Optimization

The better GIF animation tools allow you to optimize the GIF when exporting it. The optimization process saves only the pixels that change from frame to frame and throws out redundant pixels. The result is a big savings in file size with no change in the animation's appearance.

The choices are Bounding Box, in which the new animated area in the frame is saved in a rectangle, or Delete Redundant Pixels, in which only the unique pixels in each frame are saved and the rest is transparent (Figure 17-3).

Creating an Animated GIF, Step by Step

At last, it's time to roll up our sleeves and get started making an animated GIF. I will be using Adobe ImageReady (bundled with Photoshop) in this demonstration. Afterwards, we'll take a brief look at other tools.

Step 1: Create the artwork

The first thing you need to do is create the artwork for the animation. I find it is useful to take advantage of layers to store the various states of the animation. I'm starting with the Photoshop file, *smile.psd*, which has a background color and the letters s-m-i-l-e stored on separate layers (Figure 17-4). The goal is to create a simple animation in which each letter appears one at a time and the word "smile" flashes at the end.

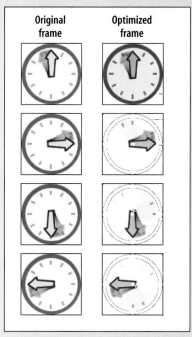

Figure 17-3. Optimized frames contain just the pixels that change from frame to frame. The result is a smaller file size than if you stored complete image information in every frame.

Figure 17-4. Each element in the animation is on its own layer.

┌─ **W O R K   A L O N G** ─────
│ *The layered Photoshop file used in this demo (smile.psd) is available in the* chap17 *materials folder. The step-by-step nature of this section will make it easy to work along.*

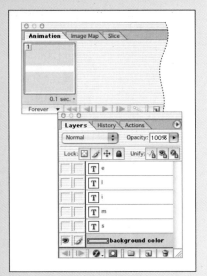

Figure 17-5. With the first frame selected, I turn on the layers I want to be visible at the beginning of the animation.

Pay attention to which frame is selected, then make the image look the way you want it to look for that frame.

Step 2: Set the first frame

You add and view animation frames in ImageReady using the Animation palette (select Window → Show Animation if it isn't visible). The palette shows a thumbnail view of the graphic that corresponds to the first frame of the animation. While this frame is selected (selected frames are highlighted with a shaded box around the thumbnail), organize the layers of your image (turning on and off layers as needed) until the image looks the way you want at the start of the animation. Turn layers on and off by clicking the Eye icon next to them.

I want the animation to start with just the blank background color, so I've turned off all the layers except the background fill layer. I can see the state of the animation in the thumbnail view (Figure 17-5).

Step 3: Add more frames

Now I'm ready to add another frame. Add a new frame by selecting New Frame from the Animation options (the triangle in the upper-right corner) or by clicking the New Frame button on the bottom bar; it looks like a page with a turned corner.

While the new frame is selected, it's time to arrange the layers so they look the way I want in the second frame of the animation. In my second frame, I want to reveal the letter "s," so I turn that layer on with the frame selected (Figure 17-6).

Continue adding frames and adjusting layers until you have completed the animation. Remember to pay attention to which frame is selected, then make the image look the way you want it to look for that frame. Use the Trash icon to delete frames if you make a mistake.

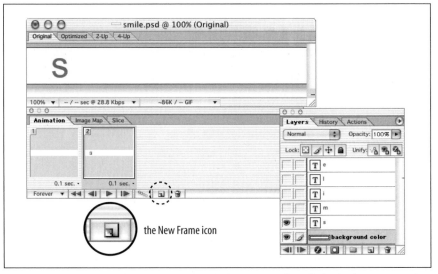

the New Frame icon

Figure 17-6. With the second frame selected, I turn on the layers I want to be visible for that frame. I can see the state of the animation (and edit the image if needed) in the Original image window.

Step 4: Check your progress

My final animation has eight frames: one for each letter, a blank frame, then a frame showing the whole word again.

The Animation palette has controls like those of a VCR at the bottom for viewing the animation in progress (Figure 17-7). When I click the Play button, the animation plays really fast and keeps repeating. I can also move through the animation one frame at a time using the "previous frame" and "next frame" buttons.

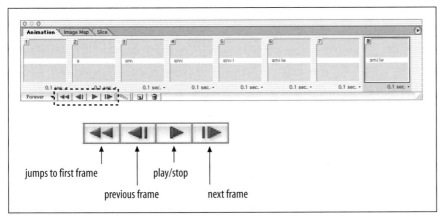

Figure 17-7. The preview controls of the Animation palette.

Step 5: Adjust the animation settings

I like the frame sequence, but now I need to adjust the behavior of the animation with the various animation settings (Figure 17-8, following page).

Looping. I usually begin by deciding whether I'd like my animation to repeat. In this case, I'd like it to play through once and stop, so I choose Once from the looping pop-up menu in the bottom corner of the Animation palette ❶.

Frame delay. Next comes the fun part: setting the timing of each frame. Do this using the pop-up delay menu that appears under each frame ❷.

It is usually necessary to play the animation a few times and continue tweaking the settings until you get the timing you want. For this animation, I ended up with the settings listed in Table 17-1.

Disposal method. By default, the disposal method is set to Automatic in ImageReady, which allows the tool to choose the best method for each frame. If I had wanted to set the disposal for a frame, I'd context-click (right-click on Windows, Ctrl-click on Mac) ❸.

Timing Tips

Here are a few tips for setting the frame delays in your animation. Always test your animation on friends and coworkers to make sure it is user-friendly.

- In general, make the animation a little slower than your initial instinct. It takes people a moment to digest new images, especially if they are in motion.

- Don't set frame delays less than .1 second, even if you want the animation to play as fast as possible. Having a small delay will help the browser play the animation more smoothly.

- If your animation contains text, make sure that you allow enough time for people to read the message. A rule of thumb is that the text should be on the screen long enough to be read aloud.

- Put a slight delay on the first frame of the animation to give users a chance to notice it and pay attention, particularly if there is a sequential text message.

Table 17-1. Animation frame delays

Delays for the sample animation

Frame 1	1.0 second
Frame 2	.2
Frame 3	.2
Frame 4	.2
Frame 5	.2
Frame 6	.5
Frame 7	.5
Frame 8	.1

(Note: the final frame delay is not used because the animation is set to play only once.)

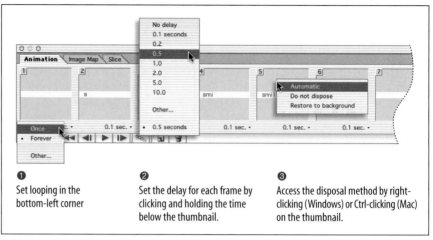

❶
Set looping in the bottom-left corner

❷
Set the delay for each frame by clicking and holding the time below the thumbnail.

❸
Access the disposal method by right-clicking (Windows) or Ctrl-clicking (Mac) on the thumbnail.

Figure 17-8. Adjusting the animation settings.

Color palette. In ImageReady, the color palette selection is made using the Optimization panel for the GIF (Figure 17-9). As with any GIF, your file will be smaller as a result of limiting the number of colors in the image. This simple image will be fine with only eight colors.

Optimization. Finally, for extra file size savings, I'm going to optimize the animation using the pop-up options menu (Figure 17-10). I'm leaving both Bounding Box and Redundant Pixel Removal options checked, so the file will be as small as possible. Bounding Box optimization crops each frame to the area that has changed from the preceding frame. Redundant Pixel Removal saves only the pixels that change in each frame, making the rest transparent.

Figure 17-9. Choose the color palette in the Optimize panel.

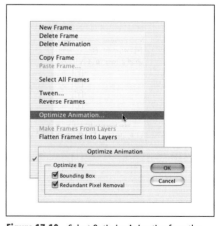

Figure 17-10. Select Optimize Animation from the Options pop-up menu (the triangle button). Leave both options checked for the smallest possible file.

Step 6: Export the GIF

Once I've made all the settings and the animation is playing the way I want, I can export the GIF by choosing File → Save Optimized, as I would for any graphic in ImageReady.

For this single animation, the Images Only format is just fine. If it had been part of a larger multipart image held together by a table, I would have chosen HTML and Images to have ImageReady generate the code for the web page (sliced images are covered in Chapter 20).

You can see the resulting GIF by opening *smile1.gif* (included in the *chap17* materials folder) in a browser.

Using animated GIF utilities

If you do not have ImageReady, you can use one of the many inexpensive or freely available standalone animation utilities. Most of these tools (such as GIFmation shown in Figure 17-11) have some sort of Frames palette where you arrange the frames and enter their settings and a preview window where you can play the animation.

The major difference is that you need to create all your frames as individual GIF images first. You then load the GIF files into the tool by importing or dragging and dropping them into the Frames palette. When you have made all of the frame settings, save or export the file.

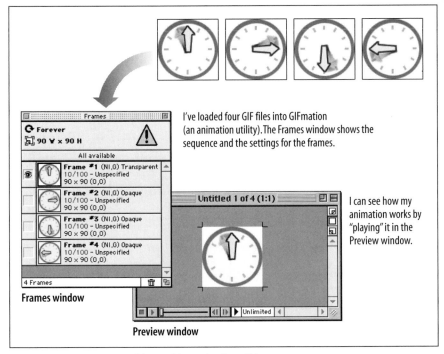

I've loaded four GIF files into GIFmation (an animation utility). The Frames window shows the sequence and the settings for the frames.

I can see how my animation works by "playing" it in the Preview window.

Frames window

Preview window

Figure 17-11. GIFmation, one of the standalone animation utilities.

Creating Animated GIFs in Fireworks

If you are using the Macromedia Studio products, you can use Fireworks to create animated GIFs. Like ImageReady, there is a Frames palette where you can control the order and settings of all the frames in the animation. However, Fireworks uses a symbol-based (rather than layer-based) model for creating animation. Animation symbols are like characters in a movie that you can move around.

If you are a Fireworks user, consult the documentation to learn how to create animations.

A Cool Shortcut (Tweening)

ImageReady and Fireworks have a great time-saving function called tweening, which generates frames for you automatically. If you want an image to move from one side of the graphic to another, or you want a graphic to fade in from light to dark, you just need to provide the beginning frame and the end frame, and the tool generates all the frames in between, thus "tweening" (Figure 17-12).

Let's go through the tweening process in ImageReady, starting with the same layered Photoshop file, *smile.psd*. This time, I'm going to use the Tween function to make the whole word "smile" move across the banner from left to right.

Step 1: Set up the first and last frames

Start by opening the file in ImageReady and view the Animation palette. If there are already frames there from the previous exercise, delete them (select Delete Animation from the Options pop-up menu).

With the first frame selected, I turned on all the layers and positioned the word in the far left corner (you can see its position in the first frame thumbnail in Figure 17-13). Then I add a new frame and, while it is selected, I alter the Original image to look the way I want in the final frame. For the last frame, have moved the whole word to the far right of the banner.

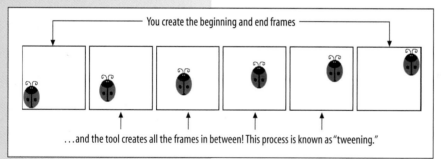

You create the beginning and end frames

...and the tool creates all the frames in between! This process is known as "tweening."

Figure 17-12. Tweening in action.

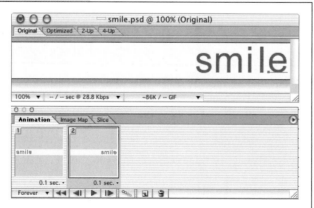

Make changes to the image in the Original view window. This shot shows where I have moved the word for the second frame.

In the first frame, the word is positioned on the left edge of the banner.

For the second frame, I have moved it to the far right edge of the banner.

Figure 17-13. Setting up first and last frames.

Step 2: Set the tweening

Now I can use the Tween function to generate the frames between the start and end frames.

Select Tween from the Options menu on the Animation palette (Figure 17-14). In the dialog box, I check Position because that is the aspect of the object that changes in the animation. The other settings allow you you change the opacity between two frames (for intance, to fade an object in or out) or change effects, such as blurring. I also set the number of frames I want the transition to take. Remember, the more frames, the larger the file, so it's best to start with a small number and go up if you need to. When I click OK, the frames are automatically inserted, as shown below.

Step 3: Save and export

At this point, I make the standard animated GIF settings such as frame delay and looping. When I am done, I select Save Optimized from the File menu. I also save the layered Photoshop file in case I want to edit it later. When the graphic is viewed in a browser, the word "smile" moves smoothly from left to right (Figure 17-15). A copy of this graphic (*smile-tween.gif*) is available in the *chap17* materials folder, so you can view it in a browser for yourself.

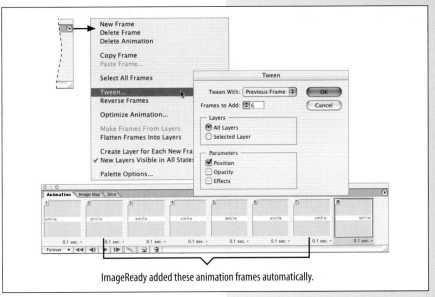

ImageReady added these animation frames automatically.

Figure 17-14. Specifying the "tween".

Figure 17-15. The final animated GIF.

TRY IT

Exercise 17-1: Fading in Text

Try tweening for yourself using the same *smile.psd* file. Use tweening to change the opacity of the object and make the word "smile" fade in gradually.

STEP 1: Start by opening the file and clearing out any existing animation frames.

STEP 2: Position the word "smile" in the middle of the banner. With the first animation frame selected, turn off all the layers except the background fill.

STEP 3: In the final frame of the animation, we want the word "smile" to be fully visible. Add a new frame and turn on all the layers so that the word "smile" is visible in the Original window. You should see a thumbnail of it in the Animation palette as well.

STEP 4: Now you can use the Tween function (located in the Options pop-up menu) to create a number of frames in between your start and end frames. Be sure to click Opacity. Add six new frames for the transition. You should see the frames added to the palette as soon as you click OK. Play the animation and see if you need to adjust the frame delays.

STEP 5: Now you can use Save Optimized to save the animated GIF.

EXTRA CHALLENGE: Can you make a version of this graphic in which the word "smile" fades in as it is moving from left to right across the banner?

Things to Remember About Animated GIFs

Animated GIFs are quite popular on the Web today, particularly in banner advertising. With the proper tool, they are simple to create and are added to the web page just like any other graphic. Here are the major points about animated GIFs we covered in this chapter:

- The ability to contain many frames of animation is a standard characteristic of the GIF file format.

- It's extremely easy to overdo animation on a web page. Consider carefully whether animation is adding or detracting from the success of your web page.

- In order to create an animated GIF, you need an animation utility. There are inexpensive (and even free) programs that do nothing but create GIF animations. In addition, animation tools are built into popular web graphics tools such as Adobe ImageReady and Macromedia Fireworks.

- When you create an animated GIF, you need to set the frame delay, disposal method, transparency, looping, color palette, and interlacing.

- Advanced animation tools may create frames for you automatically in a process called "tweening."

WHERE TO LEARN MORE

GIF Animation

You might want to check out the list of GIF animation resource links gathered by WebReference.com available at *www.webreference.com/authoring/graphics/animation.html*. They have an amazing article about animated GIF optimization, which you can find at *www.webreference.com/dev/gifanim/*.

Some of the articles have a few years on them, but GIF animation hasn't changed much since the late 90s, so they are still good resources.

TRY IT

Exercise 17-2: Practice

Looking for some extra practice at animated GIFs? Here's the homework assignment I typically give in my web design classes.

The Challenge

Choose a product (your favorite new CD, cereal, deodorant, software package, whatever) and create an animated banner ad for it. The animation should feature the product (with an image, if possible) and text (a slogan or other ad copy) in a meaningful and attention-getting way.

Specifications

The banner ad should measure 468 x 60 pixels. It must have at least 8 frames and should be optimized for web delivery.

If you want a realistic challenge, see if you can keep the file size of your banner under 6 or 7 KB, which is the K-limit for most ads on the Web.

Test Yourself

Here are a few quick questions to test your knowledge of animated GIFs. The answers appear in the Appendix.

1. What makes an animated GIF different from a static one?

2. Name three ways to reduce the file size of an animated GIF.

3. Which disposal method should you use if your image contains transparency?

4. What does "Redundant Pixel Removal" optimization do?

5. Where does the word "tween" come from?

Slicing and Rollovers 18

The last two graphics techniques we're going to explore are slicing and rollovers.

Slicing is the technique of taking a large image, slicing it into bits, then holding those bits together seamlessly with an HTML table. Why would you go through all that trouble? The main reason is so the image can contain different types of content. For instance, you could insert HTML text in the middle of a graphical page, or make part of an image a JPEG while the rest is a GIF.

A rollover is a graphic that changes when the mouse pointer rolls over it. Rollovers use JavaScript, a scripting language that works specifically in web browsers, to swap out one graphic for another when triggered by the movement of the mouse. Like imagemaps, rollovers don't require a special kind of graphic; the effect is created with code.

While you can create slices and rollovers manually, this is an area where a web-specific tool such as Adobe ImageReady or Macromedia Fireworks will really make your life easier.

Sliced Images

Let's take a look at some situations in which you might want to use a sliced image:

- If you have a large, complex image with both flat color areas and photographic areas. When you break up the image, you can save each piece in the most appropriate file format (GIF and JPEG, respectively).

- If you have a large image and you want to animate just one area of it. Instead of making the whole thing an animated GIF (with the resulting hefty file size), you can break the image into pieces and animate just the necessary parts. The remaining pieces will be ordinary GIFs.

- If you are creating a fancy rollover effect in which you want a part of the image to change when you roll the mouse over it. Instead of swapping out the whole image, you can swap out just the necessary section—again, reducing the amount of data that needs to be downloaded. Figure 18-1 shows a graphic that has been sliced to incorporate rollover effects on each numbered button.

- If you are using sliced graphic for a large part of your web page and you want it to contain HTML text. It is easier to edit HTML text on a regular basis than to recreate the entire graphic when you need to make a change.

Multipart images are made up of a number of graphics files and an HTML table that holds them all together seamlessly. Of course, the disadvantage of this is that when you have that many graphics covering a large area, the total file size can be quite large.

If you are writing the table by hand, it needs to be constructed carefully so that no extra space creeps into the cells, spoiling the illusion of a solid graphic. It is much easier to use ImageReady or Fireworks. Whichever tool you choose, the process involves creating slicing objects or dragging rules where you want the divisions to occur. The program exports the individual graphics, names them, and writes the table code for you.

Using ImageReady

There are two methods for slicing an image in ImageReady: slicing automatically along guides and drawing your own slices with the slice tool. We'll look at both here.

Slicing along guides

The simplest way to make slices is to slice along all the guides you drag onto the image. This technique is appropriate when you want to cut the image on a simple grid. In this demonstration, we'll take a navigation toolbar design, break it into individual graphics, and link each one to a page.

1. Open the file *navbar.psd* in ImageReady. Make sure the rulers are visible. If they aren't, select View → Show Rulers. Drag guides between the button labels to the points where you want the buttons to be cut. To create a guide, move the mouse into the vertical ruler, click and hold the mouse button, and drag a guide into position (Figure 18-2).

With this technique, the image automatically changes when a user points to each numbered button (known as a "rollover" effect).

border="0"

The image is actually made up of separate graphics held together by a table. The pieces are evident when the table border is turned on.

border="1"

Figure 18-1. A graphic divided into slices.

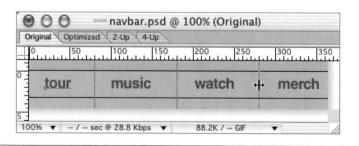

Figure 18-2. Drag guides from the ruler and position them in the image where you want the slices to occur.

2. Create slices by selecting Slices → Create Slices from Guides. The image is now divided into slices, numbered sequentially (slices are shown on an overlay over the original image, as shown in Figure 18-3).

3. Now we can make some settings for each slice (Figure 18-4). Open the Slice palette (Window → Slice) **Ⓐ**. If you do not see entries for Message and ALT, click the triangle button in the top corner and select Show Options.

4. Use the Slice Select tool (a small knife with a pointer arrow) to select the first slice. Information for that slice appears in the Slices palette. You can give the slice a name (although ImageReady names the slices automatically), enter the URL you want the graphic to link to, and provide alternative text for the graphic. Repeat this for each slice.

5. In this graphic, the images in each slice are similar, so they can share the same optimization settings. Select all the slices (Shift and click with the Slice Select tool) and enter the appropriate settings in the Optimization palette **Ⓑ**.

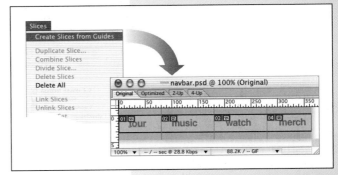

Figure 18-3. Selecting Create Slices from Guides converts the guides into slices. The Slices overlay shows the slice borders and numbers over the original image.

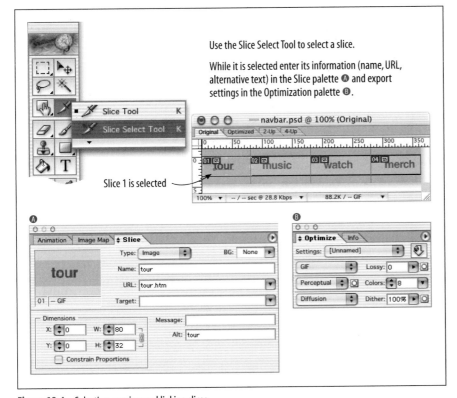

Use the Slice Select Tool to select a slice.

While it is selected enter its information (name, URL, alternative text) in the Slice palette **Ⓐ** and export settings in the Optimization palette **Ⓑ**.

Slice 1 is selected

Figure 18-4. Selecting, naming, and linking slices.

— N O T E —

You can select No Image on the Slices palette for any given slice. When you select No Image, you can specify HTML text and a solid background color for the cell. Remember, HTML is smaller and faster to download than a graphic, so if you have cells filled with only solid color, consider using a background color instead of a graphic.

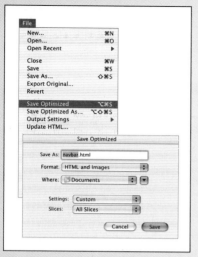

6. To export the slices and the HTML table that holds them together, select File → Save Optimized. In the dialog box, select HTML and Images under Format. Make sure All Slices is selected at the bottom (Figure 18-5). The default Output Settings are fine for most purposes, but you can use them to adjust how the slices are automatically named.

When you click Save, ImageReady creates the HTML table and a folder containing all of the image slices as separate graphics (Figure 18-6). You can cut and paste the table into your final web page. Make sure the final file and the images folder stay in the same directory or the pathnames will be incorrect and the images will not be found.

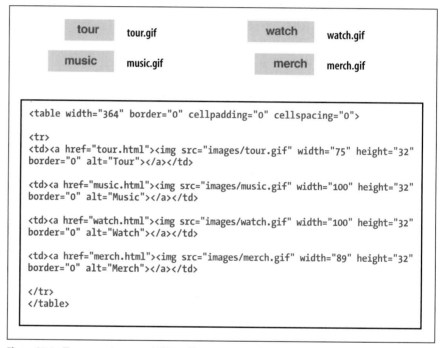

Figure 18-6. The separate images and HTML table generated by ImageReady.

7. When you are finished, save the layered ImageReady file by selecting File → Save. This saves the image, slice information, and hyperlinks in an editable, layered format. (This file format is not viewable in a web browser.)

Drawing slices with the slice tool

If you have an image in which the slices are more irregularly placed, you can draw slices using the Slice tool (Figure 18-7). Otherwise, slicing is done by following the steps we just covered.

1. Open the file *evan.psd*. Make sure the rulers and the Slice palette are visible. I know that I want the majority of this image to be saved in GIF format, so I make sure that GIF is selected in the Optimize window.

2. Using the Slice tool, I draw rectangles over the important areas of the image. For instance, I know I want to save the image within the television as a JPEG, so I draw a slice over that area.

   When you draw a slice, ImageReady automatically creates all the necessary slices around that slice. If you need to edit your slice, use the Slice Select tool (the knife with a pointer arrow) to select it, then reposition or resize the slice using the handles on its borders.

3. While the slice is selected, I can enter its settings (name and alternative text) in the Slice palette **A**. I also set its format to JPEG in the Optimization palette **B**. Individual slice settings override any optimization settings made for the whole image.

   I repeat this process for each of the elliptical buttons so I can make them into rollovers later. Each time, I give the slice a name, alternative text, a URL, and I check its Optimization settings.

4. When I am finished, I save the layered file and select File → Save Optimized as before to export the HTML table and the individual graphics.

Use the Slice Tool to draw a new slice in the image.

While it is selected enter its information (name and alternative text) in the Slice palette **A** and export settings in the Optimization palette **B**. In this case, I want the photo image to be saved as a JPEG.

Figure 18-7. Drawing slices using the Slice tool in ImageReady.

Using Macromedia Fireworks

Making sliced images in Fireworks is nearly identical to the process used in
ImageReady (Figure 18-8).

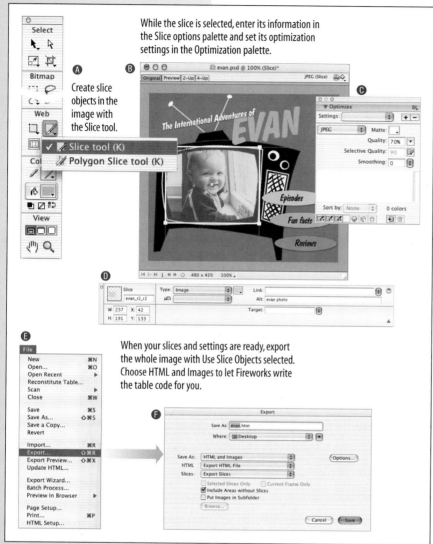

Figure 18-8. Creating slices using Macromedia
Fireworks.

1. First, create or open your image.
   Using the Slice Tool **Ⓐ** from the
   Toolbox palette, define rectangular segments of the image.
   Fireworks automatically slices
   the remainder of the image into
   the fewest number of segments
   containing the specified slice **Ⓑ**.

2. To set the default export settings
   (file format, bit-depth, dithering,
   etc.) for the entire image, make
   sure that no slicing objects are
   selected and adjust the settings
   in the Optimize palette. You can
   override the default export settings by selecting a particular
   slice and adjusting its properties
   in the Optimize palette **Ⓒ**.

3. Enter the information (such as
   URLs for links and alternative
   text) for each slice in the Slice
   options palette **Ⓓ**.

4. Once your are slices chosen and
   configured, export the file by
   selecting File → Export **Ⓔ**. In
   the Export dialog box **Ⓕ**, select
   Export Slices from the Slicing
   pop-up menu.

When you click Export, Fireworks
creates all the graphics files and the
HTML file for the sliced image. This
is by no means a complete explanation of the power of Fireworks' slicing abilities. If you use Fireworks,
read the documentation for detailed
instructions.

324

Part III: Creating Web Graphics

Producing images in tables by hand

If you don't have Fireworks or ImageReady, never fear. You can still put a sliced image together using your image-editing tool, an HTML editor, and a fair amount of patience.

1. *Plan the structure.* The first step is to plan out the divisions of the image and establish the structure of the table (Figure 18-9). (This process is reviewed in Chapter 11.) The goal is to make the table as simple as possible, with as few pieces as possible, so take advantage of any column span and row span opportunities.

2. *Divide the image.* If you are using an image-editing tool that does not support slicing, you will need to make your slices by hand. It helps to drag guidelines at the points where you want the image to be divided, using the table structure sketch as a reference. Use the rectangle marquee (make sure feathering and anti-aliasing options are turned off) to select each area of the image (Figure 18-10).

   As you go, note the exact pixel measurements for each section as you select it. This information will be needed when you create the HTML file, so it is a good idea to jot down the numbers as you go along. The measurements will indicate whether your selections have consistent heights and widths. Copy and paste each selection into a new file and save it as a GIF or JPEG, as appropriate.

3. *Write the HTML table.* Use the techniques outlined in Chapter 11 for writing the HTML table. To hold the image together seamlessly, follow these tips:

   - In the `<table>` tag, set the following attributes to 0: `border`, `cellpadding`, `cellspacing`.

   - In the `<table>` tag, specify the width of the table with an absolute pixel value. Be sure that the value is exactly the total of the widths of the component images.

   - Keep `<td>`s and their contents flush on one line with no extra spaces. If you must break the line, break it somewhere within the `<img>` tag.

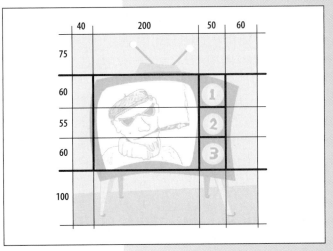

Figure 18-9. Begin by planning the structure of the table, paying attention to the total number of rows and columns, their pixel dimensions, and the possibility for column spans and row spans.

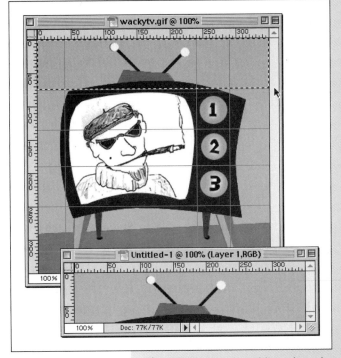

Figure 18-10. Using the guidelines, select each section of the image, copy it, and paste it into a new document (noting of the exact pixel dimensions). Save and name each new graphic.

- Set accurate width and height values in pixels for every image.

- Set border="0" for every linked image.

- Specify the width and height pixel values for every cell in the table. If you have column spans, you may consider setting up an extra row in the table with 0 height that contains the exact measurement of every column. For simple grid-like tables (such as the one in this example), you may not need to provide the individual cell dimensions; the enclosed images will force each cell into the proper dimensions.

The final HTML file for this table looks like this:

```html
<html>
<head>
  <title>TV PAGE</title>
</head>
<body bgcolor="#00CCCC">

<table width="350" height="350" cellspacing="0"
  cellpadding="0" border="0">

  <tr>
    <td colspan="4" width="350"><img src="top.gif" width="350"
      height="75"></td>
  </tr>

  <tr>
    <td rowspan="3" width="40" height="175"><img src="leftside.gif"
      width="40" height="175"></td>
    <td rowspan="3" width="200" height="175"><img src="beatnik.gif"
      width="200" height="175"></td>
    <td width="50" height="60"><img src="1.gif" width="50" height="60"
      border="0"></td>
    <td rowspan="3" width="60" height="175"><img src="rightside.gif"
      width="60" height="175"></td>
  </tr>

  <tr>
    <td width="50" height="55"><img src="2.gif" width="50" height="55"
      border="0"></td>
  </tr>

  <tr>
    <td width="50" height="60"><img src="3.gif" width="50" height="60"
      border="0"></td>
  </tr>

  <tr>
    <td colspan="4" width="350" height="100"><img src="bottom.gif"
      width="350" height="100"></td>
  </tr>

</table>

</body>
</html>
```

Rollovers

Rollovers (graphics that change when the mouse touches them) are popular because they provide a strong visual cue that the graphic is clickable; plus, they're just fun (Figure 18-11). The disadvantage is that they require two graphics instead of one, which means twice the download time. For this reason, they are becoming more scarce, particularly on high-profile commercial web sites.

As I mentioned earlier in this chapter, rollovers have nothing to do with the graphic itself. Rather, they are just a little JavaScript trick.

A word about JavaScript

JavaScript (not related to the powerful programming language Java) is a scripting language that works specifically in web browsers. It adds interactivity and conditional behavior (as in, "When this happens, do this") to web pages. The script for a rollover instructs, "When the mouse is over graphic X, replace it with graphic Y."

JavaScript is also responsible for these common web tricks (along with many more):

- Displaying notes in the status bar of the browser based on mouse position

- Opening links in pop-up browser windows

- Changing the content of the page based on certain conditions (such as browser version)

Learning to write JavaScript from scratch is tricky, particularly if you have no prior programming experience. The good news is you don't need to learn to write JavaScript to implement it on your pages.

You can use full-featured web-authoring tools such as Macromedia Dreamweaver and Adobe GoLive to write the JavaScript for basic tasks (such as pop-up windows and rollovers). If it's just rollover effects you're after, they can also be generated easily using web graphics tools such as Macromedia Fireworks and Adobe ImageReady (included with Photoshop 5.5 and higher).

Unfortunately, a tutorial on how to write JavaScript is beyond the scope of this book. However, I'm a believer that everyone should have some level of familiarity with what's happening "under the hood," so we'll take a look at the components of a script responsible for a simple rollover.

Figure 18-11. An interactive button, commonly called a "rollover," changes when the pointer is positioned over it. The rollover effect is created with JavaScript.

> **NOTE**
>
> *For another demonstration of JavaScript in action, see the section titled* Pop-up Windows *in Chapter 19.*

How rollovers work

A rollover consists of two images of the same dimensions. The original image is what displays when the page loads. The rollover image is what displays when the user's pointer passes over the original image.

The swapping process is directed by a script in the HTML file. Let's look at the JavaScript for a simple rollover in which passing the mouse over the graphic changes that graphic. It is also possible to swap out other graphics on the page, or even change several graphics at once, but we'll start simple.

```
    <html>
    <head><title>Two Rollover Images</title></head>
    <script language="JavaScript">
    <!--
Ⓐ  if (document.images) {

Ⓑ      // "On" images
        img1on = new Image();
        img1on.src = "resume-on.gif";
        img2on = new Image();
        img2on.src = "web-on.gif";

Ⓒ      // "Off" images
        img1off = new Image();
        img1off.src = "resume-off.gif";
        img2off = new Image();
        img2off.src = "web-off.gif";
    }

Ⓓ  function imgOn (imgName) {
        if (document.images) {
            document.images[imgName].src = eval (imgName + "on.src");
        }
    }

Ⓔ  function imgOff (imgName) {
        if (document.images) {
            document.images[imgName].src = eval (imgName + "off.src");
        }
    }
    //-->
    </script>
    </head>
    <body>
Ⓕ  <a href="resume.html"
Ⓖ    onMouseOver="imgOn('img1')"
Ⓗ    onMouseOut="imgOff('img1')"><img name="img1" src="resume-off.gif"></A>

    <a href="web.html" onMouseOver="imgOn('img2')"
      onMouseOut="imgOff('img2')"><img name="img2" src="web-off.gif"></A>

    </body>
    </html>
```

Ⓐ This line detects whether the user's browser supports the images object, which is a prerequisite for rollovers to work. The functions in this script are contingent on browser support and may not work on older browser versions.

Ⓑ The next four lines handle the "on" versions of the graphics (the versions that show when the mouse is over the image). The code creates an Image object for each graphic and preloads it into memory. The filename in color can be changed; the rest of the code must remain as-is to work.

Ⓒ This section handles the "off" versions of the graphics (the default images). Again, Image objects are created for each one and preloaded into memory.

Ⓓ The imgOn() function is what activates the rollover. When the user moves the mouse over an image, the onMouseOver trigger (called an event handler) in the anchor tag passes the name (established by the name attribute) of the graphic to this function. Event handlers are standard actions that trigger JavaScript functions. The function adds the "on" suffix to the name and loads the appropriate "on" GIF file.

Ⓔ The imgOff() function returns the graphic to its "off" state. When the mouse passes outside of the image, the onMouseOut event handler sends the image name to this function, which attaches the "off" suffix and loads the appropriate "off" graphic.

Ⓕ This is the HTML code for one of the rollover images. There are actually two things happening here. First, the image is assigned a name within the <img> tag. JavaScript uses this name to refer to this particular graphic slot. Second, the calls to the imgOn() and imgOff() JavaScript functions are set up using the onMouseOver and onMouseOut event handlers. These need to go in the anchor (<a>) tag along with the URL for the link.

Ⓖ This line sets up the onMouseOver event for this rollover. It says to call the imgOn() function when the mouse is over the graphic, passing the image name to that function.

Ⓗ Similarly, this line sets up the onMouseOut event handler for the rollover. It calls the imgOut() function when the mouse leaves the area of the graphic, passing the image name to that function.

Have you had enough? If you're thinking "Yes," don't worry, we'll be moving on to the methods for creating rollovers using tools that will take care of this stuff for you. If you're thinking that this JavaScript stuff is cool, see the Where to Learn More: JavaScript sidebar.

WHERE TO LEARN MORE

JavaScript

Designing with JavaScript, Second Edition
by Nick Heinle and Bill Peña (O'Reilly, 2001)
   A robust introduction to writing basic JavaScript.

JavaScript for the World Wide Web (Visual QuickStart Guide), Fourth Edition
by Tom Negrino and Dori Smith (Peachpit Press, 2001)
   Another useful beginner's guide.

JavaScript: The Definitive Guide, Fourth Edition
by David Flanagan (O'Reilly, 2001)
   A more advanced reference for once you're up and running.

Webmonkey's JavaScript Resources
hotwired.lycos.com/webmonkey/programming/javascript/
   A dozen or so useful tutorials from the experts at Webmonkey.

Figure 18-12. The "on" and "off" versions of our rollover graphics.

Making rollovers in Dreamweaver

I create my web pages in Dreamweaver so I can take advantage of its easy-to-use rollover feature. This technique requires that you create and save the "on" and "off" versions of each graphic in advance (Figure 18-12).

❶ Open a document in Dreamweaver and place the "off" versions of the graphics on the page using the graphics tool. These are the versions that users will see when the page first loads. Because these are buttons, I've added the link information for each one in the Image Options panel (Figure 18-13). You must give the image a name for it to show up in the Behaviors palette.

❷ Select the Behaviors tab (if it is not visible, choose Window → Behaviors). This is where Dreamveaver keeps all of its automatic JavaScript functions. With the graphic selected, click on the Add button and choose Swap Image from the list of behaviors. Behaviors that do not apply to graphics will be grayed out and unavailable.

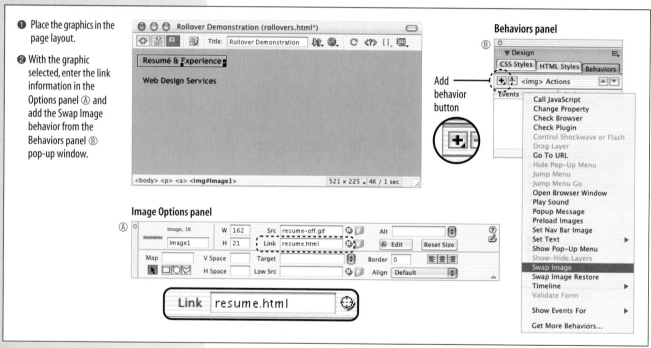

Figure 18-13. Dreamweaver's Behaviors tab.

WORK ALONG

All of the graphic files used in the Rollovers section are available in the chap18 materials folder if you would like to work along with the demonstrations.

3. In the Swap Image dialog box (Figure 18-14), enter the name of the "on" graphic that should appear on the rollover (you can use the Browse button to make sure the pathname is correct) **A**.

Check Preload Images **B**. This makes the browser preload all of the graphics into its cache, so the "on" versions will be ready to go when called for.

Check Restore Images onMouseOut **C**. This adds a function that switches to the "off" state when the mouse leaves the graphic area.

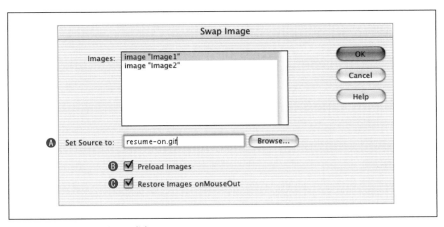

Figure 18-14. The Swap Image dialog.

4. Repeat steps 2 and 3 for the other graphics on the page. You can take a peek at the source code to see all the JavaScript work that Dreamweaver is sparing you.

5. The rollovers don't work in the Dreamweaver page view, so you need to look at the page in a browser to see them in action. Select File → Preview in Browser to open a temporary version of the document (Figure 18-15). When you are done, save the HTML document.

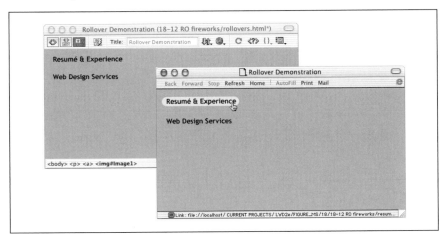

Figure 18-15. Previewing your rollover in a temporary file.

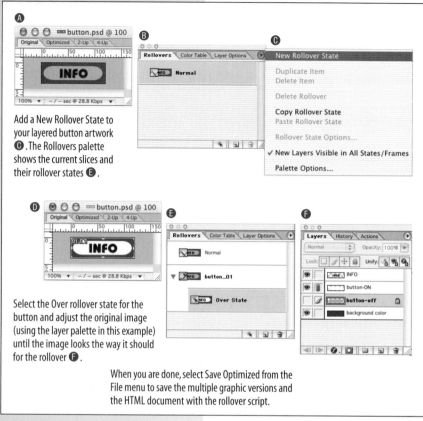

Add a New Rollover State to your layered button artwork **C**. The Rollovers palette shows the current slices and their rollover states **E**.

Select the Over rollover state for the button and adjust the original image (using the layer palette in this example) until the image looks the way it should for the rollover **F**.

When you are done, select Save Optimized from the File menu to save the multiple graphic versions and the HTML document with the rollover script.

Figure 18-16. Making a rollover button with ImageReady.

NOTE

In earlier versions of ImageReady, the Rollovers palette is located near and looks more like the Animation palette. It does not list slices, nor does it convert the image into a slice as Version 7 does. Otherwise, it is the same in that you add a state, then adjust the Original image for that state.

Making rollovers with ImageReady

ImageReady and Fireworks create the graphics for each rollover state and export the HTML and Java-Script all in one process. In the following demonstration, I will use ImageReady 7 to make a simple rollover (the process is very similar in Fireworks).

To keep things simple, I'll start with a graphic that contains just one rollover button (Figure 18-16).

1. Start with *button.psd* open in ImageReady **A**. Click on the Rollovers tab to reveal the Rollovers palette (you can also select Window → Show Rollovers). In the Layers palette, make sure that the "button-ON" layer is not visible (turn it off by clicking the eye icon).

   The Rollovers palette reveals a thumbnail-sized view of the image labeled Normal. This is the way the image will appear in the browser when the page loads and before the user interacts with it **B**.

2. Now add the rollover state by clicking on the Options menu (the arrow button) and choosing New Rollover State **C** (or click the New State icon that looks like a page with a turned corner). For ImageReady, slices and rollovers are integrated, so the entire image is now labeled as a single slice **D**. The slice and its new rollover state are added to the Rollovers palette **E**. By default, this rollover state is labeled Over, corresponding to the state when the user's mouse passes over the image.

3. While the Over state is active (you can tell because it is shaded and the label is in bold type), edit the Original image so that it looks the way you want for the "on" state of the rollover. For this image, I've hidden the "button-OFF" layer and revealed the "button-ON" layer, which contains a white version of the same button shape ❻. (Layers are turned on and off by clicking the eye icon next to them.) The button will appear to light up when the user mouses over it.

4. We're going to stop there, but you can also add states for other mouse actions. Other states include:

    Down. What the image looks like when the mouse is pressed down.

    Click. What the image looks like when the mouse button has been clicked. It stays until the mouse is moved out of the image.

    Out. What the image looks like when the mouse moves out of the image By default, the image returns to its Normal state when the mouse leaves.

    Up. What the image looks like when the user releases the mouse button (post-click) over the image.

    You can change the rollover state for a selected thumbnail by double-clicking on the label and selecting the desired state from the list of options. Keep in mind that each state requires an additional graphic to download, so only add states if there is a good reason to do so.

5. With the Over state all set, select File → Save Optimized to export the images and the HTML file containing the JavaScript. It is a good idea to save the layered file with the rollover information as well.

You can view the resulting HTML file in a browser and test the rollover. In most cases, you will copy and paste the code into another HTML document. If you do so, make sure that the pathnames to the graphic files and linked documents are correct once the code is in its final document.

> **TIP**
>
> When designing a graphic that you know will have rollovers, it helps to keep your layers well-organized and clearly labeled. Think ahead to the elements you'll want to turn on and off and put them on their own layers.

Slices and Rollovers in ImageReady

Let's combine the skills we covered in this chapter and create a number of rollover buttons from a single navigation toolbar design. This is a more efficient method than making buttons one at a time, and it shows the real power of using a web graphics tool such as ImageReady or Fireworks.

The process for adding the rollover state is exactly the same as before, only this time, we'll apply an Over state for a number of slices in the image (Figure 18-17).

1. Start by opening *navbar-roll.psd* in ImageReady. This looks like the graphic we used in the slicing demo earlier, but there are extra layers containing "glowing" versions of each label to be used for the Over states.

2. Make sure the Rollovers palette is visible by clicking on the tab or selecting Window → Rollovers.

3. As we did before, drag guides from the vertical ruler into the image where you want slices to occur. Then select Slices → Create Slices from Guides. You should now see the slices overlay on the original image. They are numbered 01–04. You will also see that each slice is listed in the Rollovers palette **Ⓐ**. Remember to add the information for each slice in the Slice palette (not shown).

4. Now we can add the rollover states one by one. Select the first slice (Tour) using the Slice Select Tool or by clicking on it in the Rollovers palette. Add a New Rollover State for that slice **Ⓑ**.

   While the Over state is active, adjust the original image to look the way you want it to look when the mouse is over the word "tour." We want the highlighted version of the text to show, so make the "tour - ON" layer visible in the Layers palette for that rollover state (and hide the "tour" layer) **Ⓒ**. It is important to make the entire image, not just the slice, look the way it should for that mouse-over position. Changes in other slices will also be triggered.

5. Next, select Slice 02 (Music). While it is selected, add a New State to the Rollover Palette **Ⓓ**. While the Over state for that slice is active, make the "Music - ON" layer visible in the Layers palette (and hide the "music" layer). Repeat these steps for the remaining two slices.

6. When you are done, select Save → Optimized from the File menu with the HTML and Images option selected. You can view the resulting file in a browser to see that the rollovers work. When you mouse over each word, it should appear to glow.

Open the file and create the slices. Enter the slice information in the Slice palette (not shown). The Rollover palette shows a list of the slices. Select a slice and add a New Rollover State.

With the Over state selected and active, adjust the Original image so it looks the way it should for the rollover. In this case, I do that by turning on my predesigned "ON" layer for the word "tour."

The word "tour" is highlighted.

Repeat this process for each slice in the image.

The predesigned ON layer is made visible for the Over state.

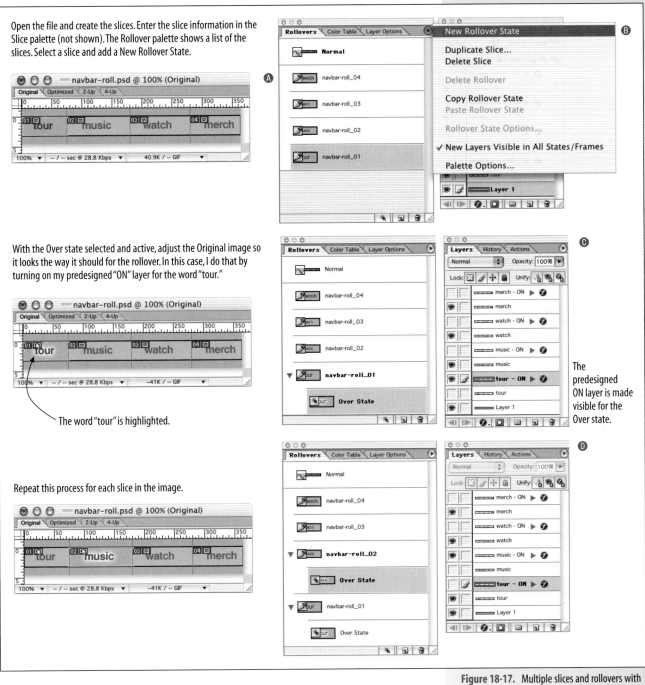

Figure 18-17. Multiple slices and rollovers with ImageReady.

TRY IT

Exercise 18-1: Complex Slices and Rollovers

This exercise will give you practice at creating slices and adding rollovers within an image. This one is a bit more complex than the exercises we've seen so far. First, you will need to use the Slice Tool because the slices are irregular. Second, the rollovers trigger a descriptive text line that appears under the buttons, in addition to the highlighting of the button text. There are more things to keep track of, but if you take it one slice at a time, the process is the same as we've seen in previous demonstrations.

1. Open *navbar-plus.psd* in ImageReady (you can use Fireworks as well, but the controls will be slightly different).

2. Make sure the Layers, Rollovers, and Slices palettes are visible. In the Layers palette, turn each layer on and off to become familiar with the elements you have to work with. It will be helpful to leave the layers with description text visible so you know how large to draw the slice for that area.

3. Using the Slice Tool, create a slice for each button and one that covers the area for the description. For each button slice, enter its information (name, URL, and alternative text) in the Slice palette.

4. Starting with the "tour" button slice, add a new Over rollover state in the Rollovers

The principle is simple: when the Over state for a slice is active, make the whole image look the way it should look when the user mouses over that slice. Applying this principle requires some practice and patience.

palette. When the user mouses over the word "tour," we want the word to be highlighted *and* we want the tour description to appear. With the Over state selected, turn on the tour-ON layer (for the highlighting) and turn on the "TOUR: schedule of upcoming gigs" layer to reveal the description.

5. Double-check that the Original view of the navigation toolbar graphic looks just as it will during the rollover: "tour" is lit up and the tour description is visible. Now we can move on to the next slice.

6. Select the slice for the "music" button and add a new Over state for that slice. Now, turn on the appropriate layers so that the navigation toolbar looks just as it should when the user mouses over the word "music": "music" is lit up and the music description is visible.

7. Repeat the process for the other two button slices. The description slice does not get a rollover state.

8. When you are done, select File → Save Optimized to save the various versions of the graphics and the HTML document containing the JavaScript. Save the layered source file as well (File → Save).

This view shows my slices and the Over state for the "merch" button.

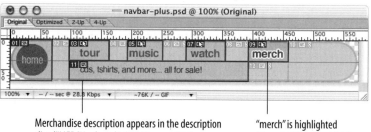

Merchandise description appears in the description slice ("MERCH: cds and tshirts" layer visible).

"merch" is highlighted ("merch-ON" layer visible).

Test Yourself

Here are five quick questions to see if you picked up the basics. The answers are in the Appendix.

1. Name three reasons for dividing a large image into slices.

2. What holds a sliced image together?

3. What is the disadvantage of using rollover images?

4. What is an event handler? Name two that are used for rollovers.

5. What other mouse events can be used to trigger a new graphic to display?

The image below shows a graphic as it might appear on a monitor that displays millions or thousands of colors (24-bit or 16-bit monitors). These monitors can smoothly display an enormous range of colors.

8-bit monitors, on the other hand, can display only 256 colors at a time. Within the browser, there are only 216 available colors to choose from.

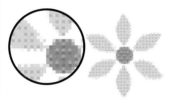

The image above shows what happens to the same graphic when viewed on an 8-bit monitor. The close-up shows how the real color is approximated by mixing colors from the available palette of colors. This effect is called dithering.

Figure 4-7. Browsers with a limited color palette will approximate unavailable colors by dithering.

| Mac | Windows |

Figure 4-8. Gamma refers to the overall brightness of monitors. Windows machines tend to be darker (the result of higher gamma settings) than Macs.

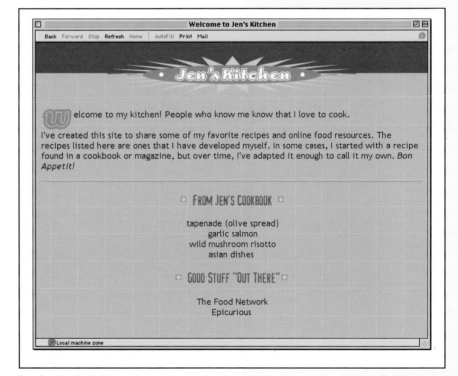

Exercise 9-3. The finished product.

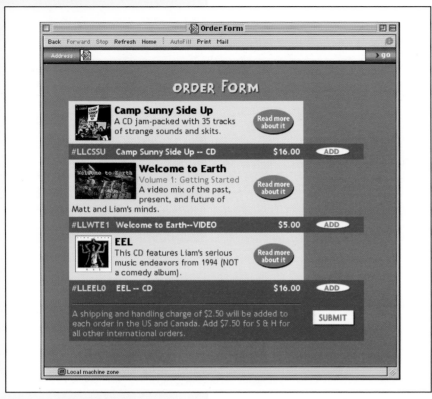

Chapter 11. The finished product.

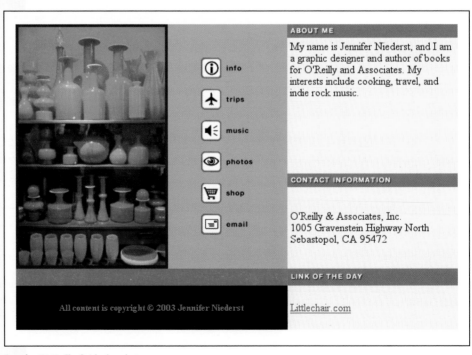

Exercise 11-5. The finished product.

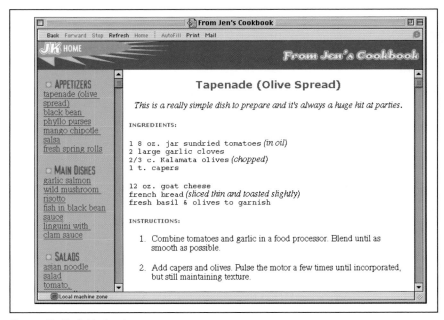

Chapter 12. The finished product.

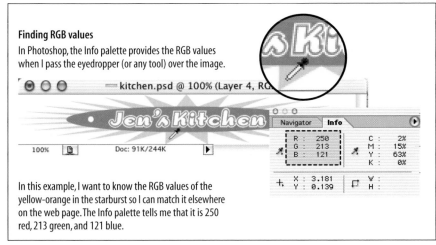

Finding RGB values

In Photoshop, the Info palette provides the RGB values when I pass the eyedropper (or any tool) over the image.

In this example, I want to know the RGB values of the yellow-orange in the starburst so I can match it elsewhere on the web page. The Info palette tells me that it is 250 red, 213 green, and 121 blue.

Figure 13-3. Photoshop has a tool to allow you to find the RGB values of a color.

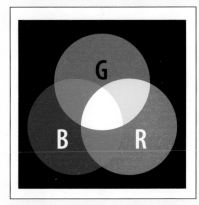

Figure 13-2. Computer monitors use the RGB color model in which colors are made up of combinations of red, green, and blue light. RGB color is additive. For example, if you mix all three colors at full intensity you get white.

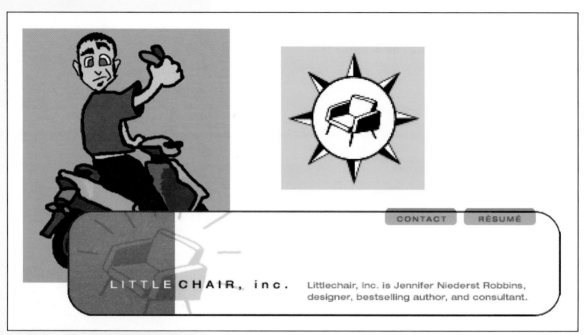

Figure 14-1. The GIF file format is best for images with sharp lines and areas of flat color.

Figure 14-2. The JPEG file format works best for images with gradient colors, such as photos or paintings.

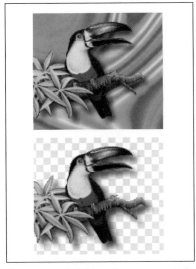

Figure 14-3. The PNG graphic supports multiple levels of transparency.

Figure 14-11. What are the best formats for these three images?

Figure 15-1. The GIF format is great for graphical images comprised mainly of flat colors and hard edges.

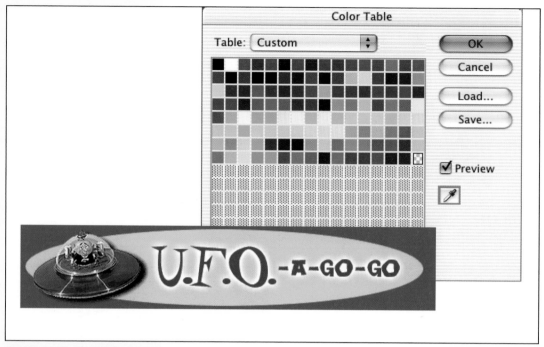

Figure 15-2. The colors in an indexed color image are stored in and referenced by a color table. The color table (also called a palette) can contain a maximum of 256 colors (8-bit). In this figure we see the color table for the U.F.O. banner graphic.

256 colors: 21 KB   64 colors: 13 KB   8 colors: 8 KB

Figure 15-16. Reducing the number of colors in an image reduces the file size.

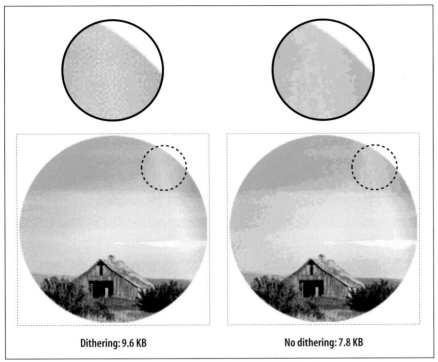

Dithering: 9.6 KB   No dithering: 7.8 KB

Figure 15-17. Turning off or reducing the amount of dithering will reduce the file size. Both images have 32 pixel colors and use an Adaptive palette.

Lossy set to 0%: 13.2 KB   Lossy set to 25%: 7.5 KB

Figure 15-18. Applying a Lossy (in Photoshop) or Loss (in Fireworks) value removes pixels from the image and results in smaller file size. Both images shown here contain 64 colors and use Diffusion dither.

 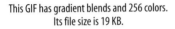  

| This GIF has gradient blends and 256 colors. Its file size is 19 KB. | Even when I reduce the number of colors to 8, the file size is still 7.6 KB. | When I create the same image with flat colors instead of blends, the size of the GIF file is only 3.2 KB. |

Figure 15-19. You can keep file sizes small by designing in a way that takes advantage of the GIF compression scheme.

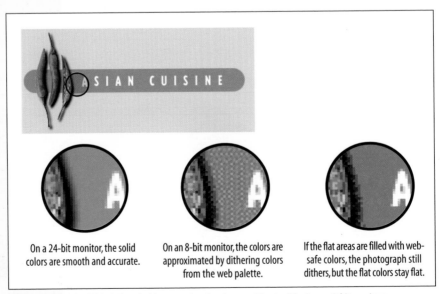

On a 24-bit monitor, the solid colors are smooth and accurate.

On an 8-bit monitor, the colors are approximated by dithering colors from the web palette.

If the flat areas are filled with web-safe colors, the photograph still dithers, but the flat colors stay flat.

Figure 15-24. This GIF is designed with non-web-safe colors, resulting in dithering on 8-bit monitors.

Figure 16-1. The JPEG file format is ideal for photographs (color or grayscale) or any image with subtle color gradations.

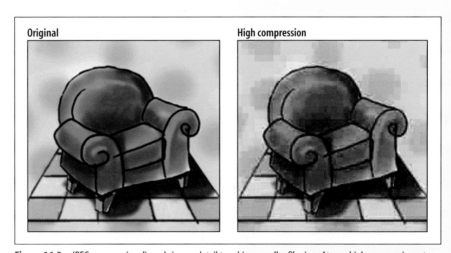

Figure 16-2. JPEG compression discards image detail to achieve smaller file sizes. At very high compression rates, image quality suffers, as shown in the image on the right.

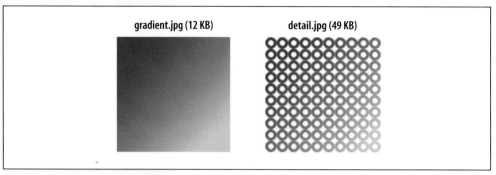

Figure 16-3. JPEG compression works better on smooth images than images with hard edges and detail. Compare the file sizes of these examples.

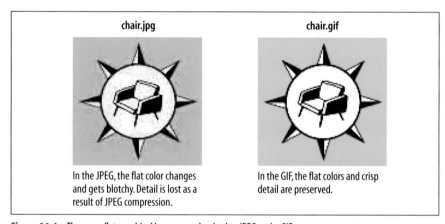

Figure 16-4. The same flat graphical image saved as both a JPEG and a GIF.

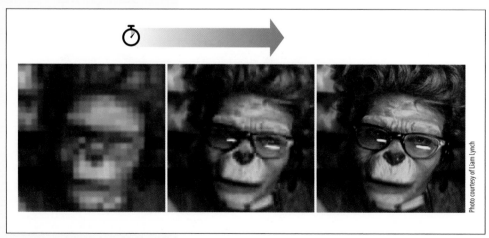

Figure 16-5. Progressive JPEGs render in a series of passes. The image detail and quality is improved with each pass.

Figure 16-8. A comparison of various compression levels in Photoshop 7 and Fireworks MX.

Quality: 20 Blur: 0 (8.7 KB)

This JPEG was saved at low quality (20 in Photoshop) with no blurring applied.

Quality: 20 Blur: .5 (6.9 KB)

In this JPEG, I applied a slight blur to the image (.5 in Photoshop) before exporting it. Although it has the same quality setting (20), the file size is 20% smaller.

In Fireworks, use the Smoothing setting to apply a blur.

Figure 16-9. Blurring the image slightly before exporting as a JPEG will result in smaller file sizes.

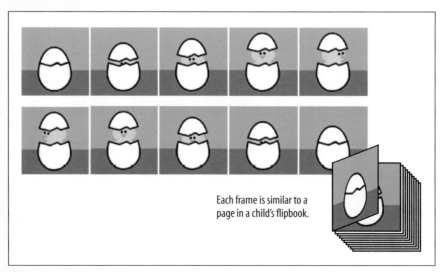

Each frame is similar to a page in a child's flipbook.

Figure 17-1.   This animated GIF contains all of the images shown above. The images play back in sequence, creating a motion effect. When this GIF is viewed in a browser, the chick pops up, takes a look around, and then goes back in its shell.

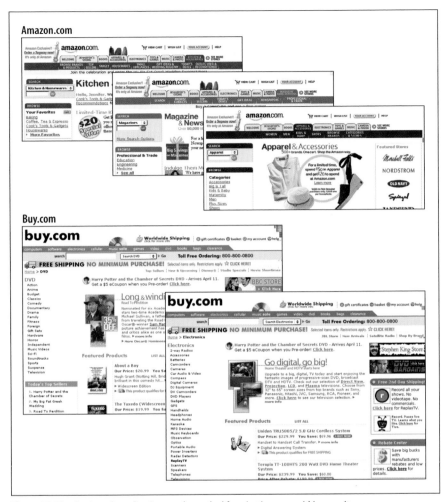

Figure 20-24. Section color coding is a popular method for orienting users within your site.

The Blue Family home page.

A typical second-level page for the Blue Family site.

Figure 20-25. Look-and-feel treatments.

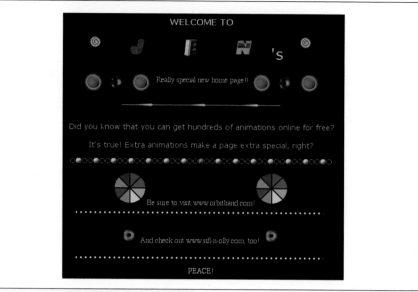

Figure 21-2. Here's an example of too much animation. Every letter, bullet, and divider bar is animated. This may look like an exaggeration, but I have seen pages like this and worse. This page (*animation.html*) is available for viewing in the *chap21* materials folder on the CD and online.

Figure 21-4. This excerpt from the Webmonkey home page (www.webmonkey.com) uses type treatments effectively to convey the structure of the information. Article listings have the same structure, with the article title given the most visual weight. Section titles are also treated similarly and are given lots of space to set them apart from other listings.

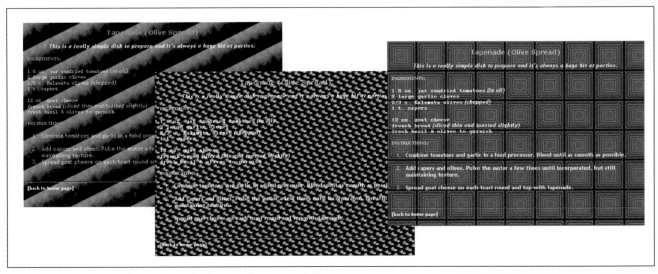

Figure 21-15. Bold background patterns can make the text on the page unreadable.

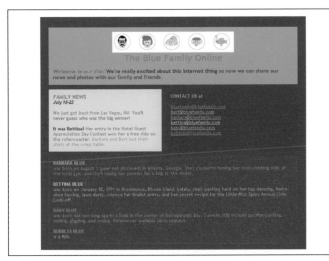

Figure 21-14. This page suffers from color overkill. Making every element a different bright color is a sure way to create visual chaos.

Figure 21-17. The web page of my nightmares! This page has it all:

- Gratuitous black background
- Animated rainbow dividers
- A spinning globe
- An unreadable link color
- Meaningless icons
- Too many colors
- Bad alignment

Scenes from a music video for Beck's "Nicotine and Gravy" (created by Fullerene Productions).

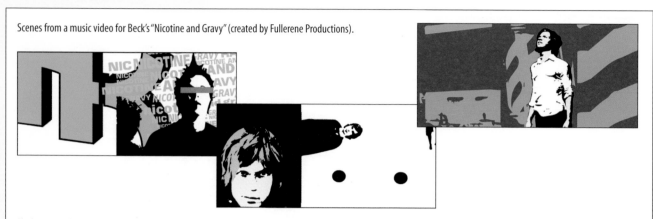

Flash intro and web site interface (screenshots from www.eye4u.com, a web design firm in Munich).

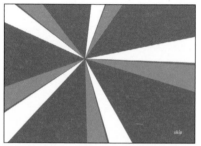

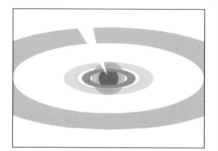

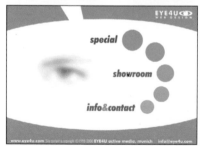

Flash animation. Shots from "A Short Smoke Break" by Rich Oakley and Fawn Scott. This and other cool animation shorts can be seen at www.animationexpress.com.

Figure 22-6. Stills from Flash animations.

Form and Function

Now that we've covered the nuts and bolts, it's time to get back to some big-picture issues. We begin by combining our new HTML and graphics skills to create some of the most common web design tricks and special elements.

Chapter 20 is an overview one of the most important and easily overlooked aspects of web design: usability. If users can't find what they're looking for on your site, or they get lost and frustrated trying, the coolest graphics in the world aren't going to save the day.

Of course, appearance counts, too, so I've provided a rapid-fire list of web design dos and don'ts in Chapter 21. They should help you avoid the tell-tale signs of amateur web design.

The book closes with a glimpse of some exciting web design topics that are just beyond the scope of this book. I want you to be familiar with advanced techniques so you can recognize them when you see them and decide for yourself if you'd like to explore further. Consider it a look at the web design horizon.

Web Design Techniques

19

Parts II and III of this book cover the nuts and bolts of creating HTML documents and web graphics. In this chapter, we'll put these skills together to create some of the common design elements that you see on professional web pages.

You'll find that a significant number of these techniques rely on HTML tables, which is why as a web designer, you'll want to have a good command of table creation. Chapter 11 is an in-depth exploration of table creation, including table-related HTML tags, the ways tables tend to go haywire, and how they are used to format whole pages.

It is worth noting that some of these techniques are kludgy workarounds to get HTML to do things it wasn't meant to do. But these days, we have Cascading Style Sheets. When there is a style-sheet alternative to a task, I'll make note of it in a sidebar. Style sheets are explained in Chapter 8.

Fancy Bulleted Lists

In Chapter 7, we saw how you can make a bulleted list using the "unordered list" tag (<ul>). This works just fine if you are happy with the browser's automatically inserted bullet styles, but what if you want a bullet with more character—such as a daisy, or a little skull? In this case, you'll need to abandon the <ul> tag and create the list manually using your own custom graphics as bullets.

The first step is to create the bullet graphic. If you want the bullet to fit into the flow of text seamlessly without adding any extra space, you should keep the height of the graphic to 10 or 12 pixels. Bullet graphics are best saved in the GIF format. See the sidebar Creating Bullets and Icons, later in this chapter, for more tips.

In this chapter

Fancy bulleted lists

Tables as sidebars and
   decorative elements

The 1-pixel square graphic trick

Vertical rules

Background tile tricks

Pop-up windows

*Keep the height of bullet
graphics to 10 or 12 pixels.*

```
<p><img src="daisy.gif" hspace="12">puppy dogs</p>
<p><img src="daisy.gif" hspace="12">sugar frogs</p>
<p><img src="daisy.gif" hspace="12">kittens' baby
teeth</p>
```

❋ puppy dogs

❋ sugar frogs

❋ kittens' baby teeth

Figure 19-1. The bulleted list was created by placing individual bullet graphics before each line.

Next, create the list in HTML. If the list consists of short entries (just a few words), you can probably separate each entry with line or paragraph breaks, depending on how much space you want between lines (Figure 19-1). I'm not using any list tags here because I don't want any bullets or numbers inserted automatically. Also notice how I've added space to the left and right of the graphic using the hspace attribute in the <img> tag in order to create an indent.

☠ **Avoid character spaces** in filenames. Although this is acceptable for local files on a Mac or Windows 95/98/NT machine, character spaces are not recognized by other systems.

☠ **Avoid special characters** such as ?, %, #, etc. in filenames. It is best to limit filenames to letters, numbers, underscores (in place of character spaces), hyphens, and periods.

```
<table border="0" width="400">
<tr>
<td width="30" valign="top" align="center"><img src="skull.gif"></td>
<td><b>Avoid character spaces</b> in filenames. Although this is acceptable
for local files on a Mac or Windows 95/98/NT machine, character spaces
are not recognized by other systems.</td>
</tr>

<tr>
<td valign="top" align="center"><img src="skull.gif"></td>
<td><b>Avoid special characters</b> such as ?, %, #, etc. in filenames.
It is best to limit filenames to letters, numbers, underscores (in place
of character spaces), hyphens, and periods.</td>
</tr>
</table>
```

Figure 19-2. Long list entries require a table to maintain an indent after the bullets.

If your list consists of longer entries, you need to use a table to control the alignment of the entry paragraphs (Figure 19-2). Use the width setting of the first table column for precise control over the amount of indentation. I've centered the bullets in their column to keep them from bumping up against the text. Adjust the column width and horizontal alignment to achieve the look you want. Remember to set the vertical alignment (valign) in each bullet cell to top to position the bullet next to the first line of text.

DESIGN TIP

Creating Bullets and Icons

There are many approaches to creating small graphic images. These are my personal techniques.

For bullets (images 12 pixels square or smaller), I usually create the graphic at actual size and draw the image, pixel by pixel, using the pencil tool in my image program. This process involves a lot of zooming in (to make the drawing process easier) and zooming out (to see the results at actual size). I find this method works well for tiny pictures because the sharp edges between colors help readability.

For icon-sized images, I usually create the image at twice or three times the final size of the graphic, then shrink the image to its final size once I'm happy with it. Working at a larger size gives me more room to play around and to take advantage of layers and image-editing tools. When the image is reduced to the smaller size, the aliased edges often help the overall quality. Sometimes I find that adding a "sharpen" filter as the final step tidies things up nicely.

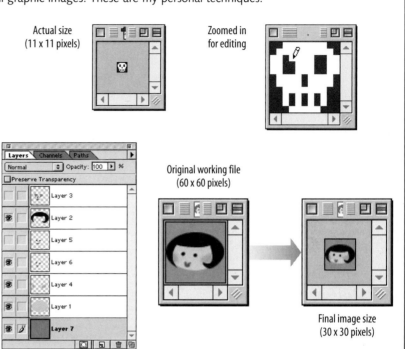

Actual size (11 x 11 pixels)

Zoomed in for editing

Original working file (60 x 60 pixels)

Final image size (30 x 30 pixels)

Fun with Boxes

A table can be used as an attention-getting device for special announcements, pull-quotes, or sidebars. You can have fun with the background color and make the box a decorative element. Once you've made the table, just place it on a page as you would a graphic (see the sidebar Text Wrap Around Tables).

Text Wrap Around Tables

You can wrap text around a table just as you would an image by setting the align attribute to left or right in the <table> tag. This is one technique for adding sidebars or call-outs to a long page of text:

```
<table align="right" width="100"
border="1" bgcolor="#003399"
cellpadding="4">
```

Simple announcement box

A single-celled table with some text centered in it can be used for a special announcement (Figure 19-3). I've adjusted the space within the cell with the `cellpadding` attribute in the `<table>` tag. You can also control the size of the box precisely using `width` and `height`. Try playing with the table background color and text color to create a box that is eye-catching yet is still in harmony with the color scheme of your page. The 3-D border can be set as thick as you like, or it can be turned off completely (`border="0"`).

```
<table border="1" bgcolor="#CC0066" cellpadding="10">
<tr>
<td align="center"><font color="white">Sale ends this week!</font></td>
</tr>
</table>
```

Sale ends this week!

Figure 19-3. A one-celled table can be used for eye-catching announcements.

Boxes with borders

If you don't like the browser's 3-D border effect, you can create a colored rule around a box of text by placing one table within another (Figure 19-4). The outer table should be slightly larger than the inner table, and it should be a different color (the color of the outer table forms the border around the box).

STYLE SHEET ALTERNATIVE

Boxes with Borders

With style sheets, you can turn any element (a paragraph or a `<div>`) into a colored box on the page. One word of warning, though: some of the following properties are buggy, even on the current browsers. If you decide to try them out, be sure to test on a variety of browser versions.

In this example, a paragraph is turned into a colored box using a multi-property style-sheet rule. Each property is explained below.

```
p { width: 200px;
    height: 50px;
    background-color: red;
    border-style: solid;
    border-weight: 4px
    border-color: #000000;
    color: #FFFFCC;
    text-align: center;
    padding: 10px;
    font-weight: bold; }
```

width and height
    Set the dimensions of the box

background-color
    Sets the color of the box

border-style
    Sets whether the border is solid, dashed, dotted, double, or grooved

border-weight
    Sets the thickness of the border around the box in pixels

border-color
    Sets the color of the border

color
    Sets the color of the text in the box

text-align
    Sets the horizontal alignment of the box contents

padding
    Adds a little space inside the box element's margins

font-weight
    Controls the boldness of the text

The rule around this box is created by filling a table with another table that is a different color and slightly smaller.

```
<table width="200" height="200" cellpadding="0" border="0">
<tr>
<td bgcolor="#333333" align="center" valign="center">
        <table width="198" height="198" border="0" cellpadding="10">
        <tr><td bgcolor="#999999">Your content here!</td></tr>
        </table>
</td>
</tr>
</table>
```

To make the border wider, make the inside table smaller (or the exterior table larger).

```
<table width="200" height="200" cellpadding="0" border="0">
<tr>
<td bgcolor="#333333" align="center" valign="center">
        <table width="180" height="180" border="0" cellpadding="10">
        <tr><td bgcolor="#999999">Your content here!</td></tr>
        </table>
</td>
</tr>
</table>
```

Figure 19-4. Creating a colored rule around a box using nested tables.

To nest the tables, place the entire contents of one table within the <td> of the other.

In Figure 19-4, I've created a table and restricted its size to 200 pixels square. Since I want the color of my box rule to be dark gray, I set the background color of this table to dark gray (#333333).

Within that table's cell, I inserted another single-celled table of a lighter gray (#999999). The thickness of the border will be one-half the difference in size between the two boxes.

— **N O T E** —

*There are some nonstandard attributes for setting border colors (*bordercolor, bordercolorlight, *and* bordercolordark*), but they work only for Internet Explorer and result in a double line or a two-tone line, not a solid line like that shown in this example.*

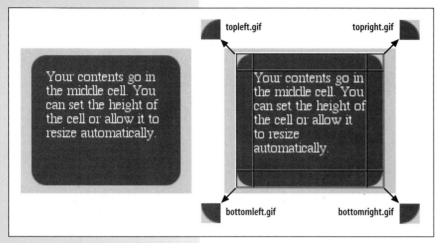

Figure 19-5. This rounded box is made of a 9-cell table with four graphics for corners.

Whenever you see rounded edges on a web page, you know they're done with graphics.

Rounded corners

There is no way to make rounded corners using HTML or style sheets, so whenever you see rounded edges on a web page, you know they're done with graphics. In most cases, rounded elements rely on tables to hold the pieces together. When you deconstruct the rounded box in Figure 19-5, you see that it is actually made of a 9-cell table and four graphic files. The side and center cells are filled with a background color that exactly matches the corner graphics.

It's not hard to create a box with rounded corners such as this one. First, decide which colors you want for the page background and for the table itself (you'll need the precise RGB values for both the graphics creation and the HTML file). In Figure 19-5, I've chosen a light gray for the background color (#CCCCCC) and a dark blue for the box (#003399).

Next, create the graphics for the corners. I make mine by taking a circle, cutting it into four pieces (see the Design Tip: Corner Creation sidebar later in this chapter) and saving each piece with a descriptive name that helps me keep track of it later (e.g., *topleft.gif*, *topright.gif*, *bottomleft.gif*, and *bottomright.gif*).

The final step is writing the code for the table. If you use a web-authoring tool, you may need to tweak the generated code to make the table behave properly. The following is the code for the example in Figure 19-5:

```
❶ <table width="150" bgcolor="#003399" cellspacing="0" cellpadding="0"
     border="0">
  <tr>
❷   <td width="15" height="15"><img src="topleft.gif"></td>
    <td width="120" height="15" bgcolor="#003399"><font
      size="-2"> </font></td>
    <td width="15" height="15"><img src="topright.gif"></td>
  </tr>
  <tr>
❸   <td bgcolor="#003399"><font size="-2"> </font></td>
❹   <td align="left" valign="top" height="100" bgcolor="#003399">
      <font color="white"> Your contents go in the middle cell. You can
      set the height of the cell or allow it to resize
      automatically.</font></td>
    <td bgcolor="#003399"><font size="-2"> </font></td>
  </tr>
  <tr>
    <td><img src="bottomleft.gif"></td>
    <td bgcolor="#003399"><font size="-2"> </font></td>
    <td><img src="bottomright.gif"></td>
  </tr>
  </table>
```

You can see that the table consists of three rows and three columns. In addition, there are some things about the code that I'd like to point out:

❶ Note that I've set the cell padding, cell spacing, and border to 0; this is crucial for creating a seamless effect between the cells. I've also used the `<table>` tag to specify the background color for the box with the `bgcolor` attribute. The page background color is set in the `<body>` tag for the document (not shown).

❷ The corner cells of the table are filled with the image files. I've set the width and height of the cells containing graphics to match the graphic dimensions exactly (15 pixels square). I've also set the width of the center column to 120 pixels wide. Setting the cell widths in this first row establishes the column widths for the whole table, so I don't need to set them in subsequent rows. (When setting cell dimensions, be sure that the total width of the cells matches the width set for the whole table.)

❸ The cells that make up the sides of the box are set dark blue and are essentially empty. I have added a nonbreaking space (` `) to ensure the cells won't collapse in Netscape Navigator. (These principles are described in detail in Chapter 11.) In this instance, I found that the height of the nonbreaking space (the same as a line of text) was too tall for the narrow top row and was adding space within the table, so I set the font size of the space to –2. This is typical of the kind of tweaks you may need to make to get your table to look right in most browsers.

❹ The content for the box goes in the center cell. You can set a specific height for this cell, as I did, or omit the height attribute and allow the table to size to fit the contents automatically.

TRY IT

Exercise 19-1: Match the Sample

Using the techniques we've covered in this chapter so far, recreate the web page element shown here. You can use any colors you like.

HINTS:

- The sample shown uses two graphic files.
- The table has two rows and two columns.
- The "new releases" label is in HTML text. You will need to set its size smaller so it will fit in the narrow top cell.
- Use line breaks to adjust space above and below the list.

new releases

✚ Cat Power

✚ The Notwist

✚ Liam Lynch

Corner Creation

This is my preferred method for creating curved corner graphics:

❶ Create a square layered file with an even pixel measurement (so it can later be divided in half easily). My graphic is 30 pixels square.

❷ Fill the background layer with the page's background color (in the example, it's light gray with an RGB value of #CCCCCC, or decimal 204, 204, 204). On a new layer, use the circle marquee to select a circle that has the same dimensions as the graphic file (30 pixels). I find it useful to use the Fixed Size style in the Marquee Options box to get a perfect fit. Fill the circle with the color you've chosen for the box (in our case, dark blue with the values #003399, or decimal 0, 53, 153). I always save my layered file in case I need to make color changes later.

❸ Divide the image into four equal parts. The easiest way is to slice it in ImageReady. I choose File → Jump to ImageReady. Drag guides to divide the image exactly into quarters, then select Slice → Create Slices from Guides.

❹ You can give each slice a descriptive name in the Slices menu. Then use Save Optimized ❺ to export just the images (you don't need the HTML).The resulting four corner graphics are ready for placement in a table.

If you don't have a slicing tool, you can copy each quarter of the image by hand and paste it into a new file. Be sure to get both the circle and the background layers when you copy (use Copy Merged or flatten the image first).

In Photoshop 7

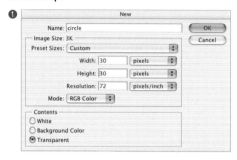

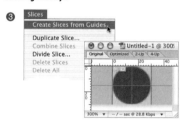

In ImageReady 7

the resulting graphics...

Using 1-Pixel Square Graphics

Very early on, designers realized that HTML did not offer the kind of layout control they were accustomed to in print. Almost immediately, a system of "cheats" were developed that used existing HTML tags in ways never intended by its developers.

Fortunately, we now have style sheets for adding indents and space around elements. I present these old-school tricks for the thoroughness of your education. Even if you do start using style sheets right away, you may still run into a problem for which these techniques offer the best solution.

One of the classic workarounds is the 1-pixel-GIF trick. This technique involves placing a transparent GIF file that is just one pixel square on the page, then stretching it to the desired size using the `width` and `height` attributes in the `<img>` tag. These invisible graphics can be used to nudge text and other page elements around on the page in specific pixel increments (Figure 19-6).

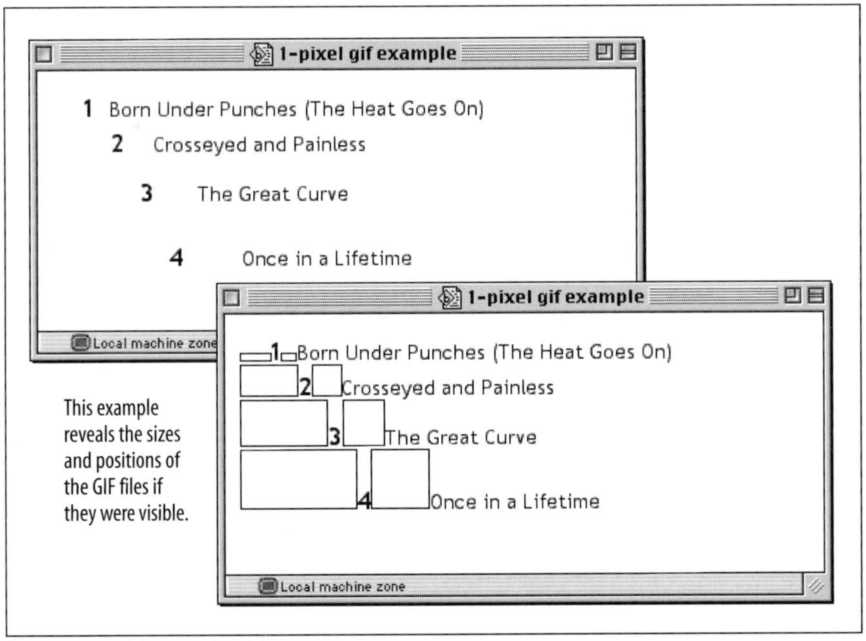

1-pixel square graphics can be used to nudge text and other page elements in specific pixel increments.

This example reveals the sizes and positions of the GIF files if they were visible.

Figure 19-6. This text is positioned using 1-pixel square transparent GIFs that have been set to various sizes.

Of course, this technique has both advantages and disadvantages. On the good side, adding graphics to the page does not interrupt the structure of the HTML document (in other words, you aren't using a "definition list" just to get an indent for a paragraph that isn't really a list). And since the graphic is only one pixel, it's just a few bytes of extra download (and once it is in the browser's cache, it can be used over and over with no load on the server).

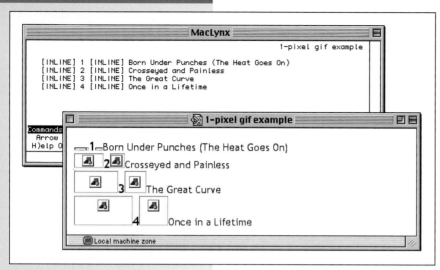

Figure 19-7. This is how 1-pixel graphics look when graphics are not available in the browser.

> ── **T I P** ──────────
>
> *When using an image for spacing, set the alternative text to an empty set of quotation marks. This should eliminate the word "inline" (as shown in Figure 19-7) or other graphic identifiers in text-only browsers.*
>
> `<img src="dot.gif" alt="">`

On the bad side, using 1-pixel GIFs all over the place adds extra junk to your document and can add to the size of your HTML file. Furthermore, this junk is apparent and distracting for users without graphical browsers or with the graphics turned off (Figure 19-7). It's just not good form.

That said, let's look at a few ways in which 1-pixel graphics can be put to work.

Paragraph indents

As we've seen, there is no way to make a standard paragraph indent using HTML alone. However, by inserting a 1-pixel GIF at the beginning of the paragraph, you can use the `width` and `height` attributes to stretch the graphic to a specific pixel width and push the text to the right (Figure 19-8).

A 1-pixel transparent GIF creates a paragraph indent.

>   The image tag places a graphic on the page. The width attribute is used to specify the width of the image in pixels. If the value of the width attribute is different than the actual image ···· dimensions, the graphic will be re-sized to match the measurement specified in the tag.

This non-transparent 1-pixel GIF reveals the shape of the graphic in the example above.

> _____The image tag places a graphic on the page. The width attribute is used to specify the width of the image in pixels. If the value of the width attribute is different than the actual image dimensions, the graphic will be re-sized to match the measurement specified in the tag.

```
<p>
<img src="1px.gif" width="36" height="1">The image tag places a graphic
on the page. The width attribute is used to specify the width of the image
in pixels. If the value...
</p>
```

Figure 19-8. Using a transparent pixel graphic to force the first line of a paragraph to indent.

First-Line Indents

Style sheets offer a simple and reliable method for indenting the first line of any text element with the `text-indent` property. See Chapter 8 for details.

```
p.first {text-indent: 50px}
```

Spacers

The graphic can be stretched in both directions, allowing you to clear larger areas of the page. In Figure 19-9, I've used a 1-pixel graphic to indent a paragraph of text. One downside to this technique is that it is difficult to know how large to size the graphic, since there is no way of knowing how many lines of text there will be when your page is viewed on others' machines.

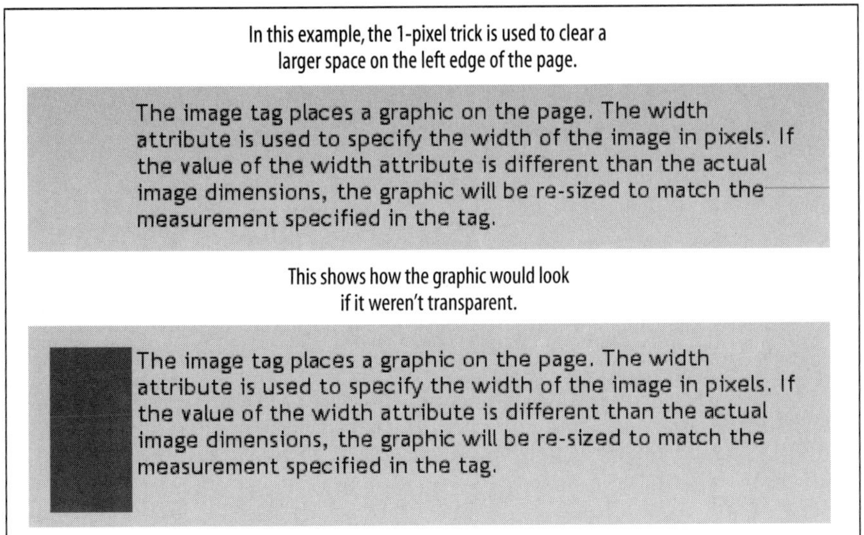

In this example, the 1-pixel trick is used to clear a larger space on the left edge of the page.

The image tag places a graphic on the page. The width attribute is used to specify the width of the image in pixels. If the value of the width attribute is different than the actual image dimensions, the graphic will be re-sized to match the measurement specified in the tag.

This shows how the graphic would look if it weren't transparent.

The image tag places a graphic on the page. The width attribute is used to specify the width of the image in pixels. If the value of the width attribute is different than the actual image dimensions, the graphic will be re-sized to match the measurement specified in the tag.

```
<p>
<img src="1px.gif" width="50" height="100" align="left">The image tag
places a graphic on the page. The width attribute is used to specify the
width of the image in pixels. If the value...
</p>
```

Figure 19-9. Using a transparent pixel graphic to force an entire paragraph to indent.

Paragraph Indents

Use one of the margin properties to indent a whole text element. `margin-left` inserts a specified margin on the left edge; `margin-right` inserts a specified margin on the right. The example below has the same formatting effect as the HTML shown in Figure 19-9:

```
<p style="margin-left: 50px">The image tag places a graphic...</p>
```

Table cell fillers

There is a bug in Navigator that causes cells to collapse if they are left empty. Some designers use 1-pixel GIFs to fill otherwise empty table cells (Figure 19-10). By setting the specific width and height of the graphic the same as the specified dimensions of the cell, you can ensure that the cell will not shrink smaller than your intended size (although if the table is constructed incorrectly, it may still stretch larger than your specifications).

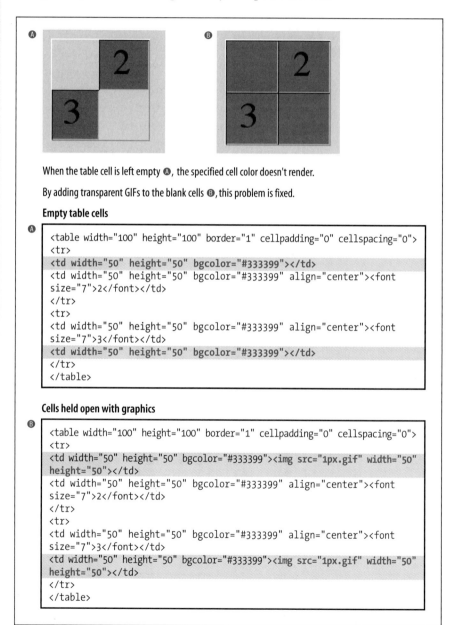

When the table cell is left empty Ⓐ, the specified cell color doesn't render.

By adding transparent GIFs to the blank cells Ⓑ, this problem is fixed.

Empty table cells

```
<table width="100" height="100" border="1" cellpadding="0" cellspacing="0">
<tr>
<td width="50" height="50" bgcolor="#333399"></td>
<td width="50" height="50" bgcolor="#333399" align="center"><font
size="7">2</font></td>
</tr>
<tr>
<td width="50" height="50" bgcolor="#333399" align="center"><font
size="7">3</font></td>
<td width="50" height="50" bgcolor="#333399"></td>
</tr>
</table>
```

Cells held open with graphics

```
<table width="100" height="100" border="1" cellpadding="0" cellspacing="0">
<tr>
<td width="50" height="50" bgcolor="#333399"><img src="1px.gif" width="50"
height="50"></td>
<td width="50" height="50" bgcolor="#333399" align="center"><font
size="7">2</font></td>
</tr>
<tr>
<td width="50" height="50" bgcolor="#333399" align="center"><font
size="7">3</font></td>
<td width="50" height="50" bgcolor="#333399"><img src="1px.gif" width="50"
height="50"></td>
</tr>
</table>
```

Figure 19-10.   1-pixel GIFs can be used to prevent table cells from collapsing in Netscape Navigator.

Rules and boxes

Colored pixels can be used to create rules and boxes of solid color. Again, the advantage is that a 1-pixel graphic will download in an instant. You can use the same graphic over and over (taking advantage of the browser cache) and just change its dimensions with the width and height attributes, rather than downloading separate solid graphics at the various sizes.

For instance, I can make a colored horizontal rule with a 1-pixel graphic (only a few bytes) and set its dimensions easily in the HTML. The length can be set as a specific pixel measurement (as shown in Figure 19-11) or as a percentage of the width of the page (for example, width="80%").

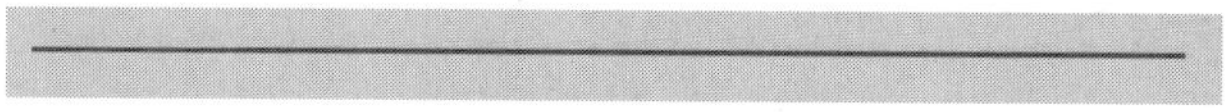

```
<p>
<img src="1px-blue.gif" width="400" height="2">
</p>
```

Figure 19-11. A colored 1-pixel GIF file can be stretched to make a horizontal rule.

Vertical Rules

As we saw in Chapter 9, there is a tag that creates an automatic horizontal rule (<hr>), but in order to get a vertical rule, you need to resort to some clever workarounds. The following are several techniques that may fit your needs.

Stretching a graphic

This is another application of the 1-pixel GIF trick we learned earlier. You can set the height of the graphic to any pixel measurement or percentage, then use the align="left" or "right" attribute to cause the text to wrap around it (Figure 19-12).

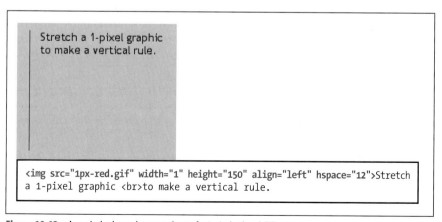

```
<img src="1px-red.gif" width="1" height="150" align="left" hspace="12">Stretch
a 1-pixel graphic <br>to make a vertical rule.
```

Figure 19-12. A vertical rule can be created out of a 1-pixel colored GIF.

Using a table cell

If you want to be sure that the height of your vertical rule always matches the surrounding contents, you may consider creating it with a table cell that is set to just one pixel wide, or whatever width you choose (Figure 19-13). That way, when the contents of the neighboring cell expand or contract, the height of the "rule" cell will expand or contract along with it. Set the color of the rule by specifying the background color (bgcolor) of the cell. Remember that the cell needs to have something in it so that it doesn't collapse in Netscape Navigator. I've used a simple line break tag (<br>) because it doesn't take up any space and won't expand the cell. I could also have used a 1-pixel graphic.

```
This rule        <table border="0" cellpadding="0" cellspacing="10">
                 <tr align="left" valign="top">
resizes                  <td width="50"><br></td>
                         <td bgcolor="darkred" width="1"><br></td>
to fit                   <td>
                                 <p>This rule</p>
your                             <p>resizes</p>
                                 <p>to fit</p>
content.                         <p>your</p>
                                 <p>content.</p>
                         </td>
                 </tr>
                 </table>
```

Figure 19-13. This rule is just the background color of a 1-pixel wide table cell.

Background Tile Tricks

There's nothing simpler than adding a tiling background image to a page using the background attribute in the <body> tag (see Chapter 9 for details). Once you've mastered that, you may want to try one of these advanced tiling techniques.

A "nonrepeating" background image

Unfortunately, HTML alone does not provide a way to prevent a background image from repeating, so if you want an image to appear only once, you need to fudge it. If you make the dimensions of the background image very large—say, larger than most monitors—then even though it repeats, there will be no way for users to open their browser windows wide enough to see the repeated images. The effect will be a single background image.

I did this for a previous version of my personal home page, as shown in Figure 19-14. My background image is a whopping 1200 × 800 pixels. This ensures that the image will be seen only once on most monitors.

If you use this technique, be careful that the file size of the graphic doesn't get out of control at such large pixel dimensions. The last thing you want is a 30-second wait just for your background to appear. Because my graphic has only four pixel colors and lots of flat, solid areas, it compresses down to just 9 KB.

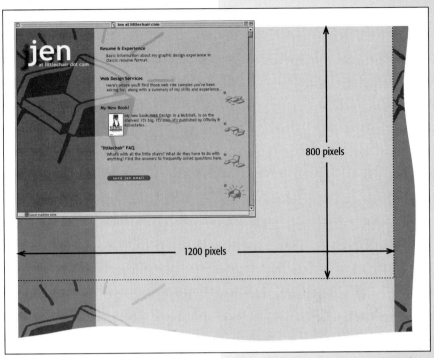

Figure 19-14. You can't prevent a background image from tiling, but you can make it so big that the repeated pattern will not be visible in even the largest of monitors.

One word of warning: be sure to check that the file size of that graphic isn't prohibitively large.

STYLE SHEET ALTERNATIVE

Nontiling Background Graphic

The best solution for preventing tiling backgrounds is to use a style sheet. When you specify a background graphic using the style-sheet `background-image` property, you can use the additional `background-repeat` property to control whether and how the image repeats.

The most popular value is `no-repeat`, which makes the background image appear only once in the upper-left corner of the window:

```
body {background-image: url(map.gif);
    background-repeat: no-repeat;}
```

Other values are `repeat-x`, which allows the image to repeat only horizontally, and `repeat-y`, which allows the image to repeat only vertically.

Another cool background image property is `background-attachment`, which determines whether the background image scrolls along with the document (`scroll`) or remains in a fixed position (`fixed`). This property is not supported by Netscape Navigator 4.

```
body {background-image: url(map.gif);
    background-attachment: fixed}
```

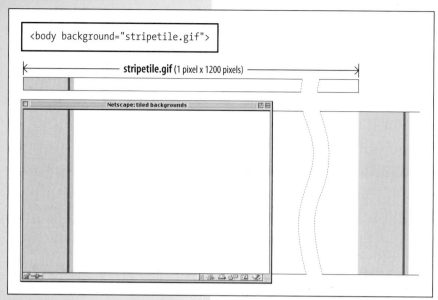

<body background="stripetile.gif">

stripetile.gif (1 pixel x 1200 pixels)

Netscape: tiled backgrounds

Figure 19-15. You can create a stripe effect by tiling a very long graphic just one pixel high. The advantage is that at only one pixel in height, the graphic file is tiny and downloads quickly.

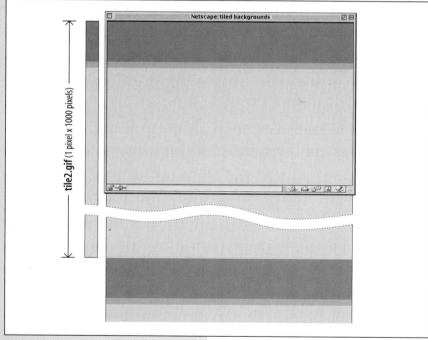

tile2.gif (1 pixel x 1000 pixels)

Netscape: tiled backgrounds

Figure 19-16. This horizontal band of color was created by tiling a very tall, skinny graphic. If you don't want the repeated tile to show, be sure that the graphic is at least taller than the contents of your page (so it won't be seen when the user scrolls) and tall enough that it won't be seen on really large monitors (approx. 1000 pixels).

Stripes

Another neat trick using the "make-it-so-wide-they-won't-see-the-repeat" technique is to create stripes with a graphic that is just one pixel thick but very long. We played with this technique a little in Chapter 9 in the background tile exercise (Exercise 9-3).

If the graphic is wide enough (greater than 1200 pixels or so), the next band of color won't be visible for most users. When this graphic tiles in the browser, the little 1-pixel-high graphics stack up to form solid bands of color (Figure 19-15).

The advantage of this trick is that, at only one pixel in height, the file size of the background image is extremely small. It's a big bang for a small byte investment.

You could also do this with a very tall graphic that is only one pixel wide to create horizontal stripes (Figure 19-16). The only drawback here is that because the graphic is tiling, the next row will be visible again if the page is long enough to scroll that far. So make sure the graphic is tall enough to span your entire page contents or use this approach only for short pages when you know users won't be able to scroll.

Pop-up Windows

One problem with putting links on your page is that when people click on them, they may never come back. One popular solution to this dilemma is to have the linked page open in a new browser window. That way, users can check out the link and still have your content available right where they left it.

The method you use for opening a new browser window depends on whether you want to control its size. If the size doesn't matter, you can use standard HTML. However, if you want to open a window of a particular size (for instance, to display an image or a small amount of text), you'll need to use JavaScript. Let's look at both of these techniques.

Targeting a new window with HTML

To open a new window using HTML, use the `target` attribute in the anchor tag (Figure 19-17). This attribute tells the browser that you want the linked document to open in a window other than the one in which the current document is displayed. You won't have any control over the size of the new window, although you can assume that it will be similar to the window size the user already has open. You have a choice of using the standard `_blank` value or giving the new window a specific name (of your choosing).

Figure 19-17. The `target` attribute opens a new window, but at an unknown size.

Opening a new window at a specific size requires JavaScript.

TIP

The easiest way to make a sized pop-up window is to use a web-authoring program to generate the code for you automatically. But it doesn't hurt to learn how it works.

Setting target="_blank" always causes the browser to open a fresh window. For example:

```
<a href="http://www.oreilly.com/" target="_blank">...</a>
```

If you use this for every link, every link will open a new window, potentially leaving your user with a mess of open windows.

A better method, especially if you have more than one link, is to give the targeted window a name, which can then be reused by subsequent links. You can give the window any name you like ("new," "sample," whatever), as long as it doesn't start with an underscore. The following link will open a new window called *display*:

```
<a href="http://www.oreilly.com" target="display">...</a>
```

If you target every link on that page to the display window, each targeted document will open in the same second window.

Opening a window of a specific size

If you want to control the dimensions of your new window, you'll need to take advantage of some simple JavaScript commands. JavaScript is a web-specific scripting language that adds interactivity and conditional behaviors to web pages. It is explained briefly as it applies to rollover effects in Chapter 18.

In the following example, we will open a new window that is 300 pixels wide × 400 pixels high (Figure 19-18). There are two parts to the JavaScript for this trick. The first is the script itself, which we will place in the <head> of the document **A**. The second is a reference to the script within the link **B**. The comment tags (<-- and //-->) hide the script from browsers that do not support JavaScript.

```
   <html>
   <head>
A  <script language="JavaScript">
   <!--
   function openWin(URL) {
   aWindow=window.open (URL,"thewindow","width=300,height=400,
   toolbar=no,status=no,scrollbars=yes,resizable=no,menubar=no");
   }
   //-->
   </script>

   </head>

   <body>
B  <p><a href="javascript:openWin('waits.html');">Tom Waits</a></p>
   <p><a href="javascript:openWin('eno.html');">Brian Eno</a></p>
   </body>
   </html>
```

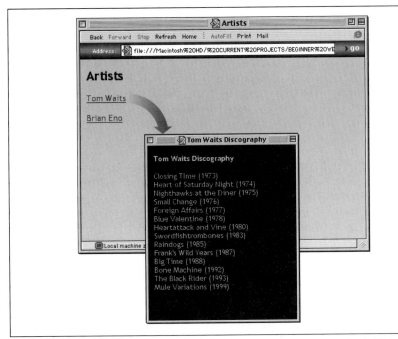

Figure 19-18. The openWin() JavaScript function allows you to open a window at specific pixel dimensions. You can also choose which elements of the browser window you want to display.

Notice in the script **Ⓐ** that you are given the opportunity to specify the width and height of the new window in pixels. You can also decide which parts of the browser window (toolbar, status bar, scrollbar, and menubar) you want to display and whether you want the user to be able to resize the window. The values for each of these are either yes or no. Do not put any character spaces or returns within the string of browser features.

The link **Ⓑ** uses a regular <a href> tag, but the value of the href is not a standard URL but a call to the JavaScript function. The word javascript tells the browser that this will be a JavaScript link. Next, the openWin() function, which was defined in the script, is called. The URL of the linked document is placed within parentheses.

This JavaScript example is easy to copy and use on your own web pages. Only the code in bold text should be replaced with your own information; the rest needs to be copied exactly. Within the function, you can change the name of the window from thewindow to any name you like. You can change the values of the browser attributes that follow, or omit them completely and allow the default browser behavior. Within the links, you need to specify the URLs of your linked pages. Be sure not to put any spaces or hard carriage returns within the function code in the script (soft text wrap is acceptable, but technically, the code needs to be on one line).

TRY IT

Exercise 19-2: Make a Pop-up Window

Try writing the code for a pop-up window based on the sample in this section. To give you a head start, the HTML documents and their respective graphics have been provided for you in the *chap19* materials folder.

Open the page *invitation.html* in a browser. You will see the word "map" at the bottom of the page. Your task is to make the word "map" a link that pops up a sized window showing the map page (*map.html*).

Open *invitation.html* in an HTML text editor. Add the necessary script to open a window that is 375 pixels wide and 375 pixels square (the same size as the map graphic). Turn off all the browser features as listed so the window displays just the graphic. It is important to copy the script exactly as it appears in the book; however, you must keep it on one line (the book shows a line break due to limited space).

The *map.html* file contains just the map graphic and has its margins set to 0 so it will be flush against the browser window. You will not need to make any changes to this file.

Once you have the pop-up window working correctly, experiment with the various settings in the script to get a feel for how they work.

Adjusting Page Margins

By default, browsers insert a margin of 10–12 pixels (depending on the browser and platform) between the edge of the browser window and the document's contents. There is no method for changing these margins using tags from the official HTML 4 specification. However, there are browser-specific attributes that can be added to the `<body>` tag that increase or decrease margin width. Not surprisingly, the major browsers use different attributes.

Interenet Explorer uses the attributes `leftmargin`, `rightmargin`, `topmargin`, and `bottommargin` to specify pixel widths of specific margins. Navigator 4 and Netscape 6 use `marginwidth` (to adjust the left and right margins) and `marginheight` (for top and bottom margins).

For all of these attributes, the measurement is a pixel measurement. The margin may be removed completely, allowing objects to sit flush against the window, by setting the value to `0`. Be aware that there is a Navigator bug that inserts a 1-pixel border even when the margins are set to `0`.

To set margins for both browsers, it is necessary to duplicate attributes. In the following example, the margins are turned off on the top and left edges using two sets of proprietary attributes:

```
<body marginwidth="0" marginheight="0" leftmargin="0" topmargin="0">
```

A Closing Word on Web Design Techniques

The true art of web design lies in the clever combination of the skills covered in this book. For instance, even a simple element such as a box with rounded corners involves the following skills:

- Writing HTML for table creation, table placement, text formatting, and color specification

- Understanding RGB colors in HTML and graphics

- Graphic production, including optimization techniques

- Knowledge of typical browser bugs (such as collapsing tables) so you can avoid them

In web design, there are often several methods for accomplishing the same task, so consider the directions in this chapter as a starting point. You can learn other techniques by viewing the HTML source of page elements you come across on the Web.

By all means, go out and experiment on your own. Be sure to test your results on different browsers and platforms to make sure things are working the way you planned. In time, your personal bag of tricks will grow and you will be creating cool and original web elements and page designs on your own.

Test Yourself

Here are some questions about the techniques covered in this chapter. The answers can be found in the Appendix.

1. What options do you have if you want to use your own graphic as a bullet in a bulleted list?

2. Name two ways to display a colored box with a 4-pixel solid colored border.

3. How do you make rounded corners on a web page?

4. The 1-pixel graphics tricks rely on two attributes to achieve spacing effects. What are they?

5. How do you make a vertical rule that gets longer when the text gets longer?

6. How do you prevent a background image from tiling altogether?

7. When do you need JavaScript to open a new browser window?

Building Usable Web Sites

20

Looks are important, but the real key to a web site's success is how well it *works*. You might have fabulous graphics and solidly coded pages, but if your users can't find the information they need or figure out how to buy your products, all of your efforts have been for nothing. Shoddy interfaces have been known to send commercial web sites right down the tubes.

Building a site that works involves attention to how the information is organized (information design) and how users get to that information (interface design and navigation systems). This planning needs to take place before you type your first HTML tag or create a single GIF.

Don't skimp on this planning phase, regardless of the scale or purpose of your site. Even a personal web site will benefit from logical organization and good navigation (Figure 20-1, following page).

In this chapter, I'll introduce the basic principles of information design, interface design, and navigation. Each of these topics is rich enough to warrant further study (see the sidebar later in this chapter, Where to Learn More: Information Design); in fact, some designers choose to become specialists in these fields. But even if you're just starting out, it's important to keep these issues in mind.

Focus on the User

All design shapes a user's experience. Print designers can affect how information is perceived on a page and in what order. An architect designs not just the building, but the visitor's experience walking through it. Similarly, a web designer needs to consider the user's experience of "moving through" the site.

In web design, it's all about the user. Terms such as "user experience" and "user-centric design" are used frequently and taken seriously. Formal studies abound, but in essence, it's about getting into the heads of your users in order to create a design that meets their needs and expectations. Interviewing users early on can give you a better idea of what they're looking for on a particular

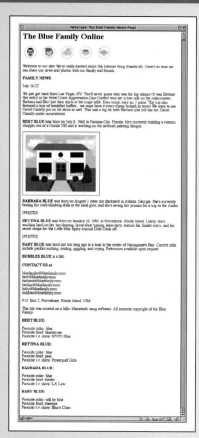

Figure 20-1. Simply throwing all your information on the home page does not create a good user experience.

site and where they expect to find it. Later in the design process, user testing is an important step in finding out if your solutions are working.

Here are some common frustrations that can kill a good user experience:

- Not being able to find the information
- Hitting dead ends
- Not being able to get back to the starting point
- Having to click through too many pages to get to the information

Many of these can be avoided by setting up a logical structure and providing clear and appropriate tools for navigating it.

The family web site pictured in Figure 20-1 needs serious help. Throughout this chapter, I'll apply principles of information and interface design to whip this simple site into shape and make it more usable.

Information Design

Information design involves both organizing information and planning how users will find it. Designers who specialize in this discipline are often called "information architects" because, like traditional architects, they are concerned with designing structures and access to areas within those structures. The information designer may also conduct testing before, during, and after the design process to make sure the information is meeting users' needs and expectations.

Information design, whether highly structured or completely informal, is the first step in any web site–creation process. Your exact process will certainly depend on the scale and goals of your site. A large commercial site may require months of research and model building before production can begin. For a personal site, a quick list of the contents and a site sketch may suffice. Either way, there are three standard steps that make up the information design process:

1. Take an inventory of the information you want to include on the site.
2. Organize the information.
3. Give it shape by designing the overall structure of the site.

Taking inventory

A good first step is to make a list of *everything* you want to include on the site. This is often referred to as the site inventory, or asset list. The list should include not only the information you want to make available, but also the things your visitors can do on the site. Remember that some content comes in the form of functionality, such as shopping, chat rooms, research tools, etc.

Once you've determined what you want (or what your client wants) to publish, you also need to give careful thought to the types of information and functionality that your users want and expect. This is a good time to do research on your site's audience and their needs.

The information-gathering process will vary from site to site. For a personal web site, it might just be time spent considering the options and making a list in a notebook. For instance, the site inventory for the Blue Family site is a manageable list of information about the family and each of its members (Figure 20-2).

At the other end of the scale, large commercial sites benefit from more in-depth research. Web development firms often spend months identifying the most effective content for a site through a process of market research and interviews, both with the client and potential users.

WHERE TO LEARN MORE

Information Design

The following books are excellent resources on information design and usability:

Information Architecture for the World Wide Web, Second Edition, by Lou Rosenfeld and Peter Morville (O'Reilly, 2002)

Web Site Usability: A Designer's Guide, by Jared M. Spool, Tara Scanlon, Will Shroeder, Carolyn Snyder, and Terri DeAngelo (Morgan Kaufmann Publishers, 1998)

Designing Web Usability, by Jakob Nielsen (New Riders Publishing, 1999)

The Art & Science of Web Design, by Jeffrey Veen (New Riders Publishing, 2001)

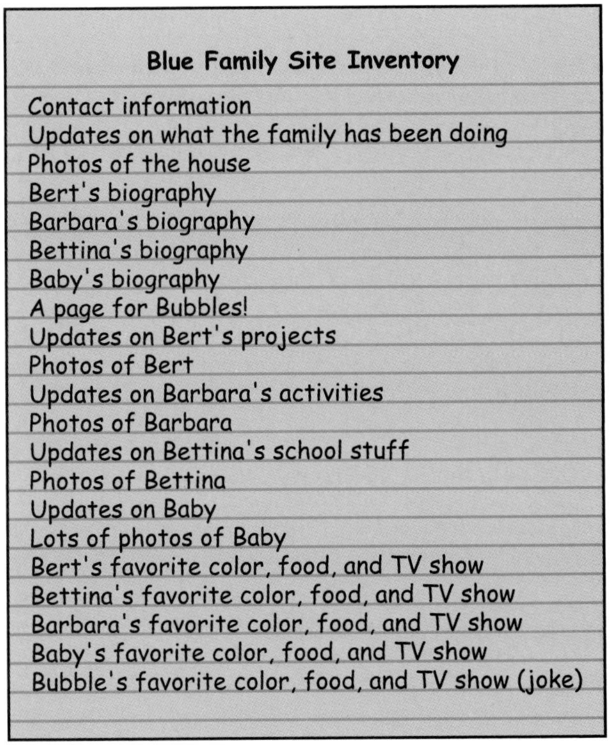

Blue Family Site Inventory

Contact information
Updates on what the family has been doing
Photos of the house
Bert's biography
Barbara's biography
Bettina's biography
Baby's biography
A page for Bubbles!
Updates on Bert's projects
Photos of Bert
Updates on Barbara's activities
Photos of Barbara
Updates on Bettina's school stuff
Photos of Bettina
Updates on Baby
Lots of photos of Baby
Bert's favorite color, food, and TV show
Bettina's favorite color, food, and TV show
Barbara's favorite color, food, and TV show
Baby's favorite color, food, and TV show
Bubble's favorite color, food, and TV show (joke)

Figure 20-2. Start by making a simple list of everything that should go in the site.

Organizing information

The next step is to organize your site's assets. Organizing information can be a complex business. Information is highly subjective in that the same set of elements can be organized in different ways, depending on the organizer's perspective.

Sorting strategies

There are standard approaches to ordering information logically. The method you choose will depend on the type of information you have. However, even a single set of data can be organized in different ways. For instance, a list of national sales data can be sorted a number of ways:

Alphabetically. Putting elements in a list from A to Z is one of the most fundamental approaches to information organization. An example is sorting sales by customer name.

Chronologically. You can organize sequential events or step-by-step information according to a timeline, usually from earliest to latest. Sorting sales by purchase date is an example of this method.

By class (or type). This approach organizes information into logical groupings based on similarities. (See the next section, Information clumping.) An example is sorting sales by product lines (office supplies, art supplies, etc.).

Hierarchically. This takes organizing by class to the next level by breaking information into large sections, then each section into subsections, and so on. It is the most popular organizational strategy for web sites; we'll discuss this method in more detail later. Examples include breaking product line sales (art supplies) down by subgroups (brushes), and sub-subgroups (sable watercolor brushes).

Spatially. Some information can be organized geographically or spatially, such as room-by-room. Organizing sales by state is one example.

By order of magnitude. You can organize some sorts of information according to a continuum, such as largest to smallest, or lightest to darkest, etc. An example of this method is sorting sales from smallest purchase amount to largest purchase amount.

Information clumping

People tend to get overwhelmed by large numbers of options. In fact, it is our nature to search for similarities among individual items and divide them into fewer, more manageable groups. In information design, this is sometimes referred to as clumping. Instead of making all of your site offerings available in a big list on the home page, I recommend that you divide them into logical groupings.

Again, there is usually more than one way to slice up the same set of information, so you may need to move things around a few times until you find the solution that works best. Even simple lists, such as the Blue Family's site inventory, present more than one option for organization by class (Figure 20-3).

```
BERT:
  email address
  birthday information
  current projects
  favorite color
  favorite food
  favorite TV show
  photos

BARBARA:
  email address
  birthday information
  current projects
  favorite color
  favorite food
  favorite TV show
  photos

BETTINA:
  email address
  birthday information
  current projects
  favorite color
  favorite food
  favorite TV show
  photos

BABY:
  email address
  birthday information
  current projects
  favorite color
  favorite food
  favorite TV show
  photos

BUBBLES:
  email address
  favorite color
  favorite food
  favorite TV show
```

```
Email addresses:
  Bert
  Barbara
  Bettina
  Baby
  Bubbles

Photographs:
  Bert
  Barbara
  Bettina
  Baby

Current events:
  Bert
  Barbara
  Bettina
  Baby

Favorite lists:
  Bert
  Barbara
  Bettina
  Baby
  Bubbles

Birthday information:
  Bert
  Barbara
  Bettina
  Baby
```

Figure 20-3. There are usually many ways to organize the same information. Here, the items from the Blue Family site inventory are arranged two different ways.

> **TIP**
>
> **The Sticky-Note Trick**
>
> One tool web developers commonly use is the old "sticky-note-on-the-wall" trick. Each sticky-note represents a chunk of information that needs to go into the site. Sometimes different colored stickies are used to differentiate types of information. With all the sticky-notes on the wall, they can be grouped and regrouped easily until the structure of the site begins to emerge.

Remember the user

While you're organizing, be sure to keep the users' perspective in mind. One of the most common mistakes that companies make is to organize their corporate web sites to match their internal department structure. While someone who works for XYZ Corporation may know which department handles special promotions, chances are that the average user will not know to look there.

A good example of designing for the user is the FedEx site (Figure 20-4). They know a significant percentage of people visiting their site are there to track a package. Although this activity makes up a small part of the functions of FedEx as a whole, it is given a prominent space on the home page of the site.

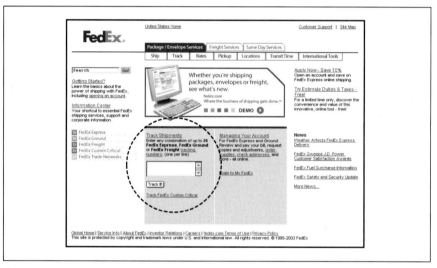

Figure 20-4. FedEx anticipated the needs of their users and put the tracking function right on the home page.

Do your research up front to learn what your users expect to find on your site and what you can do to meet their needs. Remember that the way you perceive your own information may be confusing to others.

After examining the possibilities, I've decided to divide the information for the Blue Family site into sections by family member. In addition, I've added three special pages that are updated frequently (Figure 20-5).

```
The Blue Family
Final Site Organization

Special Features:

Family News (updated frequently)

Vacation Photographs

Contact Information
(email and mailing addresses)

Family Member Sections:

Bert Page:
      Personal bio
      Current activities
      Favorites list
      Photo page

Barbara Page:
      Personal bio
      Current activities
      Favorites list
      Photo page

Bettina Page:
      Personal bio
      Current activities
      Favorites list
      Photo page

Baby Page:
      Personal bio
      Current activities
      Favorites list
      Photo page

Bubbles Page:
      Personal bio
      Favorites list
```

Figure 20-5. The organization of the Blue Family site.

Giving it a shape: Site structure

Once you've identified the contents of your site and given it a basic organization, it is helpful to create a site diagram. Professional information architects use site diagrams as tools for communicating the structure of the site to clients, and as a road map for providing guidance throughout the web-production process.

Site diagrams use boxes to represent pages with lines and/or arrows to represent the relationships (links) between pages (Figure 20-6). It's nice to have a mental model for the overall shape of the site; it creates a sense of space and begins to suggest a system for navigation.

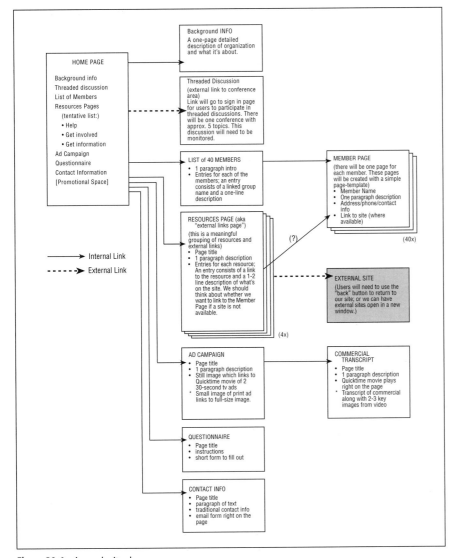

Professional information architects use site diagrams as tools for communicating the structure of the site.

Figure 20-6. A sample site plan.

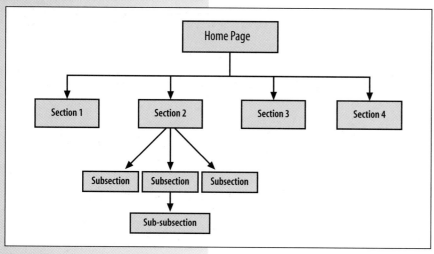

Figure 20-7. A diagram of a site with hierarchical organization.

Hierarchical structure

Most sites are organized hierarchically, starting with a top page that offers several choices and then successive layers of choices branching out below, so that a "tree" is formed (Figure 20-7).

Hierarchical organization is a tried-and-true method and, if done well, it offers the user clear, step-by-step access to material on the site. If you choose this structure, there are a few guidelines you should follow.

First, make sure that important information doesn't get buried too deeply. With each required click, you run the risk of losing a few readers who may only have time to skim through the top layers of a site.

Also, make sure that the branches of the hierarchy tree are generally balanced. For example, if the majority of the categories are shallow (only a few levels deep), avoid having one category drill down through multiple levels of information. If this is the case, chances are you can organize the information better to create consistency throughout the site.

Our family site is based on a simple hierarchical structure (Figure 20-8) with the addition of special sections on the home page. The family member sections are available from every page on the site.

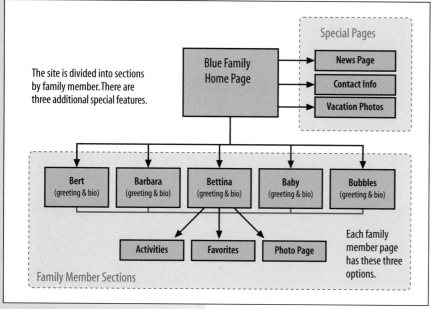

Figure 20-8. The Blue Family site diagram.

Linear arrangement

Although tree-style structure is the most popular and multipurpose, it is by no means your only option, and may not be the best suited for your type of information. You may consider organizing your site (or a part of it) linearly. In a linear arrangement, the user is guided from page to page in a particular order. This is appropriate for narratives or any information that must be viewed in sequence.

In the Blue Family site, I've chosen a linear arrangement for the vacation photographs, which have been arranged in chronological order (Figure 20-9). Notice that I've also planned for access to the home page from any page in the photo sequence, so the user never gets stuck in the flow.

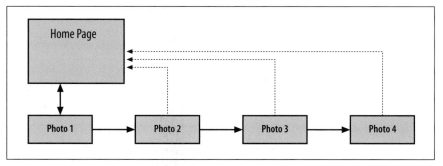

Figure 20-9. A linear site diagram. Each page offers a link to the home page.

NAVIGATION TIP

How Far Do I Have to Go?

When you're driving down a highway, you see mile markers and signs telling you how many miles it is to the next city. This is an important type of feedback for knowing where you are and for planning your trip.

Likewise, when users are clicking through a series, such as a multipart article, they need some feedback as to the total length of the trip (total number of pages) and where they are in the flow (the current page number).

Each page in a linear arrangement should be clearly labeled with this status information. There are several common approaches:

1 of 5
Lists the current page number (1) and the total number of pages (5).

1, 2, 3, 4, 5
Lists each page number individually with the current page highlighted. Each page number serves as a link to that page.

Intro
Information Design
Interface Design
Navigation Design
Conclusion
Instead of just numbers, it is more informative to provide actual titles for each page so users can make a better decision whether they want to continue or skip ahead.

Planning Server Structure

If you are building a web site that has more than a dozen or so pages, you'll probably want to divide your files into subdirectories on the server. In general, it is most convenient when the organization of your files on the server matches the structure of your site. Therefore, the information-design phase of a web design project is also a good time to set up a directory structure on the server.

There are many approaches to server management, but in general, a single directory contains all the files for a site. That directory is divided into subdirectories that reflect the site's major sections. It is common to keep all of the graphics in a directory called *graphics* or *images*. I often keep an *images* directory in each of my section subdirectories so all the common information sticks together.

www.orbitband.com

Complex structures

Not every site is going to fit nicely into a tree or a straight line. Most commercial web sites today offer so much information and functionality that the site diagrams can become enormous and quite complex. I've seen a site diagram for one popular media site that used postage-stamp sized boxes to represent pages, and the overall site diagram sprawled the length of the hallway!

But that's just the point of using a site diagram. It enables you to get a handle on the site as a whole and to keep track of its farthest corners.

TRY IT

Exercise 20-1: Take Inventory

If you bought this book, chances are you have a web site project in mind. Take this opportunity to plan the contents of your site. If you don't already have a web project on your to-do list, you can practice these skills by making up a site for your family, church, or a friend's business.

Make a detailed list of the things you want to include in the site. Don't underestimate the importance of this process; being thorough takes real work. You will probably find that the elements will fall into a natural organization, perhaps by category. Challenge yourself and see if you can take the same list of elements and put them into a different organization. Is there anything to be learned by the alternative structure?

When you can't think of anything else to add and all the pieces are organized in a balanced, logical fashion, try sketching a diagram that shows how your content inventory translates into a site structure. Start with boxes for the home page and pages that link from it. For small sites, it may be possible to sketch out every page of the site. For complex sites, you may only be able to indicate major sections.

Of course, there are no answers in the back of the book for this exercise. To see how you're doing, get feedback from your family, peers, or client.

Interface Design

Now that we have our content in shape, we need to give our visitors a way to get to it. We're entering the interface design phase.

The interface design determines how a site's logical structure appears visually on the page. It includes all the visual cues to understanding what information is available as well as navigational tools for moving through the site.

Because the interface works visually, it is closely integrated with the graphic design of the site. For instance, the interface designer might say, "This information will be accessed via a button on the home page," while the graphic designer might say, "Our buttons will be blue with yellow outlines and white type." In the real world, however, it is quite common for both of these roles to be performed by the same person or department.

Let's look at some of the visual cues and conceptual models that you can use to make the structure of your information more apparent and understandable.

Grouping like elements

Long lists of choices can be overwhelming and may discourage browsing. If there are a large number of items available on a page (and there often are), it is a good idea to break them into a small number of major groups and to indicate these groups visually (Figure 20-10).

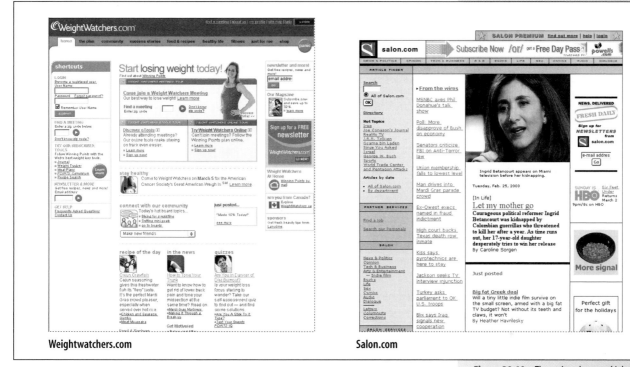

Weightwatchers.com

Salon.com

Figure 20-10. These sites do a good job of dividing a large number of page elements into manageable groups through the use of tables and color.

The magic number in interface design is seven. The theory is that the human brain tends to short-circuit when faced with more than seven options at a time. So when designing interfaces, choices are often limited to seven, plus or minus two (however, it is not a hard and fast rule). While it's unlikely that you'll have just seven elements on a page, you can break your longer list into seven or fewer groups.

For instance, you may put all of your navigational buttons in a row across the top of the page. By using a colored background for that area or similar graphical treatments for each button, the buttons will work together as one visual unit. Likewise, you may put links to archived material in a shaded table to set them apart from the main content areas of the site.

Metaphors

Another way to make the information on a site more accessible and understandable is to use a metaphor. A metaphor associates a new concept (such as a site organization or navigational tool) with a familiar model or idea. The knowledge the user has of the familiar setting will provide a head start to understanding the new environment.

Site-wide metaphors

A site-wide metaphor strives to turn the whole site into something recognizable, such as a town square or a kitchen, as the interface to information. Objects in that space correlate with sections of the site.

Site-wide metaphors were popular when the Web first started because it was easy to assume that everyone was new to the Web and needed a little handholding. There were many little villages online (Figure 20-11, middle), and even large corporations tried it out. Some infamous examples include the IRS's "Digital Daily" newspaper interface (Figure 20-11, top), Southwest Airlines' virtual ticket counter, and Kraft's "Interactive Kitchen." They've all been redesigned now. In fact, the site-wide metaphor is virtually extinct...and for good reason. Metaphors tend to break down—not every section in your site is going to have a logical association with something in the metaphorical scene. It becomes confusing quickly, and at times, even trite. For instance, where do you download tax forms in a newspaper, or look for corporate information in a kitchen? In addition, site-wide metaphors often require a graphics-heavy design to set the stage, which can slow down performance.

Use any metaphor with caution. When the symbol misses its mark, it's not only confusing, it can be comical.

So while a metaphor might be a fun and tempting solution to your home page, I advise that you resist, unless that metaphor is part of your content (like a game) or it somehow makes perfect sense for the site. For instance, it might be an entertaining and easy interface for a children's site.

Tool metaphors

Metaphors are more effective when they are used to explain specific concepts or tools (Figure 20-11, bottom). I think the best example of this is the online "shopping cart." People know what you do with a shopping cart in the real world: you load it up with the things you want to buy and then take them to the cash register for purchase. Shopping sites quickly adopted the shopping-cart metaphor for online shopping functionality.

Getty Images, a company that licenses photography, has a function for saving selected images that can be looked at later and shared with a group. They call this feature the "lightbox," referring to the backlit table that traditional designers use to view transparent artwork. The activities that take place around a traditional lightbox are a good match for what takes place on Getty's virtual photo-viewing area, making the lightbox an effective metaphor.

Examples of site-wide metaphors

The IRS (www.irs.gov) used this newspaper metaphor for years. Fortunately, they have since cut the cute stuff and have redesigned the site to make finding information and forms easier.

An example of a neighborhood metaphor on a community center web site. The assignment of topic to building is arbitrary because the drawing is not of the center itself.

Examples of tool metaphors

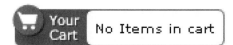

The well-established shopping-cart metaphor (this one from barnesandnoble.com).

This online lightbox tool on the Getty Images site (creative.gettyimages.com) allows designers to store and view images. When you are ready to purchase, you add the image to your cart, of course.

Figure 20-11. Site-wide and tool metaphors.

Interface design methods

Like information architects, interface designers use diagrams and flowcharts to work out the functionality of their designs. Diagrams show how pages work and are generally devoid of graphic design. You can even use them to do a round of user testing to make sure your site works before the time is spent developing the prototype.

Page diagrams

One type of diagram used in the interface-building process is a wireframe page layout of typical pages in the site. In most cases, large web sites use a limited number of page templates that can be reused for common page functions (such as login pages, top-level section pages, etc.).

I developed the interface for a site that allowed members to search through a large database of public records. Early in the design process, I created diagrams of each page type to communicate the functionality of the site to the client and to give the graphic designer a basic structure for the page design (Figure 20-12).

> *Diagrams show how pages work and are generally devoid of graphic design.*

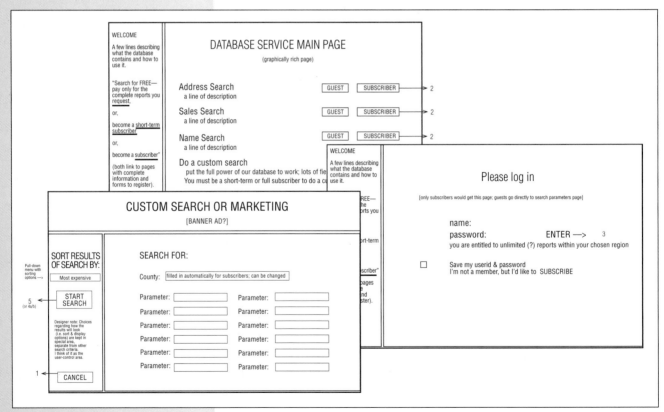

Figure 20-12. Interface designers use wireframe page diagrams to plan the functionality of the site.

Even if you are just working on a web site for yourself, you might find that sketching out the home page and representative pages within your site is a useful step to take before you dig into writing the HTML and developing the look and feel for the page. It helps you make sure that all the pieces are there. Page diagrams for the Blue Family site might look like Figure 20-13.

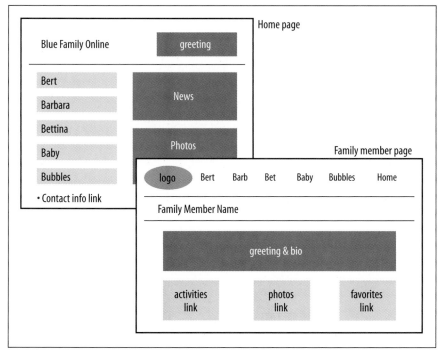

Figure 20-13. Page diagrams for the Blue Family site.

User scenarios

For complex commercial sites, particularly those with interactive functionality and step-based features such as shopping, personalized content (accessed by logging in), and so on, the interface designer might also produce typical user-scenario flowcharts. These flowcharts show how a typical user might click through the various levels and features of the site. It's a diagram of one possible pathway through the site.

The database site I mentioned earlier had a complicated interface that changed depending on the level of membership the user signed up for and the number of records that were retrieved. The development team and I used flowcharts to anticipate and plan for each of these variations (Figure 20-14). Flowcharts may be accompanied by a more descriptive narrative of the action, as shown in the flowchart sample.

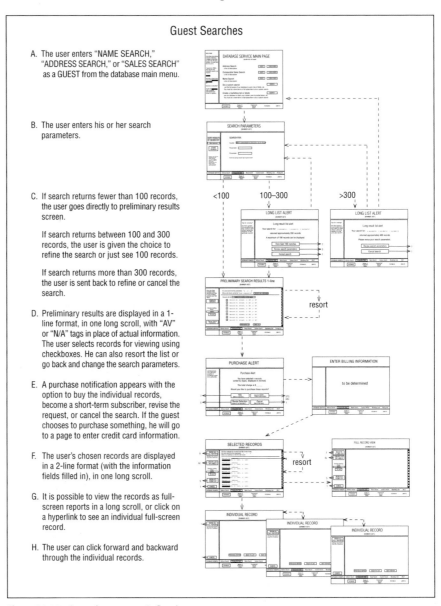

Guest Searches

A. The user enters "NAME SEARCH," "ADDRESS SEARCH," or "SALES SEARCH" as a GUEST from the database main menu.

B. The user enters his or her search parameters.

C. If search returns fewer than 100 records, the user goes directly to preliminary results screen.

If search returns between 100 and 300 records, the user is given the choice to refine the search or just see 100 records.

If search returns more than 300 records, the user is sent back to refine or cancel the search.

D. Preliminary results are displayed in a 1-line format, in one long scroll, with "AV" or "N/A" tags in place of actual information. The user selects records for viewing using checkboxes. He can also resort the list or go back and change the search parameters.

E. A purchase notification appears with the option to buy the individual records, become a short-term subscriber, revise the request, or cancel the search. If the guest chooses to purchase something, he will go to a page to enter credit card information.

F. The user's chosen records are displayed in a 2-line format (with the information fields filled in), in one long scroll.

G. It is possible to view the records as full-screen reports in a long scroll, or click on a hyperlink to see an individual full-screen record.

H. The user can click forward and backward through the individual records.

Figure 20-14. A sample user-scenario flowchart.

Navigation Design

Navigation is a subset of the site's interface, but because it's an important topic, I'll give it a little extra attention.

The information in a web site is often perceived as occupying a physical space. Like a real physical space, such as a city or airport, a web site requires a system of signage to help visitors find their way around. On web sites, this takes the form of logos, labels, buttons, links, and other shortcuts. These elements make up the navigational system for the site.

Where am I?

One of the main duties of a navigation system is to let users know where they are. Remember that users can enter your site at any point if they have the right URL or if they are clicking on a link from a list of search engine results. There's no guarantee that they will have the benefit of the home page to tell them where they've landed, so it is important that every page on your site contains some label that identifies the site.

Nordstrom's web site (*www.nordstrom.com*) uses an effective global navigation bar at the top of every page (Figure 20-15). The Nordstrom logo on the left clearly identifies the site.

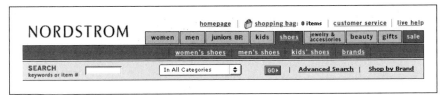

Figure 20-15. Nordstrom's global navigation toolbar clearly identifies the site and is used on every page.

In addition, if your site has different sections or levels, it is a good idea to orient the reader within the site's structure. As you can see in the Nordstrom navigational toolbar, the subsection is also identified by highlighting its name in the toolbar.

Where can I go?

The other responsibility of a navigation system is to clearly present the options for where users can go (or what they can do) next. I usually ask myself two questions when deciding exactly which navigational buttons to add. The first question is user-based: where might this person want to go next? For the second question, I play the role of the client or web site publisher: where do *we* want that person to go next?

Like a real physical space, such as a city or airport, a web site requires a system of signage to help visitors find their way around.

It is impractical to provide a link to every page on a site from every other page, so you need to choose your links wisely. By limiting choices, you can help shape the users' experience of your site while providing the flexibility they need to get around.

The navigational options for every site will be different, but there are a few standards. An expanded view of the Nordstrom site shows how it employs some standard navigational systems (Figure 20-16).

Ⓐ First, a link back to the home page from every page in the site is usually expected. If the reader ever gets lost in the maze, this provides a way to get back to the beginning with one click.

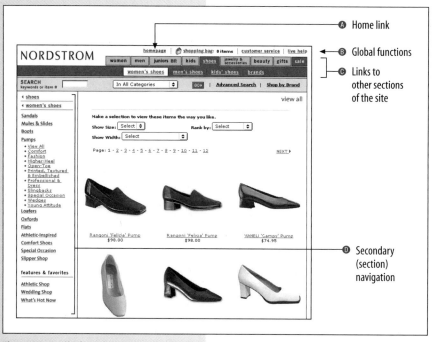

Figure 20-16. Nordstrom's navigational systems.

Ⓑ There might also be a set of links that should be accessible site-wide, regardless of the current section. These include links to a help section, personalized information, search capabilities, and other general information that should always be available to users. These can be incorporated into the global navigation system, but usually with less visual weight. Note that Nordstrom uses a shopping bag, rather than a cart.

Ⓒ If your site is divided into sections, you might choose to provide links to the main pages of the other sections as part of the navigation system on every page.

Ⓓ You may also have options that are specific to a particular section of the site. This is called secondary navigation or section navigation. On Nordstrom.com, the secondary navigation is in a column on the left. Each section has its own set of section-specific navigational options as well as the global navigation system.

Fundamentals of good navigation

Navigation systems are highly site-specific. The list of choices that are perfect for one site could totally bomb on another. However, there are a few guiding principles that apply regardless of the type of site you're building. The key characteristics of a successful navigation system are clarity, consistency, and efficiency. Let's look at what each of these means in practical terms.

Clarity

In order for navigation to work, it must be easily learned. One of the main gripes about surfing the Web is that you have to learn how to use every new site you visit. It is in your interest to make the learning process as quick and painless as possible by making your navigational tools intuitive and easily understood at a glance.

Try following these guidelines for keeping your navigation system clear and user-friendly:

Navigation should look like navigation. Your navigational tools (such as links to the home page and other parts of the site) should somehow stand out on the page. This can be accomplished by grouping them together and applying some sort of visual treatment that sets them apart from ordinary content. Buttons don't necessarily need to be in 3-D to look "clickable," but they should still read as navigation at a glance.

Label everything clearly. I can't emphasize this point strongly enough. Despite the fact that the Web is a visual medium and we've been discussing visual cues for interface design, people still find their way around with words. Nothing stands in the way of finding information more than labels that are vague or too cute to be understood. Don't call a section "A Light in the Darkness" when it's really just "Help."

User testing shows that longer, more descriptive link text is more effective in getting people where they want to go. Make sure your section names and all links are labeled in a way that everyone will understand.

Use icons with caution. Although there are a few icons that have taken on standardized meanings (such as a small house picture as a link to the "home" page), for the most part, icons are difficult to decipher and can stand in the way of usability. Can you tell what each of the icons in Figure 20-17 do?

Figure 20-17. Icons aren't necessarily intuitive.

NAVIGATION TIP

List Navigation

Here's a simple tip to save your users some clicks. If you have a number of items in a list of links, be sure that each page has a link to the next item in the list. This prevents users from needing to click back to the list page each time they want to get to the next item.

Of course, you need to provide a link back to the list as well, in case the viewer does not want to view the list in order. You might add a link to the previous item in the list as well (not shown below) to allow movement through the list both backward and forward.

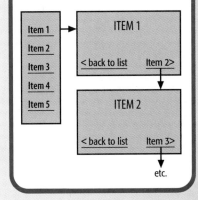

Did you guess "align elements" **Ⓐ**, "expand window" **Ⓑ**, and "News" **Ⓒ**?* This shows how, in general, icons alone do a poor job of communicating. Some icons, such as a globe, are so overused that they mean absolutely nothing. If you choose to use icons, it is best to reinforce them with clear labels in every instance. If you have just one or two carefully chosen icons, you may get away with defining them once on the home page and using the icons alone throughout the site. Either way, you should carefully consider whether icons are really aiding your navigation.

Consistency

It's important that navigational options be consistent throughout the site, in availability as well as in appearance.

Providing navigational options is not enough if they aren't predictable or dependable. It's important that navigational options be consistent throughout the site, in availability as well as in appearance.

Pages that are alike should have the same navigational options. If I could get back to the home page directly from one second-level page, I'd expect to be able to get back from all the others as well. Third-level pages might have a different set of options, but those options need to be consistent among all third-level pages, and so on.

Furthermore, it helps usability to present the options in the same fashion every time they are presented. If your home page button appears in blue at the top right-hand corner of one page, don't put it at the bottom in red on another page. If you offer a list of options, such as in a toolbar, keep the selections in the same order on each page so users don't have to spend time hunting around for the option they just used. Navigation options should stay put.

Efficiency

With every click into a site's hierarchy, you run the risk that the user will lose interest and leave. When you are designing the structure and navigation of a site, be mindful of how many clicks it takes to get to a piece of content or complete a task (such as filling out a form or purchasing something). The goal is to get users to the information they want efficiently and keep them engaged in the process.

The navigation system for a site should alleviate extra clicking, not add to it. Your navigation should include shortcuts to information—it can be as simple as providing links to other major sections of the site. You might want to supplement the global site-navigation system with specialized shortcuts such as a site map or search function.

---

* Icons were taken from Macromedia Freehand 8, RealPlayer 7, and *www.k10k.com*, respectively.

Navigational elements

There are many tools that you can use to help users move around a site. Here are some of the most popular.

Toolbars and panels

The majority of web sites group their navigational options (whether graphical buttons or text links) into some sort of horizontal toolbar or vertical panel. Toolbars are generally placed along the top of the page (sometimes below an advertising banner). The left edge of the page is another convenient location for navigation options and lists of related links (Figure 20-18).

Most web sites group their navigational options into a vertical or horizontal toolbar.

www.npr.org uses a global navigation toolbar at the top of every page.

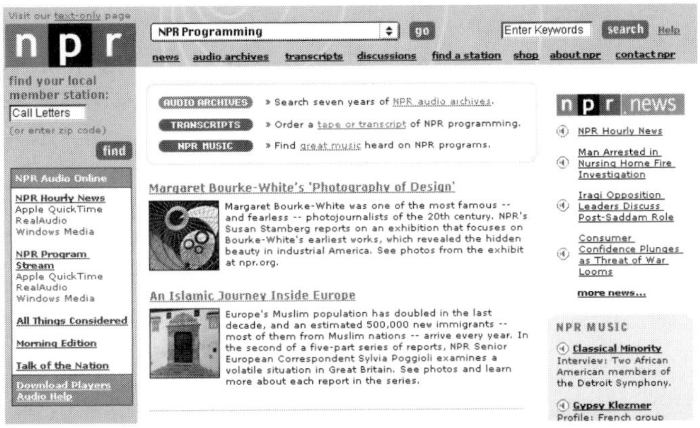

www.sfgate.com places navigational options in a panel on the left side of the page. The panel is consistent in every part of the site, while the main content area varies according to content.

Figure 20-18. Navigational toolbars and panels.

Pull-down menus

A great space-saving method for adding a large number of links on a page is to put them in a pull-down menu (Figure 20-19). That way, all the links are readily available but don't require much precious screen real estate.

The most common method for doing this today is to use DHTML menus that pop up when you mouse over them (DHTML is discussed in Chapter 22). A similar effect can be created using a pull-down menu form element. Form elements require some scripts on the server in order to function. In either case, beginners may need some assistance from a web programmer to implement this navigational shortcut.

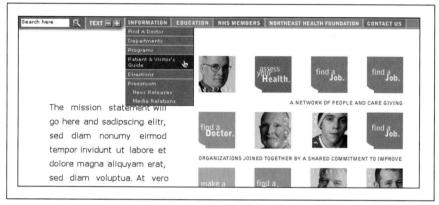

Figure 20-19. Drop-down (or pull-down) menus are a great way to add shortcuts to pages without taking up much screen real estate. This site uses DHTML to make an interactive toolbar at the top of the page.

Tabs

Navigational tabs across the top of the page have become a standard web element since their introduction in the late 90s. While they serve as a compact and fairly intuitive device for allowing access to different sections of a site, I find that they are sometimes applied inappropriately or gratuitously.

Ideally, tabs should be used to indicate similar functionality across a number of categories (Figure 20-20). Amazon.com (one of the early tab adopters) uses them correctly in this case—whether you've selected books or movies, you have the same basic options for viewing specials, reading reviews, and shopping.

All too often, tabs are used arbitrarily for access to divisions of the site. While there's nothing inherently wrong with this, the tabs aren't communicating functionality; they're just a decorative design for what otherwise would be a simple navigational toolbar.

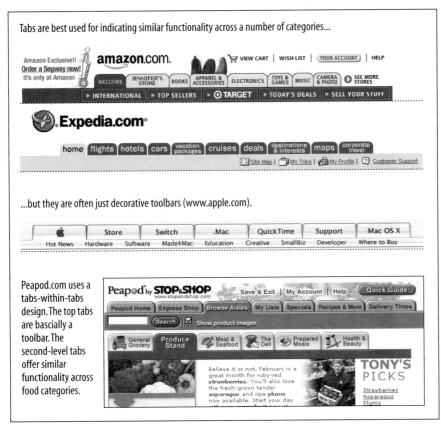

Figure 20-20. Examples of navigational tabs.

One drawback to tabs, which Amazon.com faced early on, is that graphical tabs stack up pretty quickly, and you may end up with an unwieldy mountain of tabs. Their solution was to offer only a select number of tabs with access to their full list of offerings on a separate page. Because of the limited pixel real estate across the top of a web page, tabbed interfaces are not easily scaleable.

As the Web continues to evolve, navigational approaches come and go like any fad. Buy.com, another formerly tab-reliant site, ditched its tabs altogether and now just presents options in a navigational panel. If you choose to use tabs, consider whether your interface is really benefitting from the additional graphics overhead. It may be that a simple toolbar would suffice.

"Breadcrumb" navigation

One of my favorite navigational elements is what's become known as "bread-crumb" navigation. As you click through the site's hierarchy, each successive level is indicated as a text link (Figure 20-21). Eventually, you end up with a string of section and subsection names that shows exactly where you are and where you've been (like Hansel and Gretel's breadcrumb trail through the forest). The trail also allows users to return to the higher levels they've passed through with just one click.

Perhaps the best feature is that, because they are only HTML text links, this form of navigation barely adds to the file size. That's a lot of communication and functionality packed into a few bytes.

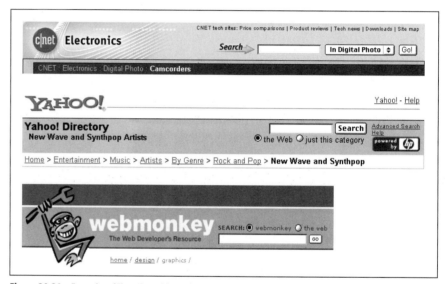

Figure 20-21. Examples of "breadcrumb" navigation.

Site maps

If your site is large and complex, you may want to supplement the navigational system on each page by providing shortcuts to your information. One approach is to provide a site map, which is a list of the contents of the site, organized to reflect the structure of the site by section and subsection (Figure 20-22). By providing an overhead view of the site's logic, you may help the user feel better oriented when travelling through the site. Each topic in the site map is also a handy link directly to that page.

As an alternative, smaller sites may be represented with a graphical site map. It is generally more difficult to do this effectively. In addition, because it is a graphic, it will take longer to download than text.

You might also choose to provide a site index, which is an alphabetical listing (like a book index) of all the topics available on your site.

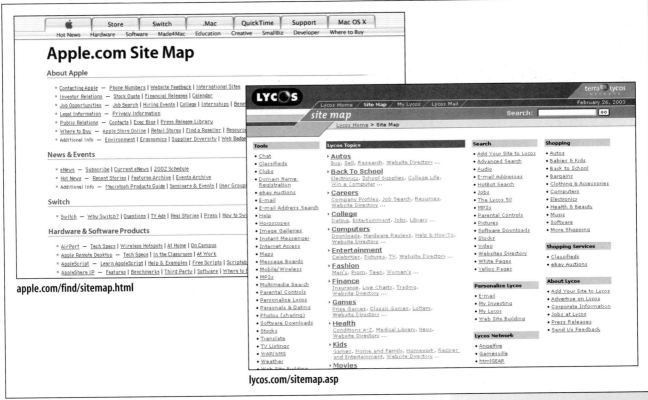

apple.com/find/sitemap.html

lycos.com/sitemap.asp

Figure 20-22. Examples of site maps.

Search functionality

One of the most widely used shortcuts for finding information on a web site is the search box (Figure 20-23). Other examples appear in nearly every navigation example in this chapter.

While it's tempting to assume that a search engine is the answer to everybody's information-seeking problems, in reality, most search functions offer a false sense of security. Search engines require special scripting on the server side, and although that can be simple to do, it's not so easy to do well. It also requires careful site indexing for it to work efficiently.

The unfortunate truth about many search engines is that they may turn up irrelevant links, or too many links to sort through. Some search engines do not provide a thorough enough description of each listing for users to make an informed choice. This can cause wasted time following links that *seem* useful, but actually aren't.

There's nothing wrong with supplementing your navigation system with search capabilities, as long as you actually take the time (and spend the money) to support it on the backend.

Figure 20-23. Search boxes are only as good as the programming behind them. Amazon.com provides a well-designed and essential search function.

Color coding

When used deliberately and thoughtfully, color is a powerful visual cue with many applications. A bright color calls attention to an element on a page. Coloring individual items with similar colors causes them to be perceived as a group. Assigning colors to each section of a site can help orient the user.

Keep in mind that the key to effective color usage is restraint and control. Too many amateur web sites make the mistake of using every available color on a single page, resulting in visual chaos. Choose a few colors, and stick with them.

I'll address a few specific examples of color use on the Web.

Link colors

The very first graphical browsers were designed to display hypertext links in bright blue, underlined text. This initial decision to assign a link color distinct from the text color was an effective method for indicating that linked text was somehow different from ordinary text. It has become the primary visual cue for "click here."

Since then, browser developers have stuck with blue text as the default link color, and it is the closest thing we have to a true interface convention on the Web. Want to get to another page? Click on the blue text!

Lately, there's been some controversy over whether designers should use HTML and Cascading Style Sheets to override the default link colors. Some more conservative designers feel that it requires more work if the user has to learn a new link color for every web site. The more popular opinion is that it is fine to change the color of links on a site as long as it is done consistently within that site. If you prefer red links, that's fine; just keep them red throughout the whole site.

Another consideration in coloring links is the difference between regular links and visited links (links that have already been followed). In general, you should set the link color to be somehow brighter or bolder than the visited link color. A toned-back visited link color better communicates a "less active" state.

TIP

For information on how to set link colors, see the sidebar, Coloring Your Links *in* Chapter 10. *Specifying colors in HTML is covered in* Chapter 13.

> *When used deliberately and thoughtfully, color is a powerful visual cue with many applications.*

DESIGN TIP

Color and Brand

Color has a big impact on the perceived "brand" of the site. Make sure the colors you choose fit the identity of the client or project.

Section color coding

If you have just a few major sections in your site, you might consider assigning each section a different color (Figure 20-24 G). This can be a useful method for orienting your user in the site, and is particularly helpful if you anticipate linking from section to section. The shift in overall color scheme is an instant indication that you've arrived in a new "place."

This advice comes with a word of caution, however. Do not rely on color alone to communicate the current section. The color-coding system should be secondary to clear labeling of the sections. Users can't be expected to memorize that corporate information is blue and small-business information is green. Furthermore, they may not see the colors at all. Make sure that color is used only as a reinforcement.

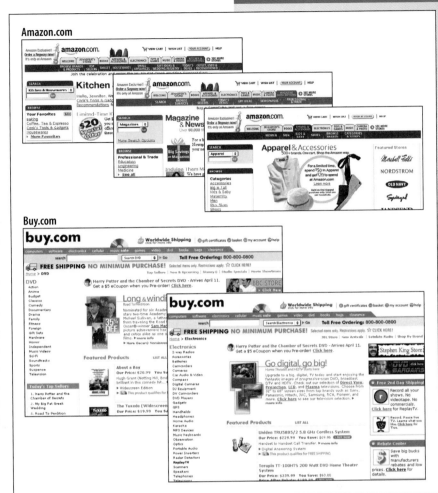

Figure 20-24. Section color coding is a popular method for orienting users within your site. G

TRY IT

Exercise 20-2: Page Diagrams

Using your site diagram as a starting point, develop wireframe page diagrams for each type of page in your site. Most sites have only a handful of different page types.

For instance, a simple site may have a home page, a section page, and a content page. Applying a single page template to similar pages on your site is one way to ensure consistent navigation options.

Consider whether your content can share page templates. Then, using the diagrams in this section as an example, sketch out the structure of your primary page types.

Don't worry about what the pages will look like; think only about which areas of the page will be allocated for which content. Think carefully about which navigational options will be available on each page and then decide where the navigational elements will be placed.

If done well, these diagrams will speed up the processes of creating a look and feel for the site and creating the working HTML template pages because all the thinking and planning will have been done ahead of time.

Some web developers use wireframe page diagrams in user testing. Using printouts, they ask users to point to "buttons" and move through pages of the site. You can use your site diagrams too see whether it is possible to smoothly move through your site. It's much easier to edit or make a new sketch on paper than to tear apart an HTML page and put it together again.

Building the Pages

Once you've carefully organized your information and planned the interface and navigation, designing and building the pages should be a fairly smooth process. Once the content and structure of the pages are designed in wireframes, the graphic designer can put a visual face on it. Using the designer's sketches, the developers can start coding.

Giving it a look and feel

The "look and feel" phase of the web design process includes choosing colors, fonts, and the graphical style for the content and navigational elements. The visual design of a site is an important factor in its usability. Colors need to be chosen not just to be pleasing to the eye, but to reinforce the structure and intended functionality of the page. Buttons and links should read as clickable at a glance. Elements need to be given appropriate visual weight on the page (for instance, the treatment of global navigation versus section navigation). These decisions typically fall into the hands of graphic designers.

The result of the visual design process is usually non-working sketches of each page type. Most designers create page sketches using Photoshop or Fireworks. Placing page elements on separate layers makes it easier to create the individual graphics later.

Figure 20-25 ⒢ shows the look-and-feel treatments I created based on the Blue Family wireframe diagrams from Figure 20-13. On the home page, I've grouped the links to the family member sections and given them a similar graphical treatment to imply that they have similar content and functionality. The news and photo page areas are given special visual treatments that are appropriate for features that will be updated frequently.

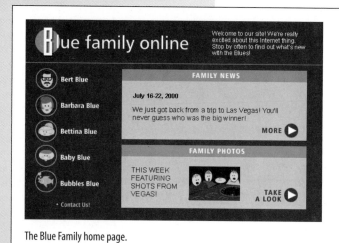

The Blue Family home page.

A typical second-level page for the Blue Family site.

Figure 20-25. Look-and-feel treatments. ⒢

Second-level pages feature a navigational toolbar that will be used on every page of the site. It features the Blue Family "logo" in the upper-left corner to identify the site from any point of entry. It also provides links to each family member section as well as the home page. The current section is identified both by the labeled area below the toolbar and by the orange dot behind the member's name in the toolbar itself.

Creating working pages

The final phase of the design process is to create working web pages from the page layouts. Web developers deconstruct the pages and create the HTML tables, text formatting, and web graphics to recreate the graphic designer's vision as closely as possible. Meanwhile, programmers may create scripts and coding for adding interactivity and functionality, if necessary. Once the site is built, it needs to be tested thoroughly (this is true for personal sites as well).

For personal and other small sites, it is common for one person to handle all the phases from interface design through the final HTML page creation. Even if you are working as a one-person web developer, it is good to be aware of how creating a web site is broken down into individual tasks.

Building Usable Web Sites: In Review

There are a lot of big, meaty topics in this chapter, all warranting further study and experimentation. Here are a few of the highlights:

- A successful web site requires attention to how the information is organized (its information design) and how users get to that information (its interface design and navigation system).

- Users' top frustrations in browsing the Web include not being able to find information, hitting dead ends, not being able to get back to where they started, and having to click through too many pages to get to the information they want.

- Information design involves organizing information and planning how users will find it. It requires taking an inventory of all the information on the site, organizing it, and giving it structure.

- Interface design determines how a site's structure is represented visually on the page. It includes all the visual cues to understanding what information is available, as well as how to get to it. It includes how items are grouped, color-coding systems, metaphors, and all the buttons and tools for navigating the site.

- Site diagrams are useful for communicating the structure of the site and developing its navigational system.

- A good navigation system must answer the questions "Where am I?" and "Where can I go from here?".

- The key characteristics of a successful navigation system are clarity, consistency, and efficiency.

- The most common navigation tool is the navigational toolbar, usually at the top (but sometimes along the side or bottom) of every page.

- You may choose to supplement the navigation system with a search function or site map.

Test Yourself

We covered a lot of juicy topics in this chapter. Answer these questions to see if you've mastered them. The correct answers are in the Appendix.

1. Name some tasks an information architect might be responsible for.

2. Name at least five standard ways information can be organized.

3. What is the most popular organization strategy for web sites?

4. What is an interface designer responsible for?

5. What are the advantages and disadvantages of using metaphors in interface design?

6. How is a user scenario different from a site diagram?

7. Describe ways to ensure clarity in navigation.

8. Name two ways to ensure consistency in navigation.

9. Name two advantages to using breadcrumb navigation in hierarchical web sites.

Web Design Dos and Don'ts

21

There is no absolute right or wrong way to design a web site. When people ask me about the best way to design a site, it always seems to come down to "It depends."

Your design decisions depend on the type of site you're publishing. Personal sites, entertainment sites, and corporate e-commerce sites all have different priorities and abide by different guidelines, both in terms of content and how that content is presented. And, as you might have already guessed, it depends a lot on your audience—the hardware and software they're using, their reason for visiting your site, etc.

Good and bad design decisions are always relative. There are no "nevers"—there's always a site out there for which a web design "don't" makes perfect sense and is really the best solution.

Consider the contents of this chapter to be general guidelines. These are some pointers to possible improvements and some red flags for common beginner traps that can be easily avoided. In the end, you'll need to decide what works best for your site.

General Page Design Advice

The following dos and don'ts apply to the formatting and structure of the whole page.

DO…
Keep all file sizes as small as possible for quick downloads.

Because…
Quick downloads are crucial for a successful user experience. If your pages take forever to download, your visitors may grow impatient and go surf elsewhere. At the very least, they'll get cranky.

In this chapter

General page design advice

Text-formatting tips

Graphics advice

Aesthetic suggestions

Jen's pet peeves

DO...

Design for a screen size of 800 × 600 pixels unless you are certain that your audience will be viewing your pages with a different configuration.

Because...

When you design larger page sizes, you risk parts not being visible for users with older, smaller monitors. If you want to be absolutely sure your whole page will be visible for all users, make sure your page fits in a browser on a 640 × 480 monitor. For more information, see Chapter 4.

DO...

Put your most important messages (who you are, what you do, etc.) in the first screenful (the top 350 pixels of the page).

Because...

Most users make judgments about a site based on that first impression, without taking the time to scroll down for more information. For details, see the sidebar Designing Above the Fold in Chapter 4.

DO...

Limit the length of your pages to two or three "screenfuls."

Because...

Longer pages that require lots of scrolling are unmanageable for online reading and make it more difficult for readers to find their place. For some reason, users do not like to scroll; they'd rather keep moving forward. It is better to break long flows of text into a few separate pages and link them together (Figure 21-1).

DON'T...

Design specifically for one browser or platform (unless you are 100% certain your audience will be viewing your pages under that configuration).

Because...

You never want to alienate your visitors. Nothing is more off-putting than arriving at a site only to find a sign that says, "You must have X browser running on X platform with X, Y, Z plug-ins to use this site." The only thing worse is to find that nothing works.

DON'T...

Use too many animations, especially on pages with content you want people to read.

Because...

While animations are effective in drawing attention, users find them annoying and distracting when they are trying to read the text on the page. Even one looping animation can be an annoyance to some people. A whole page of spinning and flashing is a disaster (Figure 21-2 [G]).

> *Put your most important messages in the first screenful.*

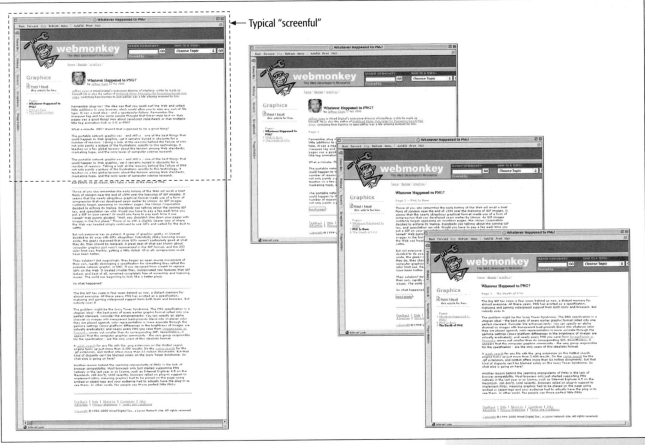

Typical "screenful"

Figure 21-1. Avoid long scrolling pages. Webmonkey (*www.webmonkey.com*) does a good job of dividing their long articles into smaller, more manageable pieces that are linked together with a clear navigational system.

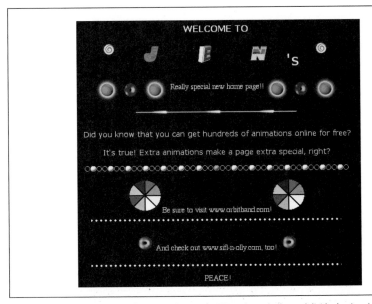

Figure 21-2. Here's an example of too much animation. Every letter, bullet, and divider bar is animated. This may look like an exaggeration, but I have seen pages like this and worse. This page (*animation.html*) is available for viewing in the *chap21* materials folder. G

DON'T...

Use "Under Construction" signs. In particular, don't make "under construction" pages that appear after a user clicks on the link. If your site or section isn't ready, simply don't post it.

Because...

While you may intend to show that you have information that will be available soon, "Under Construction" signs and other placeholders just make it look like you don't have your act together. I especially hate it when I end up on a "construction" page after I've taken the time to follow a link from the home page (Figure 21-3). Providing links that go nowhere is a waste of your visitors' time and patience.

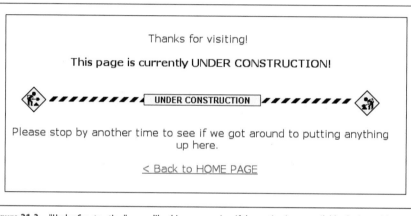

Figure 21-3. "Under Construction" pages like this are annoying. If the section is not available, don't provide a link to it.

Text-Formatting Tips

These tidbits of wisdom pertain to the formatting of text. In many cases, text on web pages follows the same design guidelines as text on a printed page. Some of these recommendations are applicable only to the special requirements of the web medium.

DO...

Take the time to proofread your site.

Because...

Typos and bad grammar reflect badly on your site and your business. If your authoring tool does not have a built-in spellchecker, be sure to have another person carefully review your content.

DO...

Make the structure of your information clear by giving similar elements the same design and important elements more visual weight (using size, space, or color) (Figure 21-4 Ⓖ).

Because...

It enables your readers to understand your content at a glance and speeds up the process of finding what they need.

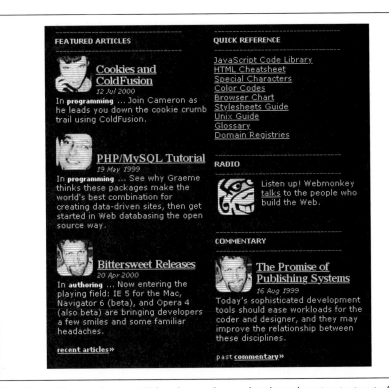

Figure 21-4. This excerpt from a past Webmonkey page (*www.webmonkey.com*) uses type treatments effectively to convey the structure of the information. Article listings have the same structure, with the article title given the most visual weight. Section titles are also treated similarly and are given lots of space to set them apart from other listings. Ⓖ

DO...

Break your content into small paragraphs or, even better, write your content specifically for web reading in the first place.

Because...

It is easier to read text on a screen when it is in small, easy-to-scan portions. Web text paragraphs should be as short as possible, or even be reduced to bulleted lists.

DO...

Change your link and visited-link colors when using a dark background color or pattern.

Because...

The default dark blue link color is readable only against light colors.

DON'T...

Set type in all capital letters.

Because...

All capital letters are harder to read than upper- and lowercase letters (Figure 21-5). In addition, it makes it look like you're shouting your message, which is just rude.

DON'T...

Set more than a few words in italics.

Because...

Most browsers just slant the regular text font to achieve an "italic" (Figure 21-5). The result is often nearly unreadable, especially for large quantities of text at small sizes.

DON'T...

Set text in all capital, bold, and italics (Figure 21-5).

Because...

Three wrongs don't make a right. This is just overkill, but I see it all the time.

Figure 21-5. Avoid setting large amounts of text in all capital letters or all italic text, because it makes it more difficult to read. A combination of capitals, italic, and bold styles is overkill.

DON'T…

Use <h5> or <h6>

Because…

In most browsers, these headings are displayed at a size even smaller than the default text. The small size along with the bold formatting makes these elements difficult to read. If level 5 and 6 headings are part of your document's structure, use style sheets to give all your headings a logical and readable format.

DON'T…

Insert line breaks unless you really mean them.

Because…

Text wraps differently for each user, depending on the browser's default text size setting and the width of the browser window. If you've inserted hard line breaks (<br>) to format lines of text, you run the risk of the text rewrapping in an awkward way (Figure 21-6).

DON'T…

Set type at size="-2" or smaller.

Because…

Type that is set to size="-2", while it may look tidy on your Windows machine, may be downright unreadable on a Mac or even on a Windows machine with its browser type set to a smaller size (Figure 21-7).

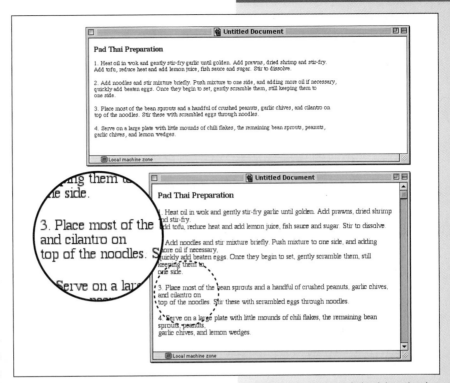

Figure 21-6. I've entered a break (<br>) at the end of each line in this example to control the width of the text. Unfortunately, with different browser settings the lines rewrap, resulting in a number of stubby little lines.

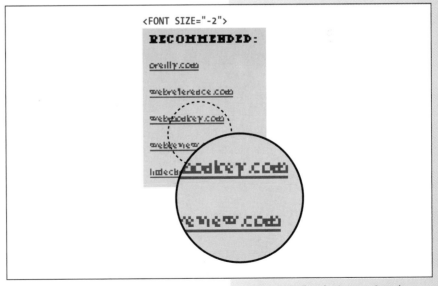

Figure 21-7. Type that is set to −2 may be completely unreadable depending on the user's browser setup and platform (Macs tend to display text smaller than PCs).

Graphics Advice

These dos and don'ts apply to both graphic production and placing graphics on the page using HTML.

Anti-aliasing smooths out the jagged edges between colors and makes your text look better. In most cases, turn on anti-aliasing for text in graphics.

Aliased

Anti-aliased

The exception is small type, which gets blurry when it's anti-aliased. Depending on the font face, you will get better results turning off anti-aliasing for type under 10 points.

Anti-aliased

Aliased

Figure 21-8. Proper use of anti-aliasing will improve the quality of your images.

Graphic with a halo

Graphic that blends well with background

Figure 21-9. Halos (the ugly fringe around transparent graphics) are easily preventable.

Clean and well-produced graphics help make your site look professional.

DO…

Use anti-aliasing for most text in graphics (except for fonts under 10 points).

Because…

Smooth anti-aliased edges will make your graphics look more polished and professional. For type under 10 points, however, anti-aliasing may blur the whole letter shape and make the text less readable. It is usually better to turn off anti-aliasing for small text (Figure 21-8).

DO…

Keep graphic files under 30 KB (unless an exception is absolutely necessary).

Because…

A 30 KB graphic could take approximately 30 seconds to download over a modem Internet connection, and that's a long time to wait for something to appear on the screen. Of course, you should keep all graphic file sizes as small as possible (I aim for under 10 KB). Ideally, the total of all the graphics on the page should be under 30 KB.

DO…

Take the time to prevent halos around transparent graphics.

Because…

Halos in your images make your graphics look sloppy and unprofessional (Figure 21-9). For detailed instructions on preventing halos, see Chapter 15.

DO…

Turn off the blue border around linked graphics.

Because…

Blue boxes around linked graphics detract from the design of the page (Figure 21-10, top). To turn off the border, set `border="0"` within the `<img>` tag. Your graphics will blend more smoothly into the page.

DO…

Provide alternate text for every graphic. Alternate text displays in the event that the graphic doesn't.

Because…

This is the easiest way to make the content of your site accessible to a wider audience, including people with text-only browsers and users who have their graphics turned off for faster page downloading. Specify alternative text using the `alt` attribute in the `<img>` tag (for more information, see Chapter 9).

DON'T…

Make graphics that look like buttons but don't link to anything (Figure 21-11).

Because…

A 3-D beveling effect is a strong visual cue for "click here." I've seen some sites that used this visual effect on ordinary graphical labels. I was duped into clicking on them, and nothing happened. Similarly, do not add a gratuitous rollover effect to a button-like graphic that is not a link.

Figure 21-10. Linked graphics look much better with borders turned off.

Figure 21-11. These section header graphics beg to be clicked because of the 3-D bevel effect. Contrary to appearances, they are not buttons and don't do anything.

DON'T...

Make thumbnail-sized images by scaling down full-sized images with the width and height attributes in the <img> tag.

Because...

It forces an unnecessarily large download. It is better to make a second graphic at the thumbnail size that will download quickly.

DON'T...

Link thumbnail graphics to similarly sized images.

Because...

It is common to use thumbnail images as links to their full-sized counterparts, so it is frustrating and a waste of time to click on a thumbnail only to get another thumbnail. Users expect a view with more detail when a thumbnail is a link. If you don't have a significantly larger image, don't link the small version.

Aesthetic Suggestions

The way your site looks communicates a certain level of professionalism. A cluttered and chaotic web site tend to reflect badly on the company the site represents. Even if corporate image isn't one of your priorities, basic readability is important for any site. Here are a few suggestions that pertain to that all-important first impression.

DON'T...

Center everything on the page.

Because...

Centering the whole page makes the content difficult to read (Figure 21-12). This is not to say that you should never center anything. For some types of information, particularly when the page contains just a few elements or when you want a formal tone, center alignment is the best choice, both logically and aesthetically.

It is best to stick with left justification for pages with a significant amount of content. I also recommend using a table to establish one or two strong lines of alignment and stick with them. This creates a clean first impression and makes it easier to find information.

> *Cluttered and chaotic web sites tend to reflect badly on the company the site represents.*

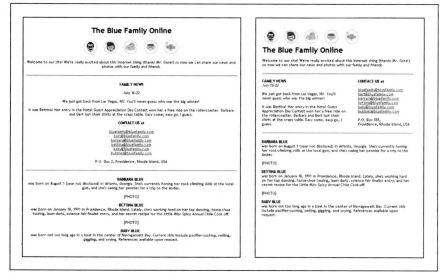

Figure 21-12. Avoid centering all the content on a page. Not only are the edges ragged and untidy, it is more difficult to read since each line starts at a different position. Notice how much clearer the page is when I use a table to create strong left alignments.

DON'T…

Mix alignments. In other words, avoid combinations of left-justified, centered, and right-justified elements on the same page (Figure 21-13).

Because…

Not only is it less elegant than a page with a single alignment, it also hinders clear communication because the readers' eyes need to jump all over the page.

Figure 21-13. The messy page on the left suffers from the combination of too many text alignments. The page on the right takes the same elements but gives the page a cleaner (and more usable!) look by sticking with a consistent alignment.

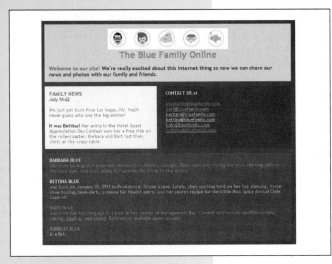

Figure 21-14. This page suffers from color overkill. Making every element a different bright color is a sure way to create visual chaos. ⒢

DON'T…

Use too many colors.

Because…

It's visually chaotic and makes it difficult to prioritize the information (Figure 21-14 ⒢). Better to choose one or two dominant colors and one highlight color and stick with them throughout the site.

DON'T…

Use wild background tile patterns (Figure 21-15 ⒢).

Because…

It makes it difficult to read the text on the page. Background patterns should be as subtle as possible. (Background tiles are discussed in more detail in Chapter 9.) I use only backgrounds that have solid colors in the text areas.

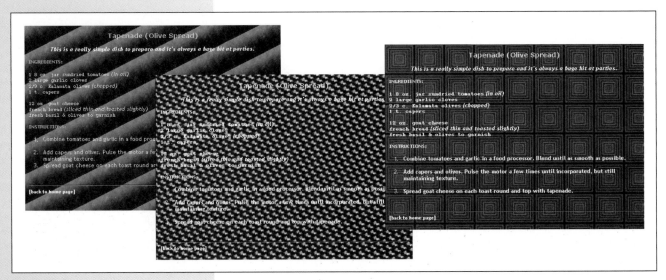

Figure 21-15. Bold background patterns can make the text on the page unreadable. ⒢

DESIGN TIP

Consider the Existing Corporate Image

Tie the look and feel of your site into your corporate identity (if one exists).

Web sites should be considered part of a unified identity package. Your audience should be able to recognize your company whether they see it in print, on television, or online. Too often, web designers take the look and feel of a web site in their own direction, which foils any attempt to build a coherent and recognizable corporate image or brand.

DON'T…

Automatically use white type on dark backgrounds, particularly for large amounts of small text.

Because...

The contrast is too high and it can be uncomfortable to read (Figure 21-16). Better to choose a very light shade instead, such as a light gray against black, or a very pale blue against dark blue. The text will still be clear, and the slightly lower contrast is more gentle on the eyes, making your page look less glaring overall.

In this line, the type is white. The contrast is as high as it can get, which is a strain on the eyes.

In this type, the type is light gray. The eye still perceives the type as white, but it is easier to read.

Figure 21-16. Lots of white type on a dark background can be uncomfortable to read. Try lightly tinting the text color instead.

Jen's Pet Peeves

Granted, these recommendations may come down to personal taste, but I would be shirking my responsibilities if I didn't at least mention them.

DON'T…

Assume a black background will automatically make your site "cool" (Figure 21-17 G).

Because...

If it isn't done right, the effect can be overly dramatic and "heavy metal." Of course, it can be handled very elegantly. But for the average site (especially a small-business site), black backgrounds are inappropriate.

DON'T…

Use a globe, especially a spinning globe (Figure 21-17 G).

Because...

Globes as icons have been so overused that they no longer carry any meaning at all. This is just a visual cliché.

DON'T…

Use rainbow dividers, especially animated rainbow dividers.

Because...

They are sure-fire indication of amateur web design and have been since the very beginning. Not cool, just tacky (Figure 21-17 G).

Figure 21-17. The web page of my nightmares! G

This page has it all:

- Gratuitous black background
- Animated rainbow dividers
- A spinning globe
- An unreadable link color
- Meaningless icons
- Too many colors
- Bad alignment

TRY IT

Exercise 21-1: Fix the Nightmare Page

It is plain to see that the page in Figure 21-17 could use some improvement.

All of the source files for this page have been provided in the *chap21* materials folder. Using the knowledge and skills you've picked up in this chapter and throughout the book, redesign the page in a professional manner.

Pay attention to readability and visual style. Think about colors, alignment, and text formatting. You may also want to create your own set of graphics.

There is no answer to this exercise in the back of the book, but it is an opportunity to combine the skills from this chapter and the rest of the book.

Test Yourself

Decide whether each of these design tips is a Do or a Don't.. The answers are in the Appendix.

1. Design specifically for Internet Explorer on Windows.

2. Change the link and visited link colors when you use dark backgrounds.

3. Design most pages to fit 800 × 600 pixel monitors.

4. Use only white type on black backgrounds.

5. Use an "Under Construction" page if your real page isn't done to let users know you're working on it.

6. Use animation to attract attention to each important thing on the page.

7. Set content in all capital letters.

8. Provide alternative text for all graphics.

9. Make text in graphics anti-aliased when it is 10 point and larger.

10. Use a spinning globe whenever possible.

How'd They Do That?
An Introduction to Advanced Techniques

22

This book has covered quite a bit of territory—enough to get you up and running with creating web pages and linking them together in well-organized sites. But if you spend any time browsing the Web, you're sure to come across pages with special effects and interactivity that will make you say, "How'd they do that?!"

While it is beyond the scope of this book to teach everything, I do want you to be able to recognize certain techniques and technologies when you see them. In this chapter, I'll zero in on some common web tricks, tell you how they're done, and provide some pointers for further learning. Bear in mind, however, that most of these topics are vast. While I'll do my best to give you the highlights, you'll need to take it from there.

Remember that you don't need to learn how to do everything yourself, so don't feel overwhelmed. The important part is knowing what *can* be done so you can speak intelligently with the folks who will be responsible for actually creating it.

Forms

How do I put a text entry field and a button on my page so people can send me messages?

Adding form elements to a web page is simple: they are created using a set of HTML form tags that define menus, text fields, buttons, and so on (Figure 22-1, following page). Form elements are generally used to collect information from a web page.

However, making a nice-looking form on a web page is only part of the story. Getting the form to actually *work* requires a script or a small program on the server that knows how to process the information the form collects. The program that does the work behind the scenes is often a CGI (Common Gateway Interface) script written in the Perl programming language

In this chapter

Introductions to:

- Forms
- Web audio
- Video for the Web
- Multimedia with Flash
- DHTML (Dynamic HTML)
- XHTML (Extended HTML)

```
┌─────────────────────────────────────────┐
│ □ ▒▒▒▒▒▒▒▒▒▒▒▒▒▒▒▒▒▒▒▒▒▒▒▒▒▒▒▒▒▒▒▒        │
│ Join the Mailing List:                    │
│ Name: [                    ]              │
│ Email: [                    ]             │
│ [Submit Query]  [Reset]                   │
│                                           │
└─────────────────────────────────────────┘
```

```html
<h2>Join the Mailing List:</h2>
<form action="/cgi-bin/mailform.p1" method="get">
<pre>
Name: <input type="text" name="name">
Email: <input type="text" name="address">
<input type="submit"> <input type="reset">
</pre>
</form>
```

Figure 22-1. You can get a general idea of how forms are created by looking at this simple example. The whole form is indicated by the `<form>...</form>` tags. Each element in the form is placed with an `<input>` tag. The `type` attribute specifies which form element to display.

WHERE TO LEARN MORE

Forms

Web Design in a Nutshell, Second Edition, by Jennifer Niederst (O'Reilly, 2002)
> Features a chapter with detailed information on creating form elements with HTML and adapting existing CGI scripts.

HTML and XHTML: The Definitive Guide, Fifth Edition, by Chuck Musciano and Bill Kennedy (O'Reilly, 2002)
> Features a chapter with detailed information on HTML form elements.

Usable Forms for the Web, by Andy Beaumont, Jon James, Jon Stephens, Chris Ullman (glasshaus, 2002)
> A whole book about creating effective forms for the Web.

(although C and C++ are also used). Form-processing programs can also be implemented as PHP scripts, Java servlets, or ASP scripts, to name a few other technologies.

If you want your site to have functioning forms, you need to get help with the programming. The scripts need to be set up on the server and you will need to include key bits of information in the forms' HTML code that feed the scripts information. Be sure to communicate your goals clearly to the person assisting you with the technical aspects.

For basic form functionality, such as a form that sends a piece of email, you may find that your hosting service provides a few canned CGI scripts that you can personalize and use for free. They generally come with clear instructions for code needs to be added to your page, and they are usually easy to implement. Be sure to ask whether these services are available.

Audio

How do I add music to a web page?

There are many options for adding music and other sound files to a web page. Of course, you need to start with some audio files. If you want to generate your audio files yourself, you need to make sure that your computer is equipped with the proper sound card and input device (such as a microphone or CD player). You also need audio-editing software that saves the audio information to a file format that can be transferred over the Web. Some popular tools for web audio include Macromedia's SoundEdit 16, Apple's QuickTime Pro, and Terran MediaCleaner Pro.

Audio downloads

The most straightforward approach to adding sound to a web site is simply making the audio file available for download. Put the file on the server and make a link to it as you would to any other file (Figure 22-2). When the users click on the link, the file is downloaded to their desktops and is played with a sound application such as

QuickTime (which comes built into recent browsers). In general, it is necessary for the whole file to download before it can start playing.*

```
<a href="http://www.ora.com/audio/song.mp3">Play the song.</a>
```

Figure 22-2. Linking to a sound file is the same as linking to another document. When the user clicks on the link, the sound file is downloaded from the server and plays with a helper application or audio browser plug-in.

The file format you use is important. Today, the most popular format is the MP3 (you can recognize it by the .mp3 suffix). You may also hear them referred to as MPEGs (pronounced "EM-peg") because they use the MPEG compression scheme. MP3s can maintain excellent audio quality even at relatively small file sizes, making them ideal for music. All of the online "jukebox" type services use MP3s to store and transfer songs.

Other common formats for web audio are WAVE (.wav), AIFF (.aif), and QuickTime Audio (.mov). All sacrifice sound quality in favor of smaller files. There's also MIDI (.mid) format, which stores synthesized musical tones in a numerical format, resulting in extremely small file sizes.

Streaming audio

Another method for delivering audio over the Web is called "streaming" audio. It differs from simple downloading in that the audio files start playing almost immediately and continue playing as the server delivers the file. This alleviates long waits for the files to download completely and begin playing. You can even deliver live broadcasts. The other significant difference is that the file is never actually downloaded to the user's machine, which alleviates some copyright concerns.

In order to truly stream audio, you must serve your files from a server equipped with the streaming software. The following are the most popular streaming formats and where to get more information about them:

RealAudio format (.ra)   www.realnetworks.com
Windows Media (.wm)   www.microsoft.com/windows/windowsmedia
Streaming QuickTime   www.apple.com/quicktime/products/qtss/

Users play these media using the appropriate player (RealPlayer, Windows Media Player, or QuickTime Player, respectively).

---

* When played with the QuickTime audio player, both MP3s and QuickTime audio files will begin playing before they are completely downloaded, simulating a streaming effect.

Optimizing Audio for the Web

Because audio files contain a lot of information, their file sizes can easily get too large for web distribution, but you can take measures to keep file sizes in check.

Current audio-editing programs typically come with built-in settings for web audio targeted at various connection speeds. While this is an excellent starting point, you might want to be familiar with the individual audio settings for reducing audio files:

Length. Keep audio clips as short as possible.

Channels. Opting for "mono" over "stereo" may cut file size roughly in half depending on format.

Bit depth. Bit depth determines the volume and overall quality of the file. MP3s are typically saved at 16-bit, and other formats at 8-bit.

Sampling rate. Sampling rate is the number of samples taken per second. Music generally requires a sampling rate of 22 kHz, sound effects work at 11 kHz, and voice only clips can be sampled at 8 kHz.

So, for example, if we start with a 1-minute music sample at CD-quality (10 MB) and change it to a mono, 8-bit, 22 kHz WAVE file, its size is reduced to 1.25 MB. By comparison, using MP3 compression, we can keep the quality at 16-bit, 44.1 kHz stereo (similar to CD quality) with a resulting file size under 1 MB. Combining these methods, you can offer 1-minute music clips at just a few hundred KB.

WHERE TO LEARN MORE

Web Audio

Designing Web Audio
by Josh Beggs and Dylan Thede (O'Reilly, 2001)
 Everything you'd ever want to know about Internet audio, including case studies and step-by-step instructions.

The MP3 and Internet Audio Handbook: Your Guide to the Digital Music Revolution
by Bruce Fries and Marty Fries (TeamCom, 2000)
 This book focuses on MP3s and dealing with digital audio on PCs.

Background sound

Sometimes when you arrive at a web page, music starts playing automatically, like a soundtrack to the page. In general, you should never force something as intrusive as an audio file on a user unless they ask for it. In fact, I almost always hit the "back" button immediately on any site that serves up an uninvited sound file. First it startles me when it comes blasting out of my speakers, then it just annoys me with its constant looping. But if you still think you have a *really* good reason for doing it, I'll show you how it's done.

To set a background sound that will work with both Microsoft Internet Explorer and Netscape Navigator, you need to use both the <bgsound> tag (for IE) and the <embed> tag (for Navigator) at the beginning of the document (Figure 22-3).

```
<embed src="audio/song.mid" autostart="true" hidden="true"></embed>
<noembed><bgsound="audio/song.mid"></noembed>
```

Figure 22-3. The <bgsound> tag works only in Internet Explorer. To make audio play automatically for Navigator users, I've added the <embed> tag. The <noembed> tag ensures that Navigator ignores the <bgsound> element.

The problem with background sound added in this method is that there are no controls on the page that allow the user to turn off the sound. Creating such a button requires JavaScript and other trickery that is, unfortunately, beyond the scope of this book.

Video

How did they get a little movie to play right on their page?

When you see a video playing right on a web page, chances are it's a QuickTime movie that has been placed on the page with an <object> tag (the World Wide Web Consortium's [W3C] preferred method) along with an <embed> tag (Apple's recommended method for Netscape and older browsers) as shown in Figure 22-4). This method is discussed in detail in the next section. In order for the movie to display on the web page, the QuickTime plug-in must be installed on the user's browser. Fortunately, this plug-in is included in current browsers' installation packages. For Windows users, code in the <object> tag automatically installs the player necessary for viewing the movie.

Optimizing Video for the Web

Most video editing tools offer automatic web video settings targeted at various Internet connection speeds. You may also want to experiment with these settings individually to find the quality that best suits your video.

Frame size. Common frame sizes for web video are 160 × 120 and 240 × 180. Some developers go as low as 120 × 90. It is not recommended that you use a frame size larger than 320 × 240 with current technology.

Frame rate. Frame rate is the measure of number of frames per second (fps). Standard video is 30 fps. For the Web, a frame rate of 15 or 10 fps is more appropriate.

Color bit depth. Reducing the number of colors from 24-bit to 8-bit will drastically reduce the size of your video, but will also sacrifice quality.

Data rate. This is the rate at which data must be transferred in order for the video to play back smoothly. Data rate is measured in kilobytes per second (Kbps). This is one of the most important settings for web video, particularly for streaming video, and it should be tailored to the targeted Internet connection speed. For 56 KB connections, aim for a data rate of 4 Kbps; 30 Kbps for DSL; and 50 Kbps for cable connections.

(continued on facing page)

Using <object> and <embed>

To ensure that videos will play properly on all browsers, it is recommended that you place the movie on the page using both the <object> and <embed> tags. The standard, minimum code for doing this is as follows:

```
<object width="240" height="196"
  classid="clsid:02BF25D5-8C17-4B23-BC80-D3488ABDDC6B"
  codebase="http://www.apple.com/qtactivex/qtplugin.cab">
  <param name="src" value="moviefile.mov">
  <param name="controller" value="true">
  <param name="autoplay" value="false">
  <embed src="moviefile.mov" width="240" height="196"
    autoplay="false" controller="true"
    pluginspage="http://www.apple.com/quicktime/download/"></embed>
</object>
```

If you look carefully, you will see that the basic directions are repeated in both the <object> tag and its parameters and the <embed> tag. Let's take a look at the minimal movie settings.

Player information. Both tags contain code that prompts the browser to download the player necessary for displaying the movie on the page. In the <object> tag, the classid and codebase attributes provide specific directions for automatically installing the required ActiveX element.

In the <embed> tag, the pluginspage takes the user to a page where they can download the QuickTime player if it is not found by the browser.

The values of these attributes (shown in color) must appear exactly as they are written here or they will not work.

Source. As for images, you must provide the source URL for the movie file in both tags. For the <object> tag, the url is provided within a parameter (<param name="src" value="moviefile.mov">). The <embed> tag uses the src attribute.

Dimensions. The width and height attributes are required in both tags. In order for the controller (the strip at the bottom with the slider and play and pause buttons), you must add 16 pixels to the height of the movie. In the previous example, the original movie is 240 x 180 pixels, so I've set the width to 240 and the height to 196.

Controller. You can decide whether you want the controller to display using the controller parameter and attribute. Setting the value to true makes it display; setting it to false hides it. Use the autoplay parameter and attribute to set whether the movie starts playing automatically when the page loads (true) or if the user needs to hit the Play button to start the movie (false).

This is just the tip of the iceberg of controls for inline video using the <object> and <embed> tags. For a complete list, see Apple's tutorial for embedding Quicktime movies at *www.apple.com/quicktime/authoring/embed.html*.

Web Video

QuickTime for the Web: For Windows and Macintosh, Third Edition
by Steven Gulie (Morgan Kaufmann, 2003)
> A complete guide to creating QuickTime content and putting it on the Web.

iMovie 2: The Missing Manual
by David Pogue (O'Reilly, 2001)
> A step-by-step guide to the movie-production process using Apple's iMovie software.

Streaming Media Bible
by Steve Mack (John Wiley & Sons, 2002)
> A comprehensive guide to putting streaming multimedia on the Web.

e-Video: Producing Internet Video as Broadband Technologies Converge (with CD-ROM)
by H. Peter Alesso (Addison Wesley, 2000)
> This book focuses on high-speed Internet.

Inside Windows Media: Learning to Combine Video, Audio, and Still Images to Create Streaming Media
by Microsoft Windows Media Team (Que, 1999)
> The definitive guide to creating Windows Media content.

Movie files

Let's talk a little more about movie files. The QuickTime Movie format (*.mov*) is ideal for delivering movies over the Web because it is a highly condensed format supported on both PCs and Macs. Movies can also be saved in MPEG (*.mpg* or *.mp2*) format or as Windows-only AVI files (*.avi*).

Making movies is easier than ever with digital video cameras that can be plugged directly into your computer. You'll need to start with a video source (from your camera or videotape). You'll also need video-editing software, such as QuickTime (by Apple), Media Cleaner Pro (by Terran Interactive, *www.terran.com*), Apple Final Cut Pro, or Adobe Premier if you want to go for professional-level editing (*www.adobe.com*). If you work on a newer Macintosh, you can take advantage of Apple's iMovie technology, which puts basic movie-making abilities in the hands of consumers (see *www.apple.com/imovie/* for more information).

Because video and audio information can be huge, the trick to making web-appropriate movies is optimization—the frame rate, the image compression, and the sound compression (see the Optimizing Video for the Web sidebar). All video-editing packages provide the tools you need for compressing your video as small as possible.

Optimizing Video for the Web (continued)

Compression scheme. Videos are compressed using compression and decompression algorithms (called codecs). There are many codecs available, but the best choices for web video are H.263 and the Sorenson Video codec, which can achieve very high image quality at lower data rates. Sorenson requires a high-performance processor for playback, so it may not work well on older computers. Sorenson 3 video is a later version which requires the latest hardware and software configurations for playback. As an alternative, the Cinepak codec is a good general-purpose codec that compresses reasonably well and is supported by older computer configurations.

Quality. You can set the overall quality of video to low, medium, or high. Medium is fine for most purposes.

Streaming video

Like audio, a video source can be streamed so that it starts playing quickly and continues playing as the data is transferred. The options for video are the same as for audio: RealMedia (*.rm*), Windows Streaming Media (*.wm*), and streaming QuickTime. For true streaming performance, the files must be served from a computer outfitted with the appropriate server software. See the companies' web sites, listed earlier in the Streaming audio section, for current information on streaming formats.

Flash

I saw this really cool page. It had music, animation, and buttons that did stuff when I touched them. How did they do that?

This sounds like a Flash page to me. Flash is a multimedia format developed by Macromedia especially for the Web (although it's now being used for other purposes as well). Flash gives you the ability to create full-screen animation, interactive graphics, and integrated audio clips, all at remarkably small file sizes.

Flash is great for putting animation and interactive elements (such as games) on web sites (Figure 22-6 Ⓖ, facing page). Some sites use Flash instead of HTML for their site's interface and content (the example in the center).

Advantages and disadvantages

There are a number of advantages to the Flash format:

- Because it uses vector graphics, files are small and download quickly.

- Vector graphics also allow Flash animations to be rescaled to any size without loss of detail. Real-time anti-aliasing keeps the edges smooth.

- It is a streaming format, which means the files start playing quickly and continue to play as they download.

- You can integrate sound files as a background soundtrack (Flash developers seem to be partial to techno music, but that's certainly not required) or as user-triggered sound effects. By compressing, looping, and reusing sound files, you can keep the file sizes in check.

- Flash 5 (and up) uses the robust ActionScript scripting language for adding behaviors and advanced interactivity to Flash movies. This allows them to be the frontend to dynamically generated content or work as games or interfaces to e-commerce functions.

Flash is a multimedia format developed by Macromedia especially for the Web. It is great for adding animation, sound effects, and interactive elements to a web page.

Scenes from a music video for Beck's "Nicotine and Gravy" (created by Fullerene Productions).

Flash intro and web site interface (screenshots from www.eye4u.com, a web design firm in Munich).

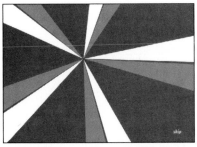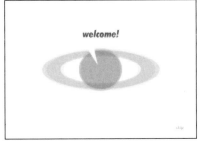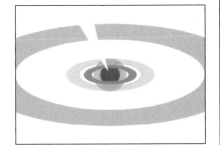

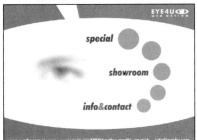

Flash animation. Shots from "A Short Smoke Break" by Rich Oakley and Fawn Scott. This and other cool animation shorts can be seen at www.animationexpress.com.

Figure 22-6. Stills from Flash animations. [G]

WHERE TO LEARN MORE

Flash

Shockwave.com
www.shockwave.com
> This site is a showcase of the latest and greatest shows, games, videos, etc. created in Flash. It's a good place to see what can be done.

"Starting Point" for Flash users
flash.start4all.com
> This is a big page o' links to everything Flash-related.

Macromedia Flash MX for Windows and Macintosh (Visual QuickStart Guide)
by Katherine Ulrich (Peachpit Press, 2002)
> Like all QuickStart Guides, this provides a no-nonsense and pictorial overview of Flash basics.

ActionScript for Flash MX: The Definitive Guide,
Second Edition
by Colin Moock (O'Reilly, 2002)
> This is the book to get when you're ready to take on ActionScript.

But of course, no technology is ideal. There are downsides (and Macromedia has an answer to most of them):

- Flash files require a plug-in to play in the browser. Many developers and clients are squeamish about sinking important navigation or content into a format that will require the user to go out and download a plug-in. But keep in mind that the Flash player plug-in is extremely popular, and as of this writing, Macromedia estimates that almost 98% of web users have Flash Version 3 or higher installed on their machines (see *www.macromedia.com/software/player_census/*).

- Content is lost for nongraphical browsers. Whenever you take content out of HTML text and put it in a picture, it is no longer available to text-only browsers. In response, Flash MX has built-in features to make Flash content accessible to text-only users. (See *www.macromedia.com/macromedia/accessibility/features/flash* for more information.)

- You need specific software to create Flash content, and it isn't cheap. As of this writing, Flash MX is $499 and Adobe's Live Motion is $399. Both are available as part of larger web development packages.

Making Flash files

Flash animations are saved in the *.swf* (ShockWave Flash) format and can be embedded right into a web page. To create a Flash file, the most obvious choice is Macromedia's new and improved Flash MX software. For more information, see *www.macromedia.com/software/flash*.

You may also want to check out Adobe's LiveMotion software, which can also save interactive animations in the *.swf* format. It is nicely integrated with other Adobe products such as Photoshop and Illustrator. For more information, see Adobe's web site: *www.adobe.com/products/livemotion/main.html*.

Before you jump on the Flash bandwagon, I want to make it clear that Flash is not appropriate for every web site, and it is certainly not going to make HTML obsolete (as some Flash enthusiasts may claim). While it is a wonderful medium for putting animations and interactive elements on web pages, it may be less successful as the navigational interface for a whole site. For every user out there who thinks Flash sites are the best, there's someone else who finds them annoying and not worth the download. Ever notice all the "Skip Intro" links on Flash sites? Even the pros tread softly.

Consider whether Flash is appropriate for your site and avoid Flash for Flash's sake.

DHTML

I saw a site that had a menu panel that slid into view when I clicked on its edge. How did they do that?

Most likely, that sliding panel was done with DHTML (Dynamic HTML). DHTML is not a programming language in itself, but rather a clever combination of HTML, JavaScript, and Cascading Style Sheets.

The HTML source controls the content of the page and its elements; JavaScript controls the functionality of the elements—the causes and effects; and Cascading Style Sheets control the appearance and positioning of objects on the page. Together, they can be used to orchestrate cool effects (Figure 22-7), such as expanding menus Ⓐ, sliding panels Ⓑ, and animated objects that float around in the browser window Ⓒ. This is by no means a complete list; DHTML can be used to many creative and practical ends.

DHTML is a combination of HTML, Cascading Style Sheets, and JavaScript.

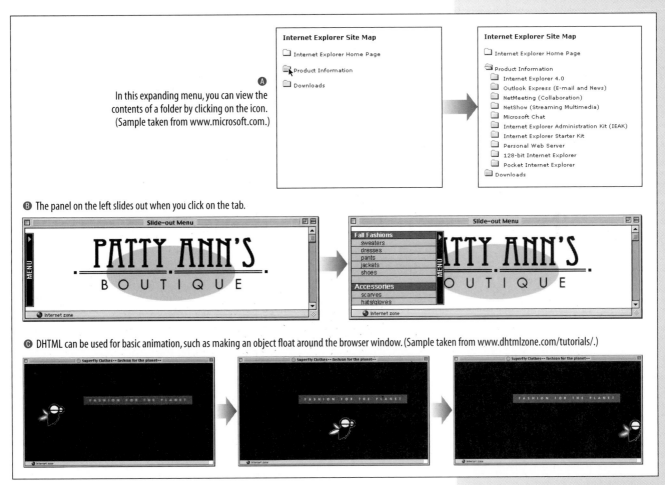

Ⓐ In this expanding menu, you can view the contents of a folder by clicking on the icon. (Sample taken from www.microsoft.com.)

Ⓑ The panel on the left slides out when you click on the tab.

Ⓒ DHTML can be used for basic animation, such as making an object float around the browser window. (Sample taken from www.dhtmlzone.com/tutorials/.)

Figure 22-7. Common DHTML tricks.

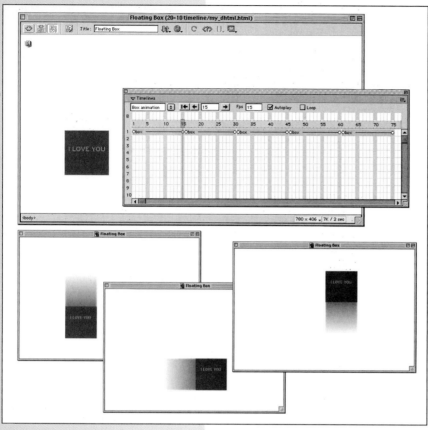

Figure 22-8. Macromedia's Dreamweaver uses a timeline interface for creating DHTML animations.

The downside to DHTML is that it is difficult to learn and implement successfully. First of all, creating DHTML effects from scratch requires an adept hand at both Cascading Style Sheets and JavaScript. But the thing that makes it a real monster is that browsers are notoriously inconsistent in the way they support DHTML objects and commands, so it is difficult to create an effect that will work for all users. In many cases, developers create several versions of a page and serve the appropriate version based on the browser making the request. Overall, DHTML is a lot of effort for questionable rewards (for instance, does the menu panel *really* need to slide out, or is that just a gratuitous effect).

For nonprogramming types who just want a basic DHTML trick (such as animation), once again, web-authoring tools come to the rescue. Macromedia Dreamweaver provides a timeline and set of tools that allow you to create the effect visually and it takes care of the coding for you (Figure 22-8). You can even specify which browsers you are targeting and let the tool worry about creating compatible code. Adobe GoLive also offers DHTML animation features. Even with the tools, however, it is important to test pages with DHTML effects thoroughly in a variety of browser environments.

XHTML (The New Standard)

While the HTML 4.01 specification went a long way in formalizing HTML, it still suffers from sloppy artifacts of HTML's fast and loose development. As a result, we have a markup language with quirky features and browsers that easily forgive basic HTML coding errors. This didn't sit well with the W3C, the committee that guides the development of web technologies, so they stepped in to finally clean things up.

The new standard they created is called XHTML. You can think of it as just a stricter version of the HTML tags you've already learned.

The rules of XML

XML is the "X" in XHTML. XML (eXtensible Markup Language) was introduced briefly in Chapter 1. It is not so much a language in itself, but rather a set of rules for creating other markup languages. Using XML, you can create new markup languages that are customized for different information types. Banking institutions can create tags that apply to banking information and then share that information in a standard way. Mathematicians can create a markup language for sharing mathematical formulas (in fact, they have, and the language is called MathML). It's powerful stuff. But with the potential for endless markup languages, the rules for how those tags are defined and implemented need to be extremely strict so browsers and other XML-compliant clients will know how to interpret them.

With the creation of XML, the W3C finally had a shiny new set of rules for defining markup languages. One of the first things they did was apply them to the somewhat clunky HMTL. The resulting XHTML specification is in line with the larger family of XML-based markup languages.

Creating XHTML documents

Marking up a document with XHTML is virtually the same as with HTML, so everything you learned in Part II of this book applies to XHTML as well. However, because it is an XML application, you need to play by the rigid rules of XML markup. Every XHTML file must begin with declarations that tell the browser which versions of XML and XHTML are used in the document. The browser uses this information to display the document correctly.

As of this writing, there are three versions of XHTML: Strict, Transitional, and Frameset. Each version is defined in an XML document called a Document Type Definition (DTD), which lists every tag and defines how it works. So when you start a new XHTML document, you need to provide code that says, "This is an XML document that uses tags from this particular XHTML DTD." The code provides actual links to the source information.

HTML DOCTYPE

Including a DOCTYPE declaration is considered proper form for all HTML documents, not just those written in XHTML.

The HTML 4.01 specification includes three DTDs. The following are descriptions of each as well as the declaration you should use to let the browser know which set of rules to follow:

Strict

This DTD includes only the elements and attributes that have not been deprecated or do not appear in frameset documents:

```
<!DOCTYPE HTML PUBLIC
"-//W3C//DTD HTML 4.01//EN"
"http://www.w3.org/TR/html4/
strict.dtd">
```

Transitional

This includes everything in the Strict DTD plus elements and attributes that have been deprecated in favor of style sheets. At the time of this writing, Transitional is the most popular flavor of HTML 4.01 because it allows developers to use common deprecated attributes (such as align). It is likely to stay the most popular until style sheets are fully supported.

```
<!DOCTYPE HTML PUBLIC
"-//W3C//DTD HTML 4.01
Transitional//EN"
"http://www.w3.org/TR/html4/
loose.dtd">
```

Frameset

This includes everything in the Transitional DTD plus frames.

```
<!DOCTYPE HTML PUBLIC
"-//W3C//DTD HTML 4.01
Frameset//EN"
"http://www.w3.org/TR/html4/
frameset.dtd">
```

The following is a minimal XHTML document. The first three lines are required and need to be copied exactly as they are shown (with the exception of which DTD is being used). We'll look at each element one at a time.

```
Ⓐ <?xml version="1.0" encoding="UTF-8"?>
Ⓑ <!DOCTYPE html PUBLIC "-//W3C/DTD XHTML 1.0 Transitional//EN"
     "http://www.w3.org/TR/xhtm11/DTD/xhtml1-transitional.dtd">

Ⓒ <html xmlns="http://w3.org/1999/xhtml" xml:lang="en" lang="en">

<head>
<title>Title is required</title>
</head>

<body>
</body>

</html>
```

Ⓐ The document begins with an XML declaration that tells the browser that the document uses XML Version 1.0. The encoding attribute specifies a common character set (8-bit Unicode), which contains the letters and characters used in most Western languages.

Ⓑ The next element is the DOCTYPE declaration that references the Transitional DTD, both by a public identifier and by providing its URL. A Strict HTML document would use this declaration:

```
<!DOCTYPE html PUBLIC "-//W3C/DTD XHTML 1.0 Strict//EN"
     "http://www.w3.org/TR/xhtm11/DTD/xhtml1-strict.dtd">
```

Framed documents use the following:

```
<!DOCTYPE html PUBLIC "-//W3C/DTD XHTML 1.0 Transitional//EN"
     "http://www.w3.org/TR/xhtm11/DTD/xhtml1-frameset.dtd">
```

Ⓒ Finally, there are a few more directions added within the <html> tag for the document. The xmlns attribute specifies the primary namespace for the document. A namespace is a unique collection of tags and attributes that can be referenced by the browser. The lang attribute is used to declare that the document language is English for both the XML and XHTML namespaces.

The remainder of the document should look familiar in that it has a <head> for information about the document and a <body> for the content. Now let's take a look at the rules that apply to tagging within the content of the document.

Well-formed XHTML documents

Browsers often recover from sloppily written or illegal HTML. This is not the case with XHTML documents. In order to display correctly in a browser, an XHTML document must be well-formed, which means that it properly follows the XML markup rules.

The primary rules for making your document well-formed are:

- There must be no whitespace (character spaces or line returns) before the XML declaration.

- All tags and attributes must be lowercase. In XML, all tags are case-sensitive, which means that `<img>`, `<Img>`, and `<IMG>` would be interpreted as different elements. In the XHTML specification, all tags were written in lowercase.

- All attribute values must be contained within quotation marks. While in HTML it was okay to omit quotation marks around numbers and single words, now you need to be careful that every value is quoted.

- Every tag must have an end tag. While it was acceptable in HTML to omit closing tags (such as `<li>`), in XHTML every container element must have a closing tag.

- Standalone (empty) elements need to be closed as well. So instead of just inserting a line break as `<br>`, XHTML also requires the closing tag (`<br></br>`). Fortunately, you can "close" empty elements simply by adding a slash before the closing bracket (`<br />`). Table 22-1 lists all the previously empty tags (standalone elements) that now need to be closed in XHTML.

- All attributes must have explicit values, which means that previously standalone attributes such as noshade or ismap become `noshade="noshade"` and `ismap="ismap"`, respectively. Table 22-2 lists the previously standalone attributes that now need explicit values. (Note that many of them have not been addressed in this book.)

- All elements must be nested correctly. While this has always been the case in HTML, the rule is strictly enforced in XHTML.

- All special characters must be represented by their character entities in any part of the document. In HTML, you may have gotten away with typing an ampersand (&), but in XHTML you must use its character entity (`&amp;`).

- Scripts must be enclosed within a CDATA section, as follows:

```
<script language="JavaScript">
  <![CDATA[
  ... JavaScript here...
  ]]>
</script>
```

Simple comment tags (`<!-- ... -->`) will no longer work.

- Finally, you must use the `id` attribute where you once used `name` (which has been deprecated).

Table 22-1. Empty tags in XHTML format

`<area />`	`<img />`
`<base />`	`<input />`
`<basefont />`	`<isindex />`
` `	`<link />`
`<col />`	`<meta />`
`<frame />`	`<param />`
`<hr />`	

Table 22-2. Explicit attribute values

```
checked="checked"
compact="compact"
declare="declare"
defer="defer"
disabled="disabled"
ismap="ismap"
multiple="multiple"
noshade="noshade"
noresize="noresize"
nowrap="nowrap"
readonly="readonly"
selected="selected"
```

Start today

XHTML is poised to become the new standard, making the current HTML standard obsolete. If you are learning HTML for the first time and anticipate becoming a web professional, you should get in the habit of writing well-formed documents with DOCTYPE declarations from the start. Web-authoring tools such as Macromedia Dreamweaver and Adobe GoLive are catching up with technology and are now making it easier than ever to write code in XHTML.

Advanced Techniques in Review

There is a world of web design beyond simple HTML and graphics. The Web is always growing and evolving. You may choose to become proficient at advanced skills such as Cascading Style Sheets or JavaScript, or you may use tools to create the basic effects. You may even choose to hire a specialist to add advanced functionality for you. Whatever your strategy, if you are in the world of web design, it is crucial that, at the very least, you have a familiarity with the more technical aspects. The following are a few tidbits from this chapter that you should keep in mind:

Forms. Forms are created with a set of form-related HTML tags. In order to be functional, they require a script or program running on the server to process the information they collect.

Audio. The most popular audio file format on the web is MP3 (*.mp3*). Other appropriate file formats include WAVE (*.wav*), AIFF (*.aif*), MIDI (*.mid*), and QuickTime Audio (*.mov*).

Audio can be made available from a web page via a link. When the user clicks the link, the audio file downloads and plays with an audio player.

Streaming audio is a method for delivering audio on a web page, in which the file starts playing immediately after the user clicks on it. The file is never downloaded to the user's machine, but is served in a stream, similar to radio. RealAudio (*.ra*), Windows Media (*.wm*), and Streaming QuickTime are three streaming media options.

Video. The most popular web video format is the QuickTime Movie (*.mov*). Other formats include MPEG video (*.mpg*) and Windows-only AVI (*.avi*).

Like audio, video material can be made available for download or via streaming.

Flash. Flash is a multimedia format developed by Macromedia that gives you the ability to create full-screen animation, interactive graphics, and integrated sound effects for web delivery.

To make Flash files (*.swf*), you need a tool such as Macromedia Flash or Adobe LiveMotion.

DHTML. DHTML is not a language in itself, but rather a combination of HTML, Cascading Style Sheets, and JavaScript. The main drawback to DHTML effects is inconsistent browser support. There is also a steep learning curve.

XHTML. XHTML is the HTML specification rewritten according to the stricter rules of XML. It will soon replace HTML as the standard way to code web pages.

Test Yourself

Even if you don't take on these advanced technologies yourself, it is good to be familiar with them. Here are a few questions to see how much you've learned. The answers are in the Appendix.

1. Name at least three languages that can be used to process information from a form.

2. Name three ways to reduce the size of an audio file for web delivery.

3. Name at least three ways to reduce the file size of a video for the Web.

4. Name two ways to make a video accessible from a web page.

5. DHTML is actually the combination of three other web technologies. What are they?

6. What is XML and how does it relate to XHTML?

Appendix:
Answers

Chapter 1: Where Do I Start?

Test Yourself

1. "Frontend" refers to the aspects of web design that appear in the browser window, such as the HTML files and graphic design. "Backend" refers to the programming that lives on the server and makes web pages work.

2. This is a trick question. Everyone who works in web design needs to learn HTML. This doesn't mean you need to memorize every tag, but you should learn enough to understand what it can do, what it can't do, and how browsers interpret it.

3. With a web-authoring tool, you can edit the elements exactly as they appear on the final web page. HTML-editing tools provide shortcuts for writing HTML, but you need to open the code in a browser to see how it looks.

4. These days, formatting text styles should be done with Cascading Style Sheets, although there are still antiquated HTML tags that will provide basic styling capabilities.

5. JavaScript is the scripting language that makes web browsers do tricks, such as popping up new windows.

Chapter 2: How the Web Works

Test Yourself

1-c, 2-d, 3-e, 4-f, 5-b, 6-a

Chapter 3: Getting Your Pages on the Web

Test Yourself

1. File Transfer Protocol, which is the protocol used for moving files from one computer to another over the Internet.

2. You'll need the domain name, your username, your password, and the proper directory in which to put your files. The last three will be provided by your server administrator or hosting company.

3. Graphic: Raw Data/Binary; Audio file: Raw Data/Binary; HTML file: Text/ASCII

4. "Get file" will download files from the server to your computer.

5. Upload a whole directory as you would a single file. Just select the directory in the FTP program and click on Put file or Upload. The program keeps the files in order and uploads them in the proper format.

6. An IP address is a 12-digit number assigned to a specific domain on a server. The domain name is a human-friendly way to refer to that IP address.

Chapter 4: Why Web Design Isn't Like Print Design

Test Yourself

1. You need to be aware that your page will look and work differently from browser to browser, so how you see and use your design on your screen is not exactly how it will appear or function for everybody on the Web. Older browser versions may not support new web technologies, such as style sheets, JavaScript, or DHTML.

2. The platform on which your page is viewed can affect how certain page and form elements are rendered, the size of the text, availability of fonts, and the brightness of the colors. Some technologies developed for the PC may not be supported on Mac or Unix platforms.

3. Users' browser settings will override the settings you make in your HTML file. It is easy for users to change the fonts, background colors, and size of the text, which affects the alignment of elements on the page. Users can also choose to turn off functionality such as Java, JavaScript, and image display.

4. Because browser windows can be resized, you never know how large your web page's screen area will be. Text will rewrap when the page is resized, unless it is controlled by a table.

5. Browsers can display a font that you specify only if it is already loaded on a user's computer. If it is not loaded, a default font (usually Times or Helvetica) will be used instead. This significantly narrows the list of fonts that are reliable for web use.

Chapter 5: The Web Design Process

Test Yourself

1. A site diagram is useful for planning and visualizing how information is organized on the site. It should be done very early in the design process, as soon as the contents and functionality of the site have been determined. The site diagram becomes a valuable reference for the whole production team.

2. A "look and feel" study is a sketch or series of sketches that propose graphic styles for the site. It focuses on how the site looks, rather than how it works.

3. The HTML documents, graphics, and backend programming.

4. On another browser version; on another platform; with the graphics turned off; with the browser window at various widths; on an 8-bit (256-color) monitor; over a slow modem connection.

Chapter 6: Creating a Simple Page (HTML Overview)

Test Yourself

1. A container tag has a closing tag. The opening and closing tags are wrapped around the text you want to affect. A standalone tag has no closing tag. It is just dropped into place.

2.
```
<html>
<head>
    <title>...</title>
</head>
<body>
...
</body>
</html>
```

3. a. Yes.

   b. No. The file must end in *.htm* or *.html* to be recognized by the browser.

   c. No. There may not be any character spaces within a filename. This is extremely important.

   d. Yes.

   e. No. There may not be any slashes within a filename. The browser will think it is a directory path name.

   f. No. Filenames may not have any special characters, like "%".

4. a. The src= part of the attribute is missing:

```
<img src="birthday.jpg">
```

   b. The closing tag is missing a slash:

```
<i>Congratulations!</i>
```

   c. Attributes go in the opening tag only:

```
<a href="file.html">linked text</a>
```

   d. The closing tag has a backslash instead of a slash:

```
<p>This is a new paragraph</p>
```

Chapter 7: Formating Text with HTML

Exercise 7-2

```
<html>
<head>
  <title>Jen's Kitchen: Tapenade</title>
</head>

<body>
<h1>Tapenade (Olive Spread) </h1>
<blockquote>This is a really simple dish to prepare and it's always a
huge hit at parties.</blockquote>

<h2>Ingredients</h2>
<p>1 8 oz. jar sundried tomatoes<br>
 2 large garlic cloves<br>
 2/3 c. Kalamata olives<br>
 1 t. capers<br>
 12 oz. goat cheese </p>
<p>french bread (sliced thin and toasted slightly)<br>
 fresh basil & olives to garnish </p>

<h2>Instructions</h2>
<p>Combine tomatoes and garlic in a food processor. Blend until as
smooth as possible.</p>
<p>Add capers and olives. Pulse the motor a few times until
incorporated, but still maintaining texture.</p>
<p>Spread goat cheese on each toast round and top with tapenade.</p>
</body>
</html>
```

Exercise 7-3

List A: This ordered lists uses capital letters for numbers.

```
<ol type="A">
<li>Spread the pesto on the pizza crust as thick or thin as you
like.</li>
<li>Cover the top evenly with tomato slices.</li>
<li>Spread the red onion (to taste) over the top and sprinkle with pine
nuts.</li>
<li>Add globs and crumbles of goat cheese randomly. (Kalamata olives
are a nice topping as well.)</li>
<li>Bake in a 400 degree oven for 10 to 15 minutes until sizzling and
fragrant.</li>
</ol>
```

List B: To get extra space between list elements, you need to insert a line break at the end of the line (see the Tip in the Unordered Lists section).

```
<p><b>5 Simple Pleasures</b></p>
<ul>
   <li>Lemonade from scratch</li><br>
   <li>Photo sticker booths</li><br>
   <li>Afros</li><br>
   <li>Saltines</li><br>
   <li>Ella (our neighbor's dog)</li>
</ul>
```

List C: This definition list features a nested unordered list. The unordered list is part of the definition (<dd>).

```
<dl>
<dt>Shrimp & Celery Bisque</dt>
<dd>This recipe makes enough for 2 or 3 meals or 4 opener soup
courses. It's one of my favorite meals in cold weather.</dd>

<dt>Wild Mushroom Bowtie Pasta</dt>
<dd>I use this wild mushroom "ragout" as the base of a number of
recipes: wild mushroom risotto, wild mushroom & brie phyllo packets,
etc. I use the following mushrooms:
   <ul>
      <li>chanterelle</li>
      <li>cremini</li>
      <li>morel</li>
      <li>shiitake</li>
   </ul>
</dd>
<dt>Chocolate-Kahlua Trifle</dt>
<dd>This is the easiest possible dessert recipe, and it's so yummy.
It's also very portable if you put it together in a tall storage
canister, so it's a good dish to bring to a party. People love dessert
in a bucket!</dd>
</dl>
```

Exercise 7-4

Note, that `<strong>` and `<b>` can be used interchangeably. The same with `<em>` and `<i>`. The sample below shows examples of both methods.

```
<html>
<head>
  <title>Jen's Kitchen: Tapenade</title>
</head>
<body>

<h1>Tapenade (Olive Spread)</h1>
<blockquote><b><i>This is a really simple dish to prepare and it's
always a huge hit at parties.</i></b></blockquote>

<h2>Ingredients</h2>
<p>
<tt>1 8 oz. jar sundried tomatoes</tt><br>
<tt>2 large garlic cloves </tt><br>
<tt>2/3 c. Kalamata olives</tt> <br>
<tt>1 t. capers</tt> <br>
<tt>12 oz. goat cheese</tt>
</p>

<p>french bread <em>(sliced thin and toasted slightly)</em><br>
  fresh basil & olives to garnish </p>

<h2>Instructions</h2>
<ol>
<li><strong>Combine tomatoes and garlic in a food processor.</strong>
Blend until as smooth as possible.</li>

<li><u>Add capers and olives.</u> Pulse the motor a few times until
incorporated, <strike>but still maintaining texture</strike>.</li>
<li>Spread goat cheese on each toast round and top with tapenade.</li>
</ol>
</body>
</html>
```

Test Yourself

❶ Works. Each element is centered with the `align` attribute.

❷ Doesn't work. `align` is an attribute, not a tag.

❸ Doesn't work. The `<div>` tag is used correctly, but its value is set to `right`, not `center`.

❹ Works. The `<center>` tag centers everything it contains.

Chapter 8: Formatting Text with Style Sheets

Test Yourself

This code is the result of steps 1 through 10, before the styles are extracted into an external style sheet in step 11.

```
<html>
<head>
<title>Laura Linen Resume</title>

<style type="text/css">
<!--
body { font-family: Verdana, Arial, sans-serif; }
h1 { font-size: 12pt; color: green; }
.intro { font-style: italic; margin-left: .5in; margin-right: .5in; }
.text { font-size: 10pt; line-height: 14pt; text-align: justify;
margin-left: .5in; margin-right: .5in; }
.list { font-size: 10pt; line-height: 11pt; margin-left: 1in; }
.course { color: purple; font-weight: bold; }
strong {font-variant: small-caps; color: purple; }
-->
</style>

</head>
<body>
<div style="text-align: center">
<h1 style="font-size: 14pt; color: purple">Laura Linen</h1>
<p>123 Sparks Street, Anytown, US 10000 | 617.555.3434 | Fax:
617.555.9878 | LL@hotmail.com</p>
<p class="intro">Seeking a full-time Interiors Assistant position in
the Anytown area to complement my B.A. studies in interior design. In
addition to advanced visual design and color skills, I have experience
managing design teams, estimating time and costs, preparing production
schedules and creating business plans.</p>
</div>

<h1>Anytown Architectural Center</h1>
<p class="text">In Fall 2001, I studied the first three of eight
required courses in the AAC's Decorative Arts Certificate Program: </p>
<p class="text"><span class="course">BASICS OF INTERIOR
DECORATION.</span> Introduction to the fundamental elements and
processes involved in designing and planning an interior space,
including drawings, space planning, space and proportion, color,
materials, lighting, and furniture.</p>
<p class="list"><strong>Project sampling:</strong><br>
   Sun Woman II Interior <br>
   Jones&#130; Sitting Room Interior <br>
   Jones&#130; Functional Analysis <br>
   Symmetry Studies <br>
</p>
<p class="text"><span class="course">DRAWING FOR INTERIOR
DECORATORS.</span> Introduction to basic skills of representation,
including plans, elevations and sections.</P>

<p class="list"><strong>Project sampling:</strong><br>
   Living Room Floorplan and Elevations <br>
   Bruce &amp; Carol&#130;s Floorplans </p>
```

```
<p class="text"><span class="course">MATERIALS, FINISHES &amp;
RESOURCES.</span> Introduction to selecting and specifying materials
for interior use. Course included multiple field trips to manufacturing
and finishing facilities, as well as job sites, to understand how a
material is decided upon, manipulated, and installed. </p>

<p class="list"><strong>Project sampling:</strong><br>
  Brownstone Kitchen Materials Board <br>
  Linoleum Flooring </p>

<h1>Interiors International</h1>
<p class="text">After realizing my skill and interests are geared
towards interior design versus decoration, I enrolled in II's 3-year
diploma in January 2002. This program consists of nine study
subjects.Within each subject, specific topics are explored extensively:
</p>
<p class="text"><span class="course">MATERIALS.</span> Natural
Materials (stone, wood, metal), Manmade Materials (brick, glass,
plastic), Applied Materials (wallpaper, paint, plaster, murals), Soft
Furnishings (textiles, carpet, drapery), Properties and Suitability of
Materials, Cataloging and Storing Materials, Dealing with Suppliers and
Manufacturers, Measuring Rooms, Estimating Materials. </p>

<p class="list"><strong>Project sampling:</strong><br>
  Materials Database in MS Access <br>
  Stone for Interiors </p>
<p class="text"><span class="course">A HISTORY OF INTERIOR
DESIGN.</span> Ancient Greece to the Middle Ages, Golden Age,
Renaissance, Age of Exuberance, European Baroque, Aristocratic Age,
Rococo and Contemporary Styles, Neo-Classicism, Empire and Regency,
Romanticism and Historicism, 19th Century Reforms, Art Nouveau, Modern
Age. </p>
<p class="list"><strong>Project sampling:</strong><br>
  Roman Interiors <br>
  Medieval Interiors </p>

<h1>Worldwide Design University</h1>
<p class="text">Upon completion of my Interiors International Diploma,
I will embark on a final year of schooling at Worldwide Design
University (WDU) to complete my B.A. in Interior Design. The final year
at WDU will include courses related to: </p>

<p class="list">Professional Business Development <br>
  Detailing Woodwork <br>
  Event Design <br>
  Innovative Design and Universal Design <br>
  Retail Store Design and Hospitality Design <br>
  Residential Design <br>
  Kitchen and Bath Design <br>
  Historic Restoration <br>
  Portfolio Presentation &amp; Marketing <br>
  Senior Thesis <br>
</p>

</body>
</html>
```

Chapter 9: Adding Graphic Elements

Test Yourself

1. The src attribute; it's required as it tells the browser which graphic to use.

2. `<img src="furry.jpg">`

3. Alternative text is what is displayed instead of the graphic if for some reason the graphic doesn't load. It allows your site to be useful and navigable even on a text-only browser or a browser with the graphics turned off.

4. It allows the page to display faster because it does not need to be redrawn each time a new graphic loads.

5. The three likely causes for a missing graphic are: 1) the URL is incorrect, so the browser looks in the wrong place or for the wrong graphic filename (remember, names are case-sensitive); 2) the graphic file is not in an acceptable format; and 3) the graphic file is not named with the proper suffix (*.gif*, *.jpg*, or *.png*, as appropriate).

6. Set border="0" in the `<img>` tag.

Chapter 10: Adding Links

Test Yourself

1. `<a href="tutorial.html">...</a>`

2. `<a href="examples/instructions.html">...</a>`

3. `<a href="examples/french/family.html">...</a>`

4. `<a href="../index.html">...</a>`

5. `<img src="../images/arrow.gif">`

6. `<a href="../instructions.html">...</a>`

7. `<a href="../../index.html">...</a>`

8. `<img src="../../images/bullet.gif">`

9. `<a href="../german/numbers.html"><img src="../../images/bullet.gif"></a>`

10. `<a href="/examples/german/numbers.html">...</a>`

11. `<body background="bkgd.gif">...</body>`

12. `<a href="http://www.learningwebdesign.com">...</a>`

Chapter 11: Tables

Exercise 11-1

```
<table>
<tr>
<td>cell 1</td>
<td>cell 2</td>
</tr>

<tr>
<td>cell 3</td>
<td>cell 4</td>
</tr>

<tr>
<td>cell 5</td>
<td>cell 6</td>
</tr>

<tr>
<td>cell 7</td>
<td>cell 8</td>
</tr>

<tr>
<td>cell 9</td>
<td>cell 10</td>
</tr>
</table>
```

Exercise 11-2

```
<table>
<tr>
<td colspan="3">cell
  1</td>
</tr>

<tr>
<td>cell 2</td>
<td>cell 3</td>
<td>cell 4</td>
</tr>

<tr>
<td>cell 5</td>
<td colspan="2">cell
  6</tc>
</tr>
</table>
```

Exercise 11-3

```
<table>
<tr>
<td>cell1</td>
<td rowspan="3">cell
  2</td>
<td>cell 3</td>
</tr>

<tr>
<td>cell 4</td>
<td rowspan="2">cell
  5</td>
</tr>

<tr>
<td>cell 6</td>
</tr>
</table>
```

Exercise 11-4

Using guides, you should have determined that the web page in the sketch requires a total of six rows and three columns. The first two cells span down four rows each. The first cells in the fifth and sixth rows span over two columns each. The resulting code is shown here:

```
<table>

<!-- the first two cells span down four rows each -->
<tr>
<td rowspan="4"></td>
<td rowspan="4"></td>
<td></td>
</tr>

<!-- in the second, third, and fourth rows, only the last cell is not
taken up by a rowspan, so there is only one <td> tag -->
<tr>
<td></td>
</tr>
```

```
<tr>
<td></td>
</tr>

<tr>
<td></td>
</tr>

<!-- the fifth and sixth rows have column spans -->
<tr>
<td colspan="2"></td>
<td></td>
</tr>

<tr>
<td colspan="2"></td>
<td></td>
</tr>
</table>
```

Exercise 11-5

```
<html>
<head>
  <title>Try It (11-5)</title>
</head>
<body>
<table width="650" height="450" border="0" cellpadding="4"
cellspacing="0">

<tr>
  <td rowspan="4" width="225" bgcolor="#003300"><img
    src="images/redbottles.jpg" width="217" height="351"
    alt="red bottles photo"></td>
  <td width="175" rowspan="4" align="center" bgcolor="#99cc66"><img
    src="images/buttons.gif" width="81" height="267"
    alt="nav buttons"></td>
  <td width="250" height="20" bgcolor="#669900"><img
    src="images/about.gif" width="66" height="12" alt="About Me"></td>
</tr>

<tr>
<td height="200" valign="top" bgcolor="#FFFFCC"><p>My name is Jennifer
Niederst, and I am a graphic designer and author of books for O'Reilly
and Associates. My interests include cooking, travel, and indie rock
music.</p>
</td>
</tr>

<tr>
<td height="20" bgcolor="#669900"><img src="images/contact.gif"
width="150" height="12" alt="Contact Info"></td>
</tr>

<tr>
<td height="120" bgcolor="#FFFFCC">O'Reilly &amp; Associates, Inc.<br>
      1005 Gravenstein Highway North<br>
      Sebastopol, CA 95472</td>
</tr>
```

```
<tr>
<td colspan="2" bgcolor="#FF0033"> </td>
<td height="20" bgcolor="#669900"><img src="images/link.gif"
width="108" height="12" alt="Link of the Day"></td>
</tr>

<tr>
<td colspan="2" align="center" valign="middle" bgcolor="#000000"><font
color="gray" size="-1"><b>All
content is copyright &copy; 2003 Jennifer Niederst</b></font></td>
<td height="70" bgcolor="#FFFFCC"><a
href="http://www.littlechair.com/">Littlechair.com</a></td>
</tr>

</table>
</body>
</html>
```

Test Yourself

1. The table (<table>), row (<tr>), and cell (<td>).

2. Space between cells is controlled by the cellspacing attribute which goes in the <table> tag.

3. Use the valign attribute set to bottom to place contents at the bottom of a cell. The valign attribute goes in the <td> tag.

4. Cell backgrounds are set with the bgcolor attribute in the <td> tag. Cell colors override background colors set at the table level (in the <table> tag).

5. The code for the table in Figure 11-31 is:

```
<table width="400" border="1" cellspacing="0" cellpadding="0">
<tr>
  <td width="50%" height="100" valign="top" align="center"
    bgcolor="red">red</td>
  <td align="right" valign="top">default</td>
</tr>
<tr>
  <td height="100" valign="middle" align="center">default</td>
  <td align="right" valign="bottom" bgcolor="yellow">yellow</td>
</tr>
</table>
```

Chapter 12: Frames

Test Yourself

1. It does not have a <body> tag at the beginning of the document. It uses the <frameset> tag instead.

2. Frames make pages difficult to bookmark and find with a search engine. They cause more work for developers and a greater load on the server. Some users also find framed documents difficult to navigate.

3.

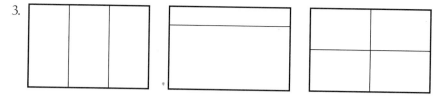

4. Set the target of the link to _top:

```
<a href="document.html" target="_top">
```

5. The frameset code is as follows (frame dimensions are approximate):

```
<frameset cols="*,2*">
    <frame src="empty.html">
    <frameset rows="80%,20%">
        <frame src="empty.html">
        <frame src="empty.html">
    </frameset>
</frameset>
```

Chapter 13: Color on the Web

Test Yourself

1. From a windowing system that runs on the Unix platform.

2. Red, Green, and Blue: the three colors of light that make up colors on a monitor.

3. R: 255, G: 255, B: 255 (or FFFFFF in hexadecimal) is the numeric equivalent of white.

4. The colors in the web palette are the cross-section of colors found in the Windows and Mac operating systems. The web palette helps colors stay solid and consistent on 8-bit monitors. When there are no more 8-bit monitors around, there will be no more use for the web palette.

5. `<table bgcolor="#E3F9BB">`

6. b. CCFF33

Chapter 14: All About Web Graphics

Test Yourself

1. GIF (Graphics Interchange Format) is the most widely used format for the Web. It is good for images with areas of flat color.

2. Bitmapped graphics are made up of a grid of tiny squares called pixels. Vector graphics are made up of shapes that are mathematically defined.

3. ppi stands for "pixels per inch," which is the technically correct way to measure the resolution of a web graphic. In common practice, people say "dpi" (dots per inch) out of habit.

4. The 7-inch graphic at 72 dpi is 504 pixels wide and is the most appropriate for a web page. The 5-inch graphic at 300 dpi is 1500 pixels wide, which is too wide to fit in most browser windows. Its file size would be much larger as well.

5. Limit their dimensions, design to take advantage of the way the format compresses images, and reuse images from the browser's cache.

6. Anti-aliasing is the slight blur around curved edges in bitmapped images that makes the transistion smoother between colors.

7. a. GIF, b. JPEG, c. GIF. (Note that you could also use 8-bit PNG instead of GIF and 24-bit PNG instead of JPEG, but it is difficult to make the file size smaller.)

Chapter 15: Creating GIFs

Test Yourself

1. Indexed color is a system of storing the pixel colors in an image in a palette or color table. Each color in the image corresponds to a numerical position in the table.

2. 8-bit graphics contain 256 colors. 5-bit graphics have 32 colors.

3. Transparency and animation.

4. An adaptive palette is a custom palette that contains the most frequently used pixel colors in the image.

5. When there is less dithering, there are more uninterrupted patches of solid color, so the GIF compression can work more efficiently.

6. The colors will stay flat and consistent even when viewed on 8-bit monitors.

Chapter 16: Creating JPEGs

Test Yourself

1. JPEG stands for Joint Photographic Experts Group, the standards body that created the file format.

2. This is a trick question. JPEGs don't use color palettes. They are 24-bit graphics capable of storing colors from the full RGB color space.

3. Cumulative compression means that more image data is thrown out every time you resave an image as a JPEG. It is good practice to avoid resaving an image in JPEG format. It is better to start with the original and export it to a fresh JPEG when you need to make changes.

4. Progressive JPEGs display in a series of passes. Optimized JPEGs use a special compression scheme to make smaller file sizes, but it does not change the display of the JPEG.

5. Optimization strategies include limiting the dimensions of the image, increasing the amount of compression, making the JPEG progressive and optimized, and adding a slight blur to all or parts of the image.

Chapter 17: Animated GIFs

Test Yourself

1. Animated GIFs store multiple images in one file. This ability is a standard feature of the GIF file format.

2. Limit its dimensions, reduce the number of frames, optimize the image, and reduce its color palette.

3. Use "do not dispose" if you have transparent areas in your frames.

4. Redundant Pixel Removal optimization stores only the pixels that change in each frame, resulting in smaller files.

5. Tween comes from the process of automatically inserting frames "between" a start and end frame.

Chapter 18: Slicing and Rollovers

Test Yourself

1. To make one portion of the image a different file format; to make one or more portion an animation; to make one or more portion a rollover; to put HTML text in the middle of the graphic.

2. An HTML table.

3. The disadvantage is that you have to download two graphics instead of one for each button.

4. An event handler is an action made by the user or browser that triggers a JavaScript function. Rollovers typically use the onMouseOver and onMouseOut event handlers.

5. Graphics can be triggered to appear when the mouse button is pressed down, when it is clicked, or when it is released.

Chapter 19: Web Design Techniques

Test Yourself

1. Add a graphic with an `<img>` tag before each entry, or apply a style sheet rule to the unordered list with the `list-style-image` property.

2. By putting an HTML table within a slightly larger table of a different color, or by using style-sheet box properties (`width`, `height`, `background-color`, `border-style`, `border-width`, `border-color`).

3. Rounded corners are always graphics. Tables are usually used to hold them in place with HTML elements.

4. `width` and `height`.

5. Create a table cell next to the text cell that is only 1-pixel wide and fill it with a color.

6. The only way to stop an image from tiling is with style sheets. Use `background-image` to specify the image and the `background-repeat` property set to `no-repeat`.

7. When you want the new window to open at a specific size.

Chapter 20: Building Usable Web Sites

Test Yourself

1. The information architect takes an inventory of the information the site should include, organizes it, and gives the site structure (usually communicated in a site diagram). User testing is another common task.

2. Information may be organized alphabetically, chronologically, by class or type, hierarchically, spatially, or by order of magnitude.

3. Hierarchical organizations are the most popular. Organization by class is also useful.

4. Designing how a site's structure appears visually on the page and giving the user intuitive tools for finding information.

5. A metaphor may give users a head start in understanding how something works because they can apply knowledge of that space or tool from the real world to the site. The disadvantage is that it is not easy to map site information logically to a metaphorical space, and the metaphor often breaks down. A metaphor can also be confusing or trite.

6. A user scenario maps the step-by-step movement of a theoretical user through the site. It is sequential and may not represent every page on the site. A site diagram is a birds-eye view of the overall structure of the site and aims to represent all of its parts.

7. To ensure clarity in navigation, make sure the navigation tools are distinctive and recognizable as navigation, label everything clearly, and use icons carefully.

8. Similar page types should have similar navigational options. These options should be presented consistently, both in appearance and location, in every instance.

9. Breadcrumb navigation shows the user where they are in relation to the site's structure and provides easy links back to any hierarchical level. Furthermore, it is text-only and adds only a few bytes to the file.

Chapter 21: Web Design Dos and Don'ts

Test Yourself

1. Don't
2. Do
3. Do
4. Don't
5. Don't

6. Don't
7. Don't
8. Do
9. Do
10. Please, don't.

Chapter 22: How'd They Do That? (An Introduction to Advanced Techniques)

Test Yourself

1. Forms are commonly scripted in Perl, C, C++, PHP, ASP, or with Java servlets.

2. You can reduce the size of an audio file by making it shorter, mono (rather than stereo), 8-bit, and by reducing the sampling rate to 22 kHz or 11 kHz.

3. You can reduce a video file by making it shorter, making the frame size smaller, reducing the frame rate, reducing the color bit-depth, reducing the data rate, and by using an advanced codec such as Sorenson.

4. You can link to an external video file or embed the video right on the web page.

5. DHTML is the combination of HTML, Cascading Style Sheets, and JavaScript.

6. XML is a set of rules for creating mark-up languages. XHTML is just HTML rewritten according to the rules of XML.

Glossary

8-bit color

A color model capable of displaying a maximum of 256 colors, the maximum number that 8 bits of information can define.

24-bit color

A color model capable of displaying approximately 16,777,216 colors.

absolute pathname

Directions to a file's location on the server, starting at the topmost level of the server. An absolute URL begins by defining the HTTP protocol, followed by the name of the server and the complete pathname.

aliasing

The jagged, "stair-stepped" edges that can appear between colors in a bitmapped graphic.

alternative text

Text provided within an image tag that will display in the browser window if the image is not visible. It is specified using the `alt` attribute within the `<img>` tag.

anchor

Another word for a link.

anti-aliasing

A slight blur added to the edges of objects and type in bitmapped graphics to smooth out the edges.

applet

A self-contained, mini-executable program, such as one written in the Java programming language.

attribute

Parameters added within an HTML tag to extend or modify its actions.

backend

Aspects of the Web and web design that pertain to functions that take place on the server.

bit depth

In web design, a measurement of the number of colors based on the number of bits (1s and 0s) allotted by the file or the system. A bit is the smallest unit of information on a computer (one bit can define two colors). Strung together, they can represent more values (8 bits can represent 256 values).

bitmapped image

A graphic that is made up of a grid of colored pixels. See also vector image.

block element

In HTML, a distinct unit of text that is automatically displayed with space above and below.

browser

The client software that requests and displays web pages.

cache
Temporary storage area that browsers use for downloaded documents, preventing the need to request the same document from the server multiple times.

Cascading Style Sheets (CSS)
An addition to HTML for controlling presentation of a document, including color, typography, alignment of text and images, etc.

CGI
Common Gateway Interface; a mechanism for communication between the web server and other programs (CGI scripts) running on the server.

character entity
A string of characters used to specify characters not found in the normal alphanumeric character set in HTML documents.

codec
An algorithm used by media files for compressing and decompressing data.

compression
A method for reducing the file size of a document. Compression is particularly important in web graphics. Different file formats use different compression techniques.

container tag
An HTML tag that has both an opening tag (e.g., <h1>) and a closing tag (e.g, </H1>).

CSS
See Cascading Style Sheets.

DHTML
Dynamic HTML; an integration of JavaScript, HTML, and Cascading Style Sheets. DHTML can be used to make content respond to user input or for adding simple animation effects.

dithering
The approximation of a color by mixing pixels of similar colors that are available in the image or system palette. The result of dithering is a random dot pattern or noise in the image.

Document Type Definition (DTD)
An XML document that lists every element and attribute in a markup language and how it works.

domain name
A name that corresponds to a specific IP address. It is easier for humans to remember than a 12-digit IP address.

event handler
A standardized description of an action that triggers a JavaScript function. Examples of events include mousing over a page element (onMouseOver), clicking (onClick), or loading a page into the browser (onLoad).

extranet
A web site or system that is available within a closed system and to select users outside that system, usually via a password.

Flash
A multimedia format developed by Macromedia for the delivery of animation, interactivity, and audio clips over the Web.

frame rate
In video and animation, the number of frames per second (fps).

frames
A method for dividing the browser window into smaller subwindows, each displaying a different HTML document.

frontend
Aspects of the Web and web design that pertain to browser functionality and display.

FTP
File Transfer Protocol; a system for moving files over the Internet from one computer to another.

gamma
Refers to the overall brightness of a computer monitor's display.

GIF
Graphic Interchange Format; common file format of web graphic images. GIF is a palette-based, 8-bit format. It is most appropriate for images with areas of flat color and sharp contrast.

hexadecimal
A base-16 numbering system consisting of the characters 0, 1, 2, 3, 4, 5, 6, 7, 8, 9, A, B, C, D, E, and F (where A–F represent the decimal values 10–15). It is used in HTML for specifying color values.

host
Another term for a server. Hosting services are companies that provide server space for web sites. See also ISP.

HTML
HyperText Markup Language; the format of web documents.

HTTP
Hypertext Transfer Protocol; the system that defines how web pages and media are requested and transferred between servers and browsers.

HTTPS
Indicates a secure HTTP protocol transaction.

imagemap
A single image that contains multiple hypertext links.

interlaced GIF
A GIF graphic that displays in a series of passes until the final image appears.

intranet

A web site or system that is available only within a closed network and is not accessible to the outside world.

IP address

A numeric identifier for a computer or device on a network. An IP address has four numbers (from 0 to 255) separated by periods (.).

ISP

Internet Service Provider; a company that sells access to the Internet computer network, whether through a dial-up modem connection, DSL, ISDN, cable, or other connection.

Java

A cross-platform, object-oriented programming language developed by Sun Microsystems. It is typically used for developing large, enterprise-scale applications, but it can also be used for creating small applications for the Web in the form of applets.

JavaScript

A scripting language developed by Netscape that adds interactivity and conditional behavior to web pages.

JPEG

A lossy graphics compression scheme developed by the Joint Photographic Experts Group. JPEG is most efficient at compressing images with gradations in tone and no sharp edge contrasts, such as photographs.

lossy

A type of compression in which data is thrown out to reduce file size. JPEG graphics use a lossy compression scheme.

MP3

A popular file format for high-quality audio that uses MPEG compression.

MPEG

A family of multimedia standards created by the Motion Picture Experts Group, commonly used to refer to audio and video files saved using one of the MPEG compression schemes.

nesting

Placing one set of HTML tags within another tag pair, usually resulting in a combination of styles or a hierarchical display (as in lists).

optimizing

Reducing file size. Optimizing is an important step in web development, where file size and transfer time are critical.

palette

A table in an 8-bit indexed color file (such as a GIF) that provides color information for the pixels in the image.

pathname

Directions to a file using a nomenclature in which directory hierarchies and filenames are separated by slashes (/).

pixel

A single square in a graphic image (short for "picture element").

PNG

Portable Network Graphic; a versatile graphics file format that features support for both 8-bit indexed images (PNG8) and 24-bit images (PNG24). PNGs also feature variable transparency levels; automatic color correction controls; and a lossless, yet highly efficient, compression scheme.

progressive JPEG

A JPEG that displays in a series of passes until the final image appears.

QuickTime

A system extension that makes it possible to view audio and video information on a computer. It was originally developed for the Macintosh but is now available for Windows as well. The term also refers to the file format.

relative pathname

Directions to a file based on the location of the current file.

resolution

The number of pixels per inch (ppi) in an online graphic. In print, resolution is measured in dots per inch (dpi).

RGB color

A color system that describes colors based on combinations of red, green, and blue light.

rollover

The act of passing the mouse pointer over an element's space or the events triggered by that action (such as a changing graphic or pop-up message).

root directory

The top-level directory on the server

sans-serif font

A font design featuring straight or squared off character strokes. Helvetica is an example of a sans-serif font.

serif font

A font that has horizontal slabs at the end of character strokes. Times is an example of a serif font.

server

A networked computer that provides some kind of service or information.

Shockwave

Proprietary technology from Macromedia for the web delivery of multimedia content.

standalone tag

An HTML tag (e.g., `<img>`) that places an object on the page and does not use a closing tag (`</>`).

tweening

A function in animation tools for automatically creating frames between a start and end frame.

Unix

A multiuser, multitasking operating system developed by Bell Laboratories. It also provides programs for editing text, sending email, preparing tables, performing calculations, and many other specialized functions that normally require separate applications.

URL

Universal Resource Locator; the address of a site or document on the Web.

vector image

A graphic that uses mathematical equations to define shapes and fills. Vector images can be resized without change in quality. See also bitmapped image.

W3C

The World Wide Web Consortium; a consortium of many companies and organizations that "exists to develop common standards for the evolution of the World Wide Web." It is run by the Laboratory for Computer Science at the Massachusetts Institute of Technology and CERN, the European Particle Physics Laboratory, where the WWW was first developed.

web palette

The set of 216 colors that will not dither or shift when viewed with browsers on 8-bit monitors.

XHTML

The new HTML standard that has been written according to the stringent rules of XML.

XML

eXtensible Markup Language; a new standard for marking up documents and data. XML allows authors to create customized tag sets that make content perform as databases and provide functionality not available with HTML.

Index

About the Author

Jennifer Niederst was one of the first designers for the Web. As the designer of O'Reilly's Global Network Navigator (GNN), the first commercial web site, she has been designing for the Web since 1993. Since then, she has been working almost exclusively on the Web, first as Creative Director of Songline Studios (a subsidiary of O'Reilly), where she designed the original interface for WebReview (*webreview.com*), and as a freelance designer and consultant since 1996. She is the author of the best-selling *Web Design in a Nutshell* (O'Reilly), and has taught web design at the Massachusetts College of Art and the Interactive Factory in Boston. She has spoken at major design and Internet events including the GRAFILL conference (Geilo, Norway), Seybold Seminars, and the W3C International Expo. In addition to designing, Jennifer enjoys cooking, travel, indie-rock, and making stuff. You can visit her site at *www.littlechair.com* or send her email at *jen@oreilly.com*.

Colophon

Our look is the result of reader comments, our own experimentation, and feedback from distribution channels. Distinctive covers complement our distinctive approach to technical topics, breathing personality and life into potentially dry subjects.

The cover image on *Learning Web Design* is a spiral. Spirals have been a part of the human experience as early as ancient Greece, and possibly since prehistory, fascinating the human imagination. In ancient times spirals were often used to represent what people believed to be portals between the present world and the world of their ancestors. In the Minoan civilization, spirals were commonly used in art and as decoration. In modern times, millions have been entertained by the spiral known as Slinky®.

The spiral shape is found throughout the natural world, most notably in the shell of the nautilus, the design of many spider webs, and the blooms of certain flowers. Another form of spiral is the double helix of DNA. In weather patterns, the spiral can be found in hurricanes, tornadoes, and the isobars surrounding high and low pressure centers. Of the known galaxies, the spiral is the most common shape.

The spiral can also be found in architecture. It tops Ionic columns, and from ancient to modern times, the spiral staircase has been a common architectural form. The helical spiral is the central structure of Frank Lloyd Wright's design of the Guggenheim Museum.

Mathematically speaking, spirals are planar curves, circling outward from a central point at a regular ratio. Archimedes discovered the first mathematical representation of a spiral: $r = a^\theta$, where r is the radius, a is any constant, and θ is the angle of rotation from the axis. This spiral is known as the Spiral of Archimedes. Many other, more complex, spirals have been found and described by mathematicians since. Spirals can also be non-planar; these three-dimensional spirals either maintain a constant radius as the central point shifts along the third axis (a helical spiral, as in the thread of a screw), or travel outward from the central point as it moves along the third axis (as in the thread of a cone-shaped drill).

Matt Hutchinson was the production editor and copyeditor for *Learning Web Design*. David Futato did the typesetting and page makeup, with assistance from Emma Colby. Jane Ellin, Genevieve d'Entremont, Claire Cloutier, and Edie Freedman provided quality control. Tom Dinse wrote the index.

Edie Freedman designed the cover of this book, with help from the O'Reilly Design team, using Photoshop 6 and QuarkXPress 4.1. Emma Colby produced the cover layout with QuarkXPress 4.1 using Adobe's Myriad Condensed font. David Futato designed and produced the CD label.

David Futato designed and implemented the interior layout using QuarkXPress 4.1. The text and heading fonts are Linotype Birka and Adobe Myriad Condensed; the sidebar font is Adobe Syntax; and the code font is TheSans Mono Condensed from LucasFont. The illustrations and screenshots that appear in the book were produced by Chris Reilley using Macromedia Freehand MX and Adobe Photoshop 7. This colophon was written by David Futato.

Other Titles Available from O'Reilly

Web Authoring and Design

HTML & XHTML: The Definitive Guide, 5th Edition

By Chuck Musciano & Bill Kennedy
5th Edition August 2002
672 pages, ISBN 0-596-00382-X

Our new edition offers web developers a better way to become HTML-fluent, by covering the language syntax, semantics, and variations in detail and demonstrating the difference between good and bad usage. Packed with examples, *HTML & XHTML: The Definitive Guide*, 5th Edition covers Netscape Navigator 6, Internet Explorer 6, HTML 4.01, XHTML 1.0, JavaScript 1.5, CSS2, Layers, and all of the features supported by the popular web browsers.

Cascading Style Sheets: The Definitive Guide

By Eric A. Meyer
1st Edition May 2000
470 pages, ISBN 1-56592-622-6

CSS is the HTML 4.0–approved method for controlling visual presentation on web pages. *Cascading Style Sheets: The Definitive Guide* offers a complete, detailed review of CSS1 properties and other aspects of CSS1. Each property is explored individually in detail with discussion of how each interacts with other properties. There is also information on how to avoid common mistakes in interpretation. This book is the first major title to cover CSS in a way that acknowledges and describes current browser support, instead of simply describing the way things work in theory. It offers both advanced and novice web authors a comprehensive guide to implementation of CSS.

Information Architecture for the World Wide Web, 2nd Edition

By Louis Rosenfeld & Peter Morville
2nd Edition August 2002
488 pages, ISBN 0-596-00035-9

This book provides effective approaches for designers, information architects, and web site managers who are faced with sites that are becoming difficult to use and maintain. Web professionals will learn how to design web sites and intranets that support growth, management, navigation, and ease of use. This thorough introduction to the field of information architecture features updated material covering classic issues as well as new approaches to Information Architecture.

Web Design in a Nutshell, 2nd Edition

By Jennifer Niederst
2nd Edition September 2001
640 pages, ISBN 0-596-00196-7

Web Design in a Nutshell contains the nitty-gritty on everything you need to know to design web pages. Written by veteran web designer Jennifer Niederst, this book provides quick access to the wide range of technologies and techniques from which web designers and authors must draw. Topics include understanding the web environment, HTML, graphics, multimedia and interactivity, and emerging technologies.

The Web Design CD Bookshelf

By O'Reilly & Associates, Inc.
Version 1.0 November 2001
(Includes CD-ROM)
640 pages, ISBN 0-596-00271-8

Six best selling O'Reilly Animal Guides are now available on CD-ROM, easily accessible and searchable with your favorite web browser: *HTML & XHTML: The Definitive Guide*, 4th Edition; *ActionScript: The Definitive Guide*; *Information Architecture for the World Wide Web*; *Designing Web Audio: RealAudio, MP3, Flash, and Beatnik*; *Web Design in a Nutshell*, 2nd Edition; and *Cascading Style Sheets: The Definitive Guide*. As a bonus, you also get the new paperback version of *Web Design in a Nutshell*, 2nd Edition.

O'REILLY®

To order: *800-998-9938* • *order@oreilly.com* • *www.oreilly.com*
Online editions of most O'Reilly titles are available by subscription at *safari.oreilly.com*
Also available at most retail and online bookstores.

Other Titles Available from O'Reilly

Web Authoring and Design

Designing with JavaScript, 2nd Edition

By Nick Heinle & Bill Pena
2nd Edition November 2001
240 pages, ISBN 1-56592-360-X

This major revision to Nick Heinle's best-selling book, is written for the beginning web designers who are the focus of our Web Studio series, teaching core JavaScript with many useful examples and powerful libraries. The second half of the book goes beyond core JavaScript, explaining objects and more powerful event models, and showing how JavaScript can manipulate not only HTML but also XML, CSS (Cascading Style Sheets), and more.

HTML Pocket Reference, 2nd Edition

by Jennifer Niederst
2nd Edition, January 2002
112 pages, ISBN 0-596-00296-3

Targeted at web designers and authors, this concise guide to every HTML tag has been brought up-to-date with the current HTML specification (4.01). Each tag entry includes detailed information on the tag's attributes and support information for the latest web browsers—Netscape 6, IE 6, and Opera 5. Author Jennifer Niederst provides context for the tags, indicating which ones are grouped together. She also offers bare-bones examples of how standard web page elements are constructed.

Perl for Web Site Management

By John Callender
1st Edition October 2001
528 pages, ISBN 1-56592-647-1

Perl for Web Site Management shows readers how to use Perl to help do everyday web tasks. Assuming no prior programming experience, this book teaches how to write CGI scripts, incorporate search engines, convert multiple text files into HTML, monitor log files, and track users as they navigate to a site. Whether the reader is a web programmer, web administrator, a designer—or simply a dabbler, this book provides a practical, hands-on introduction to Perl.

SVG Essentials

By J. David Eisenberg
1st Edition, February 2002
368 pages, ISBN 0-596-00223-8

SVG Essentials shows developers how to take advantage of SVG's open text-based format. Although SVG is much more approachable than the binary or PostScript files that have dominated graphics formats so far, developers need a roadmap to get started creating and processing SVG files. This book provides an introduction and reference to the foundations developers need to use SVG, and demonstrates techniques for generating SVG from other XML formats.

Dreamweaver MX: The Missing Manual

By David McFarland
1st Edition November 2002
792 pages, ISBN 0-596-00349-8

Dreamweaver MX: The Missing Manual is the ideal companion to this complex software. The book begins with an anatomical tour of a web page, and then walks users through the process of creating and designing a complete web site. Armed with this book, both first-time and experienced web designers can easily use Dreamweaver to bring stunning, interactive web sites to life. In addition, users new to database-driven web sites will be given an overview of the technology and a brief primer on using this new functionality in Dreamweaver.

Building Data-Driven Web Sites with Dreamweaver MX

By Simon Allardice
1st Edition May 2003 (est.)
376 pages (est.), ISBN 0-596-00340-4

The book teaches power users, step by step, how to create web pages with Dreamweaver MX (formerly UltraDev) that access a remote database using ColdFusion, ASP, ASP .Net, JSP, or PHP—without a lot of programming. Readers will benefit from the author's first-hand knowledge and polished teaching style.

O'REILLY®

To order: 800-998-9938 • *order@oreilly.com* • *www.oreilly.com*
Online editions of most O'Reilly titles are available by subscription at *safari.oreilly.com*
Also available at most retail and online bookstores.

Other Titles Available from O'Reilly

1. Visit our award-winning web site

http://www.oreilly.com/

★ "Top 100 Sites on the Web"—PC Magazine
★ CIO Magazine's Web Business 50 Awards

Our web site contains a library of comprehensive product information (including book excerpts and tables of contents), downloadable software, background articles, interviews with technology leaders, links to relevant sites, book cover art, and more. File us in your bookmarks or favorites!

2. Join our email mailing lists

Sign up to get email announcements of new books and conferences, special offers, and O'Reilly Network technology newsletters at:

http://elists.oreilly.com

It's easy to customize your free elists subscription so you'll get exactly the O'Reilly news you want.

3. Get examples from our books

To find example files for a book, go to:

http://www.oreilly.com/catalog

select the book, and follow the "Examples" link.

4. Work with us

Check out our web site for current employment opportunities:

http://jobs.oreilly.com/

5. Register your book

Register your book at:

http://register.oreilly.com

6. Contact us

O'Reilly & Associates, Inc.
1005 Gravenstein Hwy North
Sebastopol, CA 95472 USA
TEL: 707-827-7000 or 800-998-9938
        (6am to 5pm PST)
FAX: 707-829-0104

order@oreilly.com
For answers to problems regarding your order or our products. To place a book order online visit:

http://www.oreilly.com/order_new/

catalog@oreilly.com
To request a copy of our latest catalog.

booktech@oreilly.com
For book content technical questions or corrections.

corporate@oreilly.com
For educational, library, government, and corporate sales.

proposals@oreilly.com
To submit new book proposals to our editors and product managers.

international@oreilly.com
For information about our international distributors or translation queries. For a list of our distributors outside of North America check out:

http://international.oreilly.com/distributors.html

adoption@oreilly.com
For information about academic use of O'Reilly books, visit:

http://academic.oreilly.com

O'REILLY®

To order: 800-998-9938 • *order@oreilly.com* • *www.oreilly.com*
Online editions of most O'Reilly titles are available by subscription at *safari.oreilly.com*
Also available at most retail and online bookstores.